MODERN SLAVERY IN GLOBAL CONTEXT

Human Rights, Law, and Society

Elizabeth A. Faulkner

First published in Great Britain in 2025 by

Bristol University Press
University of Bristol
1-9 Old Park Hill
Bristol
BS2 8BB
UK
t: +44 (0)117 374 6645
e: bup-info@bristol.ac.uk

Details of international sales and distribution partners are available at bristoluniversitypress.co.uk

© Bristol University Press 2025

British Library Cataloguing in Publication Data
A catalogue record for this book is available from the British Library

ISBN 978-1-5292-2470-2 hardcover
ISBN 978-1-5292-2471-9 paperback
ISBN 978-1-5292-2472-6 ePub
ISBN 978-1-5292-2473-3 ePdf

The right of Elizabeth A. Faulkner to be identified as editor of this work has been asserted by her in accordance with the Copyright, Designs and Patents Act 1988.

All rights reserved: no part of this publication may be reproduced, stored in a retrieval system, or transmitted in any form or by any means, electronic, mechanical, photocopying, recording, or otherwise without the prior permission of Bristol University Press.

Every reasonable effort has been made to obtain permission to reproduce copyrighted material. If, however, anyone knows of an oversight, please contact the publisher.

The statements and opinions contained within this publication are solely those of the editor and contributors and not of the University of Bristol or Bristol University Press. The University of Bristol and Bristol University Press disclaim responsibility for any injury to persons or property resulting from any material published in this publication.

Bristol University Press works to counter discrimination on grounds of gender, race, disability, age and sexuality.

Cover design: Hayes Design and Advertising
Front cover image: Alamy/Maria Repkova

I would like to dedicate this edited collection to my 'Baby Bean'. You were there at the start, lost on the way, and I often imagine all the things you could have become.

Contents

Table of Cases	ix
Table of Acts, Treaties, and Other Instruments	xi
List of Figures and Tables	xiv
List of Acronyms	xv
Notes on Contributors	xviii
Acknowledgements	xxiii
Foreword: Against 'Newness'	xxiv
Joel Quirk	

1	**Introduction: The Interdisciplinary Kaleidoscope and Creation of Modern Slavery in Global Context**	1
	Elizabeth A. Faulkner	
	Introduction	1
	Modern slavery in global context: overview	3
	Modern slavery: rage against the machine	13
	About the edited collection: the organizing logic	14
	Conclusion: shifting the kaleidoscope	24

PART I Theoretical Perspectives

2	**From Social to Legal: Shifting Approaches to Trafficking at the Turn of 20th-Century England**	31
	Laura Lammasniemi	
	Introduction	31
	Section I: the shifting legal and social landscape of the mid-19th century	34
	Section II: towards legal framework on anti-trafficking	39
	Conclusion	47

3	**The Coloniality of Modern Slavery in Latin America**	53
	Chris O'Connell	
	Introduction	53
	Methodology: conducting fieldwork in Bolivia and Peru	55
	Problematizing approaches to modern slavery	56

	Coloniality of power and modern slavery	60
	Decolonization and modern slavery in Bolivia	67
	Conclusion	73
4	**Constructing 'Indigenous People' Reproducing Coloniality's Epistemic Violence: A Content Analysis of the Trafficking in Persons Reports**	81
	Avi Boukli, Georgios Papanicolaou and Eleni Dimou	
	Introduction	81
	Coloniality and epistemic violence	83
	Coloniality and human trafficking	86
	Data and methods	88
	Coloniality of knowledge in the TIPRs: constructing the 'Indigenous victim' of human trafficking	92
	Conclusion	102

PART II Structural Issues in Modern Slavery and Human Trafficking Practice

5	**The Ethics of Research into Human Trafficking Beyond 'Do No Harm': Developing a 'Living' Ethical Protocol**	113
	Patricia Hynes and Mike Dottridge	
	Introduction	113
	Conceptual approaches: capturing the transnational and contextual nature of trafficking	116
	Conclusion	138
6	**Governing through Indicators: Structural Biases and Empirical Challenges in Indicator-Based Approaches to Anti-Trafficking Policy, Practice, and Research**	145
	Ieke de Vries and Ella Cockbain	
	Introduction	145
	The aetiology of problem, risk, and performance indicators	147
	Indicators as the vocabulary of victimization within human trafficking discourse	150
	Empirical challenges in developing human trafficking indicators	154
	Problem frames and empirical challenges in the use of risk factors: the case of commercial sexual exploitation and trafficking of children in the US	157
	Implications for policy, interventions, and further research	159
	Conclusion	161

7	**The Criminal Investigation of Human Trafficking Crimes in the UK: Benefits and Challenges of Police Collaboration During Police Investigations**	168
	Laura Pajón	
	Introduction	168
	Human trafficking: a complex crime	172
	The benefits and challenges of police collaboration in human trafficking investigations	180
	The practice of police collaboration to investigate human trafficking crimes	184
	Conclusion	186

PART III Case Studies

8	**Brexit-Precipitated or Free Movement-Facilitated? Labour Exploitation of EU Migrants in the UK**	197
	Samantha Currie	
	Introduction	197
	Brexit: a facilitator of labour exploitation	199
	Free movement as a facilitator of labour exploitation	201
	The aggravating impact of restrictive immigration policy	210
	Conclusion	213

9	**The Modern Slavery Agenda in the UK: Labour Market Enforcement Perspectives on Law and Policy**	220
	Amy Weatherburn	
	Introduction	220
	Tackling labour market non-compliance: law and policy responses	222
	The paradox of a labour market enforcement perspective: the 'hostile environment' trumps labour market security	228
	Conclusion	233

10	**Insights from Uganda: Wartime Sexual Violence, Knowledge Production, and Power**	241
	Allen Kiconco	
	Introduction	241
	'The field': power and feminist methodology	244
	Navigating risk, access, and collaboration	248
	"I cannot tell you everything": navigating ethics and in-depth interviews	254
	Conclusion	257

11	**Beyond Victim-Centric Research: Participatory Action Research in a Trafficking 'Hotspot' of Nepal**	261
	Ayushman Bhagat	
	Introduction: reimagining the political epistemology of victim-centric anti-trafficking research	261
	Methodology, knowledge production, and unravelling power dynamics	267
	Conclusion	280
12	**Saviours or Disrupters? The Role of Non-State Actors in the Government-Centric Realm of Anti-Trafficking in Belize**	291
	Cherisse Francis	
	Introduction	291
	The rise of NSAs	294
	Belize: the good, the bad, and the ugly	297
	Conclusion	311
Index		323

Table of Cases

International

1970	Barcelona Traction, Light and Power Company Limited (*Belgium v Spain*), International Court of Justice
2001	*Prosecutor v Kunarac, Kovac and Vukovic* Case IT-96-23-T and IT-96-23/1-T, International Criminal Court
2015	*The Prosecutor v Dominic Ongwen*, International Criminal Court

Regional

1986	Case 66/85 Lawrie-Blum ECLI:EU:C: 1986:284, European Court of Justice
1986	Case 139/85 Kempf ECLI:EU:C: 1986:223, European Court of Justice
2014	Case C-333/13 Dano ECLI:EU:C: 2014:2358, European Court of Justice
2016	Case of the *Hacienda Brasil Verde Workers v Brazil*, Inter-American Court of Human Rights
2021	Case C-709/20 *CG v Department for Communities in Northern Ireland* ECLI:EU:C: 2021:602, European Court of Justice
2021	*V.C.L. & A.N. v the United Kingdom* [2021] Applications nos. 74603/12 and 77587/12, European Court of Human Rights

National

Australia

2008	*R v Tang*, (2008) 249 ALR 200, High Court of Australia

United Kingdom

2016 *G v DJ Houghton Catching Services Ltd* [2016] EWHC 1376, England and Wales High Court

2019 *Antuzis v DJ Houghton Catching Services Ltd* [2019] EWHC 843, England and Wales High Court

2022 *R (on the application of the Independent Monitoring Authority for the Citizens' Rights Agreements) v Secretary of State for the Home Department* [2022] EWHC 3274 (Admin), England and Wales High Court

Table of Acts, Treaties, and Other Instruments

International

1904	International Agreement for the Suppression of the White Slave Traffic
1910	International Convention for the Suppression of the White Slave Traffic
1921	International Convention for the Suppression of Traffic in Women and Children
1926	Convention to Suppress the Slave Trade and Slavery
1930	Convention Concerning Forced and Compulsory Labour
1933	International Convention for the Suppression of Traffic in Women of Full Age
1947	Protocol Amending the International Convention for the Suppression of Traffic in Women and Children and the International Convention for the Suppression of Traffic in Women of Full Age
1947	Labour Inspection Convention
1947	Labour Inspection Convention, 1947 (No 81)
1948	Universal Declaration of Human Rights
1949	Protocol Amending the International Agreement for the Suppression of the White Slave Traffic, and Amending the International Convention for the Suppression of the White Slave Traffic
1949	Convention for the Suppression of Traffic in Persons and the Exploitation and Prostitution of Others
1956	Supplementary Convention on the Abolition of Slavery, the Slave Trade, and Institutions and Practices Similar to Slavery
1969	Vienna Convention on the Law of Treaties
1988	Rome Statute of the International Criminal Court
1989	Convention on the Rights of the Child
2000	Convention against Transnational Organized Crime

2000	Protocol to Prevent, Suppress, and Punish Trafficking in Persons, Especially Women and Children, Supplementing the United Nations Convention against Transnational Organized Crime

Regional

1950	European Convention Human Rights
1969	American Convention on Human Rights
1995	95/46/EC Directive (Data Protection Directive)
2004	Directive 2004/38 [2004] OJ L158/77
2007	Treaty on the Functioning of the European Union

National

Albania

2008	Personal Data Protection, No. 9887

Australia

2018	Modern Slavery Act

Belize

2011	Non-Governmental Organisations Act, Revised Edition
2013	Anti-trafficking in Persons (Prohibition) Act

Brazil

1888	Lei Aurea (Golden Law)

India

1860	Indian Penal Code

United Kingdom

1824	Vagrancy Act 1824
1829	Metropolitan Police Act
1861	Offences Against the Person Act
1864–1869	Contagious Diseases Act
1885	Criminal Law Amendment Act
1905	Aliens Act
1912	Criminal Law Amendment Act
1977	Criminal Law Amendment Act
1984	Police and Criminal Evidence Act
1998	National Minimum Wage Act
2015	Modern Slavery Act
2015	The National Minimum Wage Regulations
2016	Illegal Immigration Act

2016	Trade Union Act
2020	Immigration Social Security Co-ordination (EU Withdrawal) Act
2022	Nationality and Borders Act

United States

1961	Foreign Assistance Act
2000	Trafficking Victims Protection Act

Vietnam

2013	Constitution of the Republic of Vietnam

List of Figures and Tables

Figures

5.1	IOM Determinants of Migrant Vulnerability Model with study annotations	121
5.2	Stages of informed consent	127
12.1	Partnerships in Belize's anti-trafficking field	298

Tables

1.1	Overview of the Trafficking Protocol definition of human trafficking, 2000	10
4.1	Indigenous communities mentions in Trafficking in Persons reports by country types and Tier status (2003–2020)	100
9.1	Number of LMEUs and LMEOs issued by the enforcement bodies	228

List of Acronyms

AMSH	Association for Moral and Social Hygiene
APG	Association of Guaraní Peoples
ATIPS Council	Anti-Trafficking in Persons Council
CARSI	Central America Regional Security Initiative
CDAs	Contagious Diseases Acts
CEE	Central and Eastern Europe
CEJIS	Centre for Legal Studies and Social Research
CG	Conclusive grounds
CIPCA	Peasant Research and Promotion Center
CLAA	Criminal Law Amendment Act
CNAMIB	National Confederation of Indigenous Women of Bolivia
CONAMAQ	National Council of Ayllus and Markas of Qullasuyu
CoP	Community of Practice
CSEC	Commercial sexual exploitation of children
DLME	Director of Labour Market Enforcement
DLR	Discretionary Leave to Remain
DoMV	Determinants of Migrant Vulnerability
EAS	Employment Agency Standards Inspectorate
ECAT	Council of Europe Convention on Action against Trafficking in Human Beings 2005
ECJ	European Court of Justice
EEA	European Economic Area (the EU member states plus Iceland, Liechtenstein, and Norway)
ERIC	Ethical Research Involving Children
ESF	Economic Support Fund
EU	European Union
EU2	Romania and Bulgaria (acceded to the EU in 2007)
EU8	Czech Republic, Estonia, Hungary, Latvia, Lithuania, Poland, Slovakia, and Slovenia (acceded to the EU in 2004)
EUSS	European Union Settlement Scheme

GAATW	Global Alliance Against Traffic in Women
GDP	Gross domestic product
GLAA	Gangmasters and Labour Abuse Authority
GRETA	Group of Experts on Action against Human Trafficking
HMRC NMW/NLW	His Majesty's Revenue and Customs National Minimum and Living Wage enforcement team
HT	Human trafficking
IACHR	Inter-American Commission on Human Rights
IAF	International Abolitionist Federation
IASFM	International Association for the Study of Forced Migration
ICC	International Criminal Court
IECA	Immigration Enforcement Competent Authority
IGO	Intergovernmental organization
ILO	International Labour Organization
IMA	Independent Monitoring Authority for the Citizens' Rights Agreements
IOM	International Organization for Migration
JIT	Joint investigation team
JR	Judicial review
JSA	Jobseekers' Allowance
LAPOs	Labour Abuse Prevention Officers
LMEOs	Labour Market Enforcement Orders
LMEUs	Labour Market Enforcement Undertakings
LSE	Women's Library
MIS	Minimum income standard
MSA	Modern Slavery Act 2015
MSIF	Modern Slavery Innovation Fund
NGO	Non-governmental organization
NHTRC	National Human Trafficking Resource Center
NMW	National Minimum Wage
NRM	National Referral Mechanism
NSAs	Non-state actors
NSPCC	National Society for Prevention of Cruelty to Children
NVA	National Vigilance Association
OCG	Organized criminal group
ODW	Overseas domestic workers
OEWM	On Eagles Wings Ministries
PAC	Peruvian Amazon Company
PACE	Police and Criminal Evidence Act 1984
PBS	Points-Based System of Immigration

LIST OF ACRONYMS

PPE	Personal protective equipment
PPP	Public-private partnerships
RG	Reasonable grounds
SCA	Single competent authority
SLEs	Shared learning events
SOCU	Serious Organized Crime Unit
TFEU	Treaty on the Functioning of the European Union
TIPR	Trafficking in Persons Report
TIPNIS	Isiboro Sécure National Park and Indigenous Territory
TVPA	Trafficking Victims Protection Act
UDHR	Universal Declaration of Human Rights
UK	United Kingdom
UN	United Nations
UNHCR	United Nations Refugee Agency
UNIAP	United Nations Inter-Agency Project on Human Trafficking in the Greater Mekong Sub-region
UNICEF	United Nations Children's Fund
UNODC	United Nations Office on Drugs and Crime
UNTOC	United Nations Convention Against Transnational Organized Crime
US	United States of America
VCLT	Vienna Convention on the Law of Treaties
VD	Venereal disease
WHO	World Health Organization

Notes on Contributors

Ayushman Bhagat is Lecturer in Political Geography at Brunel University London. His current research focuses on the spatial politics of anti-slavery and migration control in Nepal and the United Kingdom. He prioritizes the experiences and practices of the people on the move who are the prime targets of anti-slavery interventions in his research and activism. With a PhD in Geography from Durham University, he has previously held research and teaching positions at Tel Aviv University and Edge Hill University, respectively. Before entering academia, he was involved in India's development sector, following his master's degree in Rural Development at Xavier Institute of Social Service (XISS). During this time, he implemented various initiatives aimed at combating 'human trafficking' and bonded labour, collaborating with organizations such as the International Labour Organization (ILO), government departments, and trade unions. Moreover, Ayushman worked closely with forest-dwelling communities at the grassroots level through non-governmental organizations (NGOs). His work has been published in leading geography journals such as *Antipode* and *Political Geography*.

Avi Boukli is Associate Professor of Criminology at the University of Southampton. They hold a PhD in Law from the London School of Economics and they have previously held positions at the London School of Economics, Birkbeck, Teesside University, and The Open University. Avi's research is concerned with social harm and social justice, and with some broader questions to do with the interface between structural inequalities and social harm.

Ella Cockbain is Associate Professor in Security and Crime Science at University College London. She is also a visiting research fellow at Leiden University in the Netherlands. Ella's research mainly focuses on human trafficking, child sexual abuse, and labour market abuses. She is interested in rigorous research across qualitative, quantitative, and mixed methods. Her research often challenges received wisdom and prevailing stereotypes around complex social phenomena; Ella seeks to encourage more nuanced, evidence-informed, and context-sensitive approaches to understanding and tackling such issues. She has worked closely with organizations across the public, private, and third sectors and contributed to counter-trafficking interventions locally, nationally, and internationally, including by co-chairing the UK's national working group on the prevention of 'modern slavery'. She has published widely on these topics, including *Offender and Victim Networks in Human Trafficking*.

Samantha Currie is Associate Professor at Monash University's Faculty of Law, Australia. Her research interests focus on the engagement of victims and survivors of trafficking with law and policy processes, with a particular focus on the nexus between migration and modern slavery. She has led research projects on survivors' access to legal advice, the role of lawyers within the anti-trafficking space, and the citizenship status of EU migrants in the UK. Previously, she was a reader in Law at the University of Liverpool.

Ieke de Vries is Assistant Professor at the Institute of Criminal Law and Criminology at Leiden University. Her scholarship examines victimizations, networks, and geographies of crime involving understudied populations and motivations for and effects of certain police responses in these contexts. In the context of human trafficking, Dr de Vries seeks to challenge empirically unsupported paradigms on human trafficking and advances international research on human trafficking using rigorous qualitative, quantitative, and computational methods. She received her PhD from Northeastern University in Boston (2020), which was supported by a Graduate Research Fellowship of the National Institute of Justice in 2018, and previously worked as Assistant Professor at Florida State University.

Eleni Dimou is Lecturer in Criminology at the Open University. She has a BA in Sociology from Panteion University, Athens, and an MA and PhD in Criminology from the University of Kent. Her research explores issues around power and resistance, and how these affect configurations of crime, harm, and processes of criminalization but also cultural and social change. She particularly focuses on colonialism and its impact today. One of her latest projects for BBC Ideas is available from: www.youtube.com/watch?v=5gWGP34-4tY. She is the author of the article 'Decolonizing southern criminology: what can the "decolonial option" tell us about challenging the modern/colonial foundations of criminology?'. She is a member of the editorial board of peer-reviewed journal *Decolonization of Criminology and Justice*, available from: https://ojs.aut.ac.nz/dcj/index.

Mike Dottridge has worked in the human rights field for 45 years. He worked for two human rights NGOs (Amnesty International and Anti-Slavery International, where he was director until 2002). His work for Amnesty concerned sub-Saharan Africa. Since 1995 he has focused on the rights of adults and children who experience economic or sexual exploitation. Since 2002 he has worked independently, undertaking evaluations and institutional learning exercises for both international organizations and NGOs. He is the author of numerous articles and handbooks commenting on aspects of international law concerning slavery, servitude, forced labour, child labour, and human trafficking or suggesting ways to prevent such exploitation and how to protect and assist the victims.

Elizabeth A. Faulkner is Lecturer in Law at Keele University, having previously held a lectureship in Contemporary Slavery at the Wilberforce Institute, University of Hull. Her interests, broadly conceived, are in international child law, human rights, crime, legal history, specializing in human trafficking, slavery, children's rights, exploitation, and sexual violence. She is the author of *The Trafficking of Children: International Law, Modern Slavery and the Anti-Trafficking Machine* published in April 2023 by Palgrave Macmillan. The monograph charts the emergence, decline, and re-emergence of child trafficking law and policy during the 20th and 21st centuries, through providing a systematic and comprehensive overview of the historical origins of child trafficking through research within archives of the League of Nations. Her research seeks to centralize the neglected histories of child trafficking and the entanglements of children's rights and colonialism in relation to the mobility and exploitation of children, through deploying the theoretical framework of the 'anti-trafficking machine' to illustrate that the contemporary anti-trafficking agenda is both imperialist and a continuity of colonial attitudes.

Cherisse Francis is a doctoral researcher at the University of Warwick researching trafficking in persons and interrogating social, cultural, historical, and political aspects of anti-trafficking. She holds an LLB (Hons) from the University of the West Indies, Cave Hill Campus, and an LLM in Human Rights and Criminal Justice (Dist) from the University of Aberdeen. Cherisse is also a qualified attorney at law called to the bar in Barbados. Her broader research interests include human rights, gender, juvenile justice, criminal justice, transatlantic slavery, and colonization.

Patricia Hynes is Professor of Social Justice in the Helena Kennedy Centre for International Justice at Sheffield Hallam University. During the past decade her research has focused on human trafficking of children and adults, working closely with non-academic partners such as ECPAT UK, the IOM, and the NSPCC. Patricia has practitioner background with refugee populations in Southeast Asia, having worked along the Thailand–Burma border and other humanitarian contexts. She has published internationally including contributions for UNICEF on child sexual exploitation in humanitarian contexts and the UNHCR on the issue of trust and/or mistrust in refugee settings. She is the author of *Introducing Forced Migration* (Routledge, 2021), co-author of *Trafficked Young People: Breaking the Wall of Silence* (Routledge, 2013), co-editor of *New Directions in the Sociology of Human Rights* (Routledge, 2013), co-editor of *Sociology and Human Rights* (Routledge, 2011), and a monograph, *The Dispersal and Social Exclusion of Asylum Seekers: Between Liminality and Belonging* (Policy Press, 2011). She has also published in academic journals such as *Journal of Refugee Studies*, *Sociology*, and *International Journal of Human Rights*. She was the Principal Investigator for the four-country research study looking at 'vulnerability' to human trafficking from Albania, Vietnam, and Nigeria to the UK, detailed within Chapter 5 (this volume).

Allen Kiconco is a postdoctoral researcher at the University of the Witwatersrand, South Africa, and her research focuses upon issues related to gender and violence, modern slavery and human trafficking. Her work has concentrated on the lived experiences of African women and girls in conflict and post-conflict settings. Child soldiering, abduction, sexual slavery, forced marriage, and forced pregnancy are among these experiences. Her work includes extensive fieldwork in Uganda and Sierra Leone with ex-combatants and survivors of wartime sexual violence and forced marriage. Allen is the author of *Gender, Conflict and Reintegration in Uganda: Abducted Girls, Returning Women* (Routledge, 2021).

Laura Lammasniemi is Associate Professor at Warwick School of Law. Laura's principal research interests lie in the areas of crime, gender, and class from a historical perspective. She is working on a Leverhulme-funded project on the history of sexual consent in criminal courts, 1870–1950, and in 2021 she was chosen to deliver the British Social Sciences Award Lecture on this topic. She has published broadly on histories on trafficking and sexual offences. Laura has participated in BBC TV and radio shows as a legal history expert.

Chris O'Connell is a researcher at the School of Law and Government in Dublin City University, Ireland. His research interests centre on the nexus of human rights and ecological unsustainability, with a regional focus on Latin America. Chris is the author of various articles, book chapters, and reports, including the influential study of the relationship between climate change and modern slavery entitled, 'From a vicious to a virtuous circle: addressing climate change, environmental destruction and contemporary slavery'. He holds a PhD in Politics from Dublin City University.

Laura Pajón is Senior Lecturer in Policing at Liverpool John Moores University. Her research focuses on law enforcement and multi-agency responses to serious and organized criminality; in particular, human trafficking and modern slavery crimes. She publishes, teaches, and advises widely on these topics. In 2021, she received the 'Young Researcher of the Year Award' from the United Nations Office on Drugs and Crime (UNODC) and the International Association of Universities in recognition of her impactful research and her work with enforcement agencies and government and non-governmental organizations to tackle human trafficking.

Georgios Papanicolaou is Associate Professor at Northumbria University. He has studied Law and Criminology at the University of Athens and the University of Edinburgh. His research interests include the political economy of policing and the political economy of illegal markets. Georgios is the co-author of *Organized Crime: A Very Short Introduction* (Oxford University Press) and the author of *Transnational Policing and Sex Trafficking in Southeast Europe: Policing the Imperialist Chain* (Palgrave Macmillan). He is an associate editor of *Criminology and Criminal Justice* and a member of the editorial board of *Trends in Organized Crime*.

Amy Weatherburn is FRS-FNRS Post-Doctoral Research Fellow (*Chargée de Recherche*) at the Université Libre de Bruxelles and Doctor of Law (VUB and Tilburg, 2019). Her post-doctoral research focuses on the normalization of exploitation in the labour market and the development of law and policy that tackles exploitation beyond criminal law. Her main research areas are modern slavery, human trafficking, migration law, and fundamental rights. She has recently published the monograph *Labour Exploitation in Human Trafficking Law* (Intersentia, 2021), was co-editor of the fifth volume of the European Integration and Democracy Series, *Irregular Migration to Europe as a Challenge for Democracy* (Intersentia, 2018), and has extensively contributed to collective works and international journals.

Acknowledgements

First, I would like to thank the Society of Legal Scholars and Modern Law Review for providing the funding that enabled Laura Lammasniemi (University of Warwick) and I to host our 'Critical Perspectives on Modern Slavery: Law, Policy, and Society' Conference in October 2019 at the Wilberforce Institute, University of Hull. An event which without the advice of Professor Joel Quirk would not have materialized – nor would this edited collection – as ever I am always indebted to you for your time and guidance.

Thank you to each of the contributors for their efforts in transforming some of the papers from the conference into this edited collection and those who joined us along the way. I would also like to thank my co-authors for their patience, collegiality, and support with this project. I have been very open about the personal toll of losing the baby that I was carrying during the 2019 conference, and the subsequent grief and later joy when we were expecting our rainbow baby who safely arrived in November 2021. Thank you for your unwavering support throughout in helping to get this edited collection to the finishing line.

Finally, thanks must go to the peer reviewers of the edited collection's initial proposal, the extensive peer review obtained by BUP, and to the peer reviewers of chapters during the process; namely, Catherine Armstrong, Alex Balch, Borislav Gerasimov, Ryzard Piotrowicz, Hila Shamir, Nandita Sharma, and Dave Walsh.

Foreword: Against 'Newness'

*Joel Quirk, Professor of Political Science,
University of the Witwatersrand, South Africa*

Most experts in the field trace the origins of human trafficking and 'modern slavery' campaigns to the mid-1990s. This chronology is usually tied to the end of the Cold War, which is said to have created (1) new opportunities for organized criminal activity, especially in Eastern Europe, and (2) new opportunities for transnational activism in the wake of the 'unipolar moment' following Soviet collapse. Most stories about the origins of anti-trafficking/ slavery typically culminate with the passage of two key milestones – the Trafficking Victims Protection Act in the US, and the Palermo Protocol to Prevent, Suppress and Punish Trafficking in Persons. Both were finalized in 2000, and they have been widely depicted as constituting *the* decisive moment where anti-trafficking first came of age. According to this origin story, anti-trafficking/slavery can be primarily understood as a new innovation which arose in direct response to a series of new and distinctive challenges generated by the dark side of globalization. This embrace of 'newness' is one of the defining features of conversations about human trafficking and 'modern slavery' from the mid-1990s onwards. Most people and organizations who started specializing in issues relating to human trafficking were keen to position themselves as pioneers who were breaking entirely 'new' ground. Their target was the new slavery, the new slave trade, and the new challenges associated with trafficking in an unprecedented age of globalization.

There are fundamental problems with this origin story. First, and most obviously, this selective focus upon the mid-1990s has obscured a number of deeper histories which have important ramifications for contemporary issues. Notable examples include the history of 'white slavery', moral panics, and harmful efforts to prohibit commercial sex, together with the uncomfortable historical relationship between organized anti-slavery, European imperialism, and colonial forced labour regimes. The problems and limitations of past campaigns and official policies could have potentially informed conversations about human trafficking from the mid-1990s onwards, but the language of 'newness' helped to push these uncomfortable histories outside the frame. People and organisations in the late 1990s and early 2000s strongly self-identified as path-breaking pioneers who were doing something entirely new and different.

The second major problem with 'newness' was that it also helped to pave the way for an unhelpful and artificial separation between human trafficking and already established bodies of knowledge, experience, and expertise. If human trafficking was a distinctively new phenomenon, then it followed logically that new approaches and solutions were now needed, so efforts would be channelled into developing entirely new campaigns, laws, protocols, and interventions. This contributed to a de facto decoupling of work on trafficking from allied fields of activism and research. Too many campaigners and officials ended up setting aside existing bodies of expertise and trying to reinvent the wheel on anti-trafficking terms. One of the main points at issue here was the degree to which anti-trafficking campaigns ended up selectively targeting individualized cases of the 'worst of the worst', and thereby ended up reinforcing an analytically unhelpful – yet nonetheless politically useful – demarcation between 'exceptional' problems and everyday practices. Numerous anti-trafficking/slavery organizations came into existence during the first decade of the 20th century, and they invariably positioned themselves as standing apart from existing campaigns and organizations working on sex worker rights, migration and asylum, and labour rights and organization.

The final problem with 'newness' was that it lowered the bar for activism and research. The dominant imagery of the path-breaking pioneer made it possible for a great deal of shoddy scholarship, ineffective policy, and superficial and sensationalist activism to escape critical scrutiny (at least initially), since it was widely assumed that any problems and limitations could be attributed to initial 'teething problems' which invariably accompanied the birth of something new. Dubious 'facts and figures' which had little or no methodological basis would be disseminated with very limited pushback, since it was widely believed that they served the greater good by helping to establish the public and political profile of anti-trafficking. There is no meaningful methodological foundation to the still popular claim that there are more slaves in the world today than at any point in human history, yet this claim has been repeated all over the world thanks to its perceived value in helping to generate interest and investment. Research into trafficking which had a very thin empirical basis would still be widely endorsed, since it was calculated that some evidence – no matter how anecdotal – was still very valuable. The de facto decoupling of research on human trafficking from research in other related fields made it possible to advance claims and characterizations which might have otherwise appeared as problematic if they had been advanced in more established fields.

Huge amounts of anti-trafficking activism have proved to be ineffective at best and harmful at worst. One notable example of the larger dynamic is the widespread popularity of 'awareness raising' campaigns, especially during the early 21st century. 'Awareness raising' is the low hanging fruit of anti-trafficking activism. It requires very little specialized expertise, and many organizations are drawn to it because it helps to safely raise their organizational profile in a way that doesn't touch upon any contentious political and ideological questions, such as the nexus between anti-trafficking and punitive anti-immigration policies. How could anyone object to efforts to get the message out regarding trafficking or slavery? However, it remains an open question whether messages targeting the public have any positive effect. They may actually cause harm by contributing to forms of racial and xenophobic profiling and by foregrounding simplistic and sensationalized narratives which create a misleading impression of what 'innocent victims' are supposed to look like. Some recent awareness campaigns around #pizzagate and #savethechildren have been especially problematic. Despite these limitations, awareness campaigns have long been the bread and butter of anti-trafficking, and they continue to be justified on the grounds that disseminating 'awareness' will help to pump prime citizens to take additional action *over the longer term*. According to this logic the greater payoff can be expected in the future, not the present, yet there is a strong case to be made, especially with the benefit of hindsight, that decades of awareness campaigns have not generated the transformation which has been repeatedly promised. This is not simply a problem for awareness raising. It is also an acute problem for 'newness'.

Treating human trafficking as a 'new' challenge enabled people and organizations to lower expectations, since they were understood to be engaged in something for the first time and therefore could not be expected to get everything right. This logic proved to be very effective in the short-term. From the mid-1990s to early 2010s the logic of newness was all but universally accepted, since it was widely agreed that it would take time to evaluate whether different interventions have been working effectively. With the passage of time, it has become increasingly difficult to hide behind 'newness'. Some people and organizations continue to try and minimize and excuse their shortcomings on the grounds that the field is still 'new', but this kind of argument is much harder to make in the 2020s than in the 2000s. A great deal of water has passed under the bridge, and there is now an extensive and sophisticated critical literature which has carefully scrutinized the numerous faces of anti-trafficking/slavery. It is my belief that this critical literature has played an important yet by no means universal role in helping to significantly raise the bar for both activism and research, but not for policy. This edited collection forms part of a larger course correction which is now well underway.

The central premise of 'newness' was that responses to human trafficking and modern slavery could be expected to significantly improve as the field 'matured' over time. This expectation has not been realized. It is definitely possible to point to examples of better practice in specific areas, but from a macro-standpoint there is a strong case to be made that things have not gone as expected or planned as far as anti-trafficking/slavery is concerned. One of the main reasons for this poor track record is the extent to which anti-trafficking efforts have been channelled into new laws and criminal justice reforms. As a now extensive literature has demonstrated, human trafficking and modern slavery have been constructed as archetypes of criminality, with misleading yet compelling narratives featuring individual criminal perpetrators (buyers and sellers) and innocent victims (who are bought and sold). This powerful association with crime and policing has profound effects on remedial responses. These include, on the one hand, how problems are diagnosed (that is, as individual criminal schemes to exploit individual victims) and, on the other, how problems are addressed (that is, with criminal justice agents arresting offenders and 'rescuing' victims).

Once the problem has been defined in terms of these stylized binaries then certain kinds of responses usually follow: 'law and order' interventions targeting illicit criminal networks. More effort has been invested in criminal justice reforms than any other arena. This includes (1) the creation of new laws, definitions, and criminal offences; (2) enhanced criminal and civil penalties; (3) improved systems to streamline and strengthen prosecutions, specialized task forces, courts, and bureaucratic processes; (4) new cooperation agreements between governments and other institutions; (5) new visa categories and identification and referral mechanisms; (6) frontline training programmes for police, immigration agents, and various others; and (7) additional measures for victim protection, restitution, rehabilitation, and repatriation. These and similar measures have translated into an increasingly dense global regime specifically focusing upon both improving and expanding criminal justice models.

Despite all these efforts, criminal justice reforms have not produced the kinds of results which had been widely expected. There has been a recurring tendency to celebrate the passage of new laws and policies as positive steps without looking too closely at what they actually say and do, since it is widely assumed that something must be better than nothing. This has meant that two related issues tend to be overlooked: (1) textual limitations and loopholes, including provisions which can sometimes end up damaging people whom laws are designed to help; and (2) further problems associated with ineffective, inconsistent, and incompetent enforcement, especially in relation to labour exploitation not involving commercial sex. Despite decades of investment, relatively few prosecutions for human trafficking and modern slavery continue to be reported throughout the globe. Making police, prosecutors, and immigrant agents responsible for frontline anti-trafficking enforcement has paved the way for all kinds of collateral damages which end up harming and not helping.

The limitations of criminal justice models have been extensively documented. Even the strongest advocates of law and order accept that there are problems with established models and that further reforms are required. However, differences of opinion quickly emerge once the focus shifts to exactly what reform entails. In many circles, reform is chiefly understood in terms of further improvements to the design and operation of established criminal justice models. This leaves the dominant position of criminal justice models unchallenged since the task of reform is to ensure that the different moving pieces work better in practice. Focusing upon criminal justice models is also the politically 'safe' option, since efforts to prosecute criminals more effectively is a cause which commands high levels of public support. The primary drawback with this approach is that it consumes large amounts of institutional and political capacity and capability, herefore leaving limited scope for alternative approaches. When criminal justice models prove to be ineffective and disappointing, the dominant response in numerous cases has been to invest even further in *yet more* criminal justice.

The recent history of criminal justice models is emblematic of a larger trend when it comes to policies and interventions targeting trafficking and modern slavery. Most of the interventions which have been introduced during the last two decades have proved to be ineffective or counter-productive, yet the dominant impulse has not been to try and change course, but to instead double down with yet even more of the same. While not everyone approaches anti-trafficking from the same vantage point, it is striking how frequently similar kinds of policies and interventions have come up time and time again, with a recurring and continuing investment in criminal justice reforms, raid and rescue operations, 'raising awareness' campaigns, technology against trafficking, and discretionary schemes for ethical investment and consumption. This last example is especially important. Corporate social responsibility via transparency legislation has proved to be completely ineffective in the case of the UK, yet it has nonetheless been taken up by other countries despite its serious flaws. There are many occasions where activity – or the appearance thereof – gets prioritized over efficacy. Many policy responses to human trafficking and modern slavery are championed for reasons that have more to do with their political acceptability than their practical efficacy.

These problems with dominant anti-trafficking/slavery policies and campaigns have been extensively critiqued. One of the most important innovations which has taken place over the last two decades has been the rapid expansion of sophisticated ethnographic research (much more than individual anecdotes) specifically focusing upon specific industries, locations, experiences, and interventions associated with human trafficking and modern slavery. Many of the claims and characterizations associated with anti-trafficking/slavery have collapsed when subject to careful ethnographic scrutiny, resulting in an environment where there is now a great deal of evidence that things have not been being working as planned. Similarly, the superficial and sensationalist character of earlier anti-trafficking campaigns is also now much better documented and understood than in the past, resulting in a situation where many but no means all campaigners have made greater efforts to get their own house together. Conversations about human trafficking and modern slavery have undoubtedly 'matured', but they have matured in ways that has created a much deeper recognition and appreciation of why and how established policies and laws have proved to be harmful and ineffective.

This is where a fork in the road comes into view. The first road involves yet more of the same, with only minor refinements within an overall direction of travel which continues to fall back on an existing policy repertoire which prioritizes criminal justice reforms, raid and rescue operations, 'raising awareness', technocracy and techno-futurism, discretionary forms of social responsibility, and the strategic conflation of anti-trafficking and anti-immigration. We can expect some additions to how this repertoire gets packaged (including trying to re-activate the language of 'newness' in order to try and reset the clock), but these additions will end up being bolted on to an established superstructure without changing the status quo in significant ways. We already have evidence that this policy repertoire is not going to work, but it will also not rock the boat politically, which is why it continues to be widely favoured.

The second road involves the expansion and consolidation of trends which are already in motion. First, and most importantly, this means setting aside the unhelpful effects of 'newness' and (re)connecting conversations about human trafficking and modern slavery to larger dynamics and debates. Issues associated with human trafficking and modern slavery can be best understood as nested within established bodies of knowledge and policy relating to migration and 'crimmigration', gender and sexuality, informal and precarious labour, law and regulation, political economy and corporate power, and social reproduction and the household, among others. This also means grappling with the uncomfortable silences which still shroud histories of 'white slavery' and colonial labour abuses under the guise of 'humanitarianism'. Lastly, it means holding research into human trafficking to the same professional and ethical standards which are conventionally applied to researchers doing fieldwork in other related fields. The bar for activism and research should not be lowered. The available evidence suggests that governments and other actors will continue to call upon the same repertoire of self-serving and ineffective responses, so our critical and ethical response must be to develop alternatives approaches, connections, and forms of solidarity.

There is nothing 'new' about human trafficking and modern slavery. This edited collection provides the resources, evidence, and insights we need to continue charting a different path.

1

Introduction: The Interdisciplinary Kaleidoscope and Creation of Modern Slavery in Global Context

Elizabeth A. Faulkner

Introduction

The kaleidoscope upon the front cover was a deliberate choice, but not simply because it is aesthetically appealing. The kaleidoscope is traditionally thought of as a toy 'consisting of a tube containing mirrors and pieces of coloured glass or paper, whose reflections produce changing patterns that are visible through an eyehole when the tube is rotated'.[1] This creation of constantly changing patterns or the sequence of objects and elements illustrates the phenomenon of 'modern slavery'[2] and how the edited collection is drawn together. The umbrella concept of modern slavery cannot be studied under a singular disciplinary gaze, or methodological approach. Therefore, this collection incorporates theoretical, historical, and empirical research from different disciplines creating a unique and evolving picture of the study of modern slavery. Modern slavery has been most frequently operationalized within the UK;[3] however, within this collection the selected chapters seek to

---

[1] *Oxford English Dictionary*, Oxford Languages.
[2] The author accepts 'modern slavery' is a contestable term and prefers alternatives such as 'extreme exploitation', but concedes to the use of the term without the punctuation to reflect disquiet with the phrase.
[3] Calls have emerged for the establishment of a Global Commission on Modern Slavery and Human Trafficking, see further https://modernslaverypec.org/resources/global-commission-scoping-study#:~:text=On%20the%20basis%20of%20the%20mapping%20of%20the,political%20leadership%20building%20the%20evidence%20and%20knowledge%20base

provide context to the global growth of understanding and knowledge about exploitative practices that fall under the expansive remit of the term globally. It is perceived as a unique issue of contemporary significance, frequently used interchangeably with human trafficking. This interdisciplinary edited collection seeks to contribute to the growing body of literature under the remit of critical modern slavery studies. The chapters draw together academics from different disciplinary backgrounds, including law, crime science, geography, anthropology, sociology, criminology, and police studies. This is where the imagery of the kaleidoscope provides an insight into the logic behind the creation of this collection. As commented by the author Neil Gaiman, the 'law is a blunt instrument'[4] and that perspective has shaped and influenced the development of this collection. As a socio-legal scholar[5] I recognize the limitations or constraints of the law and that broader engagement beyond the constraints of traditional legal analysis is required. Furthermore, the law has acted throughout history as more of an enabler of injustice and in relation to anti-trafficking the chronic ineffectiveness of the law has been extensively examined (Kotiswaran, 2017: 6).

This marks the uniqueness of this collection, which brings together research to examine the intricacies of modern slavery in a variety of global contexts but not with each chapter centralizing an interrogation of the legal frameworks or of the legal history of slavery within each jurisdiction.[6] Some chapters present analyses that challenge the current orthodoxy of

---

[Accessed 15 July 2023]. It was recently advocated by the UK's Head of Foreign and Commonwealth Department Office Modern Slavery Team in wake of the OCSE Conference (www.osce.org/event/alliance23) in April 2023 that 'such a commission will inject political momentum at this critical time, and will support the global community to achieve our shared goal of eradicating modern slavery and human trafficking by 2030'. See further www.gov.uk/government/speeches/osce-alliance-conference-on-combating-trafficking-in-persons-uk-statement-april-2023 [Accessed 15 July 2023].

[4] https://journal.neilgaiman.com/2008/12/why-defend-freedom-of-icky-speech.html [Accessed 15 July 2023].

[5] Through the reference to socio-legal, I refer to the study of legal ideas, practices, and institutions in their social, cultural, and historical contexts. It has been observed that socio-legal scholarship has challenged doctrinal legal research culture by questioning the assumed centrality of law and legal institutions to many social problems. See further O'Donovan (2016) 'Socio-legal methodology: conceptual underpinnings, justifications and practical pitfalls', in L. Cahillane and J. Schweppe (eds) *Legal Research Methods: Principles and Practicalities*, Dublin: Clarus Press.

[6] For an extensive overview of slavery in different jurisdictions, see further Pargas and Schiel (2023) *The Palgrave Handbook of Global Slavery throughout History*, available from: https://link.springer.com/book/10.1007/978-3-031-13260-5?page=3&fbclid=IwAR0AODvnUzRrKLpSt-YOn5lvf9ElHjpot1lhT_0IkqnrLUISe6tnJXeIc7A_aem_AeWftkZJEFodTyYM1nxE5mPP1I7Dxyy520PYbYs3WF7TYtAHLibSJGkSGq5c94Mh2-A#toc

the discourse. What each disciplinary perspective brings with it is its own unique vision which when combined with each other creates a pattern of understanding or critique that creates the kaleidoscope. The purpose is to contribute to the debate, recognizing the significant footprint of the edited collections produced in recent years.[7]

Modern slavery in global context: overview

As a term, modern slavery serves as a powerful tool that invokes an extensive appeal to altruistic feeling, while simultaneously providing an elastic umbrella-like term for a variety of exploitative practices. Defining slavery has proven difficult in the contemporary world, with fierce debates over the parameters of what encompasses (and in turn does not encompass) modern slavery. The label slavery carries a political and emotional weight, particularly in the US with Beutin (2017, 2023) highlighting how the discourse of anti-trafficking invokes the history and exploits memory of transatlantic slavery.

Definitions are important in many different contexts, in relation to the classification of the crime of modern slavery a definition is required to enable the criminal justice system to effectively deal with the issue. However, is modern slavery purely an issue for criminal justice or is the neglected framework of human rights (so often taken for granted) the more just framing for those who have been subjected to extreme exploitation? Freedom from slavery is frequently cited as the original or first human rights treaty, yet international law has not been nor is a neutral tool and has frequently played the role of enabler rather than prohibitor for human rights violations perpetrated globally (Mutua, 2001; Anghie 2005). Herein lies a problem: crime requires punishment and within the context of anti-trafficking and slavery this involves the victim, the villain, and the rescuer, the latter of which is the neoliberal state and/or the humanitarian industrial complex. Within this framework, new representations of slavery in the Global South show colonized peoples as helplessly trapped by their repeating Sisyphean tasks, classed as objects not subjects, the eternal victims who can only be liberated by white saviours (Kempadoo, 2015; O'Connell Davidson, 2015: 73).

---

[7] Including but not limited to P. Kotiswaran (ed) (2017) *Revisiting the Law and Governance of Trafficking, Forced Labor and Modern Slavery*, Cambridge: Cambridge University Press, DOI: 10.1017/9781316675809; Bunting and Quirk (2017b) *Contemporary Slavery: The Rhetoric of Global Human Rights Campaigns*, Ithaca, NY: Cornell University Press; Kempadoo and Shih (2023) *White Supremacy, Racism and the Coloniality of Anti-Trafficking*, New York, London: Routledge; Brace and O'Connell Davidson (2018) *Revisiting Slavery and Antislavery Towards a Critical Analysis: Towards a Critical Analysis*, Basingstoke: Palgrave Macmillan.

The role of definitions: the legal origins of slavery and human trafficking

The contestation over defining what has emerged as modern slavery has a complicated history, with attempts to define slavery and categorize its unique wrongs provoking scholarly clashes among classicists, philosophers, political theorists, anthropologists, sociologists, and legal academics (Finley, 1964; Kopytoff and Miers, 1977; Patterson, 1982; Meillassoux, 1991; Allain, 2012; Chuang, 2014; and Rota, 2020). The terms human trafficking, trafficking in persons, and modern slavery are used interchangeably by politicians, charities, media, scholars, and within society. Yet, forced labour, slavery, and human trafficking are crimes that exist at the far end of what Jens Lerche identifies as the 'spectrum' of labour exploitation (Lerche, 2007: 435). These terms are used interchangeably providing a broad appeal to humanitarian feeling (O'Connell Davidson, 2015: 6) and remain intrinsically linked, exploiting the emotive quality of slavery, and affording a level of exceptionality to the phenomena. Subsequently, the issues emerged during the early 21st century as 'major sources of popular fascination and political preoccupation' (Bunting & Quirk, 2017a). The view that modern slavery is an 'urgent global social problem' has been readily accepted (O'Connell Davidson, 2022: 2), illustrated through the inclusion of modern slavery within Target 8.7 of the UN Sustainable Development Goals (SDGs),[8] with the definition of what qualifies as or does not qualify as modern slavery appearing as an increasingly important rhetorical device that serves in separating out which kinds of exploitation require political priority (Quirk, 2011). However, in legal terms a special kind of pressure emerges as the prohibition of slavery is recognized as a rule of customary international law.[9] It is also regularly identified as a legal obligation *erga omnes*[10] and as part of *jus cogens* – a peremptory norm of international law.[11]

---

[8] See further https://sdgs.un.org/goals/goal8 [Accessed 15 February 2023].

[9] See further *Prosecutor v Kunarac, Kovac and Vukovic*, Case IT-96-23-T and IT-96-23/1-T, ICTY Trial Chamber, 22 February 2001 (*Kunarac* judgment), at para 520. For an overview of this customary prohibition and its development, see M.C. Bassiouni (1991), 'Enslavement as an international crime', *New York University Journal of International Law and Politics*, 23: 445.

[10] A legal obligation *erga omnes* is considered to be universal in character giving any state a legal interest in its protection and a capacity to bring suit against another state in the International Court of Justice (ICJ). This legal right is vindicated irrespective of whether the state has suffered direct harm. The basis for this right was recognized by the ICJ in *Barcelona Traction, Light and Power Company Limited (Belgium v Spain)*, [1970] ICJ Rep 3 (*Barcelona Traction*) at paras 33–4.

[11] The international law principle of *jus cogens* is a 'peremptory norm of general international law' and is a 'a norm accepted and recognized by the international community as a whole as a norm from which no derogation is permitted and which can be modified only by a subsequent norm of general international law having the same character', Vienna Convention on the Law of Treaties (VCLT), at Art 53. See further on the status of the

In law the two respective regimes of slavery and human trafficking are conceptually distinct and have separate historical origins, which only merged with the negotiations of the UN Protocol to Prevent, Suppress and Punish Trafficking in Persons, especially women and children (hereafter, the Palermo Protocol) (Allain, 2018: 3). The continued conflation between slavery and trafficking for some commentators has been done to acknowledge other forms of exploitation that have been excluded or missed by the efforts of the international legal framework and international counter-trafficking policy regime (Allain, 2017: 61). While others have noted that the rise of modern slavery 'is a distraction: in the midst of hand-wringing over myriad forms of exploitation, attention is not being paid to the factors that contribute to and sustain such exploitation' (Segrave et al, 2018: 9). The undercurrent of colonialism and the racial hierarchies of colonial logic infiltrate contemporary response to immigration, victimhood, and othering (see further Boukli et al, this volume). As encapsulated in the foreword to this volume, the deeper histories and entanglements that inform and shape responses to modern slavery are integral to the debate. These undercurrents need to be centralized within critiques of modern slavery, as without this wider context beyond the notion of freeing slaves the ideological machine of anti-trafficking cannot be dismantled.

I will now provide a brief overview of the legal origins or regimes of regulation relating to slavery and human trafficking.

Slavery

Legal systems throughout time have sought to govern and regulate slavery in multiple manifestations, from Ancient Greece and the Roman Empire to the contemporary moves to eradicate modern slavery in the UK and Australia, through their respective Modern Slavery Acts of 2015[12] and 2018[13] to France's 'duty of vigilance' law of 2017.[14] Different forms of slavery are known to have existed in prehistoric societies and 'have been

---

    prohibition on slavery as an obligation *erga omnes* and as a *jus cogens* norm: Bassiouni, 'Enslavement as an international crime'.

[12] www.legislation.gov.uk/ukpga/2015/30/contents/enacted [Accessed 15 July 2023]. See further www.opendemocracy.net/en/beyond-trafficking-and-slavery/dangerous-appeal-of-modern-slavery-paradigm/ [Accessed 15 July 2023]; V. Mantouvalou (2018) 'The UK Modern Slavery Act 2015 three years on', *Modern Law Review*, 81(6): 1017–45.

[13] www.legislation.gov.au/Details/C2018A00153 [Accessed 15 July 2023]; see further www.opendemocracy.net/en/beyond-trafficking-and-slavery/australia-s-modern-slavery-proposal-falls-short/ [Accessed 15 July 2023]; P. Redmond (2020) 'Regulating through reporting: an anticipatory assessment of the Australian Modern Slavery Acts', *Australian Journal of Human Rights*, 26:1, 5–26. doi: 10.1080/1323238X.2020.1774844.

[14] See further F. McGaughey, H. Voss, H. Cullen, and M.C. Davis (2022) 'Corporate responses to tackling modern slavery: a comparative analysis of Australia, France and

present historically in most regions of the world' (Brace and O'Connell Davidson: 2018: 6). Indeed, 'it should be accepted that slavery has constituted the rule, not the exception in human history' (Allain, 2013: 10). The label of slavery carries a political and emotional weight (Beutin, 2023; Kempadoo and Shi, 2023). *Jus cogens* (also known as a peremptory norm of international law) means that it is norm that is accepted and recognized by the international community as a whole as a norm from which no derogation is permitted and which can be modified only by a subsequent norm of general international law having the same character[15] Yet, when it comes to defining slavery, some academics have commented that the project of trying to find a definition of slavery 'that might fit all [historical cases]' is a 'fruitless exercise in semantics' (Kopytoff and Miers, 1977: 7). The term modern slavery itself does not situate well within the context of the US with the clear preference for 'human trafficking' within legislative and policy responses.[16] This preference is replicated within Europe and within this edited collection you will see that the terms human trafficking and modern slavery are used interchangeably by contributors, with some authors such as Bhagat, Francis, and De Vries and Cockbain avoiding the use of 'modern slavery' altogether.

Most contemporary discussions of slavery and international law begin with the work of the League of Nations[17] (1919–45), which established a foundation upon which the most recent jurisprudence concerned with slavery was built (Quirk, 2012: 257). During the early 20th century, anti-slavery activists pressed for more expansive legal definitions and the political understanding of slavery (Brace and O'Connell Davidson, 2018). One example of this emerges from the Leagues' archives in Geneva, in a pamphlet entitled 'Slavery and the Obligations of the League' which identified slavery's 'barbaric cruelty, no less than its economic folly, should make a strong

---

the United Kingdom', *Business and Human Rights Journal*, 7(2): 249–70, DOI: 10.1017/bhj.2021.47.

[15] The international law principle of *jus cogens* is a 'peremptory norm of general international law'. See further VCLT, at Art 53. See further on the status of the prohibition on slavery as an obligation *erga omnes* and as a *jus cogens* norm, Bassiouni, 'Enslavement as an international crime'.

[16] For example, the Trafficking Victims Protection Act 2000, as amended, provides the tools to combat trafficking in persons both worldwide and domestically. The Act authorized the establishment of the State Department's TIP Office and the President's Interagency Task Force to Monitor and Combat Trafficking in Persons to assist in the coordination of anti-trafficking efforts. Available from: www.state.gov/international-and-domestic-law/ [Accessed 15 June 2023].

[17] See further S. Legg (2012) '"The life of individuals as well as of nations": international law and the League of Nations' anti-trafficking governmentalities', *Leiden Journal of International Law*, 25(3): 647–64.

appeal to the civilized world civilized world ... with a plea for international enquiry and action'.[18] Yet, most international attention during this period was directed towards non-European governments, most notably Liberia and Ethiopia, rather than with colonial labour regimes or European tutelage of 'backwards peoples' (Allain, 2012: 256).

The League of Nations introduced the Convention to Suppress the Slave Trade and Slavery (hereafter, the Slavery Convention) in 1926,[19] calling upon all states to criminalize enslavement, and to put an end to slavery progressively and as soon as possible. However, it is notable that the way in which the 1926 definition was 'operationalized by European authorities concerned with various slave systems which continued under colonial jurisdiction' (Quirk, 2012: 226). Article 1 of the 1926 Convention articulated that: 'Slavery is the status or condition of a person over whom any or all of the powers attaching to the right of ownership are exercised.'

This definition approaches it from a property law perspective, and for liberal thinkers this is what makes slavery uniquely abhorrent (O'Connell Davidson, 2022: 14). The definition 'is accepted as the contemporary definition, having been considered in negotiations for both the 1956 Supplementary Convention and the 1998 Statute of the International Criminal Court and found to be satisfactory as being an accurate reflection of the term'[20] (Allain, 2013: 4). The 1926 Slavery Convention definition was essentially one that fitted with what had, till then, been understood as chattel slavery but also required states to bring about the complete abolition of slavery in 'all its forms' (Brace and O'Connell Davidson, 2018). The concept of 'slavery in all its forms' has been of particular interest to Joel Quirk, who commented that it 'acquires legal and analytical currency through its incorporation within 1926 but can also be found in other international instruments such as the 1948 Universal Declaration of Human Rights'.

The definition of slavery has caused controversy since its adoption with visible differences in opinion emerging about which practices should and should not be classified as slavery and therefore designated for elimination[21]

---

[18] J.H. Harris (1922), *Slavery and the Obligations of the League*, London: The Anti-Slavery and Aborigines Protection Society.

[19] See further https://treaties.un.org/pages/ViewDetails.aspx?src=TREATY&mtdsg_no=XVIII-3&chapter=18&clang=_en [Accessed 15 July 2023].

[20] See further the 2008 *Tang* case before the High Court of Australia, which makes clear 'the definition is an applicable contemporary standard applying in situations of both de jure slavery, but more importantly in cases of de facto slavery'.

[21] See further the UN Sub-Commission on the Promotion and Protection of Human Rights, Contemporary Forms of Slavery, Updated Review of the Implementation and Follow-Up to the Convention on Slavery, working paper prepared by D. Weissbrodt and Anti-Slavery International, 52nd session, 26 May 2000, E/CN.4.Sub.2/2000/3, para 6.

(Humbert, 2009: 26), with the 1953 Report of the Secretary General indicating that the drafters of the 1926 Convention had in mind the concept of authority of the master over the slave, comparable to that of *dominica potestas* in Roman Law.[22] Some have commented that the definition provided through the 1926 and 1956 Slavery Conventions was deliberately drafted to be narrow in scope to avoid 'spiralling interpretations' (Allain and Hickey, 2012). Quirk (2012: 258) and accepts the frustrating fact that all these forms were never defined, whilst highlighting that the burden subsequently fell upon the signatories to the Slavery Convention to determine the scope of their new obligations.

Human trafficking

The history of human trafficking can be divided into three periods: first, pre-League of Nations; second, the League of Nations era from 1919 to 1945; and, finally, the United Nations era from 1945 to today, with the origins of human trafficking emerging from the focus within Europe upon the 'White Slave Traffic' (see further Lammasniemi, this volume). An in-depth discussion of each of these periods falls outside the parameters of this chapter, but they form a central foundational component of the contemporary debates unpicked within this edited collection. Although, the clear racialized term 'white slavery' shifted into the more neutral 'trafficking in women and children' during the 20th century, the racialized constructs that influence the legal responses to human trafficking and immigration more generally remain (Lammasniemi, 2017; Beutin, 2023).

The origins of the Palermo Protocol can be traced back to Argentina's interest in the issue of trafficking in minors and to its 'dissatisfaction with the slow progress on negotiating an additional Protocol to the CRC to address child prostitution and child pornography'[23] (Faulkner, 2023). Adopted as a Protocol to the UN Convention against Transnational Organized Crime 2000, framing the problem as a crime. This framing of the 'problem of human trafficking as a transnational crime, best addressed through aggressive prosecution of traffickers'[24] for the crime of violating state control of borders. The Protocol was negotiated at 'lightning speed on the UN clock' within two years (Lloyd and Simmons, 2015: 423) and

---

[22] See Report of the Secretary-General on Slavery, the Slave Trade, and Other Forms of Servitude, E/2357 (1953), para 36, fn 1, quoted in N. Lassen (1988), 'Slavery and slavery-like practices: United Nations standards and implementation', *Nordic Journal of International Law*, 57: 197–227, 205.

[23] Travaux preparatoires; 320 Argentina (A/AC.254/8).

[24] Protocol to Prevent, Suppress and Punish Trafficking in Persons, Arts 2, 4.

entering into force in 2003, the Palermo Protocol has been exceptionally well ratified to date.²⁵

Article 3(a) of the Protocol reads:

> 'Trafficking in persons' shall mean the recruitment, transportation, transfer, harboring or receipt of persons, by means of the threat or use of fore or other forms of coercion, of abduction, of fraud, of deception, of the abuse of power or of a position of vulnerability or of the giving or receiving of payments or benefits to achieve the consent of a person having control over another person, for the purpose of exploitation. Exploitation shall include, at a minimum, the exploitation of the prostitution of others or other forms of sexual exploitation, forced labour or services, slavery or practices similar to slavery, servitude or the removal of organs.

Article 3(a) establishes the three separate elements to the definition: (i) the action; (ii) the means; and (iii) the purpose or exploitation (illustrated by Table 1.1). As defined by the Palermo Protocol, trafficking does not refer to a single, unitary act leading to one specific outcome, but is rather to cover a process (recruitment, transportation, and control) that can be organized in a variety of ways and involves a range of different actions and outcomes (Anderson and O'Connell Davidson, 2003). It therefore 'offers an expansive understanding of both the means of trafficking as well as the purpose for which one is trafficked, namely exploitation' (Kotiswaran, 2017: 11). Although the Palermo Protocol contained an explicit definition of the meaning of trafficking in persons, essentially it consolidated existing international law concerning a range of forms of unacceptable exploitation (Dottridge, 2017: 59). Since the adoption of the Protocol, global anti-trafficking law and policy has evolved significantly. The 'once near-exclusive focus on the prosecution prong of the "3Ps" approach to trafficking – prosecuting traffickers, protecting victims and preventing trafficking – has given way to increased victim protection' (Chuang, 2021: 179) Yet, the concepts of coercion and exploitation that are central to the Palermo Protocol are undefined and their 'meaning under international law is far from definitive even when clear' (Kotiswaran, 2018: 11). This explicit framing of trafficking as transnational organised crime, rather than a human rights violation, can be understood by the fact that the foci of anti-trafficking was predominately upon border control. The crime of human trafficking was viewed as a violation of statist controls

---

²⁵ https://treaties.un.org/Pages/ViewDetails.aspx?src=TREATY&mtdsg_no=XVIII-12-a&chapter=18&lang=en [Accessed 25 November 2020].

Table 1.1: Overview of the Trafficking Protocol definition of human trafficking, 2000

	Action (i)	Means (ii)	Purpose (iii)
Trafficking in persons	Recruitment	Threat or use of force	Exploitation, including
	Transport	Coercion	Prostitution of others
	Harbouring	Abduction	Sexual exploitation
	Receipt of persons	Fraud	Forced labour
		Deception	Slavery or similar practices
		Abuse of power or vulnerability	Removal of organs
		Giving payments or benefits	Other types of exploitation

Source: Author

of national borders and legally constructed upon this logic through the Palermo Protocol. This leads to the question of human rights and what role these rights might have in addressing the nexus between anti-trafficking and anti-immigration.

The question of human rights

Human rights are defined as certain fundamental rights to which every human being is entitled and are inherent in all human beings irrespective of colour, ancestry, sex, ethnic origin, or social status. In the wake of the Second World War (1939–1945), it was recognized that 'no international human rights mechanisms has existed prior to and during the war which could have allowed interference between a state and its citizens in relation to even extreme human rights abuses' (Fenwick, 2018: 28). The European historical origins of human rights – namely, the protection of the emerging bourgeoisie against authoritarian monarchical regimes – are for some commentators enough to demonstrate their inadequacy to protect populations of the Global South against violations (by imperialist and neoclassicist practices) of the same rights (Ramina, 2018: 265). The politics of international human rights protection had become apparent, and by 1947 'human rights' were rapidly becoming an ideological weapon in the war of words between East and West (Lauren, 1998: 228). For some commentators the West was able to impose its philosophy of human rights upon the rest of the world due to its dominance of the UN at its inception (Ramina, 2018: 267). The colonial logics of human rights remain entrenched within the international legal framework and policy measures which have been implemented in a mission to advance human rights globally, such as through the Sustainable Development Goals (SDGs). Despite this legacy human rights are identified as the blueprint for the eradication and prevention of slavery, including the construction of modern slavery.

The Universal Declaration of Human Rights (hereafter, the UDHR) was collaboratively drafted by representatives with different legal and cultural backgrounds from all regions of the world. In the aftermath of the Second World War, attempts were concentrated on the development of legal instruments which protected human rights. The UDHR is generally agreed to be the foundation of international human rights law – adopted in 1948, it has 'inspired a rich body of legally binding international human rights treaties'.[26] The construction of international law as the protector against the abhorrent practice of slavery is problematic, as for some international law remains an instrument to pursue the interests of ancient colonial power (Gallie, 2008; Ramina, 2018). Furthermore, international law does not 'necessarily offer universal justice precisely because unequal power relations following the patterns of the colonial era are maintained through international law today' (Mayblin and Turner, 2021: 21).

The UDHR explicitly addresses slavery through Article 4, which proclaims that 'No one shall be held in slavery or servitude; slavery and the slave trade shall be prohibited in all their forms'.[27] This prohibition (albeit non-binding) gives the concept 'legal and analytical currency' (Quirk, 2012: 256) as the inclusion of slavery in all its forms arises from the 1926 Slavery Convention previously discussed. International Human Rights Law reflects the 1956 Supplementary Conventions division between slavery and servitude or 'slavery-like practices'. The UDHR and the International Covenant on Civil and Political Rights (ICCPR)[28] both prohibit slavery and the slave trade, and 'further stipulate that no person shall be held in *servitude*' – a term that, although not defined by either instrument, is related normatively to the

---

[26] www.un.org/en/about-us/udhr/foundation-of-international-human-rights-law [Accessed 15 June 2021].

[27] The Universal Declaration of Human Rights (UDHR) is a milestone document in the history of human rights. Drafted by representatives with different legal and cultural backgrounds from all regions of the world, the Declaration was proclaimed by the United Nations General Assembly in Paris on 10 December 1948 (General Assembly resolution 217 A) as a common standard of achievements for all peoples and all nations.

[28] UDHR Art 4, ICCPR Arts 8(1) and 8(2), respectively.

pre-human rights era concept of 'servile status' (Gallagher, 2012: 182). The UDHR has not been free of critique with Lauterpacht dismissing it as having 'controversial moral authority' (Lauterpacht, 1950: 279), while others note how human rights are perceived and as a mechanism to impose European standards often used as a toll for colonialist practices and interventions (Mutua, 2001; Ibhawoh, 2007, 23; Bachand, 2010; Ramina, 2018, 264). The 'savages, victims, and saviors' (SVS) metaphor coined by Mutua (2001) laid bare some of the hypocrisies of the human rights project, which 'contains a subtext which depicts an epochal contest pitting, savages on the one hand, against victims and saviours, on the other'. Certain parallels can be drawn here via the SVS metaphor under the operationalized narrative of modern slavery, with certain forms:

> made to be visually synonymous with very selective working conditions, including: child laborer's in Africa, the Caribbean, and Asia who work in small-scale mining, fishing, farming, brick and carpet making, and domestic households; migrant farmworkers in the United Sates; Asian-owned massage parlors and nail salons in the United States and United Kingdom ... and all forms of sex work globally. (Beutin, 2023: 2)

The division between practices treated as acceptable exploitation in comparison with those which are not sits at the heart of this volume. Each of the chapters evaluates exploitation, with Kiconco (this volume) and Bhagat (this volume) both illustrating how research participants and/or the gatekeepers can offer the story that is wanted or expected succinctly. The emphasis of anti-slavery/trafficking campaigns is often placed upon the victims, who have been reduced to objects of trade. This manifests into the visual imagery of women and girls as slabs of meat, or packed in jam jars or sardine tins, or with bodies barcoded ready for sale, or as inanimate objects such as puppets, or as decapitated heads or packaged as sex toys (Aradau, 2004; Andrijasevic, 2007; O'Connell Davidson, 2015: 18). Human trafficking has been consistently constructed as 'sexual slavery', with the dominant media images of the issue featuring 'young, desperate women forced to sell sex on dirty mattresses in dimly lit back rooms' (Beutin, 2023: 2). This fear of sexual slavery has been subsequently expanded through references to capture bonded and forced labour under the rubric of 'a modern form of slavery'.[29]

---

[29] Victims of Trafficking and Violence Protection Act 2000, Public Law 106–386, 28 October 2000, available from: www.govinfo.gov/content/pkg/PLAW-106publ386/pdf/PLAW-106publ386.pdf [Accessed 15 July 2023].

Modern slavery: rage against the machine

Fighting human trafficking and modern slavery over the last two decades has become a 'cause célébre' (LeBaron and Pliley, 2021: 1), despite the fact that there is nothing new to fight. In fact, advocacy against modern slavery was once situated upon the periphery, sidelined by the fascination of human trafficking for sexual exploitation, and now in the 21st century 'it has risen to the fore as the "catch-all" for a broad range of exploitative practices' (Chuang, 2014; Kotiswaran, 2017; Segrave, Milivojevic, and Pickering, 2018). It is an issue that is frequently heralded as a threat to society, and the quest to end modern slavery rests upon the premise that it constitutes a uniquely intolerable moral wrong, and that it can be separated from other social and global ills for purposes of practical intervention (O'Connell Davidson, 2015: 8) and quantification (Engle-Merry, 2017; Broome and Quirk, 2015) (Modern slavery is presented as a distinct and concrete crime, and as the worst of contemporary ills with millions of people enslaved globally. A variety of global benchmarking frameworks[30] (methodologically unsound, yet presented as hard facts) have been implemented from the 'Global Slavery Index, Global Estimates of Modern Slavery to the Trafficking in Persons Reports produced annually by the US Department of State which seeks to measure human trafficking according to Global North paradigms' (Kempadoo and Shih, 2023: 6). The Trafficking in Persons Report remains an important mechanism in the context of critical modern slavery studies and receives an interrogation from multiple authors in the collection (see further Boukli et al, De Vries and Cockbain, and Francis, this volume). Despite the adoption of the language of modern slavery, a unified understanding of what does and does not encompass 'modern slavery' is yet to be (if ever) agreed.

Within this Introduction I make references to modern slavery, anti-trafficking, and the discourse of both indiscriminately. However, as indicated previously, it needs to be acknowledged that the international legal frameworks have separate origins with human trafficking emerging from attempts to address the 'White Slave Traffic' in late 19th-century Europe (Allain, 2018: 5) and the abolition of slavery and Transatlantic Slave Trade. The issue of modern slavery is one of increasing significance in relation to research, from the plethora of funding available for research and actions that will eradicate the issue to the attention it receives globally in legal and

---

[30] For an interrogation of the global-benchmarking mechanisms such as the TIPR, see further S. Engle-Merry (2017) who crucified the reliability of such reports and any estimates as to the prevalence of trafficking. See further, A. Broome and J. Quirk (2015) 'The politics of numbers: the normative agendas of global benchmarking', *Review of International Studies*, 41(5): 813–18.

policy fora, to the continual publication of global benchmarks[31] and targets to eradicate the 'scourge of modern slavery' (Brace, 2018: 11). It is here that the collection situates, not through continuing the contestation over the term of slavery, whether it is useful or who gains from this rhetorical framing but through challenging the dominant narrative that surrounds the issues.

Exploitation is interwoven into the fabric of society, with legal efforts to curtail specific forms or types of exploitation or to better protect identified categories of people ultimately ignoring how systems perpetuate and foster the environments within which exploitation thrives. Focusing upon the international legal framework crafted under the auspices of the UN, from human rights to migration and trafficking, the question that arises is along the lines of querying whether the world is a better place? Ultimately, the answer to that depends upon your perspective. International law has long been documented as a tool of oppression and that the concerns of human rights only emerged in the wake of the suffering of white populations following the Second World War. The counter narrative of Third World Approaches to International Law (TWAIL) illustrates that it was European colonialism that formed the background for the emergence of international law as we know it today. The purpose of international law is to both rationalize and regulate the subjugation of non-European lands and people (Anghie, 2005). The discourse of anti-trafficking has a 'distinct racialized legacy that includes the history of fears about "white slavery", sex work and commercial intimacy, migration from non-Western countries, Blackness and Indigeneity' (Kempadoo and Shih, 2023: 1). It is within this context (of the deeper histories of anti-trafficking/slavery) that we consider the emergence of modern slavery under an interdisciplinary lens.

About the edited collection: the organizing logic

This interdisciplinary volume has been drawn together under the illustrative concept of a kaleidoscope, highlighting how different disciplinary positions and perspectives form and clash together to form a unique insight into critical modern slavery studies. This construct seeks to illustrate the organizational logic and framing of the collection, providing a viewpoint to understand how each chapter contributes to the creation of the kaleidoscope. It is important to recognize that the imagery is not fixed, but one that can be changed depending on your viewpoint or informed and influenced by your perspective or global outlook. This collection seeks to provide an empirically grounded interrogation of the concept of modern slavery, along with the legal, policy, and knowledge architecture

---

[31] TIPR, ILO, GEMS, GSI.

surrounding it. A central theme through the book relates to the concept of harm, its construction and interpretation in different empirical studies relating to modern slavery globally. The book is organized under three interlocking strands; namely, Part I 'Theoretical Perspectives', Part II 'Structural Issues in Modern Slavery and Human Trafficking Practice, and Part III 'Case Studies'.

Chapter overview

The chapters consider the different legal, political, and policy responses from a variety of geographical locations from around the world intended to address modern slavery. The collection utilizes specific case studies from states such as Belize, Bolivia, Nepal, Peru, Uganda, the UK, and Vietnam to provide insights into the construction of the phenomena. Through operationalizing different disciplinary perspectives, anti-colonial critiques, and interrogating the global power structures that regulate exploitation, this collection will provide a contribution to the growing critical scholarly work on the issue of modern slavery and the plethora of challenges connected thereto. It draws together issues such as the influence of the international legal responses, issues of knowledge production and extraction, coupled with the 'Western gaze' of anti-slavery efforts upon different geographical locations, featuring research conducted in the Caribbean, Latin America, North America, South America, Asia, Europe, and Africa.

Part I: 'Theoretical Perspectives'

The entanglements of history and the influence of legal and societal debates of trafficking in women or 'white slavery' can be seen within contemporary arenas, but that history is often neglected, unknown, or exploited by politicians, policy makers, society, and the humanitarian industry alike. This part of the collection draws together three chapters, one firmly a historical piece with the latter both incorporating historical context into the discussion but utilizing coloniality as a theoretical framework to challenge the dominant discourse of modern slavery. Each chapter focuses upon a different geographical location and time period, with the first centred on Great Britain in the early 20th century, the second firmly centred within Latin America in the 21st century, while the third chapter undertakes a review of trafficking internationally through analysing the Trafficking in Persons Reports[32] between 2001 and 2020.

---

[32] For the most recent annually produced report, see www.state.gov/reports/2023-trafficking-in-persons-report/ [Accessed 15 June 2023].

The methodological approach within each chapter is different but commonalities between can be traced. Together, these chapters provide a compelling argument that a full understanding and appreciation of the historical, colonial, and racialized contexts from which modern slavery have emerged is imperative to gain an understanding of the present state of exploitation globally.

Lammasniemi's chapter provides an insight into a period which is often overlooked in debates about modern slavery; namely, after the adoption of abolitionist legislation in the early 20th century prior to the adoption of international instruments to address human trafficking. Drawing upon archives the chapter catalogues the efforts of civil society organizations (namely, the National Vigilance Association and the International Abolitionist Federation) to influence laws implemented and highlight the role that civil society has played within the legislative process. The power of language and the rhetoric attached to it is interwoven through antitrafficking laws which sideline the voices of women. This chapter provides a portrayal of how the legal frameworks emerged and the social and moral context that engulfed them. Building on the historical insights provided in relation to the legislative developments in Great Britain, the subsequent chapter centralizes historical contexts in relation to the development of modern slavery in Latin America.

O'Connell's chapter draws upon both historical and contemporary evidence from Bolivia and Peru to illustrate how so-called abolition has given way to neocolonial forms of exploitation, subsequently distinguishing it from forms of exploitation elsewhere in the world such as in Europe. Through conducting extensive documentary and field research, O'Connell critiques state responses to modern slavery in the guano and rubber industries of Peru and the exploitation of indigenous Guaraní in Bolivia. Undertaking 90 qualitative interviews with a range of actors in each state including state officials, prosecutors, NGO representatives, social movement leaders and local academics, O'Connell gains an insight into the responses of the state to vulnerability to exploitation and abuse. Further, through identifying the role and power of the state, O'Connell advocates for more engagement with colonial history and global capitalism within modern slavery research. Central to the discussion is the problematic nature of the term modern slavery, and the confusion surrounding its use, asserting that the focus upon individual slaves diverts attention from the wider socio-economic and political context; something which is not isolated to the region but can be seen in subsequent chapters within the case studies in Part III (see further Currie and Weatherburn, this volume). Using coloniality as a theoretical framework for the analysis, the chapter serves as a challenge to the mainstream thinking and policy responses to the phenomena. It is through this lens that the subsequent chapter follows, providing a content analysis of the

Trafficking in Persons Reports[33] (hereafter, TIPR), which are produced annually by the US.

The TIPR are presented as a global benchmark for analysing trafficking trends, with the perceived need for quantification in the field addressed earlier in the introductory chapter. The TIPR are a prime example of soft power, as both funding and policy initiatives from the US are associated with the findings. This in turn influences the responses of states as it holds a particular dominance over the anti-trafficking field for financial, geographical, and political reasons (see Francis, this volume). The TIPR predominately focus on sex trafficking and illustrates the role of moral anxiety attached to certain forms of labour and sexual exploitation. This, in turn, serves to obscure many other forms of exploitation which have emerged globally.

The chapter undertakes a content analysis of the reports between 2001 and 2020, explicitly highlighting how policy interventions of anti-trafficking impose colonial frameworks of knowledge both locally and globally. It considers the dangers of stereotypes and the prejudice caused to certain population groups (see Hyne and Dottridge, this volume). Through centralizing racial hierarchies of colonial logic, the chapter focuses on the category of 'Indigenous' as it embodies a set of colonial constructions that are being fed both inwards and outwards, illustrating how Indigenous people become more visible over time as individuals and not in a way which alerts the reader to the basic colonial underpinning of the TIPR analysis, which reproduces power relations across the globe in specific parts of the world where victims are identified, such as the Caribbean (see Francis, this volume), Southeast Asia and Latin America. Ultimately, Boukli, Papanicolaou, and Dimou view the TIPR as a mechanism that reproduces coloniality, on a global scale. While the chapter is not explicitly connected with ethics, it does present similar observations to the following chapter in that it illustrates some of the dangers of the anti-trafficking debate.

Part II: 'Structural Issues in Human Trafficking and Modern Slavery Practice'

Building upon the theoretical frameworks evidenced in the first part of the collection, the second part moves to identify some of the key structural issues that emerge within the context of human trafficking and modern slavery practice, providing further insights into the artificial and unhelpful distinction between human trafficking and existing bodies of knowledge, experience and expertise.

---

[33] See www.state.gov/trafficking-in-persons-report/ [Accessed 21 December 2023].

Each chapter considers the UK in some capacity but speaks to the core theme of this collection; namely, 'global context' through drawing upon research relating to four continents, including Africa, Asia, Europe, and North America. The chapters demonstrate some of the issues for those working in the field, such as those which advocate simplistic solutions for incredibly complex and diverse phenomena. This is not isolated to contemporary discussions, as these proposed solutions often cause harms for those they purport to protect and compound structural inequalities and injustices.

De Vries and Cockbain provide an examination of the way that indicators are used to explain and enumerate the trafficking nexus in most countries, building upon the previous chapters' examination of colonial constructions and the subsequent development of quantitative solutions. The chapter highlights how indicators provide a false sense of reliability and solidity, far removed from giving a proper account of the trafficking process, and effectively serving to obscure rather than reveal the 'real' data. Additionally, indicators are not 'neutral nor unskewed' and can be manipulated to present a particular picture for differing actors concerned politically about the phenomenon.[34] For the authors, the use of indicators both perpetuates and reinforces stereotypical views and ideals of victimhood.[35] The production and use of indicators shape the focus upon specific dimensions of human trafficking, which are driven by Western hegemony[36] (see O'Connell and Boukli, this volume), knowledge production, and political motivations. Through focusing on the commercial sexual exploitation of children in the US, the chapter identifies the empirical challenges in developing human trafficking indicators and the need for empirically stronger and more robust mechanisms. In essence, the US report system establishes the US as the world's arbiter on anti-trafficking initiatives and agendas. The impact of the position of the US as the global sheriff (Chuang, 2006)[37] is that the conceptions may not align with local realties, and this is subsequently discussed later in the volume (see Francis). The authors contend that those working within the field need to rethink their dependence on current

---

[34] See further www.opendemocracy.net/en/beyond-trafficking-and-slavery/the-victims-of-unknown-exploitation-hiding-within-the-uk-national-referral-mechanism/ [Accessed 15 June 2023].

[35] See further Lammasniemi (Chapter 2, this volume) for discussion of victimhood in the early 20th century.

[36] White Western hegemony dominates cultures in nations that were colonized by countries in Western Europe. These colonial logics have infiltrated anti-trafficking logics.

[37] J.A. Chuang (2006) 'The United States as global sheriff: using unilateral sanctions to combat human trafficking', *Michigan Journal of International Law*, 27(2). Available from: https://ssrn.com/abstract=990098

indicators and recognize that the process may be more complex than can effectively be captured by numerical approaches. Ultimately, the chapter observes that calls for indicator-based approaches require greater scrutiny, transparency, and efficient testing and improvement. Through hinting that indicators perpetuate harms through their lack of neutrality and skewed status, a link to the subsequent chapter arises.

The link that emerges between the chapter by Hynes and Dottridge and the discussion by De Vries and Cockbain transpires through the notion of unintended harms. This concept of 'unintended harms' has been extensively analysed, resulting in the contestation that they can no longer be classified as such due to the growing body of evidence (Kempadoo, 2005). The notion of 'collateral damage'[38] is extensively examined within the literature (Kempadoo and Shih, 2023: 1) and the authors seek to address this through developing a 'living ethical protocol' to minimize the impact. Collateral damage has particular significance when undertaking research into modern slavery and the authors identify their disquiet with the notion of the unintended harms of law and policy in this area. Through a large-scale project conducted in Albania, Nigeria, Vietnam, and the UK, this chapter contributes to the unfolding debates surrounding the question of ethics in relation to modern slavery studies. Through carefully avoiding constructing migration as a problem to be dealt with, the chapter talks through existing frameworks and that through the adoption of a trafficking lens to migration everything is inherently wicked. The notion of harm and how individuals at local levels perceive harm and how those harms are categorized while recognizing agentic individuals serves as a challenge to the classical cultural imperialism that often pervades this area (see further Bahgat, this volume). The authors seek to frame research into modern slavery and trafficking in a different way; they consider the construction of methodological nationalism,[39] and ecological models of child abuse and human trafficking. This overarching aim underlies the chapter's call for greater prudence when designing research or presenting findings – something addressed in the previous chapter.

Ethics undoubtedly play a role within the context of human trafficking investigations, but how do ethical considerations sit within the criminal justice context? It is here that Pajon's chapter shifts the focus of this part to critique the criminal investigation[40] process. The chapter considers two

---

[38] See further GAATW (2007) 'Collateral damage: the impact of anti-trafficking measures on human rights around the world', available from: https://gaatw.org/resources/publications/908-collateral-damage-the-impact-of-anti-trafficking-measures-on-human-rights-around-the-world [Accessed 15 July 2023].

[39] See further Chapter 6 for definition of methodological nationalism.

[40] The criminal investigation of modern slavery offences remains relatively new and unique to the UK as save for Australia; it remains one of the only legal jurisdictions in the world

police investigations within England and Wales, but each respective operation focuses on non-British nationals; namely, the labour exploitation of Czech nationals (Operation Green) and the sexual exploitation of Romanian nationals (Operation Blue). This chapter offers a specific examination of the nature of police collaboration with partner agencies in two large human trafficking investigations from the UK, but in doing so links to the successful (due to the creativity) development of the relationship between the police and non-state actors in Belize alluded to later in the volume. Offering a UK-based case study of practice, it situates as an example of contemporary practice and a critique of the framing of modern slavery and human trafficking as criminal justice issues. The empirically rich chapter draws upon interviews conducted with lead investigators, coupled with reviews of police files and other official documents. Through documenting the intricacies of the investigative process, and implied power dynamics between the police and other agencies, the author highlights the exclusion of alternative frameworks to approach the issues. Pajon emphasizes that multi-agency collaboration is needed within the field, indicating to the points raised later in the volume about what that collaboration could and should look like, and how to ensure it is successful.[41]

We shall now turn to the final part of the book, which includes chapters with geographically focused specific case studies.

Part III: 'Case Studies'

The regional or country-focused studies create a map for exploring some of the significant issues within the field of modern slavery studies that are depicted in the first two parts of the collection. The intention is not to use examples that can be extrapolated or generalized across the world, but to enrich the book's focus on global context. The synergies between chapters are more discrete in this part in some contexts, with the accounts of Weatherburn and Francis offering contrasting reviews focusing on state and non-state actors respectively. However, the chapters included form pieces of the interdisciplinary kaleidoscope that serves to illustrate the internal logics of the collection. The impact of the anti-trafficking and anti-slavery movements

---

to specifically enact modern slavery legislation. See further www.legislation.gov.uk/ukpga/2015/30/contents/enacted; www.legislation.gov.au/Details/C2018A00153. Although the phrase 'modern slavery' is not specifically referenced, the state of California in the US has enacted the Transparency Supply Chains Act as the 'California Legislature found that slavery and human trafficking are crimes under state, federal, and international law; that slavery and human trafficking exist in the State of California and in every country, including the United States'; see further https://oag.ca.gov/SB657 [Accessed 15 June 2023].

[41] See Francis (Chapter 12).

is not uniform, nor isolated to one disciplinary angle, but embedded through the infrastructures created and compounded by the global order – an order that has been built on what Césaire (2000) identified as the 'self-centred economic exploitation of the colonized'.

The first two chapters of this part focus on the UK, which has seen significant changes to immigration law and policy in recent years, including the Nationality and Borders Act 2022[42] and the Illegal Migration Act 2023,[43] which in July 2023 was passed following a record number of defeats in the House of Lords with clashes over child detention and removal of modern slavery protections under the often-lauded Modern Slavery Act (MSA) 2015. What is currently omitted from the debate is the recognition that the MSA was an integral tool of the hostile environment, forming a central component of both anti-worker and anti-immigrant policies. It is within this context that the chapters from Currie and Weatherburn sit, complementing each other well due to the number of synergies between them.

The chapters are intrinsically linked due to their focus on labour within the context of law and policy in the UK. However, they cover different issues utilizing alternative perspectives for analysis; for example, the role of immigration law and policy (and that of the state and/or the EU – more generally) in both establishing vulnerabilities for workers and making precarity, and exploitation, more likely to occur. Both Currie and Weatherburn consider the exploitation of migrant workers in the labour market, but the starting points of each contribution are different, with the former focusing on migration law and policy, and the latter on labour market enforcement.

Through starting with the premise that Brexit is facilitating the labour exploitation of EU migrants, Currie's chapter then shifts to argue that labour exploitation was also part of the experiences of EU migrants under the operation of free movement, subsequently focusing on those from Central and Eastern European (CEE) accession states and centralizing the role of immigration regimes. The impact of Brexit and subsequent changes to immigration policy for EU nationals form the skeleton of this chapter, interrogating how harsher immigration rules and procedures are driving more workers underground to engage in work within the informal economy. This slippage ultimately exposes those working in this context more explicitly to exploitation. Labour law has not been utilized as a framework to protect workers from exploitation and abuse, and is subsequently excluded from the 'package of responses deemed appropriate' to address modern slavery. This provides the bridge into the next chapter which identifies the various

---

[42] www.legislation.gov.uk/ukpga/2022/36/contents/enacted
[43] https://bills.parliament.uk/bills/3429

legal and policy initiatives enacted by the state since the UK's adoption of the MSA in 2015.

Weatherburn contends that those measures will have limited impact given the wider labour market context which is simultaneously facilitating exploitation in many ways. This is exemplified by consecutive Conservative governments that have presented modern slavery as an immigration issue[44] and the poor level of resources available to enforcement officers. The chapter centralizes its analysis on the recent policy development and their contractions which sit at the heart of the current Conservative government in the UK. Ultimately, this demonstrates the real ideological basis that drives the implementation and adoption of such policies. Each chapter, then, emphasizes the uncertainty as to how the issues discussed will play out in future considering the UK's politically restrictive and regressive climate on immigration.

Building on the broader ideology surrounding the field of modern slavery studies, this next chapter shifts our exploration of modern slavery to the grassroots level working directly with research subjects rather than an analysis of the law and policy implemented. This change links to the development of an ethical living protocol from the earlier chapter by Hynes and Dottridge but contends that there is no overarching recipe for ethically good research but how even in the most difficult circumstances it is possible to pursue an ethical approach to research. The chapter focuses its empirical investigation on wartime abduction and sexual violence undertaken by Kiconco in northern Uganda. Kiconco identifies the hierarchical power structures of knowledge production, the role of 'do no harm', and challenges that present through undertaking ethnographic research focusing on lived experiences of formerly abducted women. The interwoven complexities of the insider/outsider, consent, class, age, and power imbalances create layers of complexity, playing out differently on the ground. Centralizing the importance of research methods, ethics, and fieldwork practices that are adopted are both culturally and experientially sensitive ways to ensure that survivors are protected and that the research remains ethically grounded. Ultimately, Kiconco provides an extensive reflexive account of the difficulties faced by the researcher in this kind of enquiry and points towards the unexpected or unintended difficulties which together form the basis for the conclusion that it is not possible to adequately prepare for this kind of research. This

---

[44] The UK government reclassified modern slavery as an immigration issue rather than a safeguarding one in October 2022. www.theguardian.com/world/2022/oct/13/home-office-reclassifies-modern-slavery-as-immigration-issue#:~:text=The%20Home%20Office%20has%20taken,updated%20online%20ministerial%20profiles%20show [Accessed 15 June 2023].

is where we move to the next chapter, which touches upon some of the difficulties facing a researcher when conducting human trafficking research in a different geographical location – namely, Nepal.

Bhagat undertakes fieldwork in Nepal to approach the political classification of victims within Nepal, utilizing a participatory action research (hereafter, PAR) framework to challenge the positionality of non-governmental actors and emphasize the importance of unintentionally deepening the divisions between deserving and undeserving subjects of protection and knowledge, and the need for non-exploitative or extractive empirical research. Within the growing literature of modern slavery, there has been an increased recent focus on victim empowerment and the centralization of the survivors of exploitation. It is within this context that the chapter contributes a challenge to the dominant narrative of a silent and vulnerable victim (see Lammasniemi and De Vries and Cockbain, this volume), through adopting a research paradigm that is centred on involving participants as collaborators within the research to enact social change.

This chapter builds on the theoretical framework of a 'living ethical protocol' proposed by Hynes and Dottridge, in addition to the reflective work of Kiconco, within which she grappled with whether truly ethical research can be undertaken within the contexts of extreme exploitation and/or violence, attempting to tackle the complexities of life's realities for people who wanted to leave the region of Nepal. Explicitly, those who, in turn, faced restricted mobility options and the position of non-governmental organizations (hereafter, NGOs) that frequently blocked mobility through ingrained anti-migration sentiment and government action upon the 'geographies of rumour'. The position of NGOs is significant not only in the context of Nepal, but also reflecting upon earlier chapters in this collection which have focused on the UK. Within the UK, NGOs have insofar been an integral aspect of partnerships which have been explicitly developed with their inclusion to address modern slavery, particularly at local level. The humanitarian industry has capitalized in the misery of others, as 'human misery and suffering is one of the primary currency earners for humanitarian organisations'.[45] It is here that the collection shifts to consider the role of non-state actors in more detail, through a specific analysis of their role within the field of trafficking.

Francis uses Belize as a case study to examine the way that the TIPR (see Boukli, this volume) are effectively used to direct the work of the Belizean government by using funding as a control mechanism. Francis illustrates that

---

[45] D. Kennedy (2009) 'Selling the distant other: humanitarianism and imagery-ethical dilemmas of humanitarian action', *Journal of Humanitarian Assistance*, 28: 1–25. Available from: https://sites.tufts.edu/jha/archives/411 [Accessed 4 January 2024].

the trafficking in persons reports are used as a skewed and politically driven tool. Moreover, the disputed effectiveness of the TIPR ultimately provides a narrow anti-trafficking module. Francis contends that for numerous developing nations, such as Belize, this narrow module does not work well because it contradicts with existing cultural and regulatory systems. This plays into earlier discussions of the coloniality of global benchmarking processes such as the TIPR. The role of moral anxiety and/or societal concern is not isolated to 21st-century Belize with the first chapter by Lammasniemi neatly illustrating some historical context to the moral anxiety that enshroud the field. The TIPR perpetuate colonial structural violence that creates dangerous environments to begin with and attaches moral anxiety to certain forms of exploitation, such as sex trafficking. What this chapter argues is that the majority of law and policy enacted appears to overlook the role of non-state actors, choosing to focus on governments.

Conclusion: shifting the kaleidoscope

Editing this collection has been challenging for me in a multiplicity of ways, through exposing me to different disciplines and the methodological considerations within the respective disciplines. The experience has not only been a humbling one but also has significantly enhanced my own knowledge and perception of the phenomena. The collection seeks to offer a range of insights into modern slavery around the world, from scholars at different career stages, and contribute to the growing body of literature that challenges the power, racism, and colonialism of the contemporary anti-trafficking as a discourse.

There remains nothing new or uniquely modern about human trafficking and/or modern slavery. Yet, we could shift away from the moral anxiety of modern slavery towards more equitable, ethical, and just responses to exploitation. This collection serves as a challenge for many working within the field, and the predominant orthodoxy that exists. Ultimately the collection makes a powerful contribution to critical modern slavery studies.

References

Allain, J. (2012) *The Legal Understanding of Slavery: From the Historical to the Contemporary*, [Online]. United Kingdom: Oxford University Press.

Allain, J. (2013) *Slavery in International Law: Of Human Exploitation and Trafficking*, Boston, MA: Brill.

Allain, J. (2017) 'White slave traffic in international law', *Journal of Trafficking and Human Exploitation*, 1(1): 1–40.

Allain, J. (2018) 'Genealogies of human trafficking and slavery', in R. Piotrowicz, C. Rijken and B. Uhl (eds) *Routledge Handbook of Human Trafficking*, Abingdon: Routledge.

Allain, J. and Hickey, R. (2012) 'Property and the definition of slavery', *The International and Comparative Law Quarterly*, 61(4): 915–938.

Anderson, B. and O'Connell Davidson, J. (2003) *Is Trafficking in Human Beings Demand Driven?* Geneva: IOM.

Andrijasevic, R. (2007) 'Beautiful dead bodies: gender, migration and representation in anti-trafficking campaigns', *Feminist Review*, 86(86): 24–44.

Anghie, A. (2005) *Imperialism, Sovereignty and the Making of International Law*, Vol 37, Cambridge: Cambridge University Press.

Aradau, C. (2004) 'The perverse politics of four-letter words: risk and pity in the securitisation of human trafficking', *Millennium*, 33(2): 251–77.

Bachand, R. (2010) 'Critical approaches and the third world: Towards a global and radical critique of international law'. Available from: https://www.studocu.com/row/document/kabarak-university/international-criminal-law/bachand-3rd-world-critical-approaches-and-the-third-world/39966111 [Accessed 4 January 2024].

Bassiouni, M.C. (1991) 'Enslavement as an international crime', *New York University Journal of International Law and Politics*, 23: 445–518.

Beutin, L.P. (2017) 'Black suffering for/from anti-trafficking advocacy', *Anti-Trafficking Review*, 9: 14–30.

Beutin, L.P. (2023) *Trafficking in Antiblackness: Modern-Day Slavery, White Indemnity, and Racial Justice*, Durham, NC: Duke University Press.

Brace, L. and O'Connell Davidson, J. (2018) *Revisiting Slavery and Antislavery: Towards a Critical Analysis*, Basingstoke: Palgrave Macmillan.

Broome, A. and Quirk, J. (2015) 'The politics of numbers: the normative agendas of global benchmarking', *Review of International Studies*, 41(5): 813–18.

Bunting, A. and Quirk, J. (eds) (2017a) *Contemporary Slavery: Popular Rhetoric and Political Practice*, Vancouver: UBC Press.

Bunting, A. and Quirk, J. (eds) (2017b) *Contemporary Slavery: The Rhetoric of Global Human Rights Campaigns*, New York: Cornell University Press. http://www.jstor.org/stable/10.7591/j.ctt1w1vjxf

Césaire, A. (2000) *Discourse on Colonialism*, New York: Monthly Review Press.

Chuang, J. (2006) 'The United States as global sheriff: using unilateral sanctions to combat human trafficking', *Michigan Journal of International Law*, 27(2): 437.

Chuang, J. (2014), 'Exploitation creep and the unmaking of human trafficking law', *American Journal of International Law*, 108(4): 609–49.

Chuang, J. (2021) 'Preventing human trafficking: the role of the IOM and the UN Global Compact on Migration', in G. Lebaron, J. Pliley, and D. Blight (eds) *Fighting Modern Slavery and Human Trafficking: History and Contemporary Policy*, Cambridge: Cambridge University Press, pp 179–202.

Dottridge, M. (2017) 'Trafficked and exploited: the urgent need for coherence in international law', in P. Kotiswaran (ed) *Revisiting the Law and Governance of Trafficking, Forced Labour and Modern Slavery*, Cambridge: Cambridge University Press, pp 59–83.

Faulkner, E.A. (2023) *The Trafficking of Children: International Law, Modern Slavery, and the Anti-Trafficking Machine*, Cham: Springer.

Fenwick, H. and Fenwick, D. (2018) 'The case for a more ready resort to derogations from the ECHR in the current "war on terror"', *European Human Rights Law Review*, 4: 303–10.

Finley, M.I. (1964) 'Between slavery and freedom', *Comparative Studies in Society and History*, 6(3): 233–49.

Gallie, M. (2008) 'Les théories tiers-mondistes du droit international (TWAIL): un renouvellement?', *Études internationales*, 39(1): 17–38.

Gallagher, A.T. (2012), *The International Law of Human Trafficking*, Cambridge: Cambridge University Press.

Humbert, F. (2009) *The Challenge of Child Labour in International Law*, New York: Cambridge University Press.

Ibhawoh, B. (2007) 'Second world war propaganda, imperial idealism and anticolonial nationalism in British West Africa', *Nordic Journal of African Studies*, 16(2): 221–43.

Kempadoo, K. (ed.) (2005) *Trafficking and Prostitution Reconsidered: New Perspectives on Migration, Sex Work, and Human Rights*, New York: Routledge.

Kempadoo, K. (2015) 'The modern-day white (wo)man's burden: trends in anti-trafficking and anti-slavery campaigns', *Journal of Human Trafficking*, 1(1): 8–20.

Kempadoo, K. and Shih, E. (2023) *White Supremacy, Racism and the Coloniality of Anti-Trafficking*, Vol 1, New York; London: Routledge.

Kennedy, D. (2009) 'Selling the distant other: humanitarianism and imagery-ethical dilemmas of humanitarian action', *Journal of Humanitarian Assistance*, 28: 1–25. https://sites.tufts.edu/jha/archives/411

Kopytoff, I. and Miers, S. (eds) (1977) *Slavery in Africa: Historical and Anthropological Perspectives*, Madison, WI: Wisconsin University Press.

Kotiswaran, P. (ed) (2017) *Revisiting the Law and Governance of Trafficking, Forced Labor and Modern Slavery*, Cambridge: Cambridge University Press.

Lammasniemi, L. (2017) 'Anti-white slavery legislation and its legacies in England', *Anti-Trafficking Review*, 9: 64–76.

Lauren, P. (1998) '"A very special moment in history": New Zealand's role in the evolution of international human rights', *New Zealand International Review*, 23(6): 2–9.

Lauterpacht, H. (1950) *International Law and Human Rights*, London: Stevens.

LeBaron, G., Pliley, J.R., and Blight, D.W. (eds) (2021) *Fighting Modern Slavery and Human Trafficking: History and Contemporary Policy*, Cambridge: Cambridge University Press.

Legg, S. (2012) '"The life of individuals as well as of nations": international law and the League of Nations' anti-trafficking governmentalities', *Leiden Journal of International Law*, 25(3): 647–64.

Lerche, J. (2007) 'Global alliance against forced labour? Unfree labour, neoliberal globalization and the International Labour Organization', *Journal of Agrarian Change*, 7(4): 425–52.

Lloyd, P. and Simmons, B.A. (2015) 'Frames and consensus formation in international relations: the case of trafficking in persons', *European Journal of International Relations*, 21(2): 323–51.

Mayblin, L. and Turner, J. (2021) *Migration Studies and Colonialism*, Cambridge: Polity Press.

McGaughey, F., Voss, H., Cullen, H., and Davis, M.C. (2022) 'Corporate responses to tackling modern slavery: a comparative analysis of Australia, France and the United Kingdom', *Business and Human Rights Journal*, 7(2): 249–70. doi: 10.1017/bhj.2021.47

Meillassoux, C. (1991) 'The anthropology of slavery: the womb of iron and gold', *Ufahamu*, 19(2–3).

Mutua, M. (2001) 'Savages, victims, and saviors: the metaphor of human rights', *Harvard International Law Journal*, 42(1): 201–45.

O'Connell Davidson, J. (2015) *Modern Slavery: The Margins of Freedom*, Basingstoke: Palgrave Macmillan.

O'Connell Davidson, J. (2022) *What Do We Know and What Should We Do About Slavery?*, New York: SAGE.

O'Donovan, D. (2016) 'Socio-legal methodology: conceptual underpinnings, justifications and practical pitfalls', in L. Cahillane and J. Schweppe (eds) *Legal Research Methods: Principles and Practicalities*, Dublin: Clarus Press.

Pargas, D.A. and Schiel, J. (eds) (2023) *The Palgrave Handbook of Global Slavery throughout History*, London: Palgrave Macmillan Cham.

Patterson, O. (1982) *Slavery and Social Death: A Comparative Study*, Cambridge, MA: Harvard University Press.

Quirk, J. (2012) 'Defining slavery in all its forms: historical inquiry as contemporary instruction', in J. Allain (ed) *The Legal Understanding of Slavery*, Oxford: Oxford University Press.

Ramina, L. (2018) 'TWAIL – "Third World Approaches to International Law" and human rights: some considerations', *Revista de Investigações Constitucionais*, 5(1): 261–72.

Rota, M. (2020) 'On the definition of slavery', *Theoria (Lund, Sweden)*, 86(5): 543–64.

Segrave, M., Milivojevic, S., and Pickering, S. (2017) *Sex Trafficking and Modern Slavery: The Absence of Evidence* (2nd edn), Abingdon: Routledge.

PART I

Theoretical Perspectives

2

From Social to Legal: Shifting Approaches to Trafficking at the Turn of 20th-Century England

Laura Lammasniemi

Introduction

In 1930, the Secretary of the International Abolitionist Federation (IAF) wrote that the anti-trafficking campaigners were being led down 'the path of repression'; that is, of relying on law and police to stop traffic in women and to promote good morals. In this chapter, I argue that those concerns were raised far too late. By 1930, trafficking in women was already viewed as a legal issue that required international and national criminal law responses, not social or political ones. Solutions offered by the IAF in its early days in the 1870s and 1880s, such as deregulation of sex work and improving worker and women's rights, were simply out of fashion. Instead, the trafficking attracted criminal and immigration measures. When and how did trafficking then become understood as a legal issue?

In this chapter, I will argue that trafficking in women came to be seen as a distinct legal issue at the turn of the 20th century. The chapter will first focus on the legal and social landscape at the turn of 20th-century England and demonstrate how that understanding of sexual labour and commercial sex changed within that period. That understanding became more nuanced and complex, particularly in the second half the 19th century as women's rights campaigners entered social and political discussions and debates. In the first part of the chapter, I will explore how the emergence of the language of victimhood, coercion, and social restraints in relation to the campaign to repeal the Contagious Diseases Acts (CDAs) impacted both legal and social framing of sex work. Women's rights campaigners attempted to publicly reframe prostitution as a social and gendered concern, yet ultimately fell short of that aim. Through the campaigns against the punitive CDAs, a new way of conceptualizing and responding to the issue came into existence – through and in law. This language of victimhood morphed into the white slavery discourse, inadvertently, creating space for more punitive laws to be enacted in the name of protecting women. Through these interventions, sex work, and closely related traffic in women, became understood as legal issues that required legal, and, in particular, criminal law, solutions. In the second part of the chapter, I will explore how the legal framework came into existence through civil society action, and how those who campaigned for it understood and spoke of law's power and potential.

While some women's rights activists tried to complicate the distinction between exploited labour, prostitution, and coercion, in legal terms, white slavery and trafficking were solely understood as prostitution, unlike the modern slavery discourse which includes all forms of exploited labour.[1] One dominant narrative of white slavery was constructed around the crude juxtaposition between dangerous, foreign men and innocent, white women. This narrative has had a long-lasting legacy in media representation of trafficking in particular, as demonstrated by Jo Doezema (2000, 2010). This particular notion of white slavery was based on a distinct idea of victimhood and protection of white womanhood from harmful and corruptive sexual experiences, but it was not the only narrative of white slavery in existence at the time. There was also a great deal of focus on procurement and procurers, often women, who led young women astray. In some of the feminist and suffrage campaigning in the early 20th century, white slavery was also used as a metaphor for 'sweated' or low-paid labour that women were forced to undertake, often in factories, paid at a lower rate than men's labour (Tickner, 1988: 157). Despite these different ways of framing, in all these contexts, white slavery was a highly 'racialized metaphor' (Irwin, 1996; Attwood, 2013). Beyond the explicit focus on white womanhood, and the use of the term 'white slavery', fear of immigration and miscegenation underlined much of the debates on trafficking from the onset. The term 'white slavery' was important as a rhetorical tool, juxtaposing the notion of slavery with that of whiteness; distinguishing it from transatlantic slavery while emphasizing its victimhood.

There is a vibrant and rich historiography on sex work and the women's rights movement in the 19th century in particular (Walkowitz, 1980; Bristow, 1977; Nead, 1988; Mahood, 1995). This chapter builds on that scholarship and owes a particular debt to Judith Walkowitz's (1980) groundbreaking analysis of prostitution and class structures in the 19th century. While

---

[1] However, the focus remains skewed towards trafficking for the purposes of sexual exploitation as illustrated in Chapter 6 in this volume.

histories of trafficking are still a developing field, in recent years, important scholarship has emerged on white slavery in the international sphere (Knepper, 2009; Limoncelli, 2010), in England (Doezema, 2010; Attwood, 2015; Lammasniemi, 2017; Laite, 2021), and in the US (Donovan, 2006 and Pliley, 2014) in particular. These works have investigated the concept of white slavery, and often sex work, through its social and racialized context. As this chapter centres law, as understood and advanced by women's rights and social reform groups, it engages extensively with social history on the period. Lucy Bland's *Banishing the Beast: Feminism, Sex and Morality* (2002) and other work (Bland, 1985 and 2005) give a particularly brilliant overview of the women's rights movement in the era: the tensions, rhetoric, and complexities that impacted the campaigns on moral regulation and has helped me to locate the emergence of the white slavery rhetoric in that context. Most of the historical studies, while relating the reform efforts to law as Paula Bartley (2000) does, do not engage with law or law enforcement in great detail. The exception to this is Julia Laite's *Common Prostitutes and Ordinary Citizens: Commercial Sex in London, 1885–1960* (2012), which analyses the policing of prostitution laws in particular through women's encounters with the criminal justice system. Building on this rich existing scholarship, the chapter locates anti-trafficking and anti-white slavery legislation and legal activity in that wider context.

A distinct feature of the white slavery laws and reforms was that, rather than states and state officials, it was certain organizations that were incremental in shaping both public understanding and legislation.[2] The chapter, therefore, draws extensively from archival research conducted at various locations, and in particular from the archives of the key organizations working in the field, particularly the Association for Moral and Social Hygiene (AMSH), the International Abolitionist Federation (IAF), and the National Vigilance Association (NVA), as well as their international counterparts, the International Abolitionist Federation and the International Bureau, also held in the Women's Library (LSE). The public records of these organizations reveal the extent to which they were invested in the process of law reform and creation both in England and in the international arena. For example, the first attempt to define trafficking in international law is found in the archives of the International Bureau as part of the minutes from the first International Congress of the International Bureau on the White Slave Trade in London in 1899 (International Bureau, 1899 ref WL 4/IBA). The Women's Library has enabled me to go beyond the published works to access conference papers, correspondence, and brief notes of

---

[2] See further Chapters 11 and 12, which consider the role and power of non-state actors in the contemporary context.

Josephine Butler, Alison Neilans, and William Coote, all of whom occupied leadership positions within the women's rights and vigilance movements respectively. These archives reveal shared aims and the very different means utilized to reach those aims. They also include discussions about law: its power and dangers. They reveal contested gender dynamics at the top, and prolonged debates through correspondence on the key issues behind law reform, on consent, victimhood, and immigration. The records are at times contradictory: Josephine Butler's huge legacy more so than any others. Beyond the tensions between organizations and state bodies, these archives illuminate how legal concepts were understood and created.

Section I: the shifting legal and social landscape of the mid-19th century

The narrative of trafficking in women in 19th-century England entered the public consciousness with the words of Alfred Dyer, who described the dungeon-like brothels where English girls were enslaved in Continental Europe as 'veritable slavery'. In his reports on the 'Belgian scandal' as he also called it, Dyer painted a vivid image of the European 'houses of ill-fame' and wrote that the enslavement of English girls was 'infinitely more cruel and revolting than negro servitude' because it was slavery 'not for labour but for lust; and more cowardly' as it fell upon 'the young and the helpless of one sex only' (Dyer, 1880: 4). In his 1880 booklet, *The European slave trade in English girls*, Dyer reveals how he rescued four English girls from registered brothels in Brussels. His account, full of moral judgement, paints a story of naïve female innocence, sexual betrayal, and ultimately the disgrace felt by the fallen women. Dyer's sensationalist account of the trade in English girls captured the public imagination and it was an important part of the events that led to the first laws against white slavery in England (House of Lords, 1881).

Yet, to say that the trafficking laws came into existence purely due to Dyer's reportage on Brussels, or the sudden focus on English girls languishing in continental brothels, is an over-simplification. Instead, I argue, it is the culmination of the decades-long reimagination of sex work through the lens of victimhood, as influenced by the emergence of the women's rights movement. The intellectual legacy of this reimagination can be traced back to the campaigns against the Contagious Diseases Acts 1864–69 (CDAs). Those campaigns, particularly ones run by women's rights activists, were strongly against all forms of regulation of sex work and those who practise it (Nield, 1973; Bristow; 1977; Walkowitz, 1980; Howell, 2009; Harrington, 2010; Legg, 2012). They were by no means proponents of sex work but rather viewed sex work as a social problem, a culmination of gendered inequalities. Alison Neilans, a long-standing leader of the IAF, referred to at the beginning of the chapter, wrote, thinking back on that early movement, that it:

> was not especially dealing with sex morality but fighting for the suffrage, for university education for women, for the married woman to be recognised in law as a human being, to have equal rights in her children, and to be acknowledged as the mistress of her own property. It was fighting to attain economic independence for women: in short, it was challenging all artificial limitations and injustices with which women were surrounded in 1867. (Neilans, 1936)

This positioning of sex work as a culmination of all forms of gendered oppression was a new way of thinking, radically different from the mainstream perceptions about sex work and those who practised it. It is demonstrative of a clear shift in how prostitution, and those who were suspected of working in it, were viewed, and regulated in the late 19th century.

For most of the 19th century, the language of threat and disease is still inescapable in the writings on prostitution by medical experts, politicians of the era, and even in the language of the law. William Tait had described in *Magdalenism: An Inquiry into its Extent, Causes and Consequences of Prostitution*, how prostitution was infiltrating every aspect of society and thus posing a threat to the nation (Tait, 1840: 31, 203). Tait's concerns over moral erosion were shared by many, and prostitution was widely referred to as the Great Social Evil of the era (Newman, 1869; Logan, 1871). Tait argued there was 'no bound to its extent' when discussing the harm and moral threat that prostitution imposed on the daily lives of ordinary citizens (Tait, 1840: 154). The women defined as prostitutes were isolated from society, for the protection of the latter, and Lynda Nead has argued (1988, 2000: 144) that the response to and the associated venereal disease (VD) 'can be seen as displacement of condemnation and fear of the prostitute' herself.

The laws regulating prostitution prior to a wave of regulation in the 1880s were a patchwork; and they were mainly aimed at controlling and criminalizing women who worked in prostitution. The sale and purchase of sex was not explicitly criminalized but various activities related to prostitution were. The laws most frequently used against women working in prostitution were public nuisance laws such as the Vagrancy Act 1824 and, in London, the Metropolitan Police Act 1839. These laws constructed prostitution in public as a public nuisance, and therefore were used primarily against the 'streetwalkers', the most visible and stigmatized of prostitutes (Laite, 2006; Hall, 2013: 45). While various activities relating to prostitution were covered by this patchwork of legislation, trafficking in women was not expressly criminalized and there were no laws women could turn to for protection or for compensation if harmed. Under the Offences Against the Person Act

1861 there were several procurement and seduction-related offences that could be applied if a girl was unlawfully taken from her parents', or more explicitly father's, care. These laws were not specific to trafficking or forced prostitution but were rather enacted to protect young girls, particularly those with property, from being seduced.

To add to this complex patchwork of laws, a series of Acts called the Contagious Diseases Acts were enacted between 1864 and 1869. The CDAs, and their enforcement and impact, have been analysed at great length by others (Nield, 1973; Bristow; 1977; Walkowitz, 1980; Howell; 2009; Harrington, 2010; Legg, 2012) and here they will be only considered insofar as relevant to the changing representation of prostitution from the mid-19th century onwards. The Contagious Diseases Act 1864 was initially enacted to remain in force for only three years, and it applied to 11 garrisons and port towns in England. The 1864 Act was not, however, repealed after three years; instead, its scope was gradually extended. The subsequent Acts were increasingly draconian and allowed for a woman suspected of being a common prostitute to be summoned, medically examined for signs of VD, and ultimately under the 1869 Act, if found suffering from VD, incarcerated for up to nine months in a Lock Hospital. The Lock Hospitals where women were treated had a dual function: as penitentiaries and as a place where women were offered spiritual guidance as much as medical treatment in the hope that they would 'reform'. Women detained under the Acts were required to receive 'moral and religious instruction' as part of their treatment and so the limited medical treatment in synthesis with moral guidance was meant to clean, or arguably punish, the soul as much as the body.

The emergence of women's rights activism

Against the incredibly punitive landscape of the 1860s, the relatively rapid shift from effectively imprisoning sex workers, to creating national and international laws for their protection seems at least on the surface remarkable. This section shows how the reimagination of the prostitution in the language of victimhood, and the emergence of white slavery rhetoric, was linked to the wider philanthropic reform initiatives of the era, and in particular women's rights activism.

In 1870, Elizabeth Wolstenholme Elmy and Josephine Butler founded the Ladies National Association for the Repeal of the Contagious Diseases Acts (hereafter, the LNA). The aim of the LNA was to campaign for the repeal of the CDAs, and by so doing simultaneously to challenge and alter the prevailing perceptions of prostitution (Ladies National Association, 1870; Butler, 1896; Walkowitz, 1980; Jordan, 2003; Jordan, 2007). Before the establishment of the LNA, Butler had already engaged in 'private rescue work', work aimed at 'rescuing' and assisting street sex workers, for years and was a known advocate against state regulation of prostitution (Carpenter, 2009; Wardle Fredrikson, 2011). Butler and the LNA argued that lax male morals and female poverty were the true causes of prostitution, so women who were driven to the trade by societal inequalities should not have to bear the cost of legal and medical interventions (Butler, 1896: 149; Pankhurst, reprint 1994). The campaign was focused beyond the immediate aim of repealing the legislation, on tackling the wider structural inequality, as the campaigners fought also for access to higher education, medical care, and equal legal and property rights (Butler, 1896; Walkowitz, 1980). For Butler, prostitution was the epitome of gendered inequality and she sought to fight it at its roots; the blame, she argued, should be traced back to the oppressor – the state, the client, or the procurer – rather than the one oppressed (Bristow, 1977: 85). The framing of prostitution through gender oppression and exploitation and the focusing of attention on the client was radical, marking a notable departure from writings such as those of Tait, as previously discussed. The LNA and Butler, therefore, were able to crystallize a discourse which identified the mistreatment of sex workers within the larger framework of inequality.

Within the repeal campaign, law was framed as the oppressor, and so, addressing the social circumstances that created prostitution was the only solution to the 'problem' of prostitution. The manifesto and literature from the LNA members focused on the underprivileged circumstances under which women took to prostitution: identifying poor wages and lack of opportunities available to them, the urban poor working-class women in particular, as the underlying factors behind prostitution (Bartley, 2000: 16, 76–7). Many involved in the repeal also highlighted the class discrimination represented by the CDAs. For instance, Edmond Beales, the then President of the Reform League, stated that every 'step in these Acts which are the worst description of class legislation, as directed against the poorer class ... are contrary to the spirit of our laws, and to every righteous, generous, and moral principle' (Wardle Fredrickson, 2011: 521).

The CDAs were relatively unknown to the public before the LNA and the National Association were established, but they soon became a topic of national debate as the LNA and National Association members travelled from town to town holding meetings, recruiting new members, and intervening in trials where women were summoned under the CDAs. As the campaigns grew into nationwide efforts, the campaigners became increasingly focused on victimhood. Medical examinations, rather than imprisonment, became the central aspect of the campaign as it progressed. Butler introduced the term 'instrumental rape'[3] to describe the

---

[3] The harms perpetrated under the guise of law and policy mechanisms implemented have been documented and some of those harms are addressed within this collection.

procedure women suspected of prostitution were subjected to in order to emphasize the demeaning and invasive nature of the speculum examination (Walkowitz, 1980: 200–1). Towards the later years of the repeal campaign, stories told in the campaign meetings held in towns came from the virtuous working-class women who had been harassed by the police and possibly forced into examination under the CDAs. The sex worker and her right to bodily autonomy was no longer the centre of the campaigns by then and was often acknowledged only through her oppression. Those who were registered prostitutes under the CDAs were described as passive victims of their own naivety or male lust, now trapped in the life of vice with no way out. Towards the end of the campaign, the agitation meetings included stories of virgins being examined, and concepts such as 'forced', 'violation', 'outraged', and 'degrading', associated with sexual violence and victimhood, were used ever more frequently (Trumble, 2003: 61). These personal stories recounted in the agitation meetings consisted of detailed descriptions of painful experiences of virgins summoned for examinations, left traumatized with a broken hymen. The agitation meeting stories and increased focus on sexual violence absolved the prostitutes from their perceived sins but also framed them as non-threatening victims, objects of the rescue efforts.

There was a great paradox at the core of Butler's work that was reflected in the movement more broadly. On the one hand, she put forward a radical constitutional rights argument of non-intervention and absolute autonomy but, on the other, this absolute autonomy was limited by propriety and chastity – and class (Summers, 1999; Bland, 2002; Attwood, 2011: ch 3). She denounced regulation in absolute terms and stated: 'for God has given to woman, for good and wise ends, an absolute sovereignty over her own person, and of this no man, no legislation on earth has any right to deprive her' (Butler, 1870a: 17). Butler's mission, while radical in rejecting the legal system, the state, and existing constructions of prostitution, remained firmly rooted in the notion of respectable female behaviour (Summers, 1999. No woman would have willingly worked in the trade, according to Butler, and nor did Butler recognize or advocate female sexual agency (1870b). Therefore, all prostitution was involuntary and exploitative in her view.

The importance of this rhetoric and reimagination of prostitution through the language of victimhood to the emergence of white slavery cannot be underestimated. The repeal campaign had introduced a radical call to abolish all laws on prostitution and frame it as a social issue with social solutions. Yet, invertedly, through the campaigns, the figure of the 'prostitute' became reframed in the language of victimhood, giving rise to an entirely new way of conceptualizing and responding to the issue. The campaigns against the CDAs gave the 19th-century women's rights activists a unified cause and gave influential women's rights campaigners such as Josephine Butler and Elizabeth Wolstenholme Elmy a national platform. Furthermore, through the anti-CDA campaigns, the women's rights' movement gained the language and tools for political and legal activism as echoed in the quest to criminalize trafficking later.

Section II: towards legal framework on anti-trafficking

The repeal campaigns were successful and the CDAs were formally suspended in 1883 and finally repealed in 1886. As the repeal campaign had reached it aims, the campaigners turned their attention to a new social ill: 'white slavery'. Talking about the first International Congress in Geneva, and the series of resolutions made there that laid the foundation for the International Convention against traffic in women, the Society of Friends said:

> The great movement for the repeal of the English Contagious Diseases Acts, begun in 1869, by Mrs Butler and others, laid firmly and broadly and deeply the foundation principles on which the subsequent work for the Abolition of the White Slave Traffic was based. Practically all the English workers and founders of this latter work were Abolitionists and received their training in the Repeal Movement. (Association for Moral and Social Hygiene, 1928)

While trafficking and white slavery explicitly entered the public domain with Dyer's reportage on the Belgian scandal in the early 1880s, I have shown that the intellectual legacy of both that public imagination and the modes of campaigning date back to the CDA repeal campaign. Following the stories, particularly those of Dyer, of girls trafficked into brothels in Brussels in particular, the Foreign Minister commissioned Thomas Snagge to conduct an inquiry into the issue, which was eventually heard in the House of Lords (Snagge, 1881). The Home Secretary ordered the inquiry reluctantly and only after excessive campaigning from Dyer and his supporters, including Butler. Butler wrote in her memoirs that once the independent inquiry was established, it marked the beginning of white slavery action and no one attempted to deny its existence any longer (Attwood, 2013: 54).

After hearing the testimonies, the House of Lords Select Committee (Snagge, 1881) made recommendations for law reform, but it took a number of bills and notable public pressure for transnational trafficking to be criminalized in 1885, with the Criminal Law Amendment Act (CLAA). When the CLAA 1885 was finally enacted, the trafficking provisions received far less attention than the provision that changed the age of consent from 13 to 16 for girls. The Bill might not have passed at all had it not been for

The Maiden Tribute of Modern Babylon, a scandalous reportage on the London underworld published in the *Pall Mall Gazette* in 1885, as evidenced by frequent references to the piece in the parliamentary debates (Hansard HC Deb., 30 July 1885). *The Maiden Tribute* was first and foremost a tool for campaigning, aimed at rousing the public's interest and passing the Criminal Law Amendment Bill. In *The Maiden Tribute*, Stead (1885) recounted lurid tales of forced prostitution in London, 'the greatest market in human flesh the world has ever seen'. He told of young girls selling their virginity for they did not understand its value, he writes about parents selling their daughters to the highest bidder, and through these tales, he paints a picture of London's East End full of moral corruption and crime (Walkowitz, 1992: 81; Lammasniemi, 2020a). The campaign was supported by the many notable members of the clergy and the Archbishop of York created his own campaign materials (Archbishop of York, 1885) to support the Bill. There was already considerable public and political support for more criminal laws to protect girls from falling into prostitution at the time of its publication (Hansard HL Deb., 18 June 1883) but the public interest in the topic reached a peak following *The Maiden Tribute*.

The CLAA 1885 was the first law to tackle and recognize the concept of 'traffic in women' by criminalizing the procurement of women to work in prostitution in England and in brothels abroad (Lammasniemi, 2017). It was, however, followed in quick succession by many laws dealing with the issue. In the years to come, hysteria over white slavery peaked, fuelled by frequent newspaper reporting on the matter (Billington-Greig, 1913), and led to the second Criminal Law Amendment Act in 1912, at times called the White Slavery Act. Simultaneously, the International Agreement for the Suppression of the 'White Slave Traffic' came into existence in 1904 and the International Convention for the Suppression of the White Slave Traffic in 1910 following action from the very same voluntary organizations that were influential in the making of CLAAs (Knepper, 2009; Limoncelli, 2010; Lammasniemi, 2020b). Each of the accords and laws explicitly dealt with the issue of traffic in women. The international accords placed obligations on signatories to cooperate to prevent traffic, and domestic laws created criminal penalties for procurement.

While these laws were ostensibly brought in to protect women, in reality, the overwhelming majority of prosecutions under the white slavery laws in fact targeted women (Laite, 2012: 58–60). In addition to these anti-traffic laws, the era saw criminalization of migrant sex workers through other measures, such as the Aliens Act 1905, which restricted the movement of foreign-born women and created measures for their expulsion (Gainer, 1972; Glover, 2012). The NVA was particularly keen on stronger immigration control in England and in the international arena, driven by a desire to restrict the immigration of women into England. Coote was strongly of the view that 'any woman pursuing the trade of prostitution in any nation other than that to which she belongs should be repatriated' (Royal Commission on Alien Immigration, 1903: 426). In his testimony to the Royal Commission on Alien Immigration in 1903, he spoke about 'the most destructive forms of vice' that were brought 'in contact with our young men, who are simply demoralised, body, soul, and spirit' by foreign women (Royal Commission on Alien Immigration, 1903: 426).

As the laws became more numerous and complex, so did the role that civil society and religious and philanthropic organizations played in the field. Ultimately, the NVA took the lead in both campaigning for laws and ensuring their enforcement. They collaborated with various organizations, including at times with women's rights and religious groups. Some Church leaders, such as then Bishop Rochester, took an active role in campaigning and in leadership of organizations. In the early days, Butler lent her support to the legal interventions such as the CLAA 1885, convinced that the law was needed to better protect women and girls from exploitation. In accordance with this aim, the leaders of the women's rights movements such as Butler joined forces with more conservative campaigners whose goal was to enforce public morality, by coercion if needs be (Coote, 1910: 5). Soon after the CLAA was enacted, ideological rifts became evident, both between organizations and within. Some of the women who had so vehemently fought for deregulation and repeal of the CDAs had now embraced the new wave of legal reforms. Elizabeth Wolstenholme Elmy, co-founder of the LNA, raised concerns when her colleagues and fellow women's rights activists 'by a strange perversion, now sanction and command the means and the methods of a cruel repression' (as quoted in Bland, 2002: 99). As the NVA campaigned for more rigorous enforcement of the CLAA 1885 and joined forces with the Public Morality Council (PMC) for the clean-the-streets of prostitution campaign, the *Journal of the Personal Rights Association*, edited by Wolstenholme Elmy, accused the NVA of exploiting and persecuting 'the poorest, most helpless and most forlorn of womankind' (as quoted in Walkowitz, 1980: 252).

Similarly, Butler grew increasingly anxious about the direction that vigilance associations had taken, and wrote in 1897, wanting to distinguish herself from their actions, that 'it may surprise and shock some who read those lines that I should say (yet I must say it) beware of purity workers in our warfare. Beware of "Purity Societies" which seek affiliation with our Society' (as quoted in Higson, 1955: 35–6). She called out the hypocrisy inherent in increasingly draconian legal measures taken to tackle street prostitution in particular, and said (as quoted in Higson, 1955: 35–6):

> We have learned that it is not unusual for men and women to discourse eloquently in public, of the home, of conjugal life, of the divinity of

womanhood ... and yet to be ready to accept and endorse any amount of coercive and degrading treatment of their fellow creatures, in the fatuous belief that you can oblige human beings to be moral by force, and in so doing that you may in some promote social purity!

Based on correspondence and notes from Butler and her organizations, their relationship with the NVA was tumultuous. They collaborated on some campaigns and clearly shared some ideals, yet Butler described W.A. Coote, the long-time leader of the NVA as 'most unsound' and argued that he loved 'coercion' (as quoted in Bristow, 1977: 188).

This divide and breaking down of relationships was far more meaningful than a spat between two leading voices on these matters in England, and de facto in Europe. The divide was an ideological one, concerning the role and potential of law and legal power. The CLAA 1885 was hailed as a 'symbolic victory for feminists and puritans alike' by Edward Bristow (1977: 114) but later laws faced fierce criticism from many supporters of the women's rights movement. For Coote, the leader of the NVA, law and law enforcement were the only way forward to protect girls and the society at large from vice. For Butler and those who followed her, law's potential was far more oppressive. Law was the oppressor and a threat to the dignity and autonomy of women and girls. Law after all was what had sanctioned coverture for centuries, it had prevented women from having legal personality, and it allowed women to be imprisoned and forcibly examined at the whim of a man, a policeman. How could law then be the solution to a problem that was law's creation?

The strong distrust of state authorities and law was not unique to Butler but was shared by many of the more radical women's rights voices. When on trial for suffragette actions, Alison Neilans, Butler's successor who became the long-standing Secretary of the AMSH, called for liberty for the oppressed and argued that 'England has won every privilege on which liberty dwells by struggles against constituted authorities' (as quoted in Laite, 2008). Similarly, Butler's close ally and friend, Elizabeth Wolstenholme Elmy, was said to have argued that the institutions like the state, the legal system, and Christianity are 'crippling the weak' and reinforcing models of oppressive patriarchy as they work only for their own aggrandisement (Wilson, 1875, Letter to Wilson). While there were plenty of women's rights campaigners who were members of the NVA and supported more moral purity action, even paradoxically Butler herself at times, the broader feminism of Butler and her followers was characterized by deep distrust in the state and law itself.

The women's rights movement had been crucial in creating a new understanding of sex work that allowed the concept of white slavery to emerge and the exploitation of women and girls within the sex industry to be recognized. Yet, as the term white slavery, a term that Butler is said to have popularized (Irwin, 1996), became the focus of legislative interventions, women's rights voices were increasingly sidelined. It was the social purity organizations, increasingly drawn to punitive criminal laws, which dominated the social reform platforms and processes. This division of power was undoubtedly an ideological one, related to perceptions about law and state, but it was also a deeply gendered one. Legal forums and committees – as discussed in the next section – became increasingly male-dominated spaces where women's voices, either as activists, or let alone as sex workers, were increasingly sidelined.

Dominance of the NVA: embracing legal power

The Belgian scandal and House of Lords Select Committee Report 1881, discussed in the first part of this chapter, brought about a different understanding of prostitution, white slavery, and victimhood; one that was directly linked to the transnational movement of women, foreign traffickers, and continental brothels (Knepper, 2009; Attwood, 2013). This understanding of white slavery focused on individual criminality, physical exploitation, and restrictions rather than social or economic victimhood. This framing of white slavery – void of its social context – undoubtedly allowed the matter to be legislated more easily. Instead of focusing on root causes of that exploitation and vulnerability to that exploitation, the law attempted to address its manifestation – procurement and brothel keeping.

Unlike most laws in the period, the early legal measures were drafted and campaigned for by civil society organizations such as the NVA, with the support of some state officials who were sympathetic to the cause. I have examined the relationship between these leading organizations and the state elsewhere and argued that the state willingly delegated its powers when it came to drafting and enforcing laws to voluntary organizations, the NVA in particular (Lammasniemi, 2017). The organizations drafted bills, passed resolutions, organized international conferences, and created cooperative networks that ultimately led to the enactment of the international accords against white slavery (International Bureau, 1899). The International Agreement and subsequent Convention are therefore a direct consequence of voluntary organizations in the field, rather than state action. Praising Coote, Gregory Maurice, who was active in the international abolitionist campaigning, said the first international conference on white slavery and the securing of the Agreement were the climax of the movement, and called Coote's work, and the 'remarkable manner' in which he had brought the Agreement about, one of the great 'romances of philanthropy' (Maurice, 1908).

The NVA was founded just as the CLAA 1885 was passed by those who had campaigned for it, with the explicit aim of enforcing it. Its first resolution stated: 'this Conference recommends the formation of a National Vigilance

Association of men and women for the enforcement and improvement of laws for the repression of criminal vice and public morality' (Coote, 1916: 5). The understanding was that the NVA would work with and through the law to aid public morality. In its early decades and most influential years, the NVA was steered by W.A. Coote. Coote came to the movement through union organizing, having attempted a career in politics (Attwood, 2015). His trust in law and legal power is inescapable in all his written work. His memoir on the work of the NVA, *A Romance of Philanthropy: Being a Record of Some of the Principal Incidences Connected with the Exceptionally Successful Thirty Years' Work of the National Vigilance Association*, reveals a figure of a man who pursued what he felt was a righteous cause with utmost conviction, letting nothing and no one stand in his way. He, and the NVA under his leadership, centred law, legal action, and legal power. Coote (1916: 24) himself wrote that 'the legal side of the work was recognised as the most immediate and important to undertake'. In the early years, half of the NVA budget was spent on legal work, mainly on funding prosecutions for cases that the state would not prosecute. Although in later years, their case work became far more varied (National Vigilance Association, 1920–30), in the 1880s and 1890s, these prosecutions mainly consisted of cases of brothel keeping, prostitution-related offences, and of obscenity-related offences.

According to Coote, they were 'compelled to undertake' this legal work due to the inaction of the police and prosecutors. He did not hold officials in the same esteem as he did law itself. If anything, officials were at times an inconvenience standing in the way of his laws, his cases, and his righteous task. In *A Romance of Philanthropy*, he recounts multiple frustrating encounters with lawmakers and the courts. Coote clearly held the system of justice and courts in high esteem but at times found himself in opposition to individual judges and magistrates who, he felt, were trying to hinder the NVA's proceedings (Coote, 1916: 30). He wrote about overcoming these uncooperative judges and, through perseverance, being able to 'shame authorities into a degree of activity' (Coote, 1916: 31). This rejection of what he called 'officialism' was a common theme in Coote's work, and *A Romance of Philanthropy* in particular. This officialism manifested itself through lethargic lawmakers, inactive police, and cynical judges, and it was clearly a source of great inconvenience for Coote, and something that was standing in the way of the NVA's work. As the officials could not be trusted with this work, according to Coote, it was the NVA's role and mission therefore to draft bills, to ensure their passing, and to enforce the Acts. This mission is best described by Coote (1916: 26) as 'supplying the eyes, ears, feet and hands to the Criminal Law Amendment Act, so that its advantages might be obtained for the girlhood of the nation'.

The White Slave Traffic Bill (referred to as the CLAA 1912 Bill) was also a result of intense campaigning by these organizations. During the years

1907 and 1908 a Conjoint Committee was established from representatives from the NVA, the Jewish Board of Deputies, the Jewish Association for the Protection of Girls and Women, and the London Council for the Promotion of Public Morality to review and propose changes to the CLAA 1885 (Alexander, 1912). While the final Act did not include all the clauses the Conjoint Committee argued for, it extended the scope of the CLAA 1885 and the powers of arrest, to include arrest without a warrant. Extending the powers of arrest was a triumph for the Committee, as it attributed further importance to the NVA patrol groups that were already monitoring ports and stations. The women's rights groups were notably absent from this Conjoint Committee. Instead, zealously anti-prostitution organizations such as the London Council for the Promotion of Public Morality (Lammasniemi, 2017) were present. The Committee had a large Deputation with the Home Office where their proposals for change were discussed, and according to their records, finally a bill was agreed that the Home Office approved of. Despite this, there was a distinct lack of enthusiasm from the Home Office, which did not introduce the Bill as a government bill (Alexander, 1912). There is a clear sense of frustration on the part of the Committee and the NVA, that Parliament was not more enthusiastic about the Bill. It was introduced multiple times by opposition MPs but as it did not have government backing, it was defeated many times before it became law. The NVA called MPs 'unreasonably obdurate' and said that the public was becoming restless 'under the arbitrary and tyrannical power' exercised by the opposing MPs (National Vigilance Association and the International Bureau, 1912).

A look into the parliamentary discussions reveals several reasons why MPs had resisted these Bills, such as the welfare of disadvantaged women. When the Bill was debated in the Houses throughout 1912, it was introduced as the White Slavery Bill. Unlike the CLAA 1885, which was, apart from a few exceptions, welcomed by the parliamentarians, the CLAA 1912 faced opposition from many, both in the Commons and in the Lords, and many were also quick to point out that the Bill had nothing to do with white slavery or protection of women. The main impact of the CLAA 1912 was to deepen the measures set out in the CLAA 1885 on the suppression of brothels. Under section 5 of the CLA Bill 1912, a landlord was given the right to terminate a lease and withhold the rent paid by a person charged with a prostitution-related offence. Some MPs strongly contested this provision and argued that it was unjust and imposed a financial penalty on top of a criminal one. Sir Frederick Banbury argued that the provision was 'utterly contrary to the spirit of the English law' and had 'nothing to do with the sentimental desire which has brought forward the agitation for this Bill, because it has nothing to do with the white slave traffic' (Hansard HC Deb., 10 June 1912). The suppression of brothels provisions, giving police the powers to raid brothels and evict those working there under the CLAA 1885, was not popular with several MPs. Colonel Josiah Wedgwood, a well-known Liberal MP, opposing the Bill, stated that: 'the objection is to making it more difficult for these women to find a shelter. You chase them off the streets, and then you chase them out of their houses. Where are they to find shelter if the police are always after them?' (Hansard HC Deb., 10 June 1912).

In a later debate, he argued that these provisions would impact the rights of all women, regardless of whether they were engaged in prostitution, who were attempting to rent a low-cost lodging. He also raised concerns that landlords would be able to ask for extortionate rents from any woman who could not prove she was 'a respectable woman', leaving women who arrive from outside London particularly vulnerable (Hansard HC Deb., 5 November 1912). Despite these objections, the CLAA 1912 came into existence albeit with some important amendments and was used to further monitor prostitutes and brothels, in Greater London in particular.

The CLAAs (the 1912 one in particular) had a devastating impact on women working in prostitution (Laite, 2012: 58). It was women who were predominantly prosecuted under these laws; it was women who became subject to surveillance and lost their homes, as predicted by Wedgwood (Bartley, 2002; Laite, 2012; Lammasniemi, 2017). Coote never acknowledged this. Fighting for higher standards of public morality were righteous tasks, if not a calling, for the NVA and Coote. He talks in his memoirs about a 'Divine Vision, or a Day-Dream inspired from on high' that became impressed on his mind. In his Vision, he was told that he should go and travel Europe in order to identify and to bring together leaders from each country to discuss white slavery in an international congress in London. That conference, according to his Vision, would put pressure on European governments to create international laws on the topic – at a time when international law was in its infancy (Coote, 1916: 173). He reflected on the vastness of the work that God had laid before him and explained how one meeting, a congress, and a conference, for which he had set the wheels in motion, would become the 1904 International Agreement for the Suppression of the 'White Slave Traffic'. On completion of the final Congress on the matter, where the first international law in the field was agreed on, Coote and the NVA received personal messages of congratulations from leaders, royalty, Church leaders, and state representatives worldwide (Coote, 1916: 194).

The 1904 Agreement did not make provision for the criminalization of procurement, nor created an offence of trafficking, but it did focus on collaboration and on repatriation of 'foreign prostitutes'. The Agreement primarily made administrative provisions that aimed to enable cooperation between participating states by establishing central bureaus for the exchange of information (Article 1) and by sharing information regarding relevant domestic convictions. The focus of the Agreement was clearly on keeping a watch on 'women and girls destined for an immoral life' as they might enter the country, and to make provision for their repatriation (Article 2). The Agreement was followed in 1910 by the International Convention for the Suppression of the White Slave Traffic that created a basis for criminal prosecution for those suspected of being in breach of the Convention, creating the first international definition for the offence of trafficking.

Conclusion

In this chapter, I have analysed the work of those who were responsible for drafting the first anti-trafficking laws in England. The anti-trafficking laws, unusually, came into existence after prolonged, tireless campaigns by civil society and philanthropic organizations, many driven by religious beliefs. Speaking at the Fourth International Congress in 1913, the Earl of Aberdeen said that 'no future historian of our time will be able to question the need and the worth of this crusade, for it depends not on opinion, or creed, or policy, but upon the eternal distinction between right and wrong and the sacred claims of justice and humanity' (Vigilance Record, 1913: 51). The quote from the Earl of Aberdeen could be applied to the work of any campaigners discussed in this chapter. The social reformers, women's rights activists, and moral purity campaigners all believed that law and the state were failing women and that white slavery was a serious issue that needed responding to. They all held convictions, whatever those convictions were, and believed in their own methods. The methods of achieving those aims, however, differed.

The organizations involved entered deep disagreements on the nature of law and its potential in ensuring equality, and morality. The women's rights organizations continuously, and unsuccessfully, pushed for state regulation of prostitution to be abolished and felt uneasy about cooperation with the state and a focus on policing. They were critical of laws yet attempted to leave their mark on the laws that they were often critical of. These groups participated in institutional spaces, and were incremental in creating those spaces and platforms, as shown by the discussion on the CDA repeal campaign, yet never dominated the lawmaking sphere.

By the early 20th century, it was clear that the NVA had created a world of its own when it came to legislative action in the field, by centring law both in its action and rhetoric, as shown in the second part of the chapter. This world was far more punitive and restrictive than the 1880s women's rights campaigners would ever have imagined. Not only was the focus on criminalization of individuals, but there was also increasingly more focus on immigration control and preventing the transnational movement of poor women at a time when immigration control was in its infancy.

Through these measures, white slavery became permanently ingrained in both domestic and international legal systems. Beyond the laws, the very notions of victimhood and the assumption that all sex work is inherently rooted in criminality, as was central to 19th-century reform campaigns, have had a long-lasting legacy, out-living the campaigners and organizations that articulated them.

References

Archbishop of York (1885) 'New Slave Trade', pamphlet. Held at Women's Library. Ref: 3AMS/B/01/01-04.

Alexander, D. (1912) 'A Response to Spectator article the Economics of Hell', *The Spectator*, 2 March 1912.

Association for Moral and Social Hygiene (1928) 'Josephine Butler and the Traffic in Women and Children'. Held at Women's Library. Ref: WL 3MS/H/01/05.

Attwood, N. (2011) *The Prostitute's Body: Rewriting Prostitution in Victorian Britain*, London: Routledge.

Attwood, R. (2013) *Vice Beyond the Pale: Representing 'White Slavery' in Britain, c.1880–1912*. Thesis. UCL.

Attwood, R. (2015) 'Stopping the traffic: the National Vigilance Association and the international fight against the "white slave" trade (1899–c.1909)', *Women's History Review*, 24(3): 325–50.

Bartley, P. (2000) *Prostitution: Prevention and Reform in England, 1860–1914*, London: Routledge.

Billington-Greig, T. (1913) 'The truth about white slavery', *English Review*, June, 428–46.

Bland, L. (1985) 'In the name of protection: policing of women in the First World War', in J. Brophy and C. Smart (eds) *Women-in-law: Explorations in Law, Family, and Sexuality*, London: Routledge & Kegan Paul.

Bland, L. (2002) *Banishing the Beast: Feminism, Sex and Morality*, London: Tauris Parke.

Bland, L. (2005) 'White women and men of colour: miscegenation fears in Britain after the Great War', *Gender History*, 17(1): 29–61.

Bristow, E.J. (1977) *Vice and Vigilance: Purity Movements in Britain since 1700*, Dublin: Gill And Macmillan; Totowa, NJ.

Butler, J. (1870a) *An appeal to the people of England, on the recognition and superintendence of prostitution by governments*. Held at Women's Library.

Butler, J. (1870b) Conference Paper on the Moral Reclaimability of Prostitutes. London, 6 May 1870. Held at Women's Library. Ref: 3AMS.

Butler, J. (1896) *Personal Reminiscences of a Great Crusade*, Horace Marshall.

Carpenter, M. (2009) *Health, Medicine, and Society in Victorian England*, Westport, CT: Praeger.

Coote, W.A. (1910) *A Vision and its Fulfilment: Being the History of the Origin of the Work of the National Vigilance Association for the Suppression of the White Slave Traffic: with a Record of Visits Paid to the Capitals of Europe, and to America, Egypt, and South Africa, for the Purpose of Organising National Committees for the Suppression of the Traffic*, London: National Vigilance Association.

Coote W.A. and Baker, A. (1916) *A Romance of Philanthropy: Being a Record of Some of the Principal Incidents Connected with the Exceptionally Successful Thirty Years' Work of the National Vigilance Association*, London: National Vigilance Association.

Doezema, J. (2000) 'Loose women or lost women? The re-emergence of the myth of white slavery in contemporary discourses of trafficking in women', *Gender Issues*, 18(1): 23–50.

Doezema, J. (2010) *Sex Slaves and Discourse Masters: The Construction of Trafficking*, London: Zed.

Donovan, B. (2006) *White Slave Crusades: Race, Gender, and Anti-Vice Activism, 1887–1917*, Urbana, IL: University of Illinois Press.

Dyer, A. (1880) *The European Slave Trade in English Girls*, Dyer Brothers.

Gainer, B. (1972) *The Alien Invasion: The Origins of the Aliens Act of 1905*, London: Heinemann.

Glover, D. (2012) *Literature, Immigration and Diaspora in Fin-de-siècle England: A Cultural History of the 1905 Aliens Act*, Cambridge: Cambridge University Press.

Hall, L. (2013) *Sex, Gender and Social Change in Britain since 1880* (2nd edn), Basingstoke: Macmillan.

Harrington, C. (2010) *Politicization of Sexual Violence: from Abolitionism to Peacekeeping*, London: Routledge.

Higson, J. (1955) *The Story of a Beginning: An Account of Pioneer Work for Moral Welfare*, London: SPCK.

House of Lords (1881) *Select Committee of the House of Lords on the Law Relating to the Protection of Young Girls; together with the proceedings of the committee, minutes of evidence, and appendix*. London. Held at British Library (BL). Ref: B.S.Ref.18/4. (6).

Howell, P. (2009) *Geographies of Regulation: Policing Prostitution in Nineteenth-century Britain and the Empire*, Cambridge, UK; New York: Cambridge University Press.

International Bureau (1899) Minutes of the International Congress on the White Slave Traffic (Westminster Palace Hotel, London, 21 and 23 June 1899). Held at Women's Library. Ref: 4/IBA.

Irwin, M. (1996) ' "White slavery" as metaphor – anatomy of a moral panic', *Ex Post Facto: The History Journal*, Vol V. Available from: www.walnet.org/csis/papers/irwin-wslavery.html

Jordan, J. (2007) *Josephine Butler*, London: Hambledon Continuum.

Jordan, J. and Sharp, I. (2003) *Josephine Butler and the Prostitution Campaigns: Diseases of the Body Politic*, London; New York: Routledge Curzon.

Knepper, P. (2009) *The Invention of International Crime: A Global Issue in the Making, 1881–1914*, Houndmills, Basingstoke; New York: Palgrave Macmillan.

Ladies National Association (LNA) (1870) 'Manifesto of the Ladies National Association for the Repeal of the Contagious Diseases Acts', *Daily News*, 1 January 1870.

Laite, J. (2006) 'Paying the price again: prostitution policy in historical perspective', *History & Policy*, [online]. Available from: www.historyandpolicy.org/policy-papers/papers/paying-the-price-again-prostitution-policy-in-historical-perspective

Laite, J.A. (2008) 'The Association for Moral and Social Hygiene: abolitionism and prostitution law in Britain (1915–1959)', *Women's History Review*, 17(2): 207–23.

Laite, J. (2012) *Common Prostitutes and Ordinary Citizens: Commercial Sex in London 1885–1960*, London: Palgrave Macmillan.

Laite, J. (2021) *The Disappearance of Lydia Harvey: A true story of sex, crime and the meaning of justice*, London: Profile Books.

Lammasniemi, L. (2017) 'Anti-white slavery legislation and its legacies in England', *Anti-Trafficking Review*, (9): 64–76.

Lammasniemi, L. (2020a) '"Precocious girls": age of consent, class and family in late nineteenth-century England', *Law and History Review*, 38(1): 241–66.

Lammasniemi, L. (2020b) 'International legislation on white slavery and anti-trafficking in the early twentieth century', in J. Winterdyk and J.M. Jones (eds) *The Palgrave International Handbook of Human Trafficking*. Cham, Switzerland: Palgrave Macmillan.

Legg, S. (2012) 'Stimulation, segregation and scandal: geographies of prostitution regulation in British India, between registration (1888) and suppression (1923)', *Modern Asian Studies*, 46(6): 1459–505.

Limoncelli, S. (2010) *Politics of Trafficking: The First International Movement to Combat the Sexual Exploitation of Women*, Stanford, CA: Stanford University Press.

Logan, W. (1871) *The Great Social Evil: Its Causes, Extent, Results, and Remedies*, London: Hodder and Stoughton.

Mahood, L. (1995) *Policing Gender, Class, and Family: Britain, 1850–1940*, London: UCL Press.

Maurice, G. (1908) Historical Sketch of the English Section of the Movement at the request of the 'Commission Administrative' of the International Federation for the Geneva Congress. Held at Women's Library. Ref: 3AMS/E/01-02.

National Vigilance Association (1920–30) Case files. Held at Women's Library. Ref: 4NVA/6.

National Vigilance Association and the International Bureau, the Criminal Law Amendment (1912) (White Slave Traffic) Bill: Why the Amendment of Law is Needed (National Vigilance Association, 1912). Held at Women's Library.

Nead, L. (1988). *Myths of Sexuality: Representations of Women in Victorian Britain*, Oxford: Basil Blackwell.

Nead, L. (2000) *Victorian Babylon: People, Streets and Images in Nineteenth-century London*, New Haven, CT; London: Yale University Press.

Neilans, A. (1936) 'Changes in sex morality', in R. Strachey (ed) *Our Freedom and its Results*, London: Leonard and Virginia Woolf at The Hogarth Press.

Newman, F.W. (1869) *The Cure of the Great Social Evil, with Special Reference to Recent Laws Delusively Called Contagious Diseases Acts*, London: Trübner & Co.

Nield, K. (ed) (1973) *Prostitution in the Victorian Era: Debates on the Issue from 19th-Century Critical Journals*, New Jersey: Gregg International Publishers.

Pankhurst, C. (1994) 'Plain facts about a great evil', in M. Mulvey Roberts and T. Mizuta (eds) *The Campaigners: Women and Sexuality*, London: Routledge.

Pankhurst C. (1994) 'Plain facts about a great evil' and 'Chastity and the health of men', reprinted in M. Roberts and T. Mizuta, *The Campaigners: Women and Sexuality*, London: Routledge/Thoemmes.

Pliley, J.R. (2014) *Policing Sexuality: The Mann Act and the Making of the FBI*, Cambridge, MA: Harvard University Press.

Royal Commission on Alien Immigration (1903) *Report of the Royal commission on alien immigration, with minutes of evidence and appendix ... Presented to both houses of Parliament by command of His Majesty*, London, printed for H.M. Stationery Office by Wyman and Sons.

Snagge, T.W. (1881) *Report of T.W. Snagge on the Alleged Traffic in English Girls for Immoral Purposes in Foreign Towns*, London: HMSO.

Stead, W.T. (1885) 'The Maiden Tribute of Modern Babylon I', *Pall Mall Gazette*, London, 6 July 1885.

Summers, A. (1999) 'The constitution violated: the female body and the female subject in the campaigns of Josephine Butler', *History Workshop Journal*, 48(1): 1–15.

Tait, W. (1840) *Magdalenism: An Inquiry into its Extent, Causes and Consequences of Prostitution in Edinburgh*, Edinburgh: P. Richard.

Tickner, L. (1988) *The Spectacle of Women: Imagery of the Suffrage Campaign, 1907–14*, Chicago, IL: Chicago University Press.

Trumble, K. (2003) *'Her Body Is Her Own': Victorian Feminists, Sexual Violence, and Political Subjectivity*. Thesis. Florida State University.

Vigilance Record (1913) July & August issue. Held at Women's Library.

Walkowitz, J.R. (1980) *Prostitution and Victorian Society: Women, Class and the State*, Cambridge: Cambridge University Press.

Walkowitz, J.R. (1992) *City of Dreadful Delight: Narratives of Sexual Danger in Late-Victorian London*, Chicago, IL: University of Chicago Press.

Wardle Fredrickson, K. (2011) *Josephine E. Butler and Christianity in the British Victorian Feminist Movement*, Charleston, SC: BiblioBazaar.

Wilson, W. (1875) Henry Wilson (20 December 1875). [Letter]. Held at Women's Library. Ref: 3/JBL/14/11.

3

The Coloniality of Modern Slavery in Latin America

Chris O'Connell

Introduction

The issue of modern slavery is highly disputed (Chuang, 2014; O'Connell Davidson, 2015; Segrave, Milivojevic, and Pickering, 2018). The dual emergence of 'new' slavery (Bales, 2004) and the codification of human trafficking in the Protocol to Prevent, Suppress and Punish Trafficking in Persons Especially Women and Children (hereafter, the Palermo Protocol) supplementing the UN Convention against Transnational Organized Crime in 2000, led eventually to their coming together under the umbrella of modern slavery. Subsequently, the emergence of the language of modern slavery has engulfed a broad range of exploitative practices due to its elasticity, absorbing everything related to it from forced marriage to child pornography into a meta-category (Faulkner, 2023). Characterized by effective control rather than legal ownership, the concept has expanded to incorporate all recognized forms of human bondage, among them forced labour, debt bondage, child labour, and forced marriage (Alliance 8.7, 2017). Nevertheless, the inclusion of recognized legal concepts and scholarly initiatives, such as the Bellagio-Harvard Guidelines (Allain, 2017), cannot obscure the fact that there is no internationally agreed definition of 'modern slavery'. It remains a 'slippery' and confusing concept (LeBaron, 2020: 7) that is significantly shaped by discourses articulated by an uncomfortable coalition of NGOs, corporations, national governments, and UN bodies (Natarajan et al, 2020).

The dominant approach treats modern slavery as an individualized relationship, characterized by extreme exploitation and explained by underdevelopment, which is viewed as exclusion from global markets. For example, eliminating modern slavery is incorporated into the UN Sustainable Development Goals (SDGs) under SDG8, which frames development in terms of economic growth.[1] Accordingly, slavery is presented as an 'anachronism' to be resolved by economic modernization and strong criminal laws (O'Connell Davidson, 2015: 57). Critical scholarship has outlined several problems associated with this hegemonic approach. This chapter seeks to develop two strands of critique. The first relates to its weak historicity, in particular its shallow reading of the history of slavery and abolition, and associated legacies of colonialism[2] and racialization (Diptée, 2018). The second strand relates to a lack of careful analysis of power relations, particularly regarding the role of the state,[3] which is an under-studied topic (Bravo, 2015; LeBaron and Phillips, 2019).

This chapter seeks to deepen analysis in these areas through engagement with the literature on decolonization, and in particular Anibal Quijano's concept of 'coloniality of power' (2000). The chapter argues that a focus on coloniality's two core processes – racialization and articulation with forms of labour control linked to global markets – challenges mainstream approaches to the study of modern slavery. According to Quijano (2000: 535), all forms of control and exploitation of labour – including slavery, serfdom, and wages – were 'deliberately established and organized' to produce commodities for the world market. This 'new global model of labour control' (2000) was in turn associated with racialized social categories, a powerful method of classifying people as 'fit' for exploitation (Martinez, 2012). In these ways, a coloniality lens reveals a need for modern slavery scholarship to engage more deeply with the history of slavery and servitude beyond simple binaries and individualized relationships, to examine how those relationships link to societal norms and wider economic structures. This highlights the importance of analysing power relations at multiple scales, and problematizing the state beyond visions of it as a 'neutral' entity (LeBaron and Phillips, 2019).

Through focusing on the ambiguous role of the state in enabling or challenging the colonial matrix of power, the chapter analyses the state as a strategic social relation that is both shaped and informed by a prevailing balance of forces and shifting narratives. The chapter proceeds in four main sections. The first presents a critical analysis of dominant approaches to the study of modern slavery, highlighting significant shortcomings in terms of historicity and analyses of power, particularly as to the role of the state. The

---

[1] See further https://sdgs.un.org/goals [Accessed 13 January 2023].

[2] The author recognizes that referencing the 'legacy' of colonialism implies that it is extinct. However, the continued impact of colonialism continues to influence and control law, policy, politics, and society globally.

[3] The role of the state is considered later in the collection, with the contribution from Francis asserting that the state-centric focus within the Belizean context is problematic.

next section introduces the concept of coloniality of power, which centres on two historic processes: the creation of racialized categories (see further Boukli et al, this volume), and the articulation of different forms of labour control with those categories, thereby ensuring that the legacies of coloniality persist beyond direct rule and the abolition of slavery. The following two sections concentrate on applying this framework to instances of forced labour and modern slavery in two neighbouring countries with varying contexts: post-independence Peru's neocolonial nation state and Bolivia's 'decolonizing' state, drawing on both documentary and field research in both countries.

Methodology: conducting fieldwork in Bolivia and Peru

This chapter uses a comparative case study approach, which allows for a deeper understanding of the dynamics and allows for comparison over time (Landman, 2008: 69). As recent scholarship on modern slavery has noted, there is a need for more comparative research of the role of states in shaping responses (Cockbain, 2018; LeBaron and Phillips, 2019: 3). To do this I draw on a mix of primary and secondary research, including fieldwork conducted in both Bolivia and Peru in 2018 and 2019 as part of a broader research project on state responses to modern slavery. The author carried out 90 qualitative interviews with state officials, prosecutors, NGO representatives, and social movement leaders, as well as local academics, with questions focusing on state responses to vulnerability to exploitation and abuse. Research participants were identified through a mix of purposive and snowball sampling. All research participants provided their informed consent in writing and have been anonymized for the purposes of this chapter.

The data gleaned from these interviews helped to inform both case study sections below, with four interviews explicitly referenced in the section entitled 'Decolonization and modern slavery in Bolivia'. To further contextualize this data and improve the rigour of the findings, this material was triangulated through analysis of laws, national plans, and other official documents, along with grey literature, press releases, and statements emanating from civil society organizations. For the section on post-independence Peru, entitled 'Coloniality of labour in post-independence Peru: rubber and guano', the chapter draws upon a mix of contemporaneous sources and later analysis by historians and anthropologists, including Peruvian scholars.

This analysis finds that a coloniality framework helps to deepen understandings of the power relations at different scales – societal, national, and international – that underpin modern slavery. It reveals the close connection between racialized divisions and exploitation, although the identity of those being exploited varies and is mediated by sociopolitical factors. Second, variations in global demand are closely connected to instances of labour exploitation, with states tending to facilitate rather than challenge this situation. These findings indicate that legacies of colonialism live on via globalized capitalism and raise questions over whether states are truly capable of 'decolonizing' and addressing the roots of modern slavery.

Problematizing approaches to modern slavery

The dominant approach to modern slavery privileges a narrow vision centred on an individualized relationship between 'slaveholder' and 'slave' (Bales, 2016). In this way, the focus of attention is restricted to the point of exploitation, divorced from the wider socio-economic context (Natarajan et al, 2020). As such, this modern form of slavery is presented as a 'residual' phenomenon (Phillips and Sakamoto, 2012: 296) which exists 'outside the purview of state scrutiny and market capitalism' (Natarajan et al, 2020: 243). This conceptualization of the issue lends itself in turn to a limited range of actions, typically incorporating the criminalization of 'slaveholders' and the 'rescue' and liberation of victims (Kotiswaran, 2019; Natarajan et al, 2020). As Quirk (2011: 8) highlights, those who adopt this approach seek to evoke the imaginary of a modern version of legal abolition, rather than engage in the real battle for 'effective emancipation'. Framed in this way, modern slavery has found a 'receptive audience' among political elites (2011: 158), business leaders (LeBaron, 2020), non-state actors,[4] and multilateral institutions (Lerche, 2007).

In turn, these institutional and policy changes have inspired a range of critical analyses. This chapter focuses on two critiques. The first relates to the level of engagement with history. Despite its use of the language of slavery, the literature on contemporary forms has been criticized for the largely ahistorical nature of its analysis (Quirk, 2009; Diptée, 2018; Faulkner, 2023). A notable example relates to the issue of race and ethnicity, which is largely glossed over in this literature, but recent contributions have sought to address this, notably the works of Beutin (2017, 2023) and Kempadoo and Shih (2023). The tone is set by the highly influential account of Kevin Bales (2004: 10) which asserts that race has 'little' to do with modern slavery. Similarly, the International Labour Organization (hereafter, ILO) views the issue as one of a range of so-called 'risk factors' that serve to render some more vulnerable to exploitation (Alliance 8.7, 2017). In practice, this issue tends to be associated with supposedly 'traditional forms of serfdom' in the 'developing world' (Plant, 2017: 431). Thus, while Indigenous[5] peoples and

---

[4] The positions of NGOs, NSAs, and civil society organizations and religious organizations are touched upon in the chapters by Lammasniemi, Bhagat, and Francis.

[5] See Chapter 4 for an in-depth review of the constructed category of Indigenous in the context of the TIPR.

ethnic minorities are acknowledged as accounting for the 'vast majority' of those in conditions of modern slavery worldwide, the situation is attributed to their economic marginalization in a context of underdevelopment (Plant, 2017: 431). Accordingly, race and caste are considered less important than 'wealth and power' (Bales, 2004: 17).

This focus on economic underdevelopment, however, reveals significant blind spots. This approach sidesteps the colonial logics of slavery and abolition – presenting what Diptée (2018) argues is a 'sanitised' version of events. As scholars have noted, British abolitionism did not reject existing social norms or advocate for enslaved peoples being viewed as the equals of white Europeans (Quirk, 2011; Diptée, 2018), nor did it seek to criticize capitalism or colonialism. According to Quirk (2011), this qualified approach to abolition, which avoided challenging social hierarchies, facilitated the later use of racialized tropes to justify forced labour in colonial Africa, caste-based bondage in India, and debt peonage among Indigenous peoples in Latin America. These contemporary forms of slavery are therefore deeply rooted in ideas of colonial power and racial superiority – ultimately race and slavery were integral to the spectacular success of the project of colonialism.

The failure to adequately engage with these historical roots has both intellectual and practical implications, influencing as it does the formulation and implementation of policy. As noted by Kempadoo and Shih (2023: 5), 'racism is not simply an effect, or an unintended outcome (see further Hynes and Dottridge, this volume) of anti-trafficking policies and interventions but is instead central to the formulation of the very idea of "human trafficking"'. This view is supported by evidence from Brazil – the last country in the Americas to abolish slavery in 1888,[6] and one that today gathers reliable data on modern slavery. According to Sakamoto (2020), of the 54,000 people released from slave-like conditions up to 2016, the majority were Black – a situation he attributes an incomplete abolition that failed to achieve real inclusion. Piscitelli (2008) and Blanchette and Silva (2012, 2018) among others have been 'systematically analysing anti-trafficking policies in Brazil for more than ten years on several levels and scales' (Olivar and Melo, 2023: 147). What is evident within this body of research is the racial issue, 'showing how anti-trafficking policies in Brazil have been built upon moral economies that fundamentally target the sexualities and displacements of poor, rural and afro-Brazilian or darker skin women' (Olivar and Melo, 2023: 147).

---

[6] On 13 May 1888, Brazilian Princess Isabel of Braganca signed Imperial Law number 3,353. Containing only 18 words, it is one of the most important pieces of legislation in Brazilian history – The 'Golden Law' (Lei Aurea) abolished slavery in all its forms. For 350 years, slavery was the heart of the Brazilian economy. See further www.blackhistorymonth.org.uk/article/listings/region/online-event/the-untold-history-of-slavery-in-brazil-juliano-moreira-december-edition/ [Accessed July 2023].

Although modern slavery, for some, is not expressly racialized, discrimination on the grounds of race and ethnicity is a key factor in determining who is made vulnerable to exploitation (Van den Anker, 2004: 19). As Munck (2018: 16) notes, 'the boundaries between economic and non-economic compulsion ... class and race/ethnicity are far more porous than generally allowed for'. Rather than focusing on the shared roots of historical and modern slavery, however, much of the literature on modern slavery relies on 'comfortable tropes' and shallow parallels (Diptée, 2018: 408). In the words of Bravo (2011: 581), 'the racism that arose from the trans-Atlantic slave trade prevents users of the analogy from delving more deeply into the substantive meanings and similarities of the modern traffic and the trans-Atlantic slave trade'.

This links to the second critique, which is a lack of deep analysis of or challenges to the power relations underpinning modern slavery, particularly capitalism. For example, a 2015 UN University report recognizes that vulnerability to exploitation is relational rather than absolute, describing it as 'a form of extreme inequality, sustained by a range of vested interests', but limits those interests to 'unscrupulous business actors, corrupt police and officials' (Cockayne, 2015: 4). Similarly, Bales' work mentions in general terms the power of multinational corporations (2004) and the role of consumer demand (2016) but focuses attention on illegal activities and 'criminal slaveholders' rather than global capitalism. This issue links to that of the weak historicity of the mainstream anti-slavery movement (Diptée, 2018). As Bunting and Quirk (2017: 20) note, efforts to end historical slavery 'were firmly aimed at the profits and privileges of the rich and powerful'. To use Diptée's phrase (2018: 416), abolitionists sought to 'cut slavery apologists off at the knees'.

This approach contrasts with contemporary efforts to tackle slavery. Ample evidence now exists to demonstrate that modern slavery, rather than an anachronistic phenomenon, is inextricably linked with globalized capitalism (Bravo, 2015; O'Connell Davidson, 2015; LeBaron, 2020). The critical literature on modern slavery argues persuasively that, while not responsible for its occurrence, neoliberal globalization fundamentally shapes contemporary forms of slavery (Van den Anker, 2004; Lerche, 2007; LeBaron and Phillips, 2019). In particular, the steady 'flexibilisation' of labour and erosion of rights and protections has exposed a growing section of the population to exploitation (Harvey, 2007: 76). As a result, modern slavery has become a consistent feature of global business (LeBaron, 2020) – a 'regularised management practice' (Crane, 2013), directly linked to profitability (Sakamoto, 2020). Corporate pressure pushes down prices and lowers labour standards, creating conditions for exploitation and abuse (LeBaron, 2020). Nonetheless, unlike early abolitionism, mainstream approaches to modern slavery instead cast corporations as 'heroes that save the day' (LeBaron, 2020: 9).

At the centre of this 'cocooned' (Lerche, 2007), 'sanitised' (Phillips and Mieres, 2015) approach to modern slavery there is the state; or rather, there is a state-shaped hole. The state is 'the principle of order and authority in a society' (Foweraker, 2018: 67). While the regime type (authoritarian, democratic, hybrid, and so on) determines the forms of state relationship with society and modes of authority (Foweraker, 2018: 67), the nation state remains highly relevant to social outcomes. Mainstream modern slavery approaches focus predominantly on state-imposed forced labour and largely ignore more prevalent forms within the private economy (LeBaron and Phillips, 2019: 2). For example, states have driven trends towards reducing regulatory capacity and empowering corporate over workers' rights (LeBaron, 2020: 68). Nevertheless, mainstream academic publications and policy documents on modern slavery tend to regard the state in a largely unproblematized manner as the creator and enforcer of laws (Bravo, 2015; LeBaron and Phillips, 2019). This approach overlooks the fact that states are frequently responsible – directly or indirectly – for facilitating exploitation and abuse (Le Baron and Phillips, 2019). On the other hand, much of the critical literature also abstracts the state, reducing it to a mere appendage of capitalism (Kotiswaran, 2019; LeBaron and Phillips, 2019).

This chapter agrees with scholars who reject the notion that the state is a neutral entity, much less a 'benevolent agent' (Jessop, 2016: 3). However, the state is not a simple instrument of capitalist accumulation or colonial power (Brand, 2013). Instead, I argue that the state must be understood as a strategic social relation, essentially that the state is both a reflection and a refraction of the changing balance of forces within a society that seeks to influence policy and politics (Jessop, 2016). To study the state, therefore, it is imperative to also analyse wider societal forces and narratives. In the context of Latin America, it is particularly important to consider state autonomy. From their formation, states in the region have lacked autonomy from oligarchic interests and international powers (Foweraker, 2018). Yet as Jessop (2008) asserts, state power is maintained through a balance of facilitating capital accumulation and establishing legitimacy – particularly under democratic governance. This fact transforms the state into contested terrain and, under the right conditions, renders it more accessible to other actors – such as civil society (Cannon and Kirby, 2012) and subsequently to progressive change.

This gap has remained neglected within the existing literature on modern slavery, with recent works emerging that address this gap (Costa, 2009; Bravo, 2015; Kotiswaran, 2019; LeBaron and Phillips, 2019). Through highlighting the agency of states in driving globalization, LeBaron and Phillips (2019: 5–6) note altering relations with private actors and the adoption of laws and policies which favour business, but which create conditions for modern slavery to thrive. The ambiguous nature of the state illustrates variations between states that see many themselves exploited by more powerful states and private actors (Bravo, 2015: 28). This approach is particularly relevant for formerly colonized states across the Global South, where the state apparatus was created and evolved along very different lines to Europe. An analysis of India's 'postcolonial developmental state' reveals a hybrid model that combines promoting growth with interventionism and welfare provision (Kotiswaran, 2019). Similarly in Brazil, a left-led developmental state built an anti-slavery system that is considered a model (Costa, 2009).

At international level, the judgment of the Inter-American Court of Human Rights in the *Hacienda Verde*[7] case broke ground by explicitly outlining the positive obligations of states under the American Convention on Human Rights to prevent slavery and trafficking (Milano, 2018). While an acknowledgement of the agency of states, the judgment nevertheless departs from the mainstream view of the state as a neutral actor. This chapter contributes to this ongoing scholarly and practice-oriented debate[8] by analysing the state as a strategic social relation that shapes and is shaped by a shifting correlation of forces and dominant narratives in the context of post-independence Latin America.

Coloniality of power and modern slavery

The concept of coloniality of power grew from different roots than the mainstream and critical approaches to modern slavery, both of which depart from a shared understanding of wage labour as the defining feature of capitalism (Boatcă, 2013: 291). Dependency theorists and world-systems analysts by contrast argued that uneven development and wide variations in the prevalence of wage labour were in fact characteristics of capitalism as a historical world system (Wallerstein, 2000). Latin Americanists rejected this as a 'myth' (Frank, 1967) and the links drawn between feudalism/ underdevelopment on the one hand, and capitalism/development on the other. Under this conceptualization of a single capitalist world system, underdevelopment was explained by the history of colonial rule and the neocolonial domination that succeeded it after independence (Frank, 1967). Therefore, modern forms of serfdom and slavery are not 'anomalies' but

---

[7] See further https://ohrh.law.ox.ac.uk/hacienda-brasil-verde-workers-v-brazil-slavery-and-human-trafficking-in-the-inter-american-court-of-human-rights/

[8] For a more in-depth discussion of some of the structural issues in modern slavery and human trafficking practice, see Part II of this volume.

rather the product of the process of the commodification of labour that began in the 16th century (Boatcă, 2013: 293).

Coloniality of power is an analytical concept which emerged from this 'epistemic shift' in Latin America (Mignolo, 2011: 46). The so-called Coloniality/Modernity School comprised important thinkers from the region and is differentiated from post-colonialism by its point of departure: the European Conquest of the Americas. A cornerstone of this school of thought is that coloniality is constitutive of modernity (Mignolo, 2007). In other words, the coloniality of power is 'the darker side of modernity and the global reach of Imperial capitalism', without which it would not exist (Mignolo, 2007: 162). Due to its distinct departure point, the genealogy of thought that underpins decoloniality is broader than, while encompassing of, post-coloniality. For Mignolo (2007, 2011) the writings of Indigenous activist Waman Puma de Ayala in colonial Peru and former slave turned abolitionist Ottabah Cugoano serve as foundational texts.

The concept of coloniality of power was developed by Peruvian sociologist Aníbal Quijano. According to Quijano's pivotal work (2000), the establishment, consolidation, and perpetuation of a new model of global power were achieved via two key processes. The first was the use of the idea of race and racial identity based on supposed biological differences as instruments of social classification. These categories, and their associated classifications of 'superior' or 'inferior', were internalized by both colonizers and the colonized as 'natural' (see further Boukli et al, this volume). As Munck (2018: 15) notes, 'race was made by colonialism, but it also makes colonialism what it was and is'. In the view of Quijano, while this novel system of social classification was colonial in origin and nature, it would prove 'more durable and stable' than colonialism itself (2000: 533). In other words, the mindsets and practices developed under Spanish and Portuguese rule persisted even after that rule ended (Alimonda, 2015: 152).

The second key process was the construction of a new system of labour control which involved the articulation of all historically known structures, including slavery, serfdom, independent production, and reciprocity, 'around and upon the basis of capital and the world market' (Quijano, 2000: 534). The result of these dual processes, according to Quijano, was the association of these social roles with racialized identities as a means of legitimating their domination and exploitation (Quijano, 2000: 534). In other words, the coloniality of power represents a 'carry-over of both racial/ethnic hierarchies and the international division of labour' from colonial times (Boatcă, 2013: 309). In this way, a 'systematic racial division of labour was imposed' in which each racialized group was linked to a particular form of labour control (Quijano, 2000: 536–7).

As Dussel (2000: 49) puts it, the enslavement of these supposedly 'backward' groups were made in the cause of 'modernisation'. Coloniality, as the 'violent side' of modernity, was integral to the expansion of capitalism and Western epistemology (Martínez, 2012: 12) – what Mignolo terms the 'colonial matrix of power' (2007). This process created a 'hierarchical ranking of humanity', which presented not only the labour power, but also the lives, cultures, and knowledges of racialized 'Others' as disposable (Martínez, 2012: 5). This concept of 'disposability' links to the writings of ex-slave Cugoano who, according to Mignolo (2011: 62), 'constantly' insisted that Black lives were treated as lacking value. It also has echoes in the highly influential book by Kevin Bales (2004), itself a foundational text for modern slavery scholars and advocates.

Coloniality of power, however, challenges mainstream modern slavery narratives in at least three ways. First, it permits analysis of the links between labour control and different racialized groups beyond the abolition of slavery to the present. While strict comparisons between different forms of bondage and exploitation may not be possible, as Boatcă notes it is nonetheless helpful to consider them 'as instances of the coloniality of labour of global capitalism' (2013: 312). Second, it problematizes the dominant reading of the history of slavery as an individualized relationship, bringing into the frame multi-scalar relations of power between societal groups and nations that influence vulnerability to exploitation beyond anodyne references to risk factors. Such an approach undermines interpretations of both slavery and abolition as primarily concerned with laws, indicating the need for greater analysis of the macroeconomic structures and incentives.

Finally, and crucially, however, this approach permits deeper analysis of continuities and changes in the correlation of forces and associated narratives over time. In particular, it provides a framework through which to assess the role of the state in challenging or advancing coloniality (Mignolo, 2011). In the Spanish Americas, the issue of labour control was a source of contention between Spanish-descended Creoles and the Crown. While some protections for the Indigenous population were introduced, the Crown's capacity to mediate racialized divisions was weak (Williamson, 1992: 115). Accordingly, the states that emerged from the Wars of Independence in the early 19th century were 'colonial nation states', characterized by an 'internal colonialism' through which Eurocentric Creoles embedded racialized hierarchies and legitimated the colonial development model (Williamson, 1992: 157–8).

In the view of Mignolo, it is this failure to break with the colonial rules of the game, and the maintenance of 'the very idea of the state within a global capitalist economy', that accounts for the lack of success of previous decolonization movements (2011: 50). Mignolo notes the need for different thinking and approaches, citing left-leaning Latin American governments in Venezuela, Bolivia, and Brazil as instances of state projects that sought to change the rules and 'plant the flag of decolonial pluri-versality' (2011: 51).

The following sections explore the utility of coloniality to the issue of state responses to modern slavery through analysis of labour exploitation in contrasting cases: Peru's post-independence neocolonial state, and Bolivia's left-led 'decolonizing' state.

Coloniality of labour in post-independence Peru: guano and rubber

In post-independence South America, new products were brought to market and new territories were colonized, but the extractive nature of its economic structure that relied on exporting primary products to Europe was unchanged (Meade, 2010). Regarding labour control, there was a realignment of the colonial system in response to both internal dynamics and external pressures. Of particular significance were the gradual abolition of chattel slavery and the removal from Indigenous peoples the limited protections provided by the Spanish Crown, opening their territories to incursions and exposing them to exploitation (Skidmore and Smith, 2005). These legal changes, nevertheless, were accompanied by the material impoverishment of all racialized groups, while large landowners enjoyed 'near complete control' over resources (Meade, 2010: 182–3).

Peru was a prototypical neocolonial state, run by and for the interests of a racialized 'white' (Creole) minority who ruled over a similarly racialized Indigenous majority – typically depicted as 'beyond redemption' (Skidmore and Smith, 2005: 182). Analysis of the role of the state in relation to two post-independence systems of labour control linked to emblematic commodities – guano and rubber – largely supports Quijano's coloniality thesis. In both cases, the rise and fall of these 'industries' respond closely to overall trends in global capitalism. On the other hand, it reveals the importance of domestic actors and their interests in defining the contours of these systems, highlighting the state's role in facilitating exploitation. In other words, the 'how' of labour exploitation was locally defined. This analysis also reveals the importance of racialization to the creation and justification of these systems of exploitation. In contrast to the strict hierarchy under direct colonial rule, however, in the post-independence era the 'who' of exploitation was flexible – groups might occupy varying levels on a hierarchy, but differentiation based on racialized categories was a consistent feature.

Following the independence wars, Peru's economy was extremely fragile until 'Nature came to (its) rescue' (Skidmore and Smith, 2005: 185). Beginning in the 1840s, demand for guano – a rich fertilizer made up of bird droppings – grew rapidly in soil-depleted countries like Britain. Peru was indebted to Britain and guano seemed to offer a means to repay its debts. In fact, the guano boom predominantly benefited the British, who enjoyed a trade monopoly on the product, although the trade also made fortunes for local elites (Clark and Foster, 2009: 320). The Peruvian state rapidly became highly dependent on guano, but the terms of the trade overwhelmingly favoured English bondholders, while providing little stimulus for long-term growth (Skidmore and Smith, 2005: 186). An estimated one million tons of guano were exported during the boom period, but Peru nonetheless remained in debt.

With regard to labour control, the guano boom revealed a degree of flexibility around a core of racialization. For example, even though guano extraction was highly labour-intensive, in 1854 President Ramon Castilla issued decrees emancipating African slaves and abolishing the Indigenous contribution (Skidmore and Smith, 2005: 187). While some scholars have attributed this outcome to the fundamental irreconcilability of slavery and capitalism, most believe that slavery and capitalism accommodated one another (Ramirez, 1996). As Gonzalez (1989) notes, chattel slavery in Peru had already declined significantly due to the impact of war and low reproduction. More proximately, abolition resulted from a combination of British anti-slavery campaigning, new sources of capital, and persistent slave resistance which had severely weakened the institution (Ramirez, 1996). As Ramirez notes, by 1854 abolition had become 'politically expedient' (Ramirez, 1996: 3). Furthermore, the rents from guano enabled the Peruvian state to compensate slaveholders at above market rates, thereby recapitalizing them from the public purse (Gonzalez, 1989: 390).

Although the guano boom contributed to enhanced liberty for some racialized groups, it worsened the situation of others. Castilla's decrees contributed to a labour shortage amid high global prices for guano, an issue he initially planned to address by forcibly transporting Indigenous Ashaninka people from the rainforest region to the coast (Chirif, 2017: 31). In the end, however, former slaveholders invested the capital gained from the state indemnity into the systematic importation of Chinese indentured servants, known as 'coolies' (Gonzalez, 1989: 390). In the words of Jose Carlos Mariategui – a Peruvian socialist thinker who inspired Quijano's work – 'when the agricultural worker has not been an Indian, he has been an African slave or Chinese coolie who is, if possible, held in more contempt' (cited in Webber, 2017: 123–4).

Around 90,000 indentured Chinese labourers were transported to Peru, a system which was subsidized by the Peruvian state following an 1839 immigration law (Gonzalez, 1989: 390). Once on the guano islands, 'coolies' were subjected to sub-human conditions, including dangerous and unsanitary work, exhausting working hours, and poor nutrition. Such exploitation and abuse were justified by a 'common belief' in the supposed racial inferiority of the Chinese (Gonzalez, 1989: 423). The workers were quickly entrapped in a system of debt bondage that further limited their mobility – a situation that enjoyed state support (Gonzalez, 1989: 393). Nevertheless, such was the demand for guano that most employers preferred to avoid lost labour time by using physical punishment rather than legal sanctions, with floggings and other violent measures common (Clark and Foster, 2009: 323). Both Peru and Britain were complicit in this '*de facto* slavery' for almost 30 years,[9] and when Britain eventually came to oppose the trade, it was primarily for commercial rather than humanitarian reasons (Gonzalez, 1989: 391).

The history of rubber in Peru in the early 20th century also supports the thesis of coloniality and state facilitation of exploitation, with some variations. The wild rubber boom was relatively short-lived, beginning in the 1870s but declining steeply after 1912, when British plantation rubber became widely available. Nonetheless, rubber extraction deepened the wealth asymmetries between regions, as raw materials fed the emerging automobile industry in Europe and the US (Mitchell, 2010). In Peru the boom made fortunes for some, but left scars on the landscape and bodies of its Indigenous peoples, including the extinction of some Indigenous groups (Meade, 2010: 242). Nowhere was this clearer than in the Putumayo – an Amazon region at the centre of a territorial dispute between Peru and Colombia. This uncertainty was seized upon by Julio Cesar Arana, who employed a usurious system of lending known as '*habilitación*' to acquire his first rubber holdings (Chirif, 2017: 32). Arana used the same system to entrap Indigenous Andokes, Bora, Huitoto, and Ocaina with 'unpayable' debts via the 'exchange' of overvalued industrial products for undervalued rubber (Chirif, 2017: 33).

Even by the standards of the rubber boom, the system put in place by Arana was notably brutal. Indigenous men, women, and children were forced to bring quotas of rubber under threat of violence. Torture, floggings, rape, and murder were regularized mechanisms of production; attempts at organized resistance resulted in massacres; and many died from disease and a famine caused by an inability to cultivate crops. The result was the death of an estimated 40,000 Indigenous people (Chirif, 2017: 38, 43) and the violence of the system almost brought Indigenous groups to extinction. The Andokes, for example, disappeared in Peru and were almost wiped out in Colombia (Chirif, 2017: 227), while Indigenous people in the region recall the extinction of other Indigenous groups (Michiles, 2021).[10] For these reasons, scholars have portrayed the rubber extraction system in the Putumayo as genocidal (Mitchell, 1997: 50).

According to research, the degree of barbarity can be explained by a combination of global and local concerns. Rising demand for rubber

---

[9] According to Gonzalez (1989), the Peruvian 'coolie trade' was concentrated between 1847 and 1874.

[10] In the words of Ocaina Indigenous shaman Blas Caimera: 'We do know that many tribes were extinct. We don't know that group, that clan, because they no longer exist' (Michiles, 2021: 80).

provided the context, but the proximate cause was increased tension between Colombia and Peru. To protect his interests, Arana sought to register his Peruvian Amazon Company (PAC) on the London Stock Exchange. Doing so, however, required a rapid rise in profitability, which was achieved by ramping up production while keeping labour costs close to zero (Chirif, 2017). Although Arana succeeded in 1907, reports of atrocities committed by a British company filtered out and an investigative commission was convoked.

At the urging of the Anti-Slavery and Aborigines' Protection Society[11] the commission was led by Roger Casement, the foremost human rights investigator of his day (Goodman, 2010: 68). Much of what we know about the Putumayo comes from Casement's report and journal (Mitchell, 1997), wherein he detailed the workings of a racialized system of de facto slavery.[12] In a revealing journal entry, a rubber merchant describes 'tribes of savages' who were 'no use to ... the white man' unless 'conquered and made to work' (Mitchell, 1997: 78–9).[13] Thus, economic imperatives only partially account for the violence of the regime, which was facilitated by an 'accumulated imaginary' of Indigenous people as non-human (Chirif, 2017: 46). The task of brutalizing the Indigenous was delegated to another racialized group: imported Black Barbadians who, as British subjects, provided key evidence of the atrocities. These workers were forced to inflict torture, violence, and even death on Indigenous labourers, and were thus themselves victims, as Casement noted (Mitchell, 1997). Presiding over the system was a racialized group of '*blancos*' (whites), a term which, in the Putumayo, 'connoted power over indigenous people' (Goodman, 2010: 99).

Casement pointed the finger at the Peruvian state that 'stood by passive' while these abuses occurred (Mitchell, 1997: 278). In fact, the state contribution to exploitation was both passive and active. From the mid-19th century, Peru was encouraging immigration by 'white' Europeans who were 'axiomatically' considered hardworking and intelligent (Chirif, 2017: 31). This 'colonialist and segregationist mentality' was reflected in the 1893 Immigration and Colonization Law that incentivized the settlement of the Amazon, ignoring Indigenous rights (Romero, 1978: 7–8). To support the rubber 'boom', in 1909 the state introduced Law 1220 that provided guarantees of legal stability to the sector (Romero, 1978: 7–8), incentivizing land expropriation, forced displacement, 'slavery and genocide' (Merino,

---

[11] The forerunner of today's Anti-Slavery International.

[12] Following interviews with Barbadians and conversations with those in the Amazon city of Iquitos – in this case British Consul David Cazes – Casement notes 'again and again I find slipping from his lips and those of others in Iquitos the unconscious admission of this system of wholesale slavery' (Mitchell, 1997: 110).

[13] The merchant goes on to tell Casement that he 'owned them (the indigenous people) as much as he owned the rubber trees on his "territory"' (Mitchell, 1997: 80).

2020: 517). The scandal that followed the publication of Casement's report in 1912 – accompanied by external pressure from the British, the US, and the Vatican – forced the Peruvian state to convoke its own commission of investigation (Goodman, 2010: 144). Despite the best efforts of Judge Carlos Valcarcel, however, no substantive reform ensued (Goodman, 2010: 144).

Instead, it was left to the vagaries of global markets to deconstruct what they had enabled the construction of, as increased production on British, Dutch, and French plantations reduced the demand for wild Amazonian rubber (Goodman, 2010: 244). For the Indigenous groups, however, this did not signify their liberation. As Chirif (2017) reveals, they remained subjugated to a colonial power matrix: following moves by Colombia to take over the Putumayo region, thousands of Indigenous people were forcibly transported by PAC employees to Peruvian territory and forced to work to meet new global demands for timber, resins, and animal hides (Chirif, 2017: 39). Peruvian scholars have traced the legacies of coloniality to present-day policies promoting the extraction of natural resources and their export into global markets (Chirif, 2017; Merino, 2020). This reflects the view of Casement who, by the end of his time in Peru, concluded the true villain was 'the unchecked power of modernisation' (Mitchell, 2010: 13).

Decolonization and modern slavery in Bolivia

On its face, the case of contemporary Bolivia appears to offer a counterpoint to post-independence Peru. The election of a self-identified Indigenous Aymara in 2005, the now former President Evo Morales[14] (offered the promise of a break with coloniality (Mignolo, 2011) after years of social upheaval. The 'process of change' that came to be spearheaded by Morales' MAS (Movement to Socialism) Party was chiefly driven by a Unity Pact of Indigenous and peasant social movements intent on re-founding the nation and decolonizing the state (Postero, 2015: 398). The primary tool for achieving decolonization was Indigenous self-determination, to be achieved through a constituent assembly to re-write the Constitution as a means of 'reversing centuries of racism against the majority indigenous population' (Postero, 2015: 398). A key manifestation of this racism was through forced labour and modern slavery.

For over a century, the exploitation of Guaraní in lowland Bolivia followed a regional pattern of abuse of Indigenous groups rendered vulnerable by

---

[14] See further www.theguardian.com/world/2014/oct/13/bolivia-evo-morales--presid ent-third-term [Accessed July 2023]; https://theconversation.com/evo-morales-champi ons-indigenous-rights-abroad-but-in-bolivia-its-a-different-story-38062 [Accessed July 2023].

systematic discrimination and exclusion (Canqui, 2011). The state played an active role in creating and maintaining vulnerability. Expansion into the Chaco region in the 19th century culminated with the 1892 Kuruyuqui Massacre by state troops of an estimated 8,000 Indigenous people, following which the remaining Guaraní were 'captured for distribution' among white settlers (Anthias, 2018: 19). The Bolivian state actively promoted racialized divisions, selling off supposedly 'idle' Guaraní lands at low prices to 'civilising' non-Indigenous settlers (Anthias, 2018: 23). Despite the promise the 1952 Bolivian Revolution, the power and militancy of the Chaco settlers saw them successfully resist the most radical aspects of the 1953 Agrarian Reform (Healy, 1983: 6). As a result, the reform extended ranchers' landholdings, further dispossessing Indigenous groups who were portrayed as 'savages' (Anthias, 2018: 25). Confined to 'more remote, less productive areas', many were obliged to labour on ranches, where they were entrapped in debt bondage (Hinojosa et al, 2015: 110)

A mix of coercive, moral, and cultural power was utilized by owners of large estates known as *haciendas* to keep Guaraní workers in a system of semi-slavery known as '*empatronamiento*'. The system involved three interrelated mechanisms of coercion and control. The first was debt bondage, involving the exchange of goods at inflated values, ensuring a state of permanent debt that facilitated exploitation (Healy, 1983). As Ventiades (1997) noted, workers laboured for 12–14 hours per day and were paid only in kind. The second element was isolation, with community's captive on *haciendas*, cut off from formal education and knowledge of the outside world. The third element was affective, with landlords assuming the role of godfathers (*patrones*) to Indigenous children (Healy, 1983; Ventiades, 1997). These mechanisms were underpinned at all stages by violence and threats (Bedoya and Bedoya, 2005; IACHR, 2009). An additional layer of control came from the state. Despite 1953 laws abolishing unpaid work and debt bondage, not only were labour inspectors unwilling to challenge the power of landowners, but also state authorities actively supported the system by capturing, detaining, and returning 'escaped' workers (Healy, 1983: 151).

In the view of Anthias (2018), although *empatronamiento* was 'not devoid of indigenous agency', as a system it was both exploitative and culturally degrading. Ethnographic research among the Guaraní has revealed that many (though not all) considered their situation to be one of 'slavery' (Ventiades, 1997; Gustafson, 2010). This situation continued unchallenged until the 1980s, when the Guaraní began to self-organize. Anthias (2018: 26) reveals that this highly challenging process was motivated by the shared experience of 'virtual enslavement' on the *haciendas*. The loss of both land and autonomy inflicted by this colonizing process led the nascent Association of Guaraní Peoples (APG) to fix on land rights as its core demand (Anthias, 2018: 27). A difficult process of articulation between lowland Indigenous groups led to the creation of a confederation and the convoking of the 1990 March for Dignity and Territory, which 'launched lowland demands onto the national stage' (Farthing and Kohl, 2014: 10).

Despite these advances, a 2005 ILO report described the situation of the Guaraní in the Bolivian Chaco as 'the most dramatic case' of forced labour in the Andean region, with the complicity of local authorities remaining an issue (Bedoya and Bedoya, 2005: 47). The year was significant, as it saw the election of Evo Morales. The core of Morales' electoral base was the Unity Pact, a broad coalition of social and Indigenous movements that included the APG, whose central demands included Indigenous and land rights (Salazar, 2015). In response, Morales' government undertook to challenge discrimination and integrate Bolivia's Indigenous and peasant populations, as well as materially improve their conditions after decades of neoliberalization (Postero, 2015; Webber, 2017). Furthermore, government pledged to decolonize the state, opening up the possibility of a state based around shared decision making, particularly regarding natural resources (Postero, 2017: 184).

The record of the government in terms of fulfilling these pledges was mixed, however, with a notable decline over time. In contrast to post-independence Peru, under Morales the Bolivian state took action to reduce social vulnerability: establishing a 'floor' of social rights and protections, redistributing income from increased rents from extractive industries, and making legal advances towards stronger cultural rights (Grugel and Fontana, 2018). The Morales government also proactively asserted the role of the state in directing, fomenting, and regulating economic activity, including nationalizing the pension system and creating protections for informal workers (Trujillo and Spronk, 2018). Nevertheless, these reforms were predicated upon a neo-developmental economic model that sought to expand the frontiers of extraction. Over time the contradiction inherent in strengthened Indigenous rights and increased extractivism came to a head (Grugel and Fontana, 2018), exposing what Anthias terms the 'limits to decolonisation' (2018).

The 2009 Constitution encapsulates the contradictions of Bolivia's 'process of change'. The text 're-founded' Bolivia as a 'pluri-national' state made up of Indigenous 'nations' with rights to self-government (Gustafson, 2010: 53; Crabtree and Chaplin, 2013: 24, 177). However, the Constitution also established the primacy of the state over the economy, including natural resources, and imposed territorial limitations on Indigenous political representation (Postero, 2017). The case of modern slavery among Indigenous Guaraní exposed these tensions when it began to receive international attention following the ILO report and complaints to the Inter-American Commission on Human Rights and a subsequent site visit (IACHR, 2009).

On the positive side of the ledger, the government took action to address vulnerability to exploitation, albeit much of it at the normative level. For example, Article 15 of the new Constitution prohibits servitude and slavery. Furthermore, the Morales government created a new Vice-Ministry for Decolonization with the stated ambition of reshaping the state and society at large (Farthing and Kohl, 2014: 58). With regard to Indigenous rights, the government legislated for a limited form of self-government ('autonomies'), prior consultation, land reform, and collective land titling (Crabtree and Chaplin, 2013: 24–8); introduced a strong anti-racism law which gave the state a broad range of powers; and adopted indigeneity, decolonization, and plurinationalism as a legitimating discourse (Postero, 2017). These changes were extraordinary in the context of the Bolivian state, and radically altered the social position of Indigenous people.

Regarding the specific case of the exploitation of the Guaraní, in 2007 Morales passed Supreme Decree 29292 that established an Inter-Ministerial Council for the Eradication of Bondage, Forced Labour, and Similar Forms of Subjugation, with the aim of providing those families with 'dignified living conditions' (IACHR, 2009: 54). This body in turn created an Inter-Ministerial Plan to tackle the Guaraní issue, which involved close cooperation with the APG (IACHR, 2009: 54). The plan catalysed a more interventionist approach by the Labour Ministry, which strengthened state presence and accelerated inspections in the lowland region, along with raising awareness of labour rights and protections among Guaraní communities. At interview in 2018, a high-ranking official in the Directorate of Fundamental Rights in the Labour Ministry noted that Bolivia's approach continued to be framed as part of a wider campaign against racism towards Indigenous peoples.[15]

The state under Morales also acted to reduce the material vulnerability of Indigenous peoples during its early years. One example was its support for land reform, which the Bolivian state cited as a measure intended to prevent exploitation and modern slavery (IACHR, 2009). Morales introduced and implemented Agrarian Law 3545, which radically accelerated land titling and distribution (Crabtree and Chaplin, 2013: 28). Furthermore, the state invoked Article 401 of the Constitution – which established that territories needed to perform a 'social or economic function' – to justify the expropriation and redistribution of property where bondage or forced labour was documented (IACHR, 2009). In relation to Indigenous self-determination, the government titled collective Indigenous territories and created a framework for autonomies. The combined effect of these actions

---

[15] Interview with Ministry of Labour official, La Paz, 20 July 2018. The Ministry's first plan focused almost exclusively on the issue of the Guaraní.

was said to be the 'elimination' of debt peonage in some areas, and its overall diminishment in Bolivia (Crabtree and Chaplin, 2013: 29). These are unquestionably 'striking' examples of state action to curb modern slavery (Anthias, 2018: 242).

Nevertheless, closer analysis reveals that the state's response was shaped and limited by several social, political, and economic factors, both external and internal. First, many of the reforms carried out by the Morales government reflected historic demands of the Unity Pact movements, which proved a source of support but also pressure when lowland elites launched a campaign of racialized violence in resistance to reform (Gustafson, 2010; Salazar, 2015). Thus, the significant reduction in exploitative labour relations of Indigenous peoples should properly be considered an achievement of the long process of Indigenous organizing (Hinojosa et al, 2015: 115). Additionally, as Gustafson (2010) notes, the Guaraní issue offered Morales a vehicle to diminish the power of political opponents in the form of large landowners. When that support was no longer required – particularly after the government reached a consensus with landowners and agribusiness from 2010 onwards – rates of land reform dropped significantly (Defensoría del Pueblo, 2012; Webber, 2017).

Similar dynamics can be observed in relation to the implementation of other important policies. For example, Bolivia's approach to fighting racism was framed as part of a bigger decolonizing project, but 'considerable confusion' surrounded what that would look like in practice (Farthing and Kohl, 2014: 58). A recent civil society report notes the failure to make concrete advances in the fight against racialized discrimination, years after the introduction of legislation (Zarate et al, 2020: 175). In the words of a female Indigenous leader, 'passing the law is one thing, but enforcing the law is another'.[16] In the view of Indigenous rights activists, truly confronting the power structures underpinning racism and coloniality was not a state priority (Zarate et al, 2020: 174). This failure impacted upon the Guaraní, many of whom were expelled from *haciendas* and so migrated to peri-urban areas. There they face racialized discrimination and exclusion and lack 'even the smallest level of dignity', in the view of a local human rights organization.[17] Nor did the state response extend to supporting Guaraní families to ensure their 'effective liberation', resulting in some returning to the *haciendas* (Defensoría de Pueblo, 2012: 71). As a result, credible reports indicate that servitude amounting to modern slavery continues among Indigenous groups to this day (Zarate et al, 2020: 175). The Bolivian state, however, has failed

---

[16] Interview with leader of women's Indigenous movement CNAMIB, Santa Cruz, 24 August 2019.

[17] Interview with representative of CEJIS, Santa Cruz, 23 August 2019.

to gather any data, much less take any action, in response to this situation (Zarate et al, 2020: 175).

This discrimination can no longer be confined to racialized 'whites' but exists in the attitudes of highland peasant and Indigenous peoples towards lowland groups. This shift is partially explained by tensions between groups over access to land (Grugel and Fontana, 2018), but includes discourses of racialized division, with lowland Indigenous people often portrayed as 'less civilised' (Miranda, 2015: 69). A case in point is the emblematic conflict between the Morales government and Indigenous movements over the construction of a highway through the lowland Isiboro Sécure National Park and Indigenous Territory (TIPNIS). While the government sought to justify the project on grounds of 'development', many saw it as primarily benefiting agribusiness and hydrocarbon interests (Salazar, 2015). The conflict split the Unity Pact and increased racialized tensions between member groups, with lowland Indigenous groups referring to pro-government coca farmers (themselves typically of Aymara or Quechua Indigenous ethnicity) as 'colonizers'; while the peasant and coca farmers labelled lowland Indigenous groups as '*latifundistas*' (large landowners) and even 'savages' (Rivera, 2015: 47–50).

Nor is the issue simply one of whether laws were implemented, but the manner in which it occurred. Regarding land reform, research reveals that the land certified for Indigenous peoples was qualitatively inferior to that occupied by large ranchers and agribusiness (Webber, 2017; Anthias, 2018), leaving the relative vulnerability of Indigenous peoples largely untouched (Hinojosa et al, 2015). The mechanisms of land reform also ran contrary to Indigenous customs by subsuming the process to what Anthias (2018: 175) calls a 'colonial' logic of enclosure. By the same token, legal norms were 'reworked' to privilege non-Indigenous claimants, such as by allowing valid targets to escape legal expropriation (Anthias, 2018: 86). For these reasons, Anthias concludes that the implementation was profoundly shaped by 'networks of racialised power and colonial discourses' (Anthias, 2018: 86).

The third issue relates to insertion into global markets; in particular, the state's prioritization of development based on resource extraction. This growth-based model was driven by internal pressures – from elites, but also peasant and coca-farming movements that adopted a resource nationalist discourse (Farthing and Kohl, 2014) – and catalysed by a global commodities boom. Nevertheless, it took time for the contradiction between the model and Indigenous rights to become apparent. For example, the government discursively supported autonomies, but in practice restricted them by subsuming autonomous zones to existing state structures (Postero, 2017). This constituted a rejection of the Guaraní demand for the state to be reorganized around autonomies (Humphreys, 2012: 141). As a result, when a Guaraní municipality became Bolivia's first Indigenous autonomous government in 2015, it did so within 'the dominant state discourse of economic liberation' (Humphreys, 2012: 186). Specifically, the government retained full control over natural resources, which, in this case, means gas. According to Humphreys (2012), state initiatives to supply land, autonomy, and financial supports are part of a 'faustian pact involving a trading of rights and territory for extraction' (Humphreys, 2012: 135) – what Anthias (2018) calls 'hydrocarbon citizenship'.

The Bolivian model also promotes agribusiness, providing state supports to large producers. Small producers are adversely incorporated into value chains and forced to supplement their income by selling their labour on unfavourable terms (Webber, 2017). According to an official at a peasant rights NGO, 'indigenous and peasant agriculture is in crisis, it is stagnant; it is large agri-business that has been growing instead'.[18] Communities failing to accept these terms were treated as obstacles to national development that could justifiably be 'sacrificed' (Postero, 2017: 181). As a highland Indigenous leader noted at interview: 'for those that stand with the government, they get conditional support; but for the critical people, they get no support at all'.[19] In practice, then, Indigenous peoples are pushed to 'pragmatically assimilate to the state' (Miranda, 2015: 71) and its capitalist mode of production or risk a return to conditions of absolute vulnerability and exploitation. It is therefore clear that while the 'decolonizing' Bolivian state made notable advances, its ultimate failure to break with the extractive logic of capitalism ended up replicating systems that relied on racialized divisions, even if the contours of those divisions were far more complex than in the colonial period.

Conclusion

The weak historicity and analysis of power relations leads mainstream approaches to view 'modern slavery' as a product of underdevelopment, to be addressed by economic modernization. These failings have led to the invisibilization of the structural and societal drivers of existing modern slavery (Bravo, 2015; Natarajan et al, 2020). This chapter has examined the issue of modern slavery in Latin America using the framework of coloniality of power developed by Quijano (2000). The chapter focuses in particular on the role of the state, which is explored via analyses of the guano and rubber booms in post-independence Peru and attempts to 'decolonize the state' and enable Indigenous self-determination in contemporary Bolivia.

Overall, the chapter finds that adopting a coloniality approach to modern slavery as a lens for analysis has strong utility. A coloniality approach tends

---

[18] Interview with representative of CIPCA, La Paz, 19 July 2018.
[19] Interview with leader of Indigenous movement CONAMAQ, La Paz, 25 July 2018.

to focus attention on the roots of the transatlantic slave trade[20] and its contemporary legacies, shedding light on the interconnected nature of racialization, labour control, and global capitalism. The chapter argues that a focus on coloniality's two core processes – racialization and articulation with forms of labour control linked to global markets – challenges mainstream approaches to the study of modern slavery. In particular, it reveals a need for deeper engagement with the history of slavery and servitude beyond simple binaries and individualized relationships, in order to examine how those relationships linked to colonial processes that created enduring societal norms and wider economic structures. This approach challenges the application of European concepts such as feudalism to very different contexts and highlights the importance of analysing relationships of power at multiple scales (Bravo, 2015: 31).

More specifically, this approach spotlights the ambiguous role of the state. Rather than a simple enforcer of laws and protector of rights, states are frequently at the forefront of facilitating exploitation, both directly and indirectly. Examples include the adoption of laws that incentivize displacement; subsidizing activities with links to exploitation; failing to enforce laws against discrimination and exploitation; and using coercive powers to restrict the liberty of certain groups. Conceptualizing the state as a social relation helps us understand how former colonies continue to reproduce racialized divisions and to prioritize the goal of modernization, despite formal independence and abolition. In contrast to the immutable racialized hierarchy under direct colonial rule, under capitalism the identity of racialized groups deemed suitable for exploitation varies, but the logic of racialization remains a consistent feature. Colonial justifications of the 'civilizing' mission finds echoes in contemporary state discourses of 'development'. That such discourses are used to justify 'trampling' on Indigenous territorial rights (Chirif, 2017: 23–4) – thereby increasing vulnerability to exploitation – should give pause to those framing 'modern slavery' as underdevelopment.

There is strong support for Quijano's central point that the purpose of a racialized labour hierarchy was to facilitate the production of commodities for the world market, and there are two points to be made here. First, is to acknowledge the fundamental differences between manifestations of modern slavery in post-colonial contexts versus those existing in Europe, where

---

[20] Between 1501 and 1867, the transatlantic slave trade claimed an estimated 12.5 million Africans and involved almost every country with an Atlantic coastline. See further Eltis and Richardson (2015) *Atlas of the Transatlantic Slave Trade*, Yale University Press. See further www.hull.ac.uk/research/institutes/wilberforce/trans-atlantic-slave-trade-database [Accessed July 2023].

labour relations evolved along a very different trajectory (Boatcă, 2013; Munck, 2018). Second, that the findings of this chapter call into question the suitability of the state for dismantling the colonial matrix of power. Despite Mignolo's (2011) citing of Morales' Bolivia as an example, the chapter reveals the limitations of decolonization there. Although the early influence of social movements yielded important reforms, a shift in the correlation of forces in favour of economic elites and Morales' core base, allied to the availability of commodity rents for redistribution, saw his government shift to reinforce the existing colonial model of extractive development and its racialized logic. While it is beyond the scope of this chapter to assess Sharma's (2020) wider claim that the state is by necessity unable to achieve decolonization, raising important questions for modern slavery that merit further research.

References

Alimonda, H. (2015) 'Mining in Latin America: coloniality and degradation', in R.L. Bryant (ed) *The International Handbook of Political Ecology*, Cheltenham: Edward Elgar.

Allain, J. (2017) 'Contemporary slavery and its definition in law', in A. Bunting and J. Quirk (eds) *Contemporary Slavery: The Rhetoric of Global Human Rights Campaigns*, Ithaca/London: Cornell University Press.

Alliance 8.7 (2017) *Global Estimates of Modern Slavery*, Geneva: ILO.

Anthias, P. (2018) *The Limits of Decolonisation: Indigeneity, Territory, and Hydrocarbon Politics in the Bolivian Chaco*, Ithaca, NY; London: Cornell University Press.

Bales, K. (2004) *Disposable People: New Slavery in the Global Economy* (3rd edn), Berkeley, CA; London: University of California Press.

Bales, K. (2016) *Blood and Earth: Modern Slavery, Ecocide and the Secret to Saving the World*, New York: Spiegel and Grau.

Bedoya Garland, E. and Bedoya Silva-Santisteban, A. (2005) 'Enganche y servidumbre por deudas en Bolivia', *ILO Working Paper*, Geneva: ILO.

Beutin, L.P. (2017) 'Black suffering for/from anti-trafficking advocacy', *Anti-Trafficking Review*, 9: 14–30.

Beutin, L.P. (2023) *Trafficking in Antiblackness: Modern-Day Slavery, White Indemnity, and Racial Justice*, Durham: Duke University Press.

Blanchette, T.G. and Da Silva, A.P. (2012) 'On bullshit and the trafficking of women: moral entrepreneurs and the invention of trafficking of persons in Brazil', *Dialectical Anthropology*, 36: 107–125.

Blanchette, T. and Silva, A.P.D. (2018) 'Classy whores: intersections of class, gender, and sex work in the ideologies of the Putafeminista Movement in Brazil', *Contexto Internacional*, 40: 549–71.

Boatcă, M. (2013) 'Coloniality of labor in the global periphery: Latin America and Eastern Europe in the world-system', *Review (Fernand Braudel Center)*, 36(3–4): 287–314.

Brand, U. (2013) 'The role of the state and public policies in processes of transformation', in M. Lang and D. Mokrani (eds) *Beyond Development: Alternative Visions from Latin America*, Amsterdam/Quito: Transnational Institute/Rosa Luxemburg Foundation.

Bravo, K.E. (2011) 'The role of the transatlantic slave trade in contemporary anti-human trafficking discourse', *Seattle Journal for Social Justice*, 9(2): 555–98.

Bravo, K.E. (2015) 'Interrogating the state's role in human trafficking', *Indiana International and Comparative Law Review*, 25(1): 9–32.

Bunting, A. and Quirk, J. (eds) (2017) *Contemporary Slavery: The Rhetoric of Global Human Rights Campaigns*, Ithaca, NY; London: Cornell University Press.

Cannon, B. and Kirby, P. (eds) (2012) *Civil Society and the State in Left-led Latin America: Challenges and Limitations to Democratization*, London/New York: Zed Books.

Canqui, E. (2011) 'El Trabajo Forzoso y los Pueblos Indígenas', *Report for Tenth Session of the Permanent Forum on Indigenous Issues*, New York: UN.

Chirif, A. (2017) *Después del Caucho*, Lima: Lluvia Editores.

Chuang, J.A. (2014) 'Exploitation creep and the unmaking of human trafficking law', *American Journal of International Law*, 108(4): 609–49.

Clark, B. and Foster, J.B. (2009) 'Ecological imperialism and the global metabolic rift: unequal exchange and the guano/nitrates trade', *International Journal of Comparative Sociology*, 50(3–4): 311–34.

Cockayne, J. (2015) *Unshackling Development: Why We Need a Global Partnership to End Modern Slavery*, Shibuya: United Nations University.

Cockbain, E. (2018) *Offender and Victim Networks in Human Trafficking*, Abingdon/New York: Routledge.

Costa, P.T.M. (2009) *Fighting Forced Labour: The Example of Brazil*, Geneva: ILO.

Crabtree, J. and Chaplin, A. (2013) *Bolivia: Processes of Change*, London/New York: Zed Books.

Crane, A. (2013) 'Modern slavery as a management practice: exploring the conditions and capabilities for human exploitation', *Academy of Management Review*, 38(1): 49–69.

Defensoría de Pueblo (2012) *Servidumbre y empatronamiento en el Chaco*, La Paz: Defensoría del Pueblo.

Diptée, A.A. (2018) 'The problem of modern-day slavery: is critical applied history the answer?', *Slavery and Abolition*, 39(2): 405–28.

Dussel, E. (2000) 'Europa, modernidad y eurocentrismo', in E. Lander and S. Castro-Gómez (eds) *La colonialidad del saber: eurocentrismo y ciencias sociales: perspectivas*, Buenos Aires: CLACSO.

Farthing, L.C. and Kohl, B.H. (2014) *Evo's Bolivia: Continuity and Change*, Austin, TX: University of Texas Press.

Faulkner, E.A. (2023) 'Child trafficking, children's rights, and modern slavery: international law in the twentieth and twenty-first centuries', in *The Trafficking of Children: International Law, Modern Slavery, and the Anti-Trafficking Machine*, Cham: Springer International Publishing.

Foweraker, J. (2018) *Polity: Demystifying Democracy in Latin American and Beyond*, Boulder, CO; London: Lynne Rienner Publishers.

Frank, A.G. (1967) *Capitalism and Underdevelopment in Latin America: Historical Studies of Chile and Brazil*, New York/London: Monthly Review Press.

Gonzales, M.J. (1989) 'Chinese plantation workers and social conflict in Peru in the late nineteenth century', *Journal of Latin American Studies*, 21(3): 385–424.

Goodman, J. (2010) *The Devil and Mr Casement*, London: Verso.

Grugel, J. and Fontana, L.B. (2018) 'Human rights and the pink tide in Latin America: which rights matter?', *Development and Change*, 50(3): 707–34.

Gustafson, B. (2010) 'When states act like movements: dismantling local power and seating sovereignty in post-neoliberal Bolivia,' *Latin American Perspectives*, 37(4): 48–66.

Harvey, D. (2007) *A Brief History of Neoliberalism*, Oxford/New York: Oxford University Press.

Healy, K. (1983) *Caciques y Patrones: Una experiencia de desarrollo rural en el sud de Bolivia*, Cochabamba: El Buitre.

Hinojosa, L., Bebbington, A., Cortez, G., Chumacero, J.P., Humphreys Bebbington, D., and Hennermann, K. (2015) 'Gas and development: rural territorial dynamics in Tarija, Bolivia', *World Development*, 73 (September): 105–117.

Humphreys Bebbington, D. (2012) 'State-indigenous tensions over hydrocarbon expansion in the Bolivian Chaco', in A. Bebbington (ed) *Social Conflict, Economic Development and Extractive Industry: Evidence from South America*, London/New York: Routledge.

IACHR (2009) *Captive Communities: Situation of the Guaraní Indigenous People and Contemporary Forms of Slavery in the Bolivian Chaco*, Washington, DC: Inter-American Commission on Human Rights.

Jessop, B. (2008) *State Power*, Cambridge: Polity Press.

Jessop, B. (2016) *The State: Past, Present, Future*, Cambridge: Polity Press.

Kempadoo, K. and Shih, E. (2023) *White Supremacy, Racism and the Coloniality of Anti-trafficking*, New York/Oxford: Taylor & Francis.

Kotiswaran, P. (2019) 'Trafficking: a development approach', *Current Legal Problems*, 72(1): 375–416.

Landman, T. (2008) *Issues and Methods in Comparative Politics: An Introduction* (3rd edn), London: Routledge.

LeBaron, G. (2020) *Combating Modern Slavery: Why Labour Governance Is Failing and What We Can Do About It*, Cambridge: Polity Press.

LeBaron, G. and Phillips, N. (2019) 'States and the political economy of unfree labour', *New Political Economy*, 24(1): 1–21.

Lerche, J. (2007) 'A global alliance against forced labour? Unfree labour, neo-liberal globalization and the International Labour Organization', *Journal of Agrarian Change*, 7(4): 425–52.

Martínez Salazar, E. (2012) *Global Coloniality of Power in Guatemala: Racism, Genocide, Citizenship*, Plymouth: Lexington Books.

Meade, T.A. (2010) *History of Modern Latin America: 1800 to the Present*, Chichester: John Wiley & Sons.

Merino, R. (2020) 'Rethinking Indigenous politics: the unnoticed struggle for self-determination in Peru', *Bulletin of Latin American Research*, 39(4): 513–28.

Michiles, A. (2021) *Secrets from Putumayo*, São Paolo: Outside.co.

Mignolo, W.D. (2007) 'Introduction: coloniality of power and de-colonial thinking', *Cultural Studies*, 21(2–3): 155–67.

Mignolo, W.D. (2011) 'Epistemic disobedience and the decolonial option: a manifesto', *Transmodernity*, 1(2): 3–23.

Milano, V. (2018) 'Human trafficking by regional human rights courts: an analysis in light of Hacienda Brasil Verde, the first Inter-American Court's ruling in this area', *Revista Electronica de Estudios Internacionales*, 36: 1–29.

Miranda Hernandez, M.A. (2015) 'Los indígenas urbanos en Bolivia y sus derechos', in E. Torrico and M.A. Miranda Hernandez (eds) *Indígenas urbanos: Tres ensayos sobre su presencia y derechos en Bolivia*, Cochabamba: CEDIB.

Mitchell, A. (1997) *The Amazon Journal of Roger Casement*, Dublin: The Lilliput Press.

Mitchell, A. (2010) *Roger Casement in Brazil: Rubber, the Amazon and the Atlantic World 1884–1916*, São Paolo: Humanitas.

Munck, R. (2018) *Rethinking Global Labour*, Newcastle upon Tyne: Agenda Publishing.

Natarajan, N., Brickell, K., and Parsons, L. (2020) 'Diffuse drivers of modern slavery: from microfinance to unfree labour in Cambodia', *Development and Change*, 52(2): 241–64.

O'Connell Davidson, J. (2015) *Modern Slavery: The Margins of Freedom*, Basingstoke/New York: Palgrave Macmillan.

Olivar, J.M.N. and Melo, F. (2023) 'The Jaula and racialization of the Amazon', in K. Kempadoo and E. Shih (eds) *White Supremacy, Racism and the Coloniality of Anti-Trafficking*, New York/Oxford: Taylor & Francis.

Phillips, N. and Sakamoto, L. (2012) 'Global production networks, chronic poverty and "slave labour" in Brazil', *Studies in Comparative International Development*, 47(3): 287–315.

Phillips, N. and Mieres, F. (2015) 'The governance of forced labour in the global economy', *Globalizations*, 12(2): 244–60.

Piscitelli, A. (2008) 'Interseccionalidades, categorias de articulação e experiências de migrantes brasileiras', *Sociedade e cultura*, 11(2): 263–74.

Plant, R. (2017) 'Combating trafficking for labour exploitation in the global economy: the need for a differentiated approach', in P. Kotiswaran (ed) *Revisiting the Law and Governance of Trafficking, Forced Labor and Modern Slavery*, Cambridge/New York: Cambridge University Press.

Postero, N. (2015) '"El pueblo Boliviano, de composición plural": a look at plurinationalism in Bolivia', in C. de la Torre (ed) *The Promise and Perils of Populism: Global Perspectives*, Lexington, KY: University Press of Kentucky.

Postero, N. (2017) *The Indigenous State*, Oakland, CA: University of California Press.

Quijano, A. (2000) 'The coloniality of power: Eurocentrism and Latin America', *Nepantla*, 1(3): 538–80.

Quirk, J. (2009) *Unfinished Business: A Comparative Survey of Historical and Contemporary Slavery*, Paris: UNESCO.

Quirk, J. (2011) *The Anti-Slavery Project: From the Slave Trade to Human Trafficking*, Philadelphia, PA: University of Philadelphia Press.

Ramirez, S.E. (1996) 'From slavery to abolition in Peru: four recent contributions', *Colonial Latin American Review*, 5(2): 321–7.

Rivera Cusicanqui, S. (2015) *Mito y desarrollo en Bolivia: El giro colonial del gobierno del MAS*, La Paz: Plural.

Romero, A.V. (1978) 'Aspectos legales sobre las comunidades nativas de la Amazonía peruana', *Revista Panorama Amazónico*, 2(3): 5–26.

Sakamoto, L. (ed) (2020) *Escravidão Contemporânea*, São Paolo: Editora Contexto.

Salazar Lohman, H. (2015) *Se han adueñado del proceso de lucha: horizontes comunitario-populares en tensión y la reconstitución de la dominación en la Bolivia del MAS*, Cochabamba: SOCEE.

Segrave, M., Milivojevic, S., and Pickering, S. (2018) *Sex Trafficking and Modern Slavery: The Absence of Evidence* (2nd edn), London: Routledge.

Sharma, N. (2020) *Home Rule: National Sovereignty and the Separation of Natives and Migrants*, Durham, NC; London: Duke University Press.

Skidmore, T.E. and Smith, P.H. (2005) *Modern Latin America*, New York/Oxford: Oxford University Press.

Trujillo, J.L. and Spronk, S. (2018) 'Socialism without workers? Trade unions and the New Left in Bolivia and Ecuador', in E. Silva and F.M. Rossi (eds) *Reshaping the Political Arena in Latin America: From Resisting Neoliberalism to the Second Incorporation*, Pittsburgh, PA: University of Pittsburgh Press.

Van den Anker, C. (ed) (2004) *The Political Economy of New Slavery*, Basingstoke/New York: Palgrave Macmillan.

Ventiades, N. (1997) 'Slavery among the Bolivian Guarani', in *Enslaved Peoples in the 1990s*, Copenhagen: Anti-Slavery International/IWGIA.

Wallerstein, I. (2000) *The Essential Wallerstein*, New York: The New Press.

Webber, J.R. (2017) *The Last Day of the Oppression, and the First Day of the Same: The Politics and Economics of the New Latin American Left*, Chicago, IL: Haymarket Books.

Williamson, E. (1992) *The Penguin History of Latin America*, London/New York: Penguin.

Zarate, C., Bustillos, P., and Mendoza, B. (2020) *Balance de la Implementación de la Ley Contra el Racismo y Toda Forma de Discriminación*, La Paz: Comunidad de Derechos Humanos/Equal Rights Trust.

4

Constructing 'Indigenous People' Reproducing Coloniality's Epistemic Violence: A Content Analysis of the Trafficking in Persons Reports

Avi Boukli, Georgios Papanicolaou and Eleni Dimou

Introduction

The annual Trafficking in Persons Report[1] (hereafter, the TIPR) of the US Department of State (hereafter DOS) has been criticized to date for being a skewed and politically driven tool of disputed effectiveness (Merry, 2016). As we explain in our analysis, the TIPRs narrowly conceptualize the problem, by drawing on a definition of human trafficking that focuses predominantly on sex trafficking (see definition of Offence, US Department of State, 2001: 2; see also de Vries and Cockbain, this volume). This silences other forms of trafficking and provides a narrow anti-trafficking policy model. Due to its confined framings, both the ability to raise awareness of human trafficking and the capacity to promote and support anti-trafficking efforts across the globe have been areas of growing concern (US Government Accountability Office, 2006, 2007; Wooditch, 2011). At its 20th anniversary in 2021, however, it remains the most authoritative report on human trafficking globally. Its combined effect, we argue, as an exercise of imperial soft power and the sheer extent of its coverage shapes this field, in terms of policy development

---

[1] See further, www.state.gov/trafficking-in-persons-report [Accessed 15 July 2023].

and priorities. Simultaneously, it defines the issue of human trafficking itself, including Indigenous victimization.

The TIPR is a prime tool in global anti-trafficking campaigns, whose shaping of the presentation of the issue and policy responses towards particular directions has been acutely contested both politically and theoretically. It is now fairly established that the process of compiling the TIPR, leading to the more formal responses towards the issue since the end of the 1990s, has been shaped by the particular focus on sex trafficking and the division of lobbying groups around the question of prostitution/sex work (Munro, 2005; Weitzer, 2007). Since the inception of the major international anti-trafficking instruments, such as the Palermo Protocol,[2] the seriousness of all forms of human trafficking as predatory exploitation has been amply recognized. However, in theoretical terms, debates around the question of agency and the nature of trafficking victimization remain very much alive to date (see, for example, Andrijasevic, 2010; Mai et al, 2021; Oude Breuil and Gerasimov, 2021). This dimension has clear implications; it shapes the forms and focus of interventions to address trafficking. Criticisms of the (anti-)trafficking rescue industry (Aguistín, 2007; Chapman-Schmidt, 2019) very much capture the intimate connection between the conceptualization of the issue and anti-trafficking practices. For instance, whether in the form of law enforcement actions, victim support and humanitarian initiatives, or public awareness of the issue, early anti-trafficking knowledge and interventions focused solely on the sex industry (Papanicolaou and Boukli, 2011).

Our arguments are situated within and contribute to the wider critique of the TIPRs (Merry, 2016), by interrogating them both as an imperial knowledge construction apparatus and a colonial monitoring tool through the concept of coloniality (Quijano, 1992; Walter, 2016). Considering the controversies surrounding the issue of trafficking, often described as 'modern-day slavery' (US Department of State, 2001: 9; Quirk, Robinson, and Thibos, 2020), our analysis shows how the reports are infused with dominant norms, values, and racial hierarchies of colonial legacies (Walter, 2016). As such the TIPRs are central in imposing colonial frameworks of knowledge and interventions both globally and locally (Clark, 2012). Through the deconstruction of the category 'Indigenous' (and 'native') victim of human trafficking, our analysis makes a twofold contribution.

---

[2] 15 November 2000, General Assembly resolution 55/25, www.ohchr.org/en/instruments-mechanisms/instruments/protocol-prevent-suppress-and-punish-trafficking-persons [Accessed 15 July 2023]. For the definition of human trafficking under the Protocol, see Table 1.1, this volume.

First, it shows that Indigenous people have been portrayed through pejorative stereotypes that serve to construct them as problematic populations in need of enhanced state management (Walter, 2016; Cunneen and Tauri, 2017). Second, we suggest that the broad brushstrokes of 'modern slavery' conceal colonial legacies. Particularly when focusing on constructions of the 'Indigenous human trafficking/modern slavery victim', we trace the unfolding contours of coloniality's epistemic violence. We locate epistemic violence – 'the complete overhaul of the episteme' – in the redefinition of colonial subjects as modern slavery victims (Spivak, 1988). With colonial legacies spilling over into knowledge/data/definitions and ultimately policy, the systematic marginalization, exploitation, and victimization of Indigenous people remains unaddressed.

Our focus on the category 'Indigenous' stems from the observation that, unlike other categories that refer to trafficking vulnerabilities in descriptive terms (such as, age, gender), it embodies a set of colonial constructions that are both being fed inwards and outwards. What this means essentially is that as they are returned to the social contexts and particular power relations from which information of the issue of trafficking is collected through local sources and therefore communicated inwards. While on the other hand, they are fed outwards via the global imperial system of power relations wherein the monitored populations and the monitoring bodies are positioned (Patel, 2021). This two-way process arguably has the implication that constructions of vulnerability and risk, within the TIPRs, reflect and reproduce a double layer of epistemic and material dependencies animated by relations of domination and subordination. The latter stem from both historical and contemporary conditions of coloniality. The impact of these conditions not only is denied when it comes to Indigenous people's experiences of trafficking but is, in fact, reinforced by the role of TIPRs in defining the issue and setting global anti-trafficking protocols.

The next section proceeds to flesh out how the concept of coloniality relates to our investigation of epistemic violence and informs our analysis. We then proceed to explain in more detail the data and methods of our analysis. The third section is concerned with the content analysis of the category 'Indigenous' appearing in the TIPRs and the construction of geographical clusters that reflect imperial politics. With the concluding section bringing together the results of our analysis. We argue that the TIPRs through their silences, concealment of coloniality, and exposition of pejorative stereotypes of Indigenous populations are part of a continuum of colonial data systems and imperial politics.

Coloniality and epistemic violence

Coloniality depicts a complex matrix of power, and the concept of coloniality was coined as a term by Quijano and identified as emerging since the

15th-century Conquest of the Americas. Coloniality is essentially 'the underlying logic of the foundation and unfolding of Western civilization' and of modernity (Mignolo, 2011: 2). The first core axis of coloniality is grounded upon the invention of the idea of 'race' – 'a mental construction that expresses the basic experience of colonial domination' (Quijano, 2008: 181). Through the construction of 'race' the differences between 'conquerors' and 'conquered' are mobilized as part of a 'supposedly biological structure that placed some in a natural situation of inferiority to the others' (Quijano, 2008: 182). Hence, coloniality involves interpreting the colonized as 'non-human' in need of 'civilizing', and utilizing 'the civilizing mission' to justify 'enormous cruelty' (Lugones, 2010: 744).

The second axis involves an idea of labour that revolves around capitalist production from 'reciprocity, slavery and serfdom' to 'the independent production of commodities' (Quijano, 2000: 218). All these forms of production are compatible, for Quijano, with the capitalist organization of labour. In relation to slavery, Quijano (2000: 218) asserts that 'slavery was deliberately established and organized as a commodity to produce commodities for the world market' and to serve the purposes of capitalism while also maintaining control over those colonized through the weaponization of 'race'. Hence, according to decolonial theory, which we follow here, through the idea of 'race' and the imposition of the capitalist organization of labour, colonized non-white and non-Western European populations were deemed 'naturally inferior' and in a position to be exploited – alongside their lands – for profit (Mignolo, 2018; Mignolo and Ennis, 2001). As such coloniality refers to a technology of power founded upon the epistemic violence of 'the "knowledge of the other"' (Castro-Gómez, 2002: 276) that essentially serves capitalist interests of production and demand, of exploiters and exploited (Spivak, 1988).

Starting from the idea that the white, Western, cisgender, heterosexual, male, Christian body deemed itself as the supreme standard by which all bodies, spiritualities, sexualities, ways of being, and forms of social organization are to be measured, coloniality of power manifests itself in several ways. It institutes social hierarchies and hierarchies of knowledge. It consolidates economic, racial, gender, and sexual inequality, it produces economic and cultural dependency, and it is woven through and around every social institution (Moraña, Dussel, and Jáuregui, 2008: 8–9). In Quijano's work the colonial matrix of power grasps four interrelated domains:

i) control of economy (land appropriation, exploitation of labor, control of natural resources);
ii) control of authority (institution, army);
iii) control of gender and sexuality (family, education); and

iv) control of subjectivity and knowledge (epistemology, education and formation of subjectivity). (Mignolo, 2007: 156)

For instance, in relation to transatlantic slavery, a wide-reaching system of control from the economy to the formation of subjectivities was instrumental in creating the need and demand through a market for the production and consumption of goods and the 'legitimation' of the dehumanization and exploitation of the colonial difference imagined in the 'savage', the 'underdeveloped', and 'uncivilized'. As Castro-Gómez (2019: 217) argues, 'the construction of the imaginary of "civilization" required the production of its counterpart: the imaginary of "barbarism"'.

Knowledge is perhaps the most crucial aspect of the matrix as it feeds into and sustains the rest (Castro-Gómez, 2002). Epistemological hegemony and the dominance of quantitative research became an imperative technology of colonial control as it constituted an 'efficient tool for dividing, [ranking] and ruling territories, peoples, [bodies] and knowledges in the service' of the modern/colonial nation state (Brunner, 2021: 199). American Indigenous populations were defined and classified to occupy the lowest stage on the spectrum of human evolution. Whereas the most evolved stage was that of white Western Europeans (Castro-Gómez, 2002). This depredatory discourse co-constituted 'the global colonial expansion and its attendant teleology of linear progress, enlightenment, and civilization' (Brunner, 2021: 199).

The imperial politics and colonial heritage of episteme and the global/local entanglements of knowledge with violence have been well documented (Agozino, 2003; Deckert, 2016; Brunner, 2021; Smith, 2021). However, their manifestations have not been explicitly explored in the TIPRs. The deeply colonial and Western-centric underpinning of social sciences and their methodologies are imbued in the TIPRs in ways that maintain and perpetuate coloniality's epistemic violence. In locating the workings of epistemic violence, we highlight the ways in which the TIPRs engage in 'the remotely orchestrated, far-flung, and heterogeneous project to constitute the colonial subject as Other' (Spivak, 1988: 280). We observe that the discursive process of othering also involves 'the asymmetrical obliteration of the trace of that Other in its precarious Subjectivity' (Spivak, 1988: 280). Thus, central aspects of coloniality's epistemic violence are: (1) the elimination of knowledge; (2) the destruction of a 'group's ability to speak, being listened to and being heard' (Brunner, 2021: 202); (3) the unequal distribution of knowledge; (4) the unequal governance of knowledge; (5) the application of techniques rendering certain (modes of life and) cultures unintelligible (Deckert, 2016); and (6) the application of data-gathering processes that render certain knowledges unintelligible. It is this framework of coloniality of knowledge that permeates the TIPRs.

Coloniality and human trafficking

Recent accounts have highlighted the importance of coloniality in the construction of human trafficking and 'modern slavery' knowledge (Kempadoo and Shih, 2023). As noted by O'Connell Davidson (2015: 19 emphases in the original), 'transatlantic slavery *was* modern slavery'. It was with the dawn of the European Enlightenment and liberalism that actually 'European colonialism and transatlantic slavery' expanded and thrived (O'Connell Davidson, 2015: 19 emphases omitted). The epistemic violence of colonial laws justified and normalized enormous exploitation and harm against colonized and enslaved populations in the name of modernity. Hence, the exploitation and silencing of enslaved populations are not incidental but constitutive of the modern/colonial world grounded upon capitalism.

Studies that engage with the enslavement of Indigenous communities, often trace historical accounts of slavery in the 'New World'. For Valcárcel Rojas et al (2020: 518) the enslavement of Indigenous peoples by Europeans began in the Caribbean, and it is estimated that between 1493 and 1552, it involved between 250,000 and 500,000 people. Across the years, between two and five million people were enslaved (Goetz, 2016: 59). In the Caribbean seven million people were killed (Las Casas, 1992), while a total of 50 million deaths of Indigenous people have been recorded in the Americas as well as a further 28 million deaths of Africans directly linked to enslavement for labour in 'the new lands' (Vazquez, 2017: 81). Despite its centrality to the creation of the colonial Caribbean and the Americas, the enslavement of Indigenous peoples in this region is still widely underexplored (Goetz, 2016; Arena, 2017).

Returning to Quijano's definition of coloniality and particularly the expression of authority in the four interrelated domains in the previous section, colonial law has been instrumental in the control of authority. International legal instruments are not immune to coloniality. Rather, they have been directly operationalized towards the subordination of non-European people and societies to European conquest and domination (Anghie, 2006). For instance, Italy's application of the *1921 International Convention for the Suppression of the Traffic in Women and Children* to its colonies introduced a reservation lowering the age of consent for Indigenous women and children to 16 (Limoncelli, 2010). Additionally, it has been illustrated that many labour-related provisions in the Indian Penal Code were a product of colonial law: '[t]he exigencies of colonial rule in general did not permit the framing of a comprehensive policy to deal with forced labor in all its forms so that any policy or legislative changes were purely reactive' (Kotiswaran, 2014: 382).

This framework, designed to allow for forced labour, left a gap for the post-colonial state to 'address the social realities of bonded labour, forced migration, and the deplorable conditions of migrant labour' (Kotiswaran, 2014: 382). This had a direct impact on how certain groups have been affected by socio-economic disadvantage and harm through the perpetuation of forced labour conditions. Moreover, the colonial legacy of slavery still animates the fortification of criminalization anti-trafficking measures often at the expanse of labour law provisions 'which have been rendered dormant with the onslaught of neoliberal economic reforms' (Kotiswaran, 2014: 405).

Earlier publications on colonial violence and the way anti-trafficking measures affect Indigenous people in Canada suggested that retuning the lens from international trafficking of 'young Eastern European women' to 'internally trafficked' Aboriginal women and girls would highlight the 'inability of the criminal justice system to acknowledge Aboriginal women and girls as victims of all forms of sexual exploitation, including particular types of trafficking in persons' (Sikka, 2010: 201–2). It would also address their subsequent exclusion 'from the programs, services, and campaigns designed to provide redress for these crimes' (Sikka, 2010: 202). This would reflect Cunneen and Tauri's (2017) argument on the workings of coloniality through the racialization of policy making. Particularly in marginalizing and silencing Indigenous experiences of victimization, especially those of Indigenous women.

Similarly, in more recent contributions, the interconnected issues of the conditions and effects of visibility of trafficking victimhood are being explored. Kaye (2017) highlights how structures of domination that naturalize legacies of colonialism in Canada are being perpetuated through anti-trafficking law and policy. Particularly, constructions of Indigenous women, youth, and Two-Spirit people as 'at risk' of human trafficking by choosing to engage in drug and alcohol use and sex work, recreate Indigenous communities as sites of violence, vulnerability, and deviance in need of enhanced state control (Kaye, 2017: 24–8). In imposing these controls, Indigenous communities are being construed in official narratives in need of rescue by the colonial state, effectively strengthening the colonial system that created conditions of exploitation and harm in the first place, but which were simultaneously silenced, hidden, and erased behind narratives of the 'white saviour' and 'civilizing missions' (Hunt, 2015; Roots, 2019).

Premised upon the critique of harmful entanglements between quantification and trafficking, Sally Engle Merry (2016) highlights in her critique of the TIPRs the connections between thin data, overemphasis on prosecution, the disproportionate influence of the US, and the perennial tendency to construe trafficking as a sex trafficking moral panic, as well as the failure to recognize and subsequently address structural causes. The combined effect of these issues is the construction of a dominant victim narrative comprised mostly of 'faceless victims, alongside the quantitative data' (Merry, 2016: 131). The context, instead of being culturally specific, takes the form of 'a generic, poor country or a nameless, universalized victim rather than a specific political, economic, and cultural situation' (Merry, 2016: 131). These sweeping omissions underpinning the colonial logic of the TIPRs are further demonstrated in that, in stark contrast to these representations, until 2010 the US did not rank itself within the reports (Merry, 2016: 131–2).

This contrast between the over-representation of underprivileged versus the absence of the privileged nations – including the conditions that sustain and propel privilege in the first place – ensures the preservation of the imperial ideological directions of the TIPR discourse. By ways of 'othering' (Deckert, 2016: 47), TIPRs have fuelled the demand for commensurable categories. Specifically, the focus on statistics means that 'local systems of knowledge cannot be incorporated into the quantification system' (Merry, 2016: 215), while often blamed and viewed as responsible for their failed anti-trafficking efforts. Therefore, silencing methodologies and epistemic violence are imbued in the reports as those with local knowledge of the surveyed populations rarely influence key categories (Merry, 2016: 215). The coloniality of knowledge in the TIPRs and the epistemic violence that accompanies it will be further explored in the subsequent sections of this chapter.

Data and methods

In this section we first make a case for revisiting the TIPRs through the lens of epistemic violence and imperialism, and then sketch out the methodological foundations of our investigation.

Epistemic violence and imperialism

In 2001, the year the first TIPR was published, its methodology section set out the intricate mechanics mobilized for its composition: 'Worldwide 186 U.S. embassies and consulates in consultation with host governments devoted substantial time and attention compiling and reporting information about the extent of trafficking in their host countries and efforts undertaken by host governments to address the problem' (US Department of State, 2001: 4).

The data-gathering stages involve local and global NGOs, local civil society actors, victims, immigration officials, and the police (US Department of State, 2001: 4). Subsequently, the DOS and government agencies[3] review the

---

[3] These include: the State Department's Bureau for International Narcotics and Law Enforcement Affairs; the Bureau of Democracy, Human Rights, and Labor; the regional bureaus; and the Office of the Legal Adviser, with assistance from the intelligence community.

reporting from US embassies and consulates along with sources from media reports and global organizations such as the United Nations International Children's Emergency Fund (UNICEF), the United Nations High Commissioner for Refugees (UNHCR), the International Organization for Migration (IOM), Human Rights Watch, and Amnesty International (US Department of State, 2001: 4). The expansion of the TIPRs coverage over time has involved an even wider and more vigorous mobilization of the DOS apparatus and US networks of 'soft' imperialist power globally.

The imperialist logic of the TIPR becomes further explicit when looking at the foundations of the Report. The institutional foundations can be detected in the Trafficking Victims Protection Act 2000[4] (hereafter, the TVPA), a federal law that mandated the production of TIPRs. At first glance, responding to a process of anti-trafficking advocacy that unfolded in the US during the 1990s, the TVPA can be read as the US policy response to the issue. It laid out the institutional infrastructure for monitoring the extent of the problem and provided the institutional means towards such response (that is, minimum standards, criminal law, and victim relief provisions). From a closer look, the TVPA had an international dimension by requiring the inclusion of the list of those (other) countries that do/don't/partly comply with the minimum standards laid down by the Act (Sec. 2, Div. A, s. 110). Importantly, the assessment of those other countries' commitment to anti-trafficking remained connected with US economic and security assistance (as per the Foreign Assistance Act 1961) and stipulated the unambiguous policy intention for the US 'not to provide nonhumanitarian, nontrade-related foreign assistance to any government' failing to comply with the standards of that assessment (TVPA, s. 110(d)).

Therefore, the epistemic violence of the Tier classification system of the TIPRs has not only symbolic but most crucially direct material implications for the assessed countries (and governments). As such a country's standing in the Tier classification determines access to not only anti-trafficking funds,[5] but also to other forms of US financial aid. Hence, the malicious effects of epistemic violence underpinning the Act are explicit, as its scope was not merely global, but rather *imperial*, a genuine instance of colonial classification that repositioned the US hegemony in the post-Cold War, globalized world (Nye, 2004).

---

[4] For an overview of the legal frameworks implemented in the US to address human trafficking, see further: www.justice.gov/humantrafficking/key-legislation [Accessed 15 July 2023].

[5] US anti-trafficking aid involves substantive sums of funds – for example, in 2008 alone the State Department budget for anti-trafficking efforts both internal and external was in the region of US$191.3 million (Siskin and Wyler, 2013), the purpose of these funds being capacity building to prevent human trafficking, protect victims, and prosecute offenders.

The significance of these developments in maintaining US imperial power extends beyond funding. The capacity of US agencies to exert influence and pressure on foreign institutional frameworks and practice to conform to US standards and expectations has been well documented (Nadelmann, 1990, 1993; Papanicolaou, 2011). The TVPA as a global criminal justice tool, packaged into US foreign policy resources, should therefore more accurately be understood as the uninterrupted circulation of US soft imperial power through transnational networks. Simultaneously, TIPRs' methodology makes clear that the data-collection effort relies heavily on interactions and conversations with state agencies and civil society organizations in each context (Dottridge, 2014). Therefore, a decolonial exploration of the TIPRs reveals multi-layered effects of coloniality of knowledge, such as: (1) the hegemonic capacity of the US to act as a factor influencing how international regimes, both epistemic and institutional, are shaped; (2) the role of the US as an organizer of transnational policy networks steering an issue area towards a particular direction; and (3) it highlights who has the power to converse with US diplomacy and transnational actors, particularly those connected to the US through aid flows (Dottridge, 2014). Regarding the latter, the methodology of the Report shows that data collection relies heavily on established conduits of power in those contexts, which are eventually the ones that engage in knowledge construction and circulation.

Explicitly, during the so-called 'golden age' of anti-trafficking NGOs (1990s–2004), NGO-sector representatives were seen as positive forces and 'benefited from the neoliberal agenda of "rolling back the state"' (Hoff, 2014: 111). This resulted in the outsourcing of many social services, including the provision of services to victims of human trafficking (Hoff, 2014). This process shored up power and legitimacy for those local actors and, simultaneously, integrated them in transnational policy networks that operate on a currency primarily defined by US standards and expectations, both epistemic and institutional. This left very little space for established relations of power to be captured, let alone problematized by the TIPRs, and ultimately, the voices of the most vulnerable in those contexts were further suppressed. These spatialized and materialist manifestations of coloniality of knowledge show that epistemic violence is not an abstract problem at all. Its causes and effects 'are in many ways entangled with international relations and global/local hierarchies of power' (Brunner, 2021: 201), and have real-life consequences for people and whole regions.

Methodology

Although evaluations of the TIPRs have interrogated their quantification elements as an influential composite indicator of human trafficking (Merry,

2016), and a policy mechanism heavily premised on the risk posed by traffickers to 'victims of special interest' (Boukli and Renz, 2019: 75), none of these studies have explicitly addressed the epistemic violence imbued in the wider production of geopolitical knowledge conveyed by the TIPRs. We investigate *how Indigenous communities are represented in the TIPRs 2001–20*, focusing on policy recognition of Indigeneity as a form of social representation. We argue that the TIPRs oscillate between tolerance and exclusion in recognizing the 'Other'. The construction of the 'Indigenous human trafficking victim' shifting from complete invisibility to an object of risk, to the subject of sympathy, before turning to be a matter of surveillance reproduces pejorative stereotypes entangled in narratives of the 'white saviour', 'civilizing missions', and increased state controls over Indigenous populations.

We undertook a two-stage content analysis (Neuendorf, 2017) of the TIPRs 2001–20, using a process of open, axial, and selective coding. The first stage involved a manually coded analysis of the corpus of the 'manifest content' (Gray and Densten, 1998: 420 in Neuendorf, 2017: 57); that is, the countable references embedded in TIPRs. We utilized deductive coding to analyse quantitatively the references to the search term 'Indigenous' victims as they progressed over time. Upon locating certain passages, we followed the linguistic substance of the references describing the type of trafficking victimization experienced by Indigenous people; for instance, trafficking for the purposes of labour (for example, mining, agriculture, domestic work, and sex work). We then utilized inductive coding to follow the references to countries of origin and destination (see Table 4.1), to consider how Indigenous communities are represented in relation to the wider geopolitical dimensions of human trafficking (see Yea, 2020).

The set of 20 Reports provided a total of 307 passages which were transferred to Excel and analysed. The analysis focused on 'pattern content'; a process by which the content of the reports was reduced to categories, enabling us to code the specific terms such as 'Indigenous' and analyse how certain patterns emerge in the content itself (Potter and Levine-Donnerstein, 1999: 259). General trends and patterns were identified as to how combinations of types of trafficking victimization emerge. For instance, we were enabled to connect whether the words 'sex trafficking' and 'migration' featured in the same country or region. From this point, we further explored patterns of countries, and how these countries feature across the years in relation to Indigenous communities in the TIPRs (which is demonstrated through Table 4.1). The second stage utilized computer-aided text analysis via NVivo 12 Plus to count key words and phrases and involved automated tabulation of variables for target content. Both stages of the research are reproducible and based on publicly available TIPRs.

Coloniality of knowledge in the TIPRs: constructing the 'Indigenous victim' of human trafficking

In our analysis of 20 years of TIPRs, the first observation we noted was that the references to Indigenous communities and Indigenous victims gradually increase over time. In 2001 and 2002 there are no relevant references to Indigenous communities; thus, the recognition of these communities and their experiences were entirely omitted and silenced. In 2001, references to certain groups as 'extremely vulnerable' can be found only in relation 'orphans and street children' (US Department of State, 2001: 1) and to women as 'mail-order brides' (US Department of State, 2001: 20). While in 2002, references to 'most vulnerable to trafficking' and 'especially vulnerable' refer to children (US Department of State, 2002: 74, 100). This silencing is the first indication of the effect of racialization of policies globally, in misrecognizing, infantilizing, and obscuring Indigeneity (Anthony, 2013: 3), and reinforcing the 'outsider status' of these communities. The racialization of policy making is central in understanding both the over-representation of Indigenous people within all stages of the penal system in settler colonial societies and the simultaneous marginalization and silencing of experiences of victimization (Cunneen and Tauri, 2017).

The emergence of the Indigenous victim of human trafficking from 2003 onwards appears as an afterthought; subsequently, from 2003 onwards there is a progressive trend towards the proliferation of these references in each subsequent iteration of the Report (Table 4.1). From 2009 onwards there are consistently more than ten references in each Report. Three peaks are also evident: namely, in 2014 with 40 references to Indigenous people (including stemmed words), in 2018 these references increased to 42, and in 2020 there are 44 references in total out of 307 references to 'Indigenous' across the Reports. In what follows we explore the mechanisms contributing to the reproduction of epistemic and social colonial relations of power, both on a local and global level. Second, we complement this analysis with an examination of the geographic clusters in which the term 'Indigenous' appears (see Table 4.1).

Equivocality of indigeneity

The meaning of Indigeneity varies in the TIPRs. For some Reports 'indigenous' (sic) people or communities are directly linked to members of Native communities; for example, the TIPR 2020 (US Department of State, 2020: 522) contains references to 'American Indians, Alaska Natives, Native Hawaiians'. While in other references the term 'indigenous' generally indicates native populations to differentiate between 'native' and 'foreign' as seen through the TIPR 2005 (US Department of State 2005: 102). Yet in relation to Equatorial Guinea: 'Equatoguinean officials recognize the government's responsibility for caring for the victims of trafficking, whether *foreign* or *indigenous*' (US Department of State, 2009: 229).

The same double meaning is replicated with the term 'native', with specific references such as 'Deng, [...] was recruited in her native Thailand' (US Department of State, 2004: 9); and to 'Russian-speaking natives from the country's northeast' (US Department of State, 2005: 102). For other references, 'indigenous' people or communities are linked to 'tribes' and 'tribal agencies' (US Department of State, 2017, 2018, 2019, 2020). Lastly, in successive Reports 'Indigenous communities' and 'Aboriginal communities' are terms used consistently and interchangeably in relation to Canada (US Department of State, 2016, 2017, 2019, 2020). The lack of a stable pattern in how these terms are being used suggests that the Reports may not have followed a system of self-identification regarding the communities that are represented. Rather, this raises the possibility that the variance is an effect of the process through which the data and other information are collected and compiled. The way that the Reports use the ambiguous term 'indigenous', with the first letter not being capitalized and with an inconsistent meaning attached to it, suggests that the Reports do not attempt to resolve 'profoundly asymmetrical forms of recognition' (Hunt, 2014: 29) but engage in their perpetuation.

An attempt to define the category 'Indigenous' was made in the 2014 Report 11 years after the term was first used. This attempt appeared in a section titled 'Topics of Special Interest' (US Department of State, 2014: 10–55), which included a wide variety of diverse topics in its sub-sections (Boukli and Renz, 2019). These varied from the vulnerability and needs of LGBT victims of human trafficking (p 10) to 'Romani victims of trafficking' (p 19), and the vulnerability of Indigenous persons to human trafficking (p 36). In describing Indigenous communities, the Report did acknowledge definitional issues and reflected on its own inconsistent use of the term 'Indigenous' and the occasional use of 'aboriginal' (US Department of State, 2014: 36). Drawing on the UN Permanent Forum on Indigenous Issues,[6] it identified several key factors to facilitate better international understanding of the term Indigenous, including self-identification, distinct language, and culture (US Department of State, 2014: 36; UNPFII, 2021). Yet it remains elusive whether these factors were applied in the inclusion of Indigenous communities.

---

[6] https://www.un.org/development/desa/indigenouspeoples/about-us/permanent-forum-on-indigenous-issues.html#:~:text=The%20Permanent%20Forum%20is%20an,educat ion%2C%20health%20and%20human%20rights. (Accessed 15 December 2023).

According to the 2014 TIPR, Indigenous communities are 'often economically and politically marginalized', and this is linked to the 'historical continuity with pre-colonial and/or pre-settler societies'. However, the solutions to these historical injustices appear to be resolved by seeking to address a single criminal offence; namely, 'trafficking of indigenous [sic] persons' (US Department of State, 2014: 36). Hence, the systemic factors that contribute to vulnerability to human trafficking are barely raised beyond the point of a vague acknowledgement, further obliterating the historical context and reproducing coloniality.

Reproducing stereotypes: vulnerability

Across different countries and years, the Reports construe Indigenous communities as exceptionally 'at risk' and 'particularly vulnerable' (US Department of State, 2008, 2009, 2012, 2014, 2015, 2017). Recommendations for enhanced state control through increased anti-trafficking measures, but without considering Indigenous world views, voices, and structural remedies, feature regularly in the TIPRs. For instance, in relation to Bolivia the 2009 Report asserts that '[m]embers of indigenous communities are particularly at risk of forced labour within the country, especially on ranches, sugar cane, and Brazilian nut plantations' (US Department of State, 2009: 82; see also O'Connell, this volume). Concerning vulnerability: 'Groups considered most vulnerable to human trafficking in Mexico include women and children, indigenous persons, and undocumented migrants' (US Department of State, 2009: 206). Regarding Peru: 'Indigenous persons are particularly vulnerable to being subjected to debt bondage by Amazon landowners' (US Department of State, 2009: 238). While, concerning Guatemala (US Department of State, 2011: 175): 'Indigenous Guatemalans are particularly vulnerable to labor exploitation'. The Reports, therefore, by presenting Indigenous communities through this prism of vulnerability and risk, continue to reconstitute and redefine Indigenous identities and cultures 'to reinforce their outsider status' (Pollock 1988: 6 in Anthony, 2013: 3). It seems impossible to unlink these contemporary forms of human trafficking from their history of being, through which empires were established and economically maintained. Such colonial representations of Indigenous people highlight in turn, that the way in which the TIPRs construct vulnerability is a form of enduring colonial structural violence against Indigenous people (Clark, 2012).

In describing different levels of vulnerability, the Reports essentially create a hierarchy of vulnerability, which seems to reverberate from country to country and across the years: '[r]efugees, particularly from Burma, were especially vulnerable to trafficking, and Malaysians from rural communities and indigenous groups were also vulnerable' (US Department of State, 2011: 244). In a different context and a few years later the focus shifts to different 'at risk' groups. In relation to Colombia:

> Groups at high risk for internal trafficking include internally displaced persons, Afro-Colombians, indigenous Colombians, Colombians with disabilities, and Colombians living in areas where armed criminal groups are active. Sex trafficking[7] of Colombian women and children occurs within the country. Authorities reported high rates of child prostitution in areas with tourism and large extractive industries, and NGOs reported that sex trafficking in mining areas sometimes involves organized criminal groups. NGOs reported that transgender Colombians and Colombian men in prostitution are exploited in sex trafficking in Colombia. (US Department of State, 2014: 134)

The contours of vulnerability are also subject to a variety of socially mediated conditions. For instance, in 2012 the Reports identify the following categories: '[g]roups considered most vulnerable to human trafficking in Mexico include women, children, indigenous persons, persons with mental and physical disablilitys [sic], and undocumented migrants' (US Department of State, 2012: 247). While throughout the years, the groups considered most vulnerable are expanded, both in relation to Mexico where '[g]roups most vulnerable to human trafficking in Mexico include women, children, indigenous persons, persons with mental and physical disabilities, migrants, and LGBT Mexicans' (US Department of State, 2014: 271), but also more widely. For instance, in Ecuador (US Department of State, 2017: 158):

> Indigenous and Afro-Ecuadorians, as well as Colombian refugees and migrants, are particularly vulnerable to human trafficking. Women, children, refugees, and migrants continued to be the most vulnerable to sex trafficking; however, LGBTI individuals remain vulnerable to sex trafficking. ... Traffickers recruit children from impoverished indigenous families under false promises of employment and subject them to forced labor in begging, domestic servitude, in sweatshops, or as street and commercial vendors in Ecuador or in other South American countries.

And in relation to Canada (US Department of State, 2018: 132): 'Women, children from indigenous communities, migrants, LGBTI youth,

---

[7] The Report utilizes a definition of 'sex trafficking' as set out by the Trafficking Victims Protection Act (see US Department of State, 2004: 24).

at-risk youth, runaway youth, and youth in the child welfare system are especially vulnerable.'

In these vulnerability clusters, we argue, the imagery of the white, Western, cisgender, heterosexual, male, Christian body features as the non-vulnerable norm. Through these representations, Indigenous peoples – along with other communities as portrayed in the previous example – are relegated to an exceptional zone. Exceptionality functions to place individual victims and communities outside the legal order, and to construe Indigeneity as a risk and vulnerability factor in itself. This reconstruction of Indigeneity as a combined risk and vulnerability factor contributes to the demonization of Indigenous families, guardians, and, more widely, communities – portraying communities as, at worst, complicit in trafficking offences and, at best, incapable of protecting members of the communities.

Echoing Anthony's (2013) earlier observations, Walter (2016) argues that the nation state's portrayal of Indigenous populations presents a continuum of colonial pejorative stereotypes of racialized hierarchies. Under the term 5D data, 'disparity, deprivation, disadvantage, dysfunction and difference', Walter (2016: 80, 82) suggests that the collection of data on Indigenous people 'are the cloned descendants of the data imperatives of colonisation'. Unlike considering these groupings as either interchangeable or an 'at random' bricolage of different groups, we suggest that these vulnerability pyramids draw on the combined force of the stereotypes they represent. Hence, these stereotype-enhancing 5D data are constitutive of pictures of communities as 'deficits' and 'inadequacies' (Walter, 2016: 84).

Moral anxieties

The data-informed moral anxiety attached to certain aspects of labour and sexual exploitation is evident across multiple Reports (see also Lammasniemi, this volume). The 2009 Report on Australia: '[s]ome indigenous teenage girls are subjected to forced prostitution at rural truck stops' (US Department of State, 2009: 67). These references are found across regions, while the Tier categorizations differ across these regions (Table 4.1). For instance, in relation to Malaysia '[t]here were reports of Malaysians, specifically women and girls from indigenous groups and rural areas, trafficked within the country for labor and commercial sexual exploitation' (US Department of State, 2009: 198). This 'risk' is often presented as endemic to the communities; for instance, in relation to Panama: 'Government agencies indicate that indigenous girls may be trafficked by their parents into prostitution in Darien province' (US Department of State, 2009: 234). While the references in relation to Canada and Australia suggest that sex trafficking of women and girls is the main source of exploitation: 'Canadian women and girls are exploited in sex trafficking across the country, and women and girls from aboriginal communities are especially vulnerable' (US Department of State, 2012: 110). And: 'Some indigenous teenage girls are subjected to forced prostitution [...]' (US Department of State, 2009: 67).

In these constructions, the lives of Indigenous people, particularly of women and girls, are being understood primarily as victims of sex trafficking (Hunt, 2014). Hence, the recommendations presented to ameliorate these vulnerabilities are limited to anti-trafficking criminalization: 'Intensify efforts to investigate and prosecute trafficking offenses, and convict and sentence trafficking offenders using anti-trafficking laws' (US Department of State, 2012: 110). Rather than addressing the perpetuation of colonial structural violence that creates unsafe environments in the first place. This does not merely conceal disadvantaged contexts and limited options available to certain communities but, arguably, sends a deterrent message to Indigenous communities regarding their right to self-determination.

State mechanisms

Any reference to colonial legacies or the interplay between Indigenous communities and the official state mechanisms rarely feature in the Reports. Concerning Gabon, the 'Reports also indicate that some indigenous Pygmies are subjected to slavery-like conditions, without effective recourse in the judicial system' (US Department of State, 2009: 137). Equally in the TIPR 2010, the DOS asserts that '[w]ithout birth certificates, national identification cards, or other identity documents, stateless persons and some indigenous groups are vulnerable to being trafficked' (US Department of State, 2010: 31). In 2013, the Reports make explicit reference to 'Risk Factors for Victimization and Challenges of Identification', where reference is made to marginalization suffered by some populations, while silencing the perpetuation of coloniality's racialized violence in attitudes, discourses, and practices embedded in state institutions and services contributing to that marginalization:

> They prey on excluded populations – many trafficking victims come from backgrounds that make them reluctant to seek help from authorities or are otherwise vulnerable – marginalized ethnic minorities, undocumented immigrants, the indigenous, the poor, persons with disabilities – whose experiences make them reluctant to seek help from authorities. Awareness materials dated as far back as the 1890s reveal that promises of greater opportunity, a better life, or a loving and supportive relationship have long lured victims into exploitation. (US Department of State, 2013: 8–9)

Even when reference is made to structural barriers, these are only used to recommend anti-trafficking measures as the main remedy: 'In every region, governments that a decade ago insisted there was no trafficking in their jurisdiction are now aggressively identifying and assisting victims and convicting traffickers. There governments are adopting modern anti-trafficking structures and sustaining the political will to vigorously apply them' (US Department of State, 2013: 9).

Arguably a parallel is emerging between hegemony and domination as used by colonial powers in a process of 'civilizing' during the colonial period and later 'modernizing' those no longer under colonial occupation, to the present-day processes of 'rescuing' Indigenous communities (Mignolo, 2007). Often the problem is framed as a matter of interpersonal violence, with human traffickers preying upon individual victims or on certain communities. Even when structural conditions are being mentioned, such as 'lack of citizenship and access to basic services, sometimes including education' (US Department of State, 2014: 36) as well as economic marginalization, these are to be pushed aside, effectively concealing the embedded colonial structures and practices in state policies.

Therefore, this 'targeting of' is completely disconnected from wider structural conditions of coloniality and instead portrayed as the 'mere' result of human trafficking modus operandi. The Reports treat human trafficking as an interpersonal issue, without considering the structural backdrop against which trafficking plays out. Consequently, the impact of perpetuating the colonial matrix of power, as the core source of 'risk' that continues to devalue the lives and living experiences of Indigenous peoples, is omitted from the Reports effectively recreating trauma, poverty, victimization, criminalization, and exploitation (Clark, 2012; Cunneen and Tauri, 2017, 2019).

Socio-economic factors

Equally, even when a wide variety of structural socio-economic factors are mentioned, these are limited to establishing *vulnerability to trafficking* rather than an outcome of coloniality underpinning state (in-)actions in constructing insecure environments: 'Worldwide, indigenous persons are often economically and politically marginalized and are disproportionately affected by environmental degradation and armed conflict. They may lack citizenship and access to basic services, sometimes including education. These factors make indigenous peoples particularly vulnerable to both sex trafficking and forced labor' (US Department of State, 2014: 36).

Responding to these factors that 'make indigenous peoples particularly vulnerable' to human trafficking, the Reports suggest the 3Ps of prosecution, protection, prevention anti-trafficking approach:[8] 'Combating the trafficking of indigenous persons requires prosecution, protection, and prevention efforts that are culturally sensitive and collaborative' (US Department of State, 2014: 36). Often the blame of Indigenous communities in these supposedly 'culturally-sensitive and collaborative' approaches take the form of partnerships: 'by incorporating community traditions and rituals into victim protection efforts, such as use of the medicine wheel – a diverse indigenous tradition with spiritual and healing purposes' (US Department of State, 2014: 36). In doing so, however, the Reports engage in what has been termed as 'the ideology of "building partnerships"', which have been used in efforts antagonistic to the principle of self-determination (Anthony, 2010). Hence, not only do these approaches fail to scrutinize economic inequalities that have been exacerbated since the gradual annihilation of alternative economic models (Mariátegui, 1928), but they also fail to promote self-determination. Vulnerability to trafficking becomes again an interpersonal issue that takes hold of Indigenous communities.

Following the imperialist logic of the TIPRs, we observed a clear division between norm-setters and norm-followers (Faulkner and Nyamutata, 2020), in wider anti-trafficking geopolitics. For a large proportion of countries where references to Indigenous communities appear in the TIPRs, we often observe an unstable/erratic pattern of Tier ranking (Table 4.1). For instance, during the covered period, Guatemala was placed three times in the 'warning zone' of the Tier 2 Watch List, subject to anti-trafficking efforts. We also observe that two clear geographic clusters are over-represented in the Reports (Table 4.1, 'Central America' and 'South America'). We further explore this point to be discussed later.

Geographical clusters

It is impossible not to recognize the objective ramifications of the TIPRs' role as an imperial policy tool. This role, we argue, in so far as it legitimizes established relations of power in those contexts, reproduces coloniality. Table 4.1 captures the appearance in all 20 TIPRs (2001–20) of the term Indigenous, alongside the Tier classifications of the respective countries (Tiers 1, 2, 2 Watchlist [2WL], and 3), and the characterization of those countries as Sending, Transit, and Destination countries.

---

[8] The first iteration of the paradigm appears in the Preamble of the Palermo Protocol (UN, 2000). The 3Ps (prevention, prosecution, protection) anti-trafficking paradigm has been reflected in the TIPR since 2010 and appears in all subsequent publications of the Report. In the Report the paradigm has been further expanded with the addition of the 'fourth P', which stands for 'partnership' (see US Department of State, 2010 introductory note by Secretary of State Hillary Rodham Clinton).

Table 4.1: Indigenous communities mentions in Trafficking in Persons reports by country types and Tier status (2003–2020)

Cluster	Country	Tier																		Type[a]
		2003	2004	2005	2006	2007	2008	2009	2010	2011	2012	2013	2014	2015	2016	2017	2018	2019	2020	
Oceania	Australia						1	1												D
	Papua New Guinea												3		2WL	3	3	3		S/T/D
S Pacific	Fiji	(sp)																	2WL	S
C Africa	R Congo				2	2	2WL	2WL	3		2	2	2	2WL	2WL	3		2WL	2	S/D
	DR Congo							2WL	3	3	3	3	3	2WL			3			S/T/D
	C A Republic					2WL														D
	Gabon						2WL	2WL												T/D
	Eq Guinea			2																S/T/D
	Sudan													2WL						S/T
Africa	Zambia			2																S/T/D
	Cote d'Ivoire				2															S/T/D
C America	Guatemala	2							2WL	2	2	2	2	2	2	2WL	2WL	2	2	S/T/D
	Mexico								2	2	2	2	2	2	2	2	2	2	2	S/T/D
	Costa Rica								2			2	2	2WL	2WL	2	2	2	2	S/T/D
	Honduras											2WL	2	2	2	2	2	2	2	S/T/D
	Panama						2						2WL					2	2	S/T/D
	Nicaragua															2WL	2WL	2WL		S/T/D
S America	Bolivia								2	2	2	2	2WL	2WL	2WL	2WL	3	2WL	2	S/T/D

100

A CONTENT ANALYSIS OF THE TRAFFICKING IN PERSONS REPORTS

Table 4.1: Indigenous communities mentions in Trafficking in Persons reports by country types and Tier status (2003–2020) (continued)

Cluster	Country	Tier 2003	2004	2005	2006	2007	2008	2009	2010	2011	2012	2013	2014	2015	2016	2017	2018	2019	2020	Type[a]
	Brazil												2	2	2	2	2	2	2	S/T/D
	Paraguay						2	2		2	2	2	2	2	2	2	2	2	2	S/T/D
	Peru							2	2	2	2		2	2	2	2	2			S/T/D
	Ecuador								2	2WL	2WL	2	2	2	2	2	2	2	2	S/T/D
	Colombia									1	1	2	2	2	1	1	1		1	S/T/D
	Venezuela									2WL	2WL	3							3	S/T/D
E Asia	North Korea					3	3	3	3	3										S
SE Asia	Malaysia						2WL	3	2WL	2WL										S
	Burma										2WL									S
	Philippines														1	1	1		1	S/T/D
	Indonesia																	2		S
	Bangladesh																		2	S
N America	Canada						1	1	1	1	1		1	1	1	1	1	1	1	S/T/D
	US												1	1	1		1	1	1	S/T/D
Caribbean	Trinidad & Tobago																2			D/T/S

Note: [a]By 'type' here is indicated the classification of countries as 'destination', 'source', and 'transit'.

Source: U.S. Department of Justice, Trafficking in Persons reports 2003–2020

Table 4.1 shows a clear geographical clustering and a more systematic appearance of the term around the regions of Central Africa, Central and South America, and Southeast Asia. We deduce from this finding that this is likely an effect of the methodology and data-collection process of the TIPRs as local sources are brought into play. Therefore, it is likely the case that the TIPRs' local sources mobilize the category of Indigenous in their accounts, hence engaging in the two-way process described previously – reflecting and reproducing a double layer of epistemic and material dependencies animated by relations of domination and subordination. Effectively, the TIPRs do not allow for categories to emerge that would disrupt the dominant anti-trafficking paradigm. Their unquestioned default position embeds the experiences of Indigenous communities in already shaped imperialist world views.

As the Tier classifications directly link to the US minimum standards, the prioritization of punitive approaches heavily emphasizes prosecutions and convictions, in combination with the material implications of falling short of those standards. Falling short of these standards, we argue, further imposes the US-preferred conceptualizations of human trafficking on those local state and civil society actors active in the issue area, while simultaneously supporting and legitimizing the system of power relations in which these latter operate in those contexts. This echoes the criticism that the global anti-trafficking regime (to which the TIPRs feed into) operates as a mechanism of exclusion and at the detriment of affected populations (GAATW, 2007; Beutin, 2023). It also operates as an imperial knowledge construction apparatus and as a colonial monitoring tool.

Conclusion

In 2001 the TIPRs included in their remit 82 countries while by 2013 the report considered 188 countries according to its three-tier system. In this chapter we deployed the concept of coloniality to understand this global expansion. Deep-seated colonial knowledge, discourses, and practices, we argued, are embedded in mainstream supranational policies such as the TIPR. The crux of the argument running through this chapter is that any social science knowledge production that does not take into consideration the role of colonial experience past and present cannot account, understand, nor address human trafficking of Indigenous populations (Clark, 2012; Cunneen and Tauri, 2017). By failing to account for the impact of structural disadvantage and dispossession in the shaping of power relations globally and locally, such knowledge production is not only incomplete but also ideologically complicit in legitimizing coloniality (Castro-Gómez, 2002; Anthony, 2013).

By utilizing a two-stage content analysis of the Reports 2001–20 and applying the analytical framework of coloniality, we showed that policy interventions are still central to imposing colonial frameworks of knowledge and interventions globally and locally. Our findings attest to the perpetuation of coloniality through constructions such as the 'particularly' or 'most vulnerable' Indigenous victim of human trafficking. While dominant technocratic forms of knowledge, such as the TIPRs, shape crime control policies globally and locally, and gradually make Indigenous victimization more visible, they lack any consideration of the impact of colonialism and coloniality to Indigenous people's lives and, hence, to human trafficking victimization. Finally, the geographic clusters and methodology of the Reports pose certain methodological and ethical challenges that need to be prioritized before any further imposition of punitive frameworks.

We argued that epistemic violence (and its perpetuation) has real-life, detrimental consequences for people and whole regions. To undo the epistemic violence inflicted by anti-trafficking and anti- 'modern slavery', data-collection efforts should resist the imperialist drive to conflate slavery, modern slavery, and human trafficking. The vicious cycle of taking these terms as metaphors for a lack of freedom lacks reflexivity about slavery in the past (Kempadoo, 2017). Unproblematically accepting colonial slavery as the standard against which any claims to forced or compulsory labour are measured in the 21st century, as in the case of the *European Convention on Human Rights* or the *Modern Slavery Act 2015* in England and Wales (see Bhandar, 2014), further obscures the legacies of persisting inequalities. To the contrary, often to see the workings of coloniality is to reveal the continuous degradation of those colonized. Hence, it is to expose the 'colonial wound' of 'the powerful reduction of human beings to … inferiors by nature' (Lugones, 2010: 752). This is not a process of merely delving into the past, but a 'matter of the geopolitics of knowledge' (Lugones, 2010: 752), of the historicity and meaning attached to knowledge produced about Indigenous communities in relation to human trafficking victimhood that persists today.

References

Andrijasevic, R. (2010) *Migration, Agency and Citizenship in Sex Trafficking*, New York: Palgrave Macmillan.

Agozino, B. (2003) *Counter-Colonial Criminology: A Critique of Imperialist Reason*, London: Pluto Press.

Agustín, L. (2007) *Sex at the Margins: Migration, Labour Markets and the Rescue Industry*, London: Zed Books.

Anghie, A. (2006) 'The evolution of international law: colonial and postcolonial realities', *Third World Quarterly*, 27(5): 739–53.

Anthony, T. (2010) 'A new national indigenous representative body, again', *Indigenous Law Bulletin*, 7(18): Bulletin 5.

Anthony, T. (2013) *Indigenous People, Crime and Punishment*, Abingdon; New York: Routledge.

Arena, C. (2017) 'Indian slaves guiana in seventeenth-century Barbados', *Ethnohistory*, 64(1): 65–90.

Beutin, L.P. (2023) *Trafficking in Antiblackness: Modern-Day Slavery, White Indemnity, and Racial Justice*, [Online], Durham: Duke University Press.

Bhandar, B. (2014) 'Property, law, and race: modes of abstraction', *UC Irvine Law Review*, 4(1): 203–18.

Boukli, A. and Renz, F. (2019) 'Deconstructing the lesbian, gay, bisexual, transgender victim of sex trafficking: harm, exceptionality and religion-sexuality tensions', *International Review of Victimology*, 25(1): 71–90.

Brunner, C. (2021) 'Conceptualizing epistemic violence: an interdisciplinary assemblage for IR', *International Politics Reviews*, 9(3): 193–212.

Castro-Gómez, S. (2002) 'The social sciences, epistemic violence, and the problem of the "invention of the other"', *Nepantla Views South*, 3(2): 269–85.

Castro-Gómez, S. (2019) 'The social sciences, epistemic violence, and the problem of the "invention of the other"', in S. Dube and I. Banerjee-Dube (eds) *Unbecoming Modern: Colonialism, Modernity, Colonial Modernities*, London and New York: Routledge, pp 211–27.

Chapman-Schmidt, B. (2019) '"Sex trafficking" as epistemic violence', *Anti-Trafficking Review*, 12(1): 172–87.

Clark, N. (2012) 'Perseverance, determination and resistance: an Indigenous intersectional-based policy analysis of violence in the lives of Indigenous girls', in O. Hankivsky (ed) *An Intersectionality-Based Policy Analysis Framework*, Vancouver, BC: Institute for Intersectionality Research and Policy, pp 133–58.

Cunneen, C. and Tauri, J. (2017) *Indigenous Criminology*, Bristol: Policy Press.

Cunneen, C. and Tauri, J. (2019) 'Indigenous peoples, criminology, and criminal justice', *Annual Review of Criminology*, 2(1): 359–81.

Deckert, A. (2016) 'Criminologists, duct tape, and Indigenous peoples: quantifying the use of silencing research methods', *International Journal of Comparative and Applied Criminal Justice*, 40(1): 43–62.

Dottridge, M. (2014) 'Editorial: how is the money to combat human trafficking spent?', *Anti-Trafficking Review*, 3(1): 3–14.

Faulkner, E.A. and Nyamutata, C. (2020) 'The decolonisation of children's rights and the colonial contours of the Convention on the Rights of the Child', *International Journal of Children's Rights*, 28(1): 66–88. doi: 10.1163/15718182-02801009

GAATW (2007) *Collateral Damage. The Impact of Anti-Trafficking Measures on Human Rights around the World*, Bangkok: Global Alliance Against Traffic in Women, pp 1–27.

Goetz, R.A. (2016) 'Indian slavery: an Atlantic and hemispheric problem', *History Compass*, 14(2): 59–70.

Gray, J.H. and Densten, I.L. (1998) 'Integrating quantitative and qualitative analysis using latent and manifest variables', *Quality & Quantity*, 32: 419–31.

Hoff, S. (2014) 'Where is the funding for anti-trafficking work? A look at donor funds, policies and practices in Europe', *Anti-Trafficking Review*, 3(1): 109–32.

Hunt, S. (2014) 'Ontologies of indigeneity: the politics of embodying a concept', *Cultural Geographies in Practice*, 21(1): 27–32.

Hunt, S. (2015) 'Representing colonial violence: trafficking, sex work, and the violence of law', *Atlantis: Critical Studies in Gender, Culture, and Social Justice*, 37(2): 25–39.

Kaye, J. (2017) *Responding to Human Trafficking: Dispossession, Colonial Violence, and Resistance among Indigenous and Racialized Women*, Toronto: University of Toronto Press.

Kempadoo, K. (2017) '"Bound coolies" and other indentured workers in the Caribbean: implications for debates about human trafficking and modern slavery', *Anti-Trafficking Review*, 9(1): 48–63.

Kempadoo, K. and Shih, E. (eds) (2023) *White Supremacy, Racism and the Coloniality of Anti-Trafficking*, London: Routledge.

Kotiswaran, P. (2014) 'Beyond sexual humanitarianism: a postcolonial approach to anti-trafficking law', *UC Irvine Law Review*, 4(2): 353–406.

Las Casas, B. (1992) *A Short Account of the Destruction of the Indies*, N. Griffin (tr), London: Penguin Classics.

Limoncelli, S.A. (2010) *The Politics of Trafficking: The First International Movement to Combat the Sexual Exploitation of Women*, Redwood City, CA: Stanford University Press.

Lugones, M. (2010) 'Toward a decolonial feminism', *Hypatia*, 25(4): 742–59.

Mai, N. et al (2021) 'Migration, sex work and trafficking: the racialized bordering politics of sexual humanitarianism', *Ethnic and Racial Studies*, 44(9): 1607–28.

Mariátegui, J.C. (1928) *Seven Interpretative Essays on Peruvian Reality*, Austin, TX: University of Texas Press. Available from: www.marxists.org/archive/mariateg/works/7-interpretive-essays/index.htm [Accessed 30 September 2023].

Merry, S.E. (2016) *The Seductions of Quantification: Measuring Human Rights, Gender Violence, and Sex Trafficking*, Chicago, IL; London: University of Chicago Press.

Mignolo, W.D. (2007) 'Introduction: coloniality of power and de-colonial thinking', *Cultural Studies*, 21(2–3): 155–67.

Mignolo, W.D. (2011) *The Darker Side of Western Modernity: Global Futures, Decolonial Options*, Durham, NC: Duke University Press.

Mignolo, W.D. (2018) 'The decolonial option', in C.E. Walsh and W.D. Mignolo (eds) *On Decoloniality: Concepts, Analytics, Praxis*, Durham, NC: Duke University Press, pp 105–226.

Mignolo, W.D. and Ennis, M. (2001) 'Coloniality at large: the Western hemisphere in the colonial horizon of modernity', *CR: The New Centennial Review*, 1(2): 19–54.

Moraña, M., Dussel, E., and Jáuregui, C.A. (2008) 'Colonialism and its replicants', in M. Moraña, E. Dussel, and C.A. Jáuregui (eds) *Coloniality at Large: Latin American and the Postcolonial Debate*, Durham, NC; London: Duke University Press, pp 1–20.

Munro, V. (2005) 'A tale of two servitudes: defining and implementing a domestic response to trafficking of women for prostitution in the UK and Australia', *Social & Legal Studies*, 14(1): 91–114.

Nadelmann, E.A. (1990) 'The role of the United States in the international enforcement of criminal law', *Harvard International Law Journal*, 31(1): 37–76.

Nadelmann, E.A. (1993) *Cops across Borders. The Internationalization of US Criminal Law Enforcement*, University Park, PA: Pennsylvania University Press.

Neuendorf, K.N. (2017) *The Content Analysis Guidebook*, Los Angeles, CA; London; New Delhi: Sage.

Nye, J.S., Jr (2004) *Soft Power: The Means to Success in World Politics*, New York: Public Affairs.

O'Connell Davidson, J. (2015) *Modern Slavery: The Margins of Freedom*, London: Palgrave Macmillan.

Oude Breuil, B. and Gerasimov, B. (2021) 'Editorial: trafficking in minors: confronting complex realities, structural inequalities, and agency', *Anti-Trafficking Review*, 16(1): 1–9.

Papanicolaou, G. (2011) *Transnational Policing and Sex Trafficking in Southeast Europe: Policing the Imperialist Chain*, Basingstoke: Palgrave Macmillan.

Papanicolaou, G. and Boukli, A. (2011) 'Sex, trafficking and crime policy', in L. Cheliotis and S. Xenakis (eds) *Crime and Punishment in Contemporary Greece: International Comparative Perspectives*, Oxford: Peter Lang Publishing, pp 307–38.

Patel, S. (2021) 'Colonialism and its knowledges', in D. McCallum (ed) *The Palgrave Handbook of the History of Human Sciences*, Singapore: Springer, pp 1–22.

Potter, W.J. and Levine-Donnerstein, D. (1999) 'Rethinking validity and reliability in content analysis', *Journal of Applied Communication Research*, 27(3): 258–84.

Quijano, A. (1992) 'Colonialidad y modernidad/racionalidad', in R. Backburn and H. Bonilla (eds) *Los Conquistados: 1492 y la población indígena de las Américas*, Bogotá, Colombia: Tercer Mundo Editores, pp 437–47.

Quijano, A. (2000) 'Coloniality of power and Eurocentrism in Latin America', *International Sociology*, 15(2): 215–32.

Quijano, A. (2008) 'Coloniality of power, Eurocentrism, and Latin America', in M. Moraña, E. Dussel, and C.A. Jáuregui (eds) *Coloniality at Large: Latin American and the Postcolonial Debate*, Durham, NC; London: Duke University Press, pp 181–224.

Quirk, J., Robinson, C., and Thibos, C. (2020) 'Editorial: from exceptional cases to everyday abuses: labour exploitation in the global economy', *Anti-Trafficking Review*, 15(1): 1–19.

Roots, K. (2019) 'Anti-trafficking efforts and colonial violence in Canada', *Anti-Trafficking Review*, 12: 201–4.

Sikka, A. (2010) 'Trafficking of aboriginal women and girls in Canada', *Aboriginal Policy Research Consortium International*, 57(8): 201–31.

Siskin, A. and Wyler, L.S. (2013) *Trafficking in Persons: US policy and Issues for Congress*, Washington, DC: Congressional Research Service.

Smith, T.L. (2021) *Decolonizing Methodologies: Research and Indigenous Peoples* (3rd edn), London: Zed Books.

Spivak, G.C. (1988) 'Can the subaltern speak?', in N. Carry and L. Grossberg (eds) *Marxism and the Interpretation of Culture*, Champaign, IL: University of Illinois Press, pp 271–313.

UN (2000) *Protocol to Prevent, Suppress and Punish Trafficking in Persons, Especially Women and Children, Supplementing the United Nations Convention against Transnational Organized Crime*, adopted by UN General Assembly Resolution A/RES/55/67 of 15 November 2000.

UNPFII (2021) 'Report on the twentieth session (19–30 April 2021)', *Permanent Forum on Indigenous Issues*, UN, Economic and Social Council, E/2021/43-E/C.19/2021/10, Official Records 2021, Supplement no. 23.

US Department of State (2001) *Trafficking in Persons Report*. Available from https://www.state.gov/trafficking-in-persons-report/ [Accessed 15 June 2022].

US Department of State (2002) *Trafficking in Persons Report*. Available from https://www.state.gov/trafficking-in-persons-report/ [Accessed 15 June 2022].

US Department of State (2004) *Trafficking in Persons Report*. Available from https://www.state.gov/trafficking-in-persons-report/ [Accessed 15 June 2022].

US Department of State (2005) *Trafficking in Persons Report*. Available from https://www.state.gov/trafficking-in-persons-report/ [Accessed 15 June 2022].

US Department of State (2008) *Trafficking in Persons Report*. Available from https://www.state.gov/trafficking-in-persons-report/ [Accessed 15 June 2022].

US Department of State (2009) *Trafficking in Persons Report*. Available from https://www.state.gov/trafficking-in-persons-report/ [Accessed 15 June 2022].

US Department of State (2010) *Trafficking in Persons Report*. Available from https://www.state.gov/trafficking-in-persons-report/ [Accessed 15 June 2022].

US Department of State (2011) *Trafficking in Persons Report*. Available from https://www.state.gov/trafficking-in-persons-report/ [Accessed 15 June 2022].

US Department of State (2012) *Trafficking in Persons Report*. Available from https://www.state.gov/trafficking-in-persons-report/ [Accessed 15 June 2022].

US Department of State (2013) *Trafficking in Persons Report*. Available from https://www.state.gov/trafficking-in-persons-report/ [Accessed 15 June 2022].

US Department of State (2014) *Trafficking in Persons Report*. Available from https://www.state.gov/trafficking-in-persons-report/ [Accessed 15 June 2022].

US Department of State (2015) *Trafficking in Persons Report*. Available from https://www.state.gov/trafficking-in-persons-report/ [Accessed 15 June 2022].

US Department of State (2016) *Trafficking in Persons Report*. Available from https://www.state.gov/trafficking-in-persons-report/ [Accessed 15 June 2022].

US Department of State (2017) *Trafficking in Persons Report*. Available from https://www.state.gov/trafficking-in-persons-report/ [Accessed 15 June 2022].

US Department of State (2018) *Trafficking in Persons Report*. Available from https://www.state.gov/trafficking-in-persons-report/ [Accessed 15 June 2022].

US Department of State (2019) *Trafficking in Persons Report*. Available from https://www.state.gov/trafficking-in-persons-report/ [Accessed 15 June 2022].

US Department of State (2020) *Trafficking in Persons Report*. Available from https://www.state.gov/trafficking-in-persons-report/ [Accessed 15 June 2022].

US Government Accountability Office (2006) 'Human trafficking: better data, strategy, and reporting needed to enhance U.S. anti-trafficking efforts abroad' (Publication No. GAO-06- 825), Report to the Chairman, Committee on the Judiciary and the Chairman, Committee on International Relations, House of Representatives, Washington, DC.

US Government Accountability Office (2007) 'Human trafficking: monitoring and evaluation of international projects are limited, but experts suggest improvements' (Publication No. GAO-07–1034), Report to Congressional Requesters, Washington, DC.

Valcárcel Rojas, R., Laffoon, J.E., Weston, D.A., Hoogland, M.L.P., and Hofman, C.L. (2020) 'Slavery of Indigenous people in the Caribbean: an archaeological perspective', *International Journal of Historical Archaeology*, 24(3): 517–45.

Vazquez, R. (2017) 'Precedence, Earth and the Anthropocene: decolonizing design', *Design Philosophy Paper*, 15(1): 77–91.

Walter, M. (2016) 'Data politics and Indigenous representation in Australian statistics', in T. Kukutai and J. Taylor (eds) *Indigenous Data Sovereignty: Toward an Agenda*, Canberra: ANU Press, pp 79–97.

Weitzer, R. (2007) 'The social construction of sex trafficking: ideology and institutionalisation of a moral crusade', *Politics and Society*, 35(3): 447–75.

Wooditch, A. (2011) 'The efficacy of the Trafficking in Persons Report: a review of the evidence', *Criminal Justice Policy Review*, 22(4): 471–93.

Yea, S. (2020) 'Human trafficking and jurisdictional exceptionalism in the global fishing industry: a case study of Singapore', *Geopolitics*. doi: 10.1080/14650045.2020.1741548

PART II

Structural Issues in Modern Slavery and Human Trafficking Practice

5

The Ethics of Research into Human Trafficking Beyond 'Do No Harm': Developing a 'Living' Ethical Protocol

Patricia Hynes and Mike Dottridge

Introduction

Although not new phenomena, human trafficking and human smuggling have risen up the policy agendas of many countries in the past two decades (Gallagher, 2015a,b; Morrison, 2002). Prior to the landmark definition of human trafficking provided by the UN Trafficking Protocol, anti-slavery activities to 'liberate' or 'rescue' people experiencing various forms of extreme exploitation during the second half of the 20th century were already subject to critiques around their counter-productive impacts, notably the lack of provision for viable economic alternatives for those freed from slavery in the two international Conventions on slavery and practices similar to slavery adopted in 1926 and 1956. Critiques of rescue and liberation have continued after the UN Trafficking Protocol (Dottridge, 2001; LeBaron and Pliley, 2021).

The term 'collateral damage' describes the dangers of anti-trafficking measures having adverse impacts on the rights and freedoms of people who have experienced human trafficking and on related groups, such as women and child migrants more generally (GAATW, 2007; Dottridge, 2018). The term describes how harm may be inflicted upon people as a result of anti-trafficking legal measures and wider campaigns. For example, detention in immigration centres, prosecution of individuals for offences involving illegal work, raids and rescues that do not adequately consider the protection of those involved, as well as repatriation to unchanged circumstances. In other words, practices wherein the 'victim' of human trafficking is not placed at the centre of actions designed to 'combat' human trafficking and which do not make it a priority to respect the dignity and rights of these individuals, as noted by the Global Alliance Against Traffic in Women (GAATW): 'A plethora of actors on the anti-trafficking terrain do their work from the perspective of human rights including those who bundle off the trafficked and migrant women back to where they came from in the name of protection' (2007: vii). That these types of 'harms' exist within work to protect people experiencing human trafficking is a key consideration when conducting research.

Ethical issues have become increasingly more central to discussions about research more broadly due in part to historical transgressions of ethical principles, revelations of medical and scientific misconduct, and an increasing recognition that research is not conducted in a 'moral vacuum' becoming thereby invariably related to politics and the politics of knowledge production (Bryman, 2012: 149– 52). Ethical boundaries in research are also constantly being set by historically informed and socially constructed limits to voyeurism.[1] Israel and Hay (2006) have argued that researchers need a better understanding of the politics and context within which ethics are regulated. Bryman (2012) also outlines how funding research through organizations with a 'vested interest' is a key part of the politics of knowledge production. This chapter links to research on ethics and human trafficking (Cwikel and Hoban, 2005; Duong, 2015; Siegel and Wildt, 2016). It also considers what Jacobsen and Landau (2003a,b) have called a 'dual imperative' in research with forcibly displaced populations. This 'dual imperative' relates to both satisfying high academic standards and ensuring knowledge production improves the lives of people concerned, including by influencing policy and practice. In other words, research is conducted ethically with responsibility towards participants and others as well as carried out in ways that underpin confidence in results of the research with researchers, and the research community, retaining integrity throughout and recognizing tensions may exist in such an endeavour (Carling, 2019).

This chapter looks at the ethics of conducting research into human trafficking and 'modern slavery'.[2] The chapter questions whether the principle of 'do no harm' is sufficient to guide researchers through the sometimes polemical and often contentious research environment of human trafficking or modern slavery. Given that power imbalances are built into responses to people who are trafficked, it is suggested that the concept

---

[1] Two social studies that are of particular note are Stanley Milgram's studies of obedience to authority and Laud Humphrey's covert observation studies of homosexuality in the 1960s.

[2] The term 'modern slavery' is contested – see later discussion. The term was introduced in the UK through the 2015 Modern Slavery Act.

of 'harm' should be broadly conceived from the outset of research. It is suggested that social stigma, and the possibility that research might reify this, be understood within research processes from conception. It is also suggested that the framing of trafficking research includes sensitivity towards regularly used negative terminology.

The meaning of 'harm' is debatable but in bioethics is thought of as physical harm to human beings. In social research this also includes physical, psychological, social, and economic damage involving 'psychological distress, discomfort, social disadvantage, invasion of privacy or infringement of rights' (Israel and Hay, 2006: 96). Sound safeguards are therefore needed (Carling, 2019). In human trafficking research potential harms can include exposing an individual to retaliation if details of data are not held confidentially and responsibly, exposing individuals to harm from family or community members if their potentially stigmatizing experiences are revealed, impacting on the dignity of individuals through a charitable (but patronizing) approach that deflects from their rights and entitlements, distress caused through unwarranted eliciting of disclosures, as well as potential harms towards those conducting research. Future harms might include causing harm to future migrants who are not trafficked if detailed techniques, locations, and routes are provided to authorities.

To explore ethics in the context of a research study, the chapter tracks the development of a 'living' Ethical Protocol, developed over two years between April 2017 and March 2019, for a project looking at human trafficking from Albania, Nigeria, and Vietnam to the UK.[3] The creation and development of this 'living' Ethical Protocol sought to develop a 'culture of ethics' across all stages of the study and across a research team spanning four countries in which people who had experienced trafficking and associated stakeholders were interviewed. It sought to embed an iterative and continuous process of ethical thinking and ethical practice. The Protocol's authors are acknowledged herein by level of contribution.[4] While this chapter does not

---

[3] As outlined in the 'Methodology' section, Albania, Nigeria, and Vietnam have consistently seen high numbers of referrals into the UK's National Referral Mechanism (NRM) and were chosen for this study on this basis – carried out in partnership with the International Organization for Migration (IOM) and funded by the Modern Slavery Innovation Fund (MSIF) at the UK Home Office.

[4] P. Hynes, V. Lenja, H.T. Tran, L. Gani-Yusuf, A. Gaxha, P. Priest, A. Olatunde, J. Dew, and P. Burland (unpublished, 2018) *'Vulnerability' to Human Trafficking: A Study of Vietnam, Albania, Nigeria and the UK – Ethical Protocol*, University of Bedfordshire and International Organization for Migration, Hanoi, Tirana, Lagos, and London. The end of the project and partnership arrangement meant no further work was carried out to publish this document.

contain a complete account of every detail of this unpublished Protocol, important aspects are included.

Initially, this mainly qualitative research drew on established ethical frameworks and guidance in existing literature, with reflection on their relevance to human trafficking research. Following a short section on the conceptual approach of the research and methodology, these established procedural ethics are outlined and the journey through ethics in practice is described. Thereafter ethical considerations relating specifically to human trafficking and the imperative to think beyond the principle of 'do no harm' that emerged out of the study are detailed. Specific mechanisms for resolving ongoing ethical issues during this research study are described. Finally, the wider context and overall framing of human trafficking/modern slavery is considered, focusing on broader structural, global governance, and ethical considerations around the use and impact of research into migration and human trafficking. In this section we raise a series of questions relating to ethics and the use of research that require further discussion among researchers.

Conceptual approaches: capturing the transnational and contextual nature of trafficking

Conceptually, this four-country study required an approach that avoided constructing migration as a problem which, as Anderson suggests, poses 'ethical and epistemological challenges to migration scholars' relating to 'political and methodological nationalism' (2019: 1). 'Methodological nationalism' relates to research which takes the nation state as the natural social and political form of the modern world, focusing on the engagement of individuals within one country and neglecting any simultaneous and continuing ties abroad (Wimmer and Glick Schiller, 2002: 302). Researchers may unconsciously define research topics within their own 'imagined communities' (Anderson, 1991) rather than transnationally and the tendency in migration studies to define issues, develop aims, conduct studies, and analyse data simultaneous to an 'uncritical embracing' of the nation state as the 'natural social and political form' which Anderson (2019) suggests in turn implicates scholars in nation state building processes (2019: 3). Methodological nationalism critiques the idea that nation states are such natural forms of organization, suggesting instead that a fuller theoretical perspective requires consideration of social networks and links with family, places of origin, and processes that cross borders between nation states (Wimmer and Glick Schiller, 2002; Vertovec, 2020).

This also reflects what Castles referred to as 'the tyranny of the national', with knowledge and understanding constructed at national level, suggested to be a key reason why the policies of states seem to have little success in preventing unwanted immigration and why migration policies ultimately fail (Castles, 2004; Geddes, 2005). There are also neglected social dynamics of the migratory process and factors linked to globalization and transnationalism to consider (Castles, 2004).

Policy, practice, and legislation on abuse, exploitation, and forced migration are regularly constructed within a paradigm of methodological nationalism (Anderson, 2019). While national logic is applied to migration control, the forces driving migration follow an international logic (Castles, 2003, 2004). Human trafficking studies that focus on transnational migration thus require conceptualization beyond the national, to encompass social networks and understandings that migration decisions are made by family/household networks to 'minimise risk and produce benefits for all' (Vertovec, 2020: 7; see also Boyd, 1989). The four-country study sought to incorporate such transnational conceptual linkage between countries of origin and the UK.

Use of an ecological model enabled contextual 'vulnerabilities' to be understood through situation-specific analysis (UNODC, 2013: 14). A recently devised IOM 'Determinants of Migrant Vulnerability' (DoMV) model allowed for disaggregation of individual-, family/household-, community-, and structural-level factors as contributors to human trafficking.

The DoMV model is akin to ecological models originally developed for child development and child maltreatment studies which place the child at the centre and explain the way in which the immediate and surrounding environment affects child development (Bronfenbrenner, 1979; further developed by Belsky, 1993). The ILO used such an ecological model in its first global report on child labour (2002). The ecological model has also been applied to a range of other issues, including youth violence (Krug et al, 2002), violence against women (Garcia-Moreno et al, 2015), violence against children (UNICEF, nd), sexual violence (Heise, 1998), and child sexual exploitation and abuse (Radford et al, 2015a,b; UNICEF, 2020). Most recently, contextual safeguarding approaches have grown out from this work (Barter, 2009; Firmin and Rayment-McHugh, 2020). As Firmin and Rayment-McHugh suggest, responses to child abuse that only target the individuals involved miss contextual factors such as 'peer relationships, school, neighborhood and online settings' highlighting relationships between individuals and context and the consequent need to 'consider context when seeking to prevent or respond to abuse' (2020: 230). This body of work has shifted thinking around differing forms of abuse and violence from single-cause models to more multifaceted models that emphasize interacting factors and such nested ecological models. These models also recognize that risk and protective factors may change over the life course.

Applying an ecological framework specifically to human trafficking, Zimmerman et al (2016) suggest it allows for larger contextual forces to be considered alongside attributes and behaviours of people who have experienced migration and labour exploitation. They also suggest that at the individual, family, and community levels there is a potential role for 'community migration norms' to be considered; that is, common practices around migration that influence and 'lend confidence' to individuals considering their migration options (Zimmerman et al, 2016: 17).

Methodology

The study looked at the causes of human trafficking within Albania, Nigeria, and Vietnam and support needs in the UK for these populations. These three countries have consistently been among the top referral countries for people who are denoted in the UK as 'potential victims'[5] when referred into the UK's National Referral Mechanism (NRM). For example, in the four years from 2014 to 2017, these countries represented 38 per cent of referrals (5,485 referrals out of a total of 14,556) to the UK's NRM. The study was funded by Phase 1 of the Modern Slavery Innovation Fund (MSIF) established by the UK Home Office in 2016 to support operational and research projects tackling the root causes of modern slavery. The research was conducted independently by a research team led by a UK-based university research team (University of Bedfordshire) and IOM team members in the four countries involved. Country-based expert researchers with extensive experience of human trafficking research were competitively recruited. An Expert Reference Group of academics, practitioners, and policy makers was convened to provide oversight, governance, ensure high academic standards, and ensure research integrity.

The associated literature review of 'grey' and peer-reviewed literature found a significant gap in empirical studies exploring the perspectives of those who had experienced trafficking-related exploitation (Brodie et al, 2019; see also Gozdziak et al, 2015). Geographically, it was found that existing literature on Albania, Nigeria, and Vietnam gave scant reference to the UK as a destination country with a far greater focus on trafficking accounts within their respective regions.

The study was grounded in a feminist approach that is rooted in a deep commitment to applied research and knowledge production based around seeking positive change for people (Ramazanoglu and Holland, 2002), meeting the imperative to improve the lives of the people concerned. To develop this stance further and ensure knowledge about each country was incorporated from the outset, Shared Learning Events (SLEs) were organized in Tirana

---

[5] These terms are contestable, with the OSCE (2004) referring to 'presumed victims' of trafficking when there are 'reasonable grounds' for considering that someone might have been trafficked.

(Albania), Hanoi (Vietnam), and Lagos (Nigeria) (Hynes et al, 2018a,,cb). These SLEs were designed to share what was already known about trafficking and explore contextual factors that led to trafficking in each country.

Following the appointment of local-expert researchers, the SLEs allowed for discussions of the project and ethical practice when conducting research across a broad range of practitioners.[6] While the idea around co-creation of the study had some limitations given funding structures and expectations around key milestones, working on the co-development of the 'living' Ethical Research Protocol at this point allowed for co-design of research questions, information sheets, and informed consent forms, each refined to suit each country context with ethics as a foregrounding principle. The development of the 'living' Protocol formed the basis for ongoing discussions with IOM partners and from this point onwards was continually updated to ensure the involvement of people in this research was ethically sound.

From the outset it was understood that children were not to be interviewed[7] but that there was a possibility that adults interviewed had experienced trafficking when they were children. It is also the case that, under Vietnamese law, a person is a child when (s)he is under 16 years of age and the transition to adulthood is 16 rather than 18 years (Barber and Nguyen, 2016). Interviews in Vietnam for this study were only conducted with those above 18 years. As such, age reckoning was an issue that researchers needed to pay attention to in relation to national versus international standards highlighting the need to think transnationally when devising research and research questions.[8]

A method of overcoming the sometimes-static view provided by ecological models related to the use of timelines to capture change over time in relation to human trafficking, broader migration, and key socio-economic and political events relating to processes of migration. In this sense Bronfenner's (1979) chronosystem added a useful dimension to ecological approaches – time – which captures all experiences individuals have lived through, such as major life transitions and historical events, change, and continuities in the environment. Research into migration is often ahistoric and the development of historic timelines during the SLEs addressed this by capturing key political events and accounts of past migrations.

A full account of the methodology and methods have been recounted elsewhere (Hynes et al, 2019) with the development of the 'living' Ethical

---

[6] In total 94 participants took part in SLEs, including representatives from a broad range of civil society, government agencies, law enforcement, health services, and academia.
[7] The decision to not include children was taken during days 2 and 3 or the SLEs independently in each country.
[8] Including taking into account the passing of each lunar year wherein newborns start at 1 year old, with the first year of life counted as 1 instead of zero. 'Cultural age' and 'calendar age' may therefore differ.

Protocol running alongside the refinement of aims, sampling strategy, questions around access, informed consent, and fieldwork. A total of 164 qualitative semi-structured interviews were conducted in the four countries involved with key informants (n=96) and adults who had experienced trafficking and/or exploitation (n=68). Of the 68 individuals with lived experience, 21 were Albanian, 18 Nigerian, and 29 Vietnamese, interviewed either in their countries of origin to which they had returned or in the UK. Qualitative data from SLEs and interviews were audio recorded, fully transcribed, and where necessary, translated into English. All transcripts and other source material were password protected and stored securely to avoid data falling into the wrong hands.

To manage the large amount of qualitative data generated, NVivo11 social sciences software was utilized to analyse the data. This introduced a limitation at the data-analysis stage to having all team members involved in coding as, beyond the logistics of analysis across four countries, licensing considerations became a barrier. The UK-based team coded data iteratively and thematically using a range of descriptive and analytic categories (Bryman, 2012). Coding thus broke down the data into component parts with constant comparison between the study aims, data, and findings as they emerged. This led to additional codes around country-specific issues, such as the position of Roma and 'Egyptian' groups as well as 'honour' codes in Albania, oath-taking and the prestige of migration to Europe in Nigeria, and the sale or mortgage of property to fund the cost of journeys in Vietnam. A final sense check was then conducted across team members in all four countries.

Developing a logic of comparison in this cross-national research was important. During the analysis stage this led to clearer understanding that social stigma spanned all four countries and was found to be a driver of human trafficking as well as an outcome (see later; Hynes et al, 2019). Negative terminology was also found in all four countries. Thinking beyond nationally based constructs and incorporating backstories was built into data analysis by developing themes that went beyond the individual country level. Thematic codes around journeys undertaken had pre-migration, transit, destination, and return to reflect the circular nature of migration.

Data analysis – utilizing IOM's DoMV model – also allowed for contextual and thematic analysis at individual, family/household, community, and structural levels. As can be seen in Figure 5.1, the DoMV levels were then disaggregated into specific risk and protective factors. Those shown here relate to the relative quantity and order of data generated during the study. For example, at the family/household level, gender roles and dynamics within the family were key and at the structural level migration management practices were mentioned most frequently.

Beyond these four levels, and between the individual and family/household levels, the importance of relations with peers emerged out of data analysis.

DEVELOPING A 'LIVING' ETHICAL PROTOCOL

Figure 5.1: IOM Determinants of Migrant Vulnerability Model with study annotations

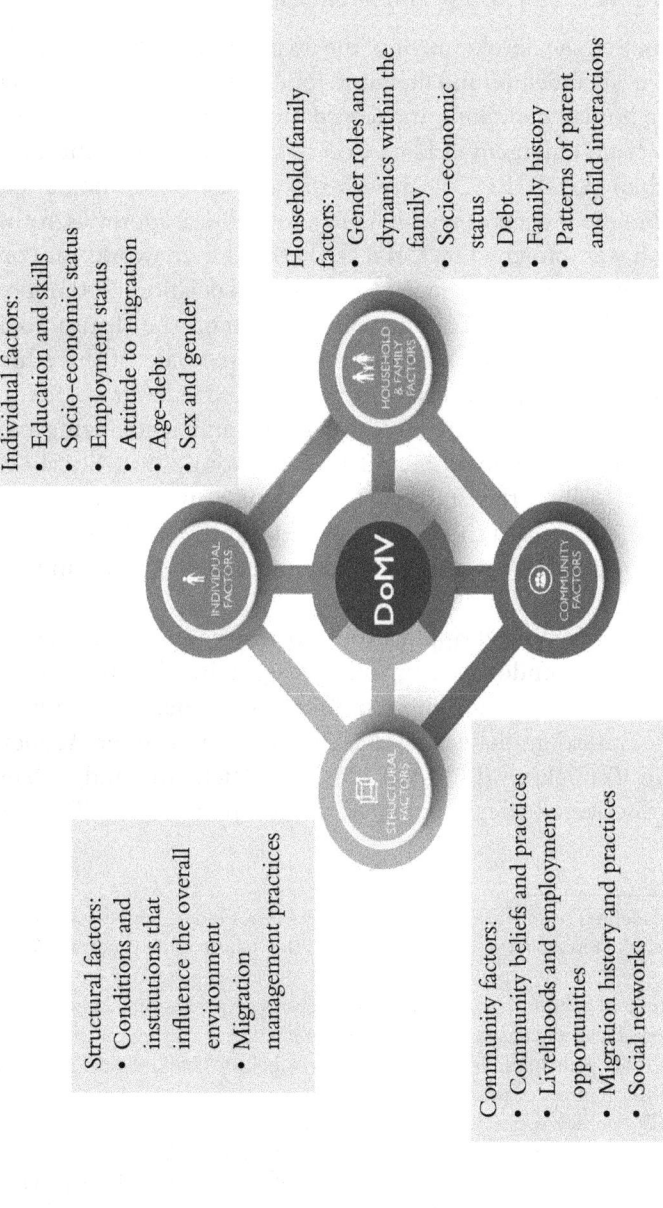

Individual factors:
- Education and skills
- Socio-economic status
- Employment status
- Attitude to migration
- Age-debt
- Sex and gender

Household/family factors:
- Gender roles and dynamics within the family
- Socio-economic status
- Debt
- Family history
- Patterns of parent and child interactions

Structural factors:
- Conditions and institutions that influence the overall environment
- Migration management practices

Community factors:
- Community beliefs and practices
- Livelihoods and employment opportunities
- Migration history and practices
- Social networks

Source: Reused with permission of the International Organization for Migration (IOM), *IOM Handbook on Protection and Assistance for Migrants Vulnerable to Violence, Exploitation and Abuse*

Peers included friends and associates who were influential in terms of function, and who had a transnational element, allowing for transnational social networks to be described.

Procedural ethics and existing ethical guidelines

From the outset, the development of the 'living' Ethical Protocol incorporated existing ethical guidelines and literature for conducting ethical social research, research on human trafficking and forced migration, as well as some reference to literature and emergent guidance on qualitative and quantitative research with children (UNICEF, 2012) with the aim of embedding a 'culture' of ethics within the process of research. To allow ethical approvals from the UK, the research was informed by UK-based ethical frameworks for conducting social science research, the Social Research Association (2003) intended to inform and advise on ethical practice in research,[9] the British Sociological Association (2017) intended to make members aware of the ethical issues that may arise during the research process and encourage them to take responsibility for their own ethical practice and recognizing conflicting interests of those involved,[10] and the Economic and Social Research Council (2010).[11] In this study, weighting of primary responsibilities was towards participants and those who carried out the field research, although ethical responsibilities towards the discipline, wider society, and the funder were considerations.

The research required applications to university-level research ethics committees, plus endorsement and oversight by national bodies within Albania and Nigeria, although no influence over methods or findings were involved.[12] Ethical guidelines by the United Nations Inter-Agency Project on Human Trafficking (UNIAP) (2008) in Vietnam[13] and in Vietnamese was only discovered after the end of the research project. There was little

---

[9] These guidelines detail ethical obligations to society, funders, employers, colleagues, and the subjects of research. For details, see: http://the-sra.org.uk/wp-content/uploads/ethics03.pdf

[10] This statement of ethical practices includes sections on professional integrity, relationships with research participants, the use of covert research, and clarifying obligations to funders and other key principles. For details, see: www.britsoc.co.uk/media/24310/bsa_statement_of_ethical_practice.pdf

[11] For details, see: www.esrc.ac.uk/funding/guidance-for-applicants/research-ethics/

[12] The National Agency for the Prohibition of Trafficking in Persons (NAPTIP) provided approval for the study in Nigeria and the Data Protection Commissioner provided approval for the study in Albania. No national oversight of research was required in Vietnam.

[13] United Nations Inter-Agency Project on Human Trafficking (2008) *Guide to Ethics and Human Rights in Counter-Trafficking: Ethical Standards for Counter-Trafficking Research and Programming*, UNIAP, Bangkok, Thailand.

available research detail of ethics in relation to human trafficking in and from Albania or Nigeria.

Beyond these nationally based frameworks, there are World Health Organization (WHO) ethical guidelines available on interviewing trafficked women (Zimmerman and Watts, 2003) – the *WHO Ethical and Safety Recommendations for Interviewing Trafficked Women*. These guidelines mirror the way human trafficking was invariably related to women at that time. These intended to address the adverse impacts that researchers and other investigators such as journalists could cause to women experiencing trafficking for sexual purposes. The WHO recommendations highlighted ten principles, beginning with 'do no harm' and how women should be treated as if the potential for 'harm' is extreme until there is evidence to the contrary. Further principles included how researchers should be prepared to provide information in a respondent's language about services and referral if requested and the need not to re-traumatize women through questions intended to provoke an emotionally charged response. Principle 10 went further, aligning with the imperative of being policy relevant: 'Put Information Collected to Good Use: Use information in a way that benefits an individual woman or that advances the development of good policies and interventions for trafficked women generally.' This echoed a recommendation in the WHO's ethical recommendations for research into domestic violence published a few years earlier. UNICEF (2003) also published a set of guidelines on how trafficked children should be protected in South East Europe, following the conflicts in former Yugoslavia. These were followed by a set of 'technical notes' for global reference (UNICEF 2006). This mentioned ethical principles, but there was no suggestion that researchers should pay attention to how findings were used by others.

Other relevant publications discuss these and other aspects of ethical conduct (Cwikel and Hoban, 2005; Duong, 2015; Siegel and Wildt, 2016).[14] There are also useful ethical guidelines available for conducting research on forced migration which prioritize relations with and responsibilities towards research participants through honouring trust, avoiding undue intrusion, and, as far as possible, involving people being studied in the planning and execution of research projects (Refugee Studies Centre, 2007). Since 2018, the International Association for the Study of Forced Migration (IASFM) has also produced a code of ethics for research in situations of forced migration

---

[14] Since the research was completed, the Nexus Institute has published a set of detailed advisory volumes on human trafficking research: see, for example, R. Surtees, A. Brunovskis, and L.S. Johnson (2019) *The Science (and Art) of Understanding Trafficking in Persons: Good Practice in TIP Data Collection*, Washington, DC: NEXUS Institute. Available from: https://nexusinstitute.net/publications/research-methods-and-ethics/

that recognizes unequal power relations, legal precariousness, and politicized research contexts in which research takes place (IASFM, 2018). Peer-reviewed papers on conducting research with refugees spell out principles of non-maleficence,[15] beneficence,[16] integrity, respect, autonomy, and justice (Mackenzie et al, 2007).

Although children were not part of this study, ethical guidelines and literature relating to children were discussed due to the possibility that adults being interviewed might have been children at the time they were trafficked and the fallibility of age assessment procedures in the UK. There are no internationally recommended ethical guidelines for research on violence against children[17] but there are useful interview guidelines available.[18] There is also a global momentum to improve the ethical treatment of children during research with useful guidelines being developed through the international Ethical Research Involving Children (ERIC) project (Graham et al, 2013).[19] These subject-specific guidelines added to the ethical frameworks outlined previously. Gilligan's (1977) 'ethics of care', with its emphasis beyond justice and rights but also stressing people's relationships with one another, was also highly relevant. Current gaps in ethical guidance include issues around boys and men who have experienced trafficking.

Beyond the WHO guidelines on interviewing women who had experienced trafficking and UNICEF's guidelines, research concerning other forms of exploitation, and the 'exploitation creep' over time discussed by Chuang (2014), has not been the subject of further ethical guidelines at global level. Given the elements of ambiguity surrounding terms used in the UN Trafficking Protocol (Gallagher, 2015a,b), these other forms of exploitation require further exploration, including looking at the ethics of conducting research into other forms of exploitation beyond sexual exploitation.

---

[15] The principle of non-maleficence relates to the expectation of minimizing risks of harm or discomfort to participants.

[16] The principle of beneficence relates to the obligation to maximize possible benefits while minimizing possible harm.

[17] Child Protection Monitoring and Evaluation Reference Group (2012) *Ethical Principles, Dilemmas and Risks in Collecting Data on Violence against Children: A Review of Available Literature*, UNICEF: New York.

[18] For example, see: B. McDonald and P. Rogers (2014) *Interviewing, Methodological Briefs: Impact Evaluation 12*, UNICEF Office of Research, Florence. Available from: https://www.unicef-irc.org/publications/pdf/brief_12_interviewing_eng.pdf [Accessed 14 May 2021].

[19] See also http://childethics.com/ – a joint initiative between UNICEF and ChildWatch – for further resources and guidelines.

From these guidelines, literature and known ethical challenges in research with vulnerable migrants (van Liempt and Bilger, 2012) plus an NSPCC[20] Ethical Protocol for work in contexts of child abuse and neglect (Radford et al, 2011), a range of pre-identified ethical considerations included:

- Risks and benefits of participating in the research.
- Minimizing 'harm' or potential distress to participants involved in the research and maximizing benefits.
- Negotiating 'informed consent' with participants and ensuring voluntary participation.
- Data protection, confidentiality, limits to confidentiality, and guarantees of anonymity.
- Child protection responsibilities if abuse, the threat or the potential of significant harm or abuse is disclosed, and reporting mechanisms to available services in Vietnam, Albania, and Nigeria and/or child protection services in the UK in such instances.
- Ensuring distress to research team members is minimized and their safety ensured.

There are also some recommended principles and guidelines on human rights and human trafficking, developed to provide rights-based policy guidance on prevention and protection in human trafficking cases, as well as facilitate the integration of human rights perspectives into anti-trafficking legislation and policy.[21]

From the outset it was known that this research fell into the University of Bedfordshire Research Ethics Committee's categorization of 'sensitive' research, defined around research topics considered in some way taboo, morally or legal ambiguous, and/or emotionally challenging. This is in line with DoCarmo's (2019) suggestion that research on trafficking intersects with other 'sensitive' domains such as gender, sexuality, sex work, and legal status. There is an expectation that some topics are considered inherently sensitive, such as child sexual abuse, rape, domestic violence, or sexual exploitation, with participants classed as 'vulnerable'. Under the Research Ethics Committee's categorization, young people working in cannabis farms would be considered 'vulnerable' and the research 'sensitive'. It is also expected that other topics are rendered sensitive by moral or political climates surrounding the activity being investigated with situations of 'vulnerability' created. People on migratory journeys can – rightly or wrongly – fall within both categorizations, dependent upon context and circumstances.

---

[20] National Society for the Prevention of Cruelty to Children (NSPCC), UK.
[21] For details, see: www.ohchr.org/documents/publications/commentary_human_trafficking_en.pdf [Accessed 14 May 2021].

Ethics in practice

As outlined earlier, ethical guidelines and literature had pre-identified a range of ethical practice which the 'living' Ethical Protocol was based upon and began to capture in a country-specific way. The pre-identified ethical issues will be discussed briefly and, thereafter, details of a mentoring process and creation of a Community of Practice are detailed. Country-specific issues, some of which are related to legacies of history, will conclude this section.

Pre-identified ethical considerations

The risks and benefits of participating in the research were clearly outlined in Information Sheets about the project relating to the desire to minimize 'harm' or distress to participants while maximizing the likely 'benefits' of the research. It was made clear that the research related to the causes, consequences, and support available for those with trafficking experiences, rather necessitating the recounting of traumatic experiences. In terms of minimizing 'harm' or potential distress to participants, up to and following initial ethical approvals, there were ongoing discussions about the balance of 'harm' and 'benefit' and the consequences of participation. A range of likely scenarios was discussed as a preparedness exercise during SLEs and prior to any interviews taking place. The potential for individual harm was explored through an informed consent process, detailed as follows. It was found that some participants wanted to disclose their accounts to researchers, particularly if they were at a point in their lives where they felt safe to do so and having someone 'bear witness' to their accounts were considered helpful even though the study did not require this. A fine line between these points must be trod by a researcher, with the recognition that ethical thinking should lead these decisions, as sharing accounts of causes and support structures might take individuals through associated abusive and exploitation memories.

Negotiating informed consent and ensuring voluntary participation was a major undertaking and the wording of Information Sheets and Informed Consent forms was debated, particularly around terms that did not translate easily.[22] These were also designed to be context-, age-, and language-appropriate. Informed consent considerations were slightly different in each country but broadly speaking followed the process outlined in Figure 5.2.

Informed consent was requested in stages and pre-discussions around criteria for involvement were part of this. For example, in Albania, first considerations around informed consent related to confining participation to those who already had access to or already receiving support and were already 'held' in some way

---

[22] For example, the term 'resilience' did not have a straightforward translation in Albania but was part of the DoMV risk and protective factors descriptors.

Figure 5.2: Stages of informed consent

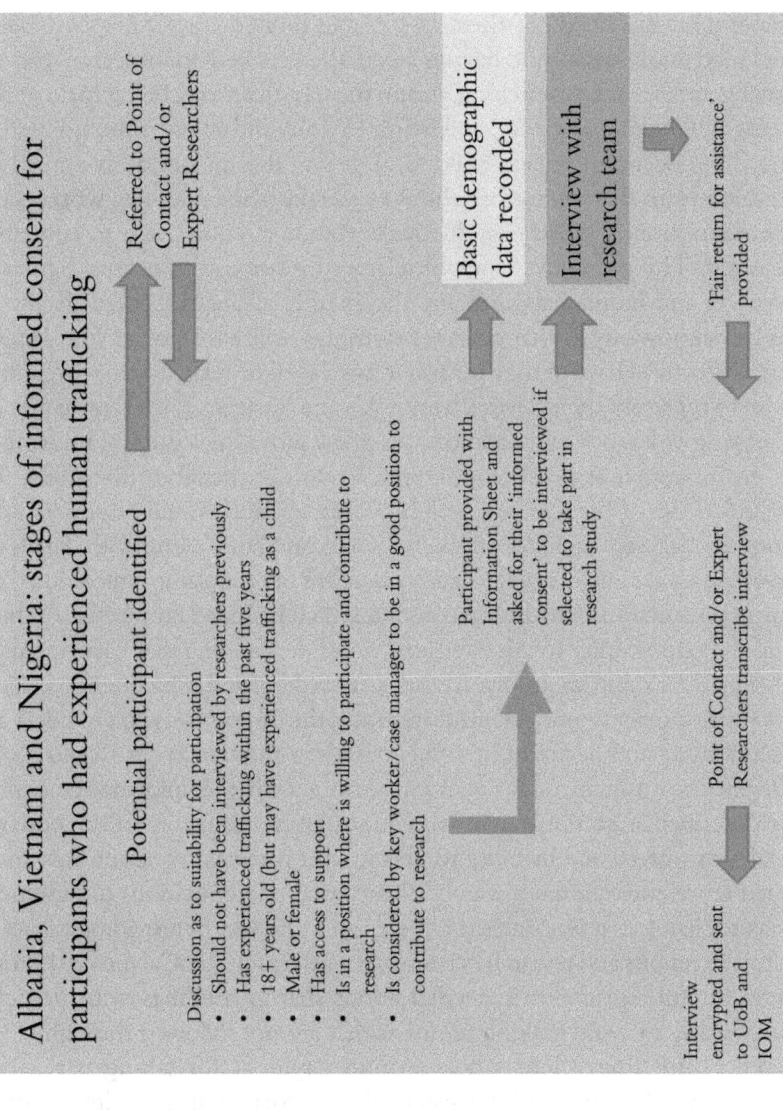

within service provision. Most knowledge about human trafficking is based on people who receive assistance rather than those who decline or avoid support (Brunovskis and Surtees, 2007; Surtees and Craggs, 2010; Tyldum, 2010; Surtees, 2014). The ethical consideration to minimize distress was considered more important in this instance. However, ethically sound research on avenues for safely sampling unidentified and/or unassisted 'victims' is warranted to understand the needs of these less visible individuals. Other considerations included individuals not having been interviewed for research previously, having experienced trafficking within the past five years, being male or female, being willing to participate, and being 18 years and above, although trafficking may have occurred during childhood. It was also unanimously agreed by the research team that discussions should also take place with key workers or case managers around whether individuals were in a 'good place' to contribute to research. This protective element relates to relationships of trust between key workers and individuals, and any therapeutic alliances formed. It also needs to be acknowledged that such relationships will have power imbalances and the protective element may be either misplaced or relate to how organizations wish to represent themselves (Brunovskis and Surtees, 2010; DoCarmo, 2019). Ensuring voluntary participation was a key aim when gaining informed, and as unambiguous as possible, consent. To do this, details of the study, funder, intended use of the research, and how information would be stored and kept confidential were included in the Information Sheets along with details of staff members and contact points for any concerns or complaints. Informed Consent forms contained a checklist for consent, which included knowledge of the study and the opportunity to ask questions; an understanding that participants could change their mind about involvement, recording, and subsequent transcription for further analysis; non-identification and the opportunity to provide a chosen pseudonym; and details of how the recording and transcripts would be stored. Despite these assurances, the question remained whether informed consent could be described as completely unambiguous given the nature of subsequent data analysis involved and inability to check with participants about how they had been represented in the research. There were also limitations of dissemination to participants as it was unclear if there was a safe way of providing copies of the ultimate reports and research briefings to participants. DoCarmo (2019) outlines how careful assessment is needed about sharing findings with participants, particularly to avoid making promises that are not followed through.

The sometimes silent taboo around payment for taking part – or the principle of 'fair return for assistance' – for participants resulted in different approaches in each country[23] based around a principle of reciprocity (Lammers, 2005; Israel and Hay, 2006; Refugee Studies Centre, 2007). For

---

[23] In Vietnam and Nigeria, money was considered most appropriate. In Albania, a small gift of toiletries was made.

example, reimbursement in Nigeria involved compensation in exchange for the time and help provided by participants for this study to take place, including costs of transportation and other logistical costs to attend interviews.

The Informed Consent checklist also included the limits of confidentiality should any information about serious abuse, exploitation, or the likelihood of someone being in danger of imminent or immediate harm be disclosed during interviews. Although the study did not interview children directly, researchers could have encountered situations wherein ethical dilemmas could arise. In the event of a disclosure of harm towards children, detailed steps were in place to respond with named points of contact. As Radford et al (2011) found in a study of child abuse in the UK, child protection responsibilities were found to legally override responsibilities for data protection. Available child protection mechanisms and services in Albania, Nigeria, and Vietnam were identified in advance.

Data protection laws in each country were discussed and made known,[24,25] as were IOM Data Protection procedures. During early discussions in Albania, it became clear that data protection is a particularly problematic area, with participants in the SLE stating this was the most important area to highlight in Information Sheets. It was also asserted that confidentiality needed to be guaranteed in respect of not sharing details with people in authority. Under Nigerian anti-trafficking law, victims of trafficking have their identities protected such that investigation, detection, evidence gathering, and interpretation of evidence are conducted in a manner that seeks to minimize intrusion into the personal histories of individuals. A particularly crucial message was about the need to anonymize identifiable details so that, in future, individuals and their family members were not discriminated against. This potential for future discrimination or harm at individual, family, or community levels related to marriage, seeking employment, and acceptance within the community.

Ensuring distress to research team members was minimized and guaranteeing their safety required attention. Debriefing of the research team involved creating a scaffold of regular debriefing sessions. These structures proved to be adequate most of the time but in need of improvement overall as the importance attached to them waxed and waned according to other priorities. This research was both sensitive and difficult and it was recognized that 'emotional labour' (Pearce et al, 2013: 44) was involved in the topic being researched.

A mentoring process was put in place to resolve ethical dilemmas as they arose, allowing for practice issues to be discussed informally, and, where

---

[24] In Albania this meant compliance with the law on Personal Data Protection, No. 9887, dated 10 March 2008 and in line with 95/46/EC Directive.

[25] In Vietnam this related to a range of legislation and Article 21 of the Final Constitution of the Republic of Vietnam, adopted in 2013.

necessary, debated within the research team. As ethical dilemmas began to emerge, they were recorded and logged during mentoring sessions held every three weeks and then discussed in team meetings between University of Bedfordshire (UoB) staff and IOM staff in London, and then via IOM offices in Albania, Nigeria, and Vietnam, which provided space for reflection and enhanced ethical practice.

The creation of a Community of Practice (CoP) across the four countries proved to be a lesson in being overly ambitious within the constraints of time and technology available. The two-year framework did not allow for sufficient time to consider practice in depth across different contexts and different time zones. Early attempts to do this were defeated by technology and the beginnings of a CoP only emerged towards the end of the study when teams met in person.

Country-specific considerations

During the SLEs, a range of country- and context-specific issues emerged that required adaptation of research tools and approaches. For example, in Nigeria, questions about sexuality were consciously omitted from research tools due to the criminalization of homosexuality within the country. To ensure a logic of comparison in the design of tools across the study, these questions were omitted across the full range of countries.

Fewer key informant interviews were conducted in Vietnam (n=9) due to the challenges around the sensitivity of the topic, a complicated procedure for getting permission from superiors to take part in research, plus an acknowledged limited knowledge of Vietnam to UK trafficking. A team-based, ethically informed decision to not seek further key informant interviews was therefore made.

Also in Vietnam, interviews with adults who had been to the UK were undertaken. However, no Vietnamese national in Vietnam who had returned from the UK was identified who was known to have been formally recognized as a victim of trafficking either through the UK NRM or within Vietnam, having been categorized in the UK as cases of irregular migration or human smuggling during their arrests, imprisonment, in some cases, and return. As such, none of the adults interviewed in Vietnam had any formal status as a 'victim' of trafficking. It was important for both the research team and IOM offices to acknowledge this lack of formal identification. Use of a Sampling Inclusion form,[26] designed to overcome this barrier, meant that

---

[26] A Sampling Inclusion form was devised to detail the form of exploitation experienced, set against ILO Operational Indicators of Trafficking in Human Beings and the 'act', 'means', and 'purpose' set out in the UN Trafficking Protocol.

all but one of the 21 interviewees were considered by the UK research team to have described experiences which would meet the definition of human trafficking under the UN Trafficking Protocol. This highlighted the need for better identification processes and also how inclusion of those not formally identified was necessary in practice.

In Albania a key focus was on people who had been trafficked to different destinations such as Italy and Greece rather than the UK and decisions were made around not highlighting aspects of individual cases that involved UK journeys.

In Nigeria, a key focus was on women and girls from Edo State to various European destinations, although a much broader range of states were reporting cases of trafficking. Also in Nigeria, the focus of most agencies and key informants (n=27) was at the time understandably on people returning from detention centres in Libya and other countries through EU-funded return programmes. This critical moment in responses to migration from Nigeria overshadowed work to understand Nigeria–UK linkages.

Ultimately, the 'living' Ethical Protocol devised to support this research provided direction for the research team. It was useful to detail ethical consideration prior to and during the research. Beyond fairly standard research and ethical considerations as outlined previously, it became clear that thinking about the 'do no harm' principle involved thinking about trafficking-specific issues of trust and mistrust, social stigma, and the use of negative terminology within current trafficking debates. These and other suggestions to go beyond 'do no harm' and standard research practice in human trafficking research are now outlined.

Beyond 'do no harm'

Moving on to what we found when considering research beyond 'do no harm' and the question of whether the principle of 'do no harm' is enough in human trafficking research, issues around social stigma and negative terminology emerged early in the study and became integral discussions on ethics and the approach to the research.

Being identified as a 'victim' of human trafficking can itself be a stigmatizing experience. This potential for 'harm' or 'risk' was identified during the SLEs and early enough to be a key consideration when interviews were being arranged. In Albania, social stigma and discrimination were outlined to be a key issue faced by 'victims' of trafficking who were often referred to as 'prostitutes' and other discriminatory labels. People working with this population in support roles were also described as being stigmatized. Support workers advised people who had experienced trafficking not to share personal details with others so they, and their children, could avoid being stigmatized. Rejection by family members was reported as being a common response to people who had experienced exploitation and/or human trafficking, as was the loss of employment and livelihood if this experience became known. Children who live in shelters were reportedly being asked to keep their addresses confidential, but teachers would sometimes identify children living in such accommodation. This stigma permeated other necessary entitlements, such as accommodation and health services. Social stigma and discrimination as a result of a trafficking experience were highly problematic. As one key informant in Albania succinctly recounted: "A victim of trafficking is not rehabilitated, she is stigmatized" (interview 91, key informant, Albania, June 2018).

Part of the explanation of this was around social stigma being made worse by poor media reporting that identifies 'victims' with their initials, names, ages, places of origin, and, in some cases, photographs. For example, in Albania, participants at the SLE described how press reports contained actual initials of 'victims' returning to Albania, such as 'AB', plus extensive family details, the initials of parents, and locations. With the relatively small population size combined with the strength of family ties and knowledge of the histories of other families, this was highly problematic for individuals, their families, and the wider community. Participants at the SLEs also outlined how, in Albania's history, there had been times when audio recording had occurred without a person's consent and the possibility of contemporary reticence around the use of recording devices. Primary and secondary data protection legislation was evident[27] but this remained a key consideration.

There was a similar focus on social stigma and discrimination in Vietnam with stigma around particular forms of exploitation, as well as returning without having made a financial 'success' of migration. As one Vietnamese man recounted after having been deported to Vietnam: "My neighbours despise me" (interview 59, Vietnam, April 2018). The neighbours he describes were aware he had returned home with little money and he was living with this stigma, plus further stigma around his divorce upon return, and he was planning to travel again. A similar scenario was found in Nigeria, with stigma directed at people who had lived abroad and had returned 'empty-handed' who were reportedly considered to be 'failures' and a disgrace to their families (see also Pennington and Balaram, 2013). A key risk of participation in research was therefore associated with this social stigma, which was often gendered in its manifestations. Civil society actors were aware of this and, as one civil society key informant suggested: "We need to raise awareness in these communities, that they are not spoiled people" (interview 159, key informant, Vietnam, February 2018).

---

[27] For example, Personal Data Protection, No. 9887, dated 10 March 2008, in line with 95/46/EC Directive.

In Nigeria, social stigma prior to trafficking was outlined in cases around the inability to conceive a child, unwanted pregnancies, abortion, as well as in cases of adoption. Family rejection was reported in cases of 'failed migration' and when return was somehow associated with shame or dishonour. As one interviewee outlined: "Even when I came back, they mocked me a lot. My family mostly. They say 'go away, you're not ashamed of yourself, you travelled, you didn't build a house, you didn't do anything and came back with shame'" (Favour, interview 18, Nigeria, July 2018).

Another interviewee discussed the stigma associated with sexual exploitation:

'You know in Nigeria, we still have the issue of "how will you marry Ashewo" [word in Yoruba for prostitute]. If they get to know that she was once a prostitute, there is stigma. But abroad, love can cover it and it is easy for that love to be blind. Nigeria love still has eyes.' (Interview 99, key informant, Nigeria, May 2018)

Negative terminology was found to be entrenched in discussions around human trafficking and perpetuated stigma and mistrust. A range of terms and associations have been revealed throughout this study – from people who have experienced trafficking being 'lazy', 'materialistic', and 'greedy'. As key informants in Nigeria outlined: "Because some of them it's greed ... the selfish and greedy search for greener pastures ..." (interview 103, key informant, Nigeria, June 2018). In Vietnam, the idea of people being 'lazy' and only interested in 'material wealth' and an 'easy life' was recurrent. During the SLE participants also recounted how children returning to Vietnam with their parents had been held up as 'bad examples' in classrooms due to the stigma associated with experiences of parents. Children had been obliged to tell their stories in class as a warning about the 'dangers' of migration.

Human trafficking and modern slavery were being described as a 'scourge' or a 'plague' on society. At the time of the study there was no specific mention of 'modern slavery' in Albania, with practitioners recounting the 'act', 'means', and 'purpose' of trafficking when this term was mentioned.

In Nigeria, there was reticence around use of the term 'modern slavery', in part as a result the history of slavery within the country. Indeed, when a different project financed by a UK government department with the title 'Stamping out slavery in Nigeria' was launched in 2019, staff in Nigeria renamed it 'Stamping out trafficking in Nigeria'. A key informant in the UK discussed how the term 'modern slavery' was not accepted by individuals who would not self-identify as either having 'been trafficked' or as being a 'modern slave': "I just think that modern slavery doesn't really encompass what really happens to the clients" (interview 130, key informant, UK, March 2018). Another linked this term with current debates and funding streams: "So with the women themselves we would never refer to modern slavery or trafficking and not hurt their feelings. We might say bad experience of something like that ... Yes. No-one wants a label like that. My goodness. But you know, for fundraising, we talk about it" (interview 131, key informant, UK, May 2018). A key informant working with young people in the UK also suggested the harmful effects of this label:

> 'I wasn't happy with them when it came along and I feel frustrated that it is something we've been forced into having to use. ... If you talk to young people, they don't relate to that term at all and don't like it, being called a modern slave, it's not a term anyone would want to describe themselves.' (Interview 132, key informant, UK, April 2018)

In addition to the pejorative terms and labels used, acronyms like 'VoT' (victim of trafficking) and 'PVoT' (potential victim of trafficking) permeated discussions. Conducting research in a way that attempted to avoid 'harm' meant engaging with the construction of these terms and acronyms in an attempt to ensure their potential stigmatizing effects were recognized but not reified during the research process. The question whether taking part in research itself could have the potential to stigmatize people simply by identifying them as 'trafficked' was keenly understood.

These questions around social stigma and terminology became key in thinking beyond the need to 'do no harm'. There was a need to go beyond 'do no harm' at the individual level to also engage in the socially constructed 'harms' surrounding this population. This led to framing enquiry around the agentic aspects of the everyday lives of people living with the impacts of stigmatizing labels and negative terminology. On reflection, and when carrying out future research, a key point of learning would be to dedicate more time, and earlier in the research, to discuss these issues around stigma and terminology. Additionally, the meaning of words used in context such as 'exploitation', 'community', 'resilience', and 'vulnerability' could themselves be fruitful areas for discussion and clarification.

Moving further towards the principle of beneficence[28] in research of maximizing possible benefits while minimizing possible harms, or 'doing good' in this type of research, Mackenzie et al (2007: 299–319) argue in relation to research with refugees:

> researchers should seeks ways to move beyond harm minimization as a standard for ethical research and recognize an obligation to design and

---

[28] A responsibility to do good.

conduct research projects that aim to bring about reciprocal benefits for refugee participants and/or communities.

This necessity of going beyond 'do no harm' – and 'doing good' – relates to Jacobsen and Landau's (2003b) policy relevance imperative and influencing legislation, policy, and practice. That research is both of a high academic standard and is policy relevant relates to the impact agenda for research in the UK. Such impact is now considered in the next section, on the context and wider construction of harm, the approach, framings, use, and impacts of research.

Context and wider considerations

Finally, we move on to what we need to consider when carrying out applied research that is rooted in a commitment to high standards of knowledge production but also policy relevance and to enable positive changes for people. The bigger picture and context in which research is being conducted is a key question – as is the impact research will have on policy, legislation, and/or practice.

Vertovec (2020) has given 'two cheers' to migration studies. The first of these 'cheers' is how this area has seen an increased number of academics involved, across a range of disciplines, producing more academic outputs and, as such, migration studies has become institutionalized. The second 'cheer' relates to how this has led to transformative concepts such as 'transnationalism' wherein it is recognized that migrants maintain extensive links with places of origin and create lives that combine origin and destination countries. The second 'cheer' also relates to progress on the avoidance of 'methodological nationalism' and the need to critique the nation state as a container of laws, people, and/or heritage – breaking free from doing research inside such containers by looking at processes, social networks, and how migration decisions are made by entire households and family networks rather than individuals (see also Chris O'Connell chapter in this volume).

The lack of a 'third cheer' for migration studies relates to impact, specifically the low level of impact that academic studies have had on public understanding or government policy in this area while good research is being done (Vertovec, 2020). Vertovec recognizes that research may have little impact on policy, with findings used selectively or, perhaps worse, disregarded. Vertovec also points to how media headlines remain misleading and how good research is still needed to provide correctives, counter these narratives with factual data, and improve understandings on the multiple causes of migration, beyond binary views.

Gallagher (2015a) has also given 'two cheers' for the UN Trafficking Protocol – outlining how the nature and pace of developments since

2000 would have been different without the impetus and foundation provided by the Protocol. Gallagher outlines how the inclusion of a definition of 'trafficking in persons' within this Protocol has provided a roadmap for change, placing trafficking firmly on the international political agenda. It is also considered that actions following the Protocol included intergovernmental bodies within and outside the UN system, along with civil society groups, who have become involved in researching the issue and initiating or supporting anti-trafficking efforts. Gallagher does then go on to suggest that there is a heavy burden of human rights violations associated with the Protocol – the 'collateral damage' detailed earlier in this chapter – which 'cast a shadow' (*sic*) (Gallagher, 2015a: 18) on the Protocol's achievements given the 'well-documented reality as measures taken in the name of addressing trafficking and related exploitation have been shown to have a highly adverse impact on individual rights and freedoms' (Gallagher, 2015a: 27–28).

This landscape of Vertovec's positives of increased academic focus and transformative concepts and Gallagher's positives of definition and increased understanding is set against the respective negatives of a lack of impact and potential for increased harms against individuals. While understanding and research throw light on the drivers and processes of migration and human trafficking, responses continue to be rooted outside of empirical enquiry. High-quality, good, and vigorous research is being carried out but this same research often has little impact.

Levy et al (2020) have documented the rise and growth of migration studies as a research field. It can be questioned where investigating the experience of people who were said to have been trafficked sits within migration studies and the need for historical analysis and interdisciplinary work that spans the social sciences, bringing in global systems theories that consider structural inequalities – studies on how 'race' and ethnicity are relevant to current debates. It can also be questioned where criminological accounts, economics, anthropology, demography, and other disciplines sit in relation to human trafficking within migration studies. In many ways it is not possible to separate research on human trafficking from research on other forms of migration, particularly where some element of forced migration is involved.

Certainly, describing and approaching human trafficking as a social problem to be solved through existing criminal justice approaches has proved to be inadequate. The way we frame human trafficking and now modern slavery is part of this bigger picture and is an ethical consideration in itself. Literature about human trafficking can locate this social 'problem' within the bodies and minds of people labelled as trafficked, rather than locating this within broader historical and contemporary understandings of the circumstances that contribute to movement, the sometimes oppressive social norms or violence that can create situations of 'vulnerability', or the simple need to migrate to fulfil family and community obligations.

It is long known that political contexts within which social research is conducted has historically concentrated on the 'poor' and/or 'vulnerable' and that to be described in these ways can itself be damaging, stigmatizing, and contribute to disempowerment (Dean, 1996: 4). Within research on human trafficking, we need to be asking what it might feel like to be approached on the basis of such constructed 'vulnerability' and associated lack of dignity. Historically, social research on a broad range of social issues has been conducted *on* rather than *with* participants, done *on* the relatively powerless *for* the relatively powerful with research processes often beyond the control of people (Dean, 1996: 32). There is a need to ensure human trafficking research moves beyond these known confines.

Impacts of the study were recorded in a final meeting of the research team and then again six months after the study ended. Impacts included raised awareness of the need to consider atypical 'victims' of human trafficking who may not fit dominant narratives, such as middle-aged men from Vietnam, a further focus on support services for boys and men, and, in Nigeria, focus on the mental health needs of people returned.

In studies around human trafficking, the use and impact of our research is an area for consideration when attempting to improve public understanding, policy, and practice. It is well known that categorizations and labels simplify the lived experiences of people and given to people who migrate rarely capture the complexities and nuances of the experience (Richmond, 1993; Zetter, 2007, 2018; Crawley and Skleparis, 2017). Should we be addressing how useful these categorizations and labels constructed by policy makers are in practice? In human trafficking debates, are the terms of 'victim' and 'survivor' suitable or dignified labels? What might we address in terms of the stigmatizing terminology regularly used in this arena?

What parts of an ecological model are focused upon – individual, family, community, or structural – is crucial as this affects how 'harms' are constructed in the context of existing social norms. These social norms may normalize violence and have unwritten rules that allow for husbands to discipline partners, boys to be considered more useful than girls, and other 'personal troubles' that are yet to become 'public issues', such as what happens in the home must stay in the home (Wright-Mills, 1973). Further, the concept of human trafficking was developed to fight crime between nation states and to hold individual criminals responsible, rather than acknowledge or modify structural issues.

The four-country study resulted in a report entitled 'Between Two Fires' which detailed some of these existing social norms and an individual participant asserting the need to move out of harmful and intolerable familial circumstances and their resistance to such social norms. It was found that several participants had resisted 'vulnerabilities' in the private sphere, attempting to resolve their own circumstances but had then encountered structural and exploitative circumstances. While this was a consistent account given by interviewees in different locations, these backstories remained largely untold and decontextualized. Individual accounts of 'vulnerability' can detract from the more structural issues then encountered, such as migration management and increased securitization of borders that constrain the abilities of people to move. Transnational realities of deterrence, hard borders, and containment of migration in regions of origin are part of the human trafficking experience, however removed they may feel to those who conduct research.

This study was about the UK as a destination country and the manifestation of these transnational realities; the 'hostile environment' policy adopted in the UK government meant that 'harm' needed to be understood broadly to incorporate contexts of hostility, disbelief, control, surveillance, and the need for some to travel under increasingly dangerous and difficult conditions to reach the UK. Many have asserted that framing the 'problem' of anti-trafficking does 'more harm than good' (LeBaron and Pliley, 2021: 3).

In light of the experience of using a 'living' Ethical Protocol and on the basis of two decades of research related to human trafficking since the introduction of the UN Trafficking Protocol, is it possible to draw conclusions about the obligations of researchers to go beyond the 'do no harm' principle and other conventional provisions of ethical protocols? The idea of such an ethical obligation is challenging both to apply and to monitor. It requires researchers to try to predict how individuals and institutions who are informed of their research findings might use them, whether law enforcement officials, policy makers, or practitioners. There is a need for strong ethical reflection on the use and dissemination of research findings. Questions remain around how aware of potential audiences researchers should be when publishing potentially sensitive findings and how 'harms' can be anticipated in such circumstances.

Along with the imperative to inform policy and practice, there is often a fear that findings might be misused in some way and, at worst, cause prejudice or stigma to people who have been trafficked and/or others who might migrate in the future (Dottridge, 2018). It is this complexity and heterogeneity that makes it undesirable to be prescriptive about ethical practice or to specify precisely how researchers should behave. Establishing a 'living' Ethical Protocol provided a valuable space for regular discussion about ethics and the possibility of recording such ethical dilemmas.

Conclusion

Social research with displaced populations can involve a 'dual imperative' to satisfy academic standards while ensuring policy and/or practice relevance. In this chapter it has been argued that there is also an imperative for 'harm' to be broadly conceived to include contexts within which people are moving from and to in human trafficking research.

When addressing human trafficking, 'harm' may emanate from policy, legislation, and global structures around migration management and it is therefore important that research does not replicate these harms or reify harmful perceptions about people who have experienced human trafficking. Locating the 'problem' of trafficking within the bodies and minds of people labelled and classified as trafficked rather than a broader understanding the circumstances that cause 'vulnerability' to trafficking needs careful consideration. Social stigma can ruin lives and avoidance of stigmatizing individuals through participation in research is key. Negative terminology, labelling, and the way trafficking is framed is part of this and needs to be challenged where necessary.

Given the policies of containment and deterrence developed around migration in recent decades, it is essential that working with and/or conducting research with those with lived experiences is carried out ethically. In contexts where power imbalances are built into responses, people can be rendered 'vulnerable' and it is vital to maintain a critical consciousness of these unequal power structures and legacies of the past. In other words, to study trafficking we have to study global migration management structures and the structural causes of 'vulnerability'. Questions around whether maintaining dignity in such contexts of disbelief are very relevant to responses to trafficking. It is challenging to consider 'what works' in a context of disbelief where people are not listened to or have their accounts believed, and simply 'bearing witness' may not be enough. Systemic issues and state policies that render people 'vulnerable' to exploitation, be it in source or destination countries, have to be factored into research into human trafficking. Such structural-level 'harms' and migration management regimes require more scrutiny. We also have to ask how we can fulfil the imperative that research improves the lives of those involved in such contexts.

The paradigm shift within migration studies towards 'transnationalism' that critiques the nation state as a natural container of social processes is relevant to human trafficking research. Understanding the backstories of individuals as well the barriers and gateways available to them also requires conscious and continuous ethical consideration. The topic of human trafficking demands that an ethical approach is undertaken and, if rights and dignity are to be at the heart of research into human trafficking, there is an imperative to conduct research ethically.

The 'living' Ethical Protocol was found to be a good way of building in these conceptual issues as well as key ethical principles and what emerged as trafficking-specific ethical questions in this study. It also allowed the research team to reflect and refine their practices during the lifetime of the study. As such, this contribution identifies key principles that could be replicated in future research on human trafficking, and it is suggested that researchers ask themselves similar questions before proceeding with research.

References

Anderson, B. (1991) *Imagined Communities*, London: Verso.

Anderson, B. (2019) 'New directions in migration studies: towards methodological de-nationalism', *Comparative Migration Studies*, 7(36): 1–13.

Barber, T. and Nguyen, H. (2016) 'Becoming adult by remaining a minor: reconfigurations of adulthood and wellbeing by young Vietnamese migrants in the UK', Becoming Adult Project, Working paper 3.

Barter, C., McCarry, M., Berridge, D. and Evans, K. (2009) *Partner Exploitation and Violence in Teenage Intimate Relationships*, Bristol and London: University of Bristol, School for Policy Studies and NSPCC.

Belsky, J. (1993) 'Etiology of child maltreatment: a developmental-ecological analysis', *Psychological Bulletin*, 114(3): 413–4. https://doi.org/10.1037/0033-2909.114.3.413

Bryman, A. (2012) *Social Research Methods*, Oxford: Oxford University Press.

Boyd, M. (1989) 'Family and personal networks in migration', *International Migration Review*, 23(3): 638–70.

Brodie, I., Spring, D., Hynes, P., Burland, P., Dew, J., Gani-Yusuf, L., Tan, H.T., Lenja, V. and Thurnham, A. (2019) *'Vulnerability' to Human Trafficking: A Study of Vietnam, Albania, Nigeria and the UK*, Geneva: IOM and University of Bedfordshire.

Bronfenbrenner, U. (1979) *The Ecology of Human Development*, Cambridge, MA: Harvard University Press.

Brunovskis, A. and Surtees, R. (2007) *Leaving the Past Behind? When Victims of Trafficking Decline Assistance*, Oslo; Vienna: Fafo AIS and NEXUS Institute.

Brunovskis, A. and Surtees, R. (2010) 'Untold stories: biases and selection effects in research with victims of trafficking for sexual exploitation', *International Migration*, 48(4).

Carling, J. (2019) *Research Ethics and Research Integrity*, MIGNEX Handbook, Chapter 4 (v1), Peace Research Institute, Oslo. Available from: www.mignex.org/d013

Castles, S. (2003) 'Towards a sociology of forced migration and social transformation', *Sociology*, 37(2): 13–34.

Castles, S. (2004) 'Why migration policies fail', *Ethnic and Racial Studies*, 27(2): 205–27.

Child Protection Monitoring and Evaluation Reference Group (2012) *Ethical Principles, Dilemmas and Risks in Collecting Data on Violence Against Children: A Review of Available Literature*, New York: UNICEF.

Chuang, J.A. (2014) 'Exploitation creep and the unmaking of human trafficking law', *American Journal of International Law*, 108(4): 609–49.

Crawley, C. and Skleparis, D. (2018) 'Refugees, migrants, neither, both: categorical fetishism and the politics of bounding in Europe's "migration crisis"', *Journal of Ethnic and Migration Studies*, 44(1): 48–64. doi: 10.1080/1369183X.2017.1348224

Cwikel, J. and Hoban, E. (2005) 'Contentious issues in research on trafficked women working in the sex industry: study design, ethics and methodology', *Journal of Sex Research*, 42(4): 306–16.

Dean, H. (1996) *Ethics and Social Policy Research*, Luton; London: University of Luton; Social Policy Association.

DoCarmo, T.E. (2019) 'Ethical considerations for studying human trafficking', in J. Winterdyk and J. Jones (eds) *The Palgrave International Handbook of Human Trafficking*, London: Palgrave.

Dottridge, M. (2001) *Is There Slavery in Sudan?*, London: Anti-Slavery International.

Dottridge, M. (2018) 'Collateral damage provoked by anti-trafficking measures', in R. Piotrowicz, C. Rijken, and B.H. Uhl (eds) *Routledge Handbook of Human Trafficking*, Abingdon; New York: Routledge

Duong, K.A. (2015) 'Doing human trafficking in research: reflections on ethical challenges', *Journal of Research in Gender Studies*, 2: 171–90.

Firmin, C. and Rayment-McHugh, S. (2020) 'Two roads, one destination: community and organizational mechanisms for contextualizing child abuse prevention in Australia and the UK', *International Journal on Child Maltreatment: Research, Policy and Practice*, 3: 229–47.

Gallagher, A.T. (2015a) 'Two cheers for the trafficking protocol', *Anti-Trafficking Review*, 4: 14–32.

Gallagher, A.T. (2015b) 'Exploitation in migration: unacceptable but inevitable', *Journal of International Affairs*, Spring/Summer 2015, 68(2): 55–74.

Garcia-Moreno, C., Zimmerman, C., Morris-Gehring, A., Heise, L., Amin, A., Abrahams, N., Montoya, O., Bhate-Deosthali, P., Kilonzo, N. and Watts, C. (2015) 'Addressing violence against women: a call to action', *Violence Against Women and Girls*, 385(9978): 1685–95.

Geddes, A. (2005) 'Chronicle of a crisis foretold: the politics of irregular migration, human trafficking and people smuggling in the UK', *British Journal of Politics and International Relations*, 7: 324–39.

Gilligan, C. (1977) 'In a different voice: women's conceptions of self and morality', *Harvard Educational Review*, 47(4): 481–517.

Global Alliance Against Traffic in Women (GAATW) (2007) *Collateral Damage: The Impact of Anti-Trafficking Measures on Human Rights around the World*, Bangkok, Thailand: GAATW.

Gozdziak, E.M., Graveline, G., Skippings, W. and Song, M. (2015) *Bibliography of Research-Based Literature on Human Trafficking: 2008–2014*, Washington, DC: Institute for the Study of International Migration.

Graham, A., Powell, M., Taylor, N., Anderson, D., and R. Fitzgerald (2013) *Ethical Research Involving Children*, Florence: UNICEF Innocenti Research Centre.

Heise, L.L. (1998) 'Violence against women: an integrated, ecological framework', *Violence Against Women*, 4(3): 262–90. doi: 10.1177/1077801298004003002

Hynes, P., Gani-Yusuf, L., Burland, P., Dew, J., Olatunde, A., Thurnham, A., Brodie, I., Spring, D. and Murray, F. (2018a) 'Vulnerability' to Human Trafficking: A Study of Viet Nam, Albania, Nigeria and the UK: Report of a Shared Learning Event held in Lagos, Nigeria, University of Bedfordshire and International Organization for Migration (IOM), London. Available from: https://www.beds.ac.uk/trafficking/nigeria

Hynes, P., Burland, P., Dew, J., Hong Thi Tran, Priest, P., Thurnham, A., Brodie, I., Spring, D. and Murray, F. (2018b) 'Vulnerability' to Human Trafficking: A Study of Viet Nam, Albania, Nigeria and the UK: Report of a Shared Learning Event in Hanoi, Viet Nam: 6–7 December 2017, University of Bedfordshire and International Organization for Migration (IOM), London. Available from: www.beds.ac.uk/trafficking/vietnam

Hynes, P., Burland, P., Dew, J., Lenja, V., Gaxha, A., Thurnham, A., Brodie, I., Spring, D. and Murray, F. (2018c) 'Vulnerability' to Human Trafficking: A Study of Viet Nam, Albania, Nigeria and the UK: Report of a Shared Learning Event in Tirana, Albania: 24–26 October 2017, University of Bedfordshire and International Organization for Migration (IOM), London. Available from: www.beds.ac.uk/trafficking/albania

Hynes, P., Burland, P., Thurnham, A., Dew, J., Gani-Yusuf, L., Lenja, V. and Hong Thi Tran with Olatunde, A. and Gaxha, A. (2019) 'Between Two Fires': Understanding Vulnerabilities and the Support Needs of People from Albania, Viet Nam and Nigeria who have experienced Human Trafficking into the UK, University of Bedfordshire and International Organization for Migration (IOM), London.

International Association for the Study of Forced Migration (2018) *Code of Ethics*, International Association for the Study of Forced Migration (IASFM).

ILO (2002) *A Future Without Child Labour*, Global Report under the Follow-up to the ILO Declaration on Fundamental Principles and Rights at Work, Geneva: International Labour Office.

Israel, M. and Hay, I. (2006) *Research Ethics for Social Scientists*, London; Thousand Oaks, CA; New Delhi: Sage.

Jacobsen, K. and Landau, L.B. (2003a) 'The dual imperative in refugee research: some methodological and ethical considerations in social science research on forced migration', *Disasters*, 27(3): 185–206.

Jacobsen, K. and Landau, L.B. (2003b) 'Researching refugees: some methodological and ethical considerations in social science and forced migration', Working Paper No. 90, *New Issues in Refugee Research*, Geneva: UNHCR.

Lammers, E. (2005) 'Refugees, asylum seekers and anthropologists: the taboo on giving', *Global Migration Perspectives*, Geneva: Global Commission on International Migration.

LeBaron, G. and Pliley, J.R. (2021) *Fighting Modern Slavery and Human Trafficking*, Cambridge: Cambridge University Press.

Levy, N., Pisarevskaya, A., and Scholten, P. (2020) 'Between fragmentation and institutionalisation: the rise of migration studies as a research field', *Comparative Migration Studies*, 8(24): 1–24.

Mackenzie, C., McDowell, C., and Pittaway, E. (2007) 'Beyond "do no harm": the challenge of constructing ethical relationships in refugee research', *Journal of Refugee Studies*, 20(2): 299–319.

McAdam, M., Surtees, R., and Johnson, L.S. (2019) *Legal and Ethical Issues in Data Collection on Trafficking in Persons*, Washington, DC: NEXUS Institute.

McDonald, B. and Rogers, P. (2014) *Interviewing, Methodological Briefs: Impact Evaluation 12*, Florence: UNICEF Innocenti Research Centre.

Morrison, J. (2002) *Human Smuggling and Trafficking*, Forced Migration Online, Oxford: University of Oxford.

Pearce, J., Hynes, P., and Bovarnick, S. (2013) *Trafficked Young People*, London; New York: Routledge.

Pennington, J. and Balaram, B. (2013) *Homecoming: Return and Reintegration and Irregular Migrants from Nigeria*, London: IPPR.

Radford, L., Allnock, D., and Hynes, P. (2015a) *Preventing and Responding to Child Sexual Abuse and Exploitation: Evidence Review*, New York: UNICEF.

Radford, L., Allnock, D., and Hynes, P. (2015b) *Promising Programmes to Prevent and Respond to Child Sexual Abuse and Exploitation*, New York: UNICEF.

Radford, L. et al (2011) *Child Abuse and Neglect in the UK Today*, London: NSPCC.

Ramazanoglu, C. and Holland, J. (2002) *Feminist Methodology Challenges and Choices*, London, Thousand Oaks and New Delhi: SAGE Publications.

Refugee Studies Centre (2007) 'Ethical guidelines for good research practice', *Refugee Survey Quarterly*, 24(3).

Siegel, D. and de Wildt, R. (eds) (2016) *Ethical Concerns in Research on Human Trafficking*, Switzerland: Springer.

Surtees, R. (2014) 'Another side of the story: challenges in research with unidentified and unassisted trafficking victims', in S. Yea and K. Pattana (eds) *Human Trafficking in Asia: Forcing Issues and Framing Agendas*, London: Routledge.

Surtees, R. and Craggs, S. (2010) *Beneath the Surface: Methodological Issues in Trafficking Research*, Washington, DC; Geneva: NEXUS Institute; IOM.

Tyldum, G. (2010) 'Limitations in research on human trafficking', *International Migration*, 48(5): 1–13.

United Nations Children's Fund (UNICEF) (2003) *Guidelines for Protection of the Rights of Children Victims Trafficking in Southeastern Europe* (amended and re-issued 2004), New York: UNICEF.

UNICEF (2006) *Guidelines on the Protection of Child Victims of Trafficking*, New York: UNICEF.

UNICEF (2012) *Ethical Principles, Dilemmas and Risks in Collecting Data on Violence Against Children: A Review of Available Literature*, New York: UNICEF.

UNICEF (2020) *Action to End Child Sexual Abuse and Exploitation: A Review of the Evidence*, New York: UNICEF.

United Nations Inter-Agency Project on Human Trafficking (2008) *Guide to Ethics and Human Rights in Counter-Trafficking: Ethical Standards for Counter-Trafficking Research and Programming*, Bangkok, Thailand: UNIAP.

United Nations Office on Drugs and Crime (2013) *Abuse of a Position of Vulnerability and Other 'Means' within the Definition of Trafficking in Persons*, New York: UNODC.

van Liempt, I. and Bilger, V. (2012) 'Ethical challenges in research with vulnerable migrants', in C. Vargas-Silva (ed) *Handbook of Research Methods in Migration*, Cheltenham, UK; Northampton, MA: Edward Elgar.

Vertovec, S. (2020) 'Two cheers for migration studies', *Comparative Migration Studies*, 8(38): 1–3.

Wimmer, A. and Glick Schiller, N. (2002) 'Methodological nationalism and beyond: nation-state building, migration and the social sciences', *Global Networks*, 2(4): 301–34.

Wright-Mills, C. (1973) *The Sociological Imagination*, London: Penguin.

Zetter, R. (2007) 'More labels, fewer refugees: remaking the refugee label in an era of globalization', *Journal of Refugee Studies*, 20(2): 172–92. doi: 10.1093/jrs/fem011

Zetter, R. (2018) 'Conceptualising forced displacement: praxis, scholarship and empirics', in A. Bloch and G. Dona (eds) *Forced Migration: Current Issues and Debates*, London: Routledge.

Zimmerman, C. and Watts, C. (2003) *WHO Ethical and Safety Recommendations for Interviewing Trafficked Women*, London: London School of Hygiene and Tropical Medicine and Daphne Programme of the European Commission.

Zimmerman, C., McAlpine, A., and Kiss, L. (2016) *Safer Labour Migration and Community-Based Prevention of Exploitation: The State of the Evidence for Programming*, London: The Freedom Fund & London School of Hygiene and Tropical Medicine.

6

Governing through Indicators: Structural Biases and Empirical Challenges in Indicator-Based Approaches to Anti-Trafficking Policy, Practice, and Research

Ieke de Vries and Ella Cockbain

Introduction

Research and policy around human trafficking builds upon an 'indicator culture' (Musto et al, 2020: 7). This culture has a tendency to simplify a complex problem such as human trafficking into quantifiable categories intended to make the concept easier for the wider public to understand, to help in identifying instances of human trafficking, or to underpin estimates of scale and other analyses. The increasing digitization of information has enabled and helped proliferate attempts to quantify human trafficking, breaking it down into tangible aspects, and guiding policy through measurable and seemingly objective standards (Merry and Conley, 2011; Merry, 2016). While various indicators shed at least partial light on the empirical realities of human trafficking, few if any apply universally to its numerous different and highly contextual manifestations. As such, the purpose of this chapter is to offer a critical reflection on the production and use of indicators.

Throughout this chapter, we use the term 'indicators' to refer broadly to any attempt to quantify and categorize information on human trafficking and anti-trafficking efforts. From this inclusive perspective, three main and interrelated types of indicators exist: namely, problem indicators, risk indicators, and performance indicators. Problem indicators have the purpose to facilitate the identification of human trafficking. For example, the United Nations Office on Drugs and Crime (hereafter, UNODC) produced an influential list of human trafficking indicators based on assumptions such as trafficked people 'believe that they must work against their will', 'show signs that their movements are being controlled', 'show fear or anxiety', or 'suffer injuries or impairments typical of certain jobs or control measures' (UNODC, nd). Such indicators have helped inform, among other things, investigative strategies such as approaches to evidence-gathering, 'spot the signs' awareness-raising campaigns (Andrijasevic and Anderson, 2009), and formal processes about whether officially to recognize someone as a 'trafficking victim'.[1]

In contrast to problem indicators, risk indicators are not so much used to detect human trafficking in real time but to determine its precedents. For example, and particularly in the US, research on commercial sexual exploitation of children (hereafter, CSEC) has indicated that prior childhood adversities such as abuse, neglect, and maltreatment put minors at increased risk of human trafficking (Choi, 2015; de Vries and Goggin, 2020). Consequently, national and local agencies commonly adopt concerns around these childhood adversities in screening and assessing individual cases. For example, the Comprehensive Human Trafficking Assessment by the Polaris Project and the National Human Trafficking Resource Center (NHTRC) in the US seek to examine concerns around CSEC through an extensive list of questions around the young people's prior childhood adversities and current behavioural and emotional concerns. Agencies at state or municipality level oftentimes capitalize on the same types of childhood concerns to assess risk to CSEC.[2]

In addition to indicators to detect human trafficking or flag vulnerability to human trafficking, 'performance indicators' (Kelley and Simmons, 2015: 55) routinely underpin comparative evaluations of anti-trafficking efforts worldwide. In particular, monitoring and ranking systems such as the US Government's Trafficking in Persons Report (TIP) integrate quantifiable information on components such as the number of victims identified, cases investigated, or people prosecuted in a given country to

---

[1] In their ongoing research into trafficking (see, for example, Cockbain and Bowers, 2019), Cockbain et al found that indicator checklists until recently formed part of the referral forms used to identify suspected victims of trafficking to the UK authorities and inform their decision making.

[2] See, for example, the Commercial Sexual Exploitation Identification Tool (CSE-IT) by the WestCoast Children's Clinic or the Human Trafficking Screening Tool (HTST) by the Florida Department of Children and Families and the Department of Juvenile Justice (see, for these and other examples, Appendix A in de Vries et al (2020b)).

rank its anti-trafficking efforts. Various other ranking systems exist both at global and regional levels (Boukli et al, this volume).

Although indicators might be useful, they are not neutral. Instead, their production and use are often inherently political, particularly given their development within a dominant anti-trafficking discourse that focuses overwhelmingly on the sexual exploitation of women and children (Farrell and Fahy, 2009; Charnysh et al, 2015; Cockbain et al, 2018). Against that background, we stress that our discussion of indicators is not an attempt to describe the empirical realities of human trafficking. Instead, we seek to examine the structural biases and significant empirical challenges in producing and using human trafficking indicators.

The remainder of this chapter is structured as follows. First, we begin with a general discussion of the aetiology of problem and performance indicators, drawing attention to these indicators' selectiveness, political biases, and skewness towards specific aspects of human trafficking. Second, we examine how indicators form the 'vocabulary of victimization' (Dunn, 2010: 6) through which boundaries around victimhood are articulated, producing false hierarchies of victimhood (Carrabine, 2004; Boukli and Renz, 2019) and influencing identification and access to support. Third, we reflect upon empirical challenges in developing human trafficking indicators, which tend to perpetuate such power imbalances and inequities. Fourth, we illustrate the combined biases in problem frames and empirical challenges through the example of the use of risk factors in the context of CSEC. We then conclude with some overall observations and considerations for future research, policy, and interventions.

The aetiology of problem, risk, and performance indicators

The drivers behind the development and proliferation of trafficking indicators can be understood through the concept of the 'seductions of quantification' of social problems more broadly (Merry, 2016, 2017). Merry (2016) coined this term to describe global efforts to collect quantifiable information on social phenomena and guide specific policies and interventions. Increasing technological opportunities to digitize information since the early 20th century have created unprecedented and globalized opportunities to collect, store, share, and present information on social phenomena. The Gross Domestic Product (hereafter GDP) is a prominent early example of an attempt to quantify economic performance, developed in the 1930s and long since established as a standardized, systematic, and internationally comparative measurement of national incomes (Merry, 2016). For international agencies such as the World Bank and the United Nations, indicators have become central building blocks to guide policies addressing global development, humanitarian problems, and human rights violations (Davis et al, 2012). When used to shape specific policies and interventions, these indicators are essentially a 'technology of governance' (Davis et al, 2012: 94) as they set the parameters of the presumed scale and nature of a given problem, thereby underpinning a specific set of responses.

The current wave of interest in human trafficking gained momentum from the 1990s onwards (Farrell and Fahy, 2009; Charnysh et al, 2015). Initially, however, there were 'as many different definitions of smuggling and trafficking as there are organizations and governments concerned with addressing this issue' (Aronowitz, 2001: 164). The watershed moment towards international consensus was the implementation of the United Nations Protocol to Prevent, Suppress and Punish Trafficking in Persons, especially Women and Children (hereafter, the Palermo Protocol) in 2000, which defined trafficking for the first time in international law (see further Table 1.1, this volume). This definition is notorious for its vagaries and consequent space for interpretation, linked in part to fierce and unresolved debate during its formulation around whether all commercial sexual activity should be defined as trafficking (Goździak and Vogel, 2020). The Palermo Protocol rallied governmental support for anti-trafficking and directly influenced numerous national laws and policies (Cockbain and Olver, 2019; Goździak and Vogel, 2020). Yet, considerable disparity persists in terms of how its definition is operationalized in national (or subnational) legislation (Farrell et al, 2010, 2014).

The Palermo Protocol's adoption also prompted a wave of national and international monitoring reports, using global indicators to operationalize and quantify human trafficking and responses thereto. Most notably, the US Department of State published its new Annual Trafficking in Persons (hereafter, TIP) report a year after the Palermo Protocol, the first in an ongoing annual series to evaluate governmental anti-trafficking efforts. These reports noticeably emphasize quantifiable information such as the number of victims identified and provided services (see further Boukli et al, this volume). Only those countries with a 'significant' number of victims – the parameters for which were unspecified – were included in the first TIP reports (US Department of State, 2001). The remit was later expanded to cover most countries, in recognition that absence of cases does not imply absence of the problem: countries with governments unable or unwilling to address human trafficking were being systematically excluded from the report (Merry, 2016). The TIP reports were followed by numerous other global reports from the UNODC, the EU, and other regional entities, which – until today – continue to be characterized by a drive to understand what proportion of victims have been identified from the larger dark figure: the unseen and unknown part of human trafficking (de Vries and Dettmeijer-Vermeulen, 2015; Farrell and de Vries, 2020).

Alongside indicators designed to describe and count human trafficking, global monitoring and evaluation reports frequently include quantitative ratings of state efforts to prevent, protect, and prosecute human trafficking (the 3P framework). Most obviously, the TIP reports use such 'performance indicators' (Kelley and Simmons, 2015: 55) to rank governmental anti-trafficking efforts. Yet the TIP reports – and indeed other such reports – have been criticized for their insufficient methodological clarity and rigour (Merry, 2016; Cockbain et al, 2018), as well as questionable underlying assumptions that perpetrate a 'politics of rescue' and erase the role of colonialism and its legacies in producing exploitation (McGrath and Watson, 2018: 25; Kempadoo and Shih, 2022). Scholars have therefore expressed concern about a hegemonic influence of the US on rankings (Beale, 2011) and global anti-trafficking efforts through the TIP reports (Merry and Conley, 2011; Chuang and Gallagher, 2012; Gallagher, 2012; Merry, 2016). A TIP ranking can have concrete ramifications, with US financial support for other countries' anti-trafficking efforts contingent on meeting minimum standards outlined in US federal legislation (or being deemed to be making significant efforts to do so). Similar monitoring arrangements exist on a regional level. For example, the Group of Experts on Action against Human Trafficking (GRETA) evaluates anti-trafficking efforts in member states of the EU through extensive questionnaires[3] that assess anti-trafficking efforts based on quantifiable information such as the number of identified victims, investigations, prosecutions, and broader anti-trafficking policies (Van Dijk and Klerx-Van Mierlo, 2014).

When used to monitor and assess countries' anti-trafficking efforts, performance indicators can alter responses both locally and globally. For example, Kelley and Simmons (2015) demonstrate a clear relationship between TIP report rankings and the criminalization of human trafficking in domestic legislation. They found that low-ranked countries were more likely to implement new anti-trafficking laws and regulations than those with higher rankings. This finding aligns with other research suggesting that transnational pressure may influence what types of responses political or social movement groups (Dai, 2007; Van Dijk and Klerx-Van Mierlo, 2014).

Although both problem and performance indicators can facilitate decision making and increase states' and organizations' accountability (Dai, 2007; Van Dijk and Klerx-Van Mierlo, 2014; Kelley and Simmons, 2015), there

---

[3] Parallels here can be drawn between the questionnaire approach adopted by GRETA and the questionnaires which shaped the League of Nations 'Summary of Annual Reports' 1922–45 which represent the most systematic and comprehensive review of trafficking conducted during the period focusing upon quantifiable information. See further E.A. Faulkner (2023) *The Trafficking of Children: International Law, Modern Slavery, and the Anti-Trafficking Machine*, [Online], Cham: Springer.

are two particularly salient issues to consider here. First, the development of indicators is rarely a neutral process. The selection and formulation of indicators, such as those underpinning the aforementioned reports, is politically driven and can all too easily reflect the unequal distribution of power, expertise, and capacity to respond (Kelley and Simmons, 2015; Merry, 2016). In the anti-trafficking arena, there is a clear Western hegemony wherein powerful actors with the means to produce knowledge and fund anti-trafficking efforts significantly influence problem definition and agenda setting (Kelley and Simmons, 2015: 56). For example, the TIP report system effectively positions the US as the world's arbiter of anti-trafficking activity, unilaterally assessing other countries against a Western-centric problem frame and metrics of success. These reports have been criticized therefore for the US' disproportionate influence in shaping global anti-trafficking efforts through performance-based indicators and rankings (Merry and Conley, 2011; Chuang and Gallagher, 2012; Gallagher, 2012; O'Connell Davidson, 2015; Merry, 2016).

Second, there are fundamental – arguably even insurmountable – challenges deriving from the fact that trafficking is not a clearly defined, neatly delineated and readily measurable issue (O'Connell Davidson, 2015). Selectivity around the boundary setting and application of indicators is further exemplified by how various states prominent in anti-trafficking such as Sweden and the Netherlands initially focused their national assessments *exclusively* on sex trafficking (Cockbain et al, 2018), systematically excluding the myriad other contexts in which people are trafficked for the exploitation of their bodies and labour. Another example is the way in which the state-sanctioned prison industrial complex is systematically excluded from much mainstream discourse around human trafficking and quantification exercises, despite prisons in countries such as the US, the UK, and elsewhere arguably constituting one of the foremost sites of labour exploitation (Smith and Hattery, 2008). As further discussed later, the production and use of indicators thus shape the focus on specific dimensions of human trafficking.

Indicators as the vocabulary of victimization within human trafficking discourse

Research examining human trafficking discourse has shown that the issue is currently typically understood and problematized through a crime frame that highlights criminal networks and nefarious offenders engaging in severe violence, particularly against women and children (Farrell and Fahy, 2009; Charnysh et al, 2015). Although the crime lens is not new and alternative perspectives on trafficking, such as lenses centring human rights violations and women's rights, persist (Farrell and Fahy, 2009; Charnysh et al, 2015), the crime and national security lens was amplified and consolidated by the

Palermo Protocol and its aftermath (Farrell and Fahy, 2009; Charnysh et al, 2015; Johnston et al, 2015; de Vries et al, 2020a). Being part of the UN Convention against Transnational Organized Crime, the Protocol explicitly frames human trafficking as a transnational security threat to be tackled primarily through crime control measures.

In foregrounding organized crime as the main driver of trafficking, this frame obscures not only individuals' human rights (Scarpa, 2020) but also broader questions about how states, businesses, and other powerful institutions can themselves create and exacerbate situations conducive to exploitation and trafficking through their policies and practices, such as restrictive migration regimes and limited labour rights and protections. The criminal justice frame thus turns the complex, multi-factorial issue of trafficking into something that influential actors can readily get behind without challenging their own self-interests or confronting broader historical, structural, and systemic issues (Farrell and Fahy, 2009; McGrath and Watson, 2018; Kenway, 2021). The Palermo Protocol also institutionalized the dominant focus on sex trafficking and reduced visibility of other victim groups by explicitly calling out 'women and children' in the title of the protocol (Gallagher, 2001; Scarpa, 2020).

The emphasis on these specific aspects of human trafficking – while filtering out other dimensions – is a clear example of a selective problem frame through which a complex issue is simplified and conceptualized in a way that a priori lends itself to certain solutions (Druckman, 2001). Yet problem frames, as we see all too clearly with trafficking, can be based on assumptions and claims about the nature or scale of an issue that do not necessarily reflect its empirical realities (Goffman, 1974; Drakulich, 2015). The problem frame around human trafficking is a social rather than empirical construction of the problem, shaped by mass media, political elites, and movement leaders (Farrell and Fahy, 2009; Gulati, 2011; Marchionni, 2012). In fact, even the 'empirical realities' of trafficking are elusive – since the construct is beset with vagaries, inconsistencies and discrepancies in its definition, conceptualization, and operationalization (O'Connell Davidson, 2015). In comparison with other problem frames on trafficking, research suggests that, in particular, the crime frame has gained strong cross-political appeal and broad public and political support for anti-trafficking efforts that align with readily available criminal justice system strategies (Farrell and Fahy, 2009; Broad, 2015; Charnysh et al, 2015; de Vries et al, 2020a). Moreover, various anti-trafficking efforts prioritize awareness raising and individualized interventions such as arrests or 'victim rescues' over broader structural and systemic change that could act on the conditions producing exploitation in the first place (Kenway, 2021).

Within these problem frames, the production of trafficking indicators thus reflects priorities on the political and social agenda. Specifically, problem and risk indicators typically reflect a central aim of identifying victims (or estimating their number), thereby providing the language for the 'social and political constructions of victimhood [that] lie at the heart of regulatory policies on sex trafficking' (Boukli and Renz, 2019: 71). Such indicator lists often reflect and perpetuate an iconic victim narrative that focuses on the younger, white, female victim of sexual exploitation experiencing extreme physical violence (Christie, 1986; Doezema, 2010; Srikantiah, 2007; Wilson and O'Brien, 2016). In doing so, these indicators purposefully and conveniently simplify a complex problem to facilitate decision making, calling for intervention in what are perceived as the worst situations.

However, by drawing attention to the more 'extreme' manifestations of human trafficking among specific populations, commonplace indicators typically provide a rather limited and non-inclusive 'vocabulary of victimization' (Dunn, 2010: 6). This vocabulary is based on sharp and false dichotomies of innocent versus blameworthy, vulnerable versus invulnerable, dignified versus undignified, and deserving versus undeserving of protection (Musto, 2009; Boukli and Renz, 2019). These dichotomies build into hierarchies of victimhood (Boukli and Renz, 2019; Carrabine, 2004), wherein the 'ideal victim' (Christie, 1986) is on top of the hierarchy representing the most innocent, traumatized and 'protection-worthy' victim (Elias, 1986; Srikantiah, 2007), while others are marginalized as less worthy of support. In idealizing innocence and casting trafficking victims as passive objects, the hierarchies of victimhood not only force victims to live up to an impossible ideal, but also downplay their agency and the decisions they take – often amid constrained circumstances and limited alternatives (Cockbain, 2018; Gerasimov and Breuil, 2021). Furthermore, these indicators overlook the considerable variation within and between different victims' experiences of trafficking in its various different forms (Cockbain and Bowers, 2019). Finally, the commonplace tendency to treat sex trafficking as the most 'egregious' form of trafficking further exceptionalizes and stigmatizes sexual labour (Smith and Mac, 2018) and rests on a rather puritanical assumption that sexual violence is automatically experienced as worse than numerous other violations.

Within these hierarchies of victimhood, anti-trafficking efforts can embody complex paradoxes. As an illustration, Boukli and Renz (2019) draw attention to how LGTBQ+[4] victims of trafficking both diverge from the iconic victim narrative – thus risking excluding them from identification and support – and are simultaneously often identified as 'victims of special interest' with 'exceptional' risk and 'extreme vulnerability' to trafficking, for example in recent US TIP reports. Those who develop and deploy trafficking indicators – often the authorities, but also non-governmental

---

[4] LGBTQ+ stands for lesbian, gay, bisexual, transgender, queer, and others.

organizations (NGOs) and others – play an important role in establishing and rearticulating the boundaries around victimhood. Even with the best of intentions, drawing attention to the real or presumed vulnerability of already marginalized groups raises several additional concerns (Boukli et al, this volume).

First, research has consistently shown that recognizing, or constructing, vulnerability within specific communities does not equal protection (Musto, 2016; Bryant-Davis and Tummala-Narra, 2017). For example, Musto's (2016) interview-based study with trans people involved in commercial sex (some of whom reported exploitation) documented experiences of victim-blaming among law enforcement and other professionals and a perceived differential response compared to their cis counterparts. The authors report how frontline responders assume a certain degree of willingness of trans people to engage in commercial sex, as a result of which they face a higher degree of criminalization for their involvement in commercial sex as opposed to cis women who are more likely to be identified through a victim-oriented approach (Musto, 2016). This victim-blaming and criminalization of behaviours in industries vulnerable to violence contradict concerns about the overrepresentation of trans people in the commercial sex industry, where research suggests they also experience more victimization and exposure to violence, coercion, and abuse (Fehrenbacher et al, 2020).

Second, identifying certain groups or communities as 'vulnerable' can increase their marginalization and stigmatization, while shifting the focus away from discrimination, inequality, and other structural problems that create vulnerabilities to trafficking in the first place (Bryant-Davis and Tummala-Narra, 2017). To illustrate, Bryant-Davis and Tummala-Narra (2017) draw attention to the colonial histories of sex trafficking, racial and ethnic stereotypes, and low-valued social roles used to justify a demand for certain labourers in industries where work is lowly paid and there is an increased risk to abuse, violence, and exploitation (Butler, 2015; Williamson, 2017). The same racialized and gendered inequalities that increase marginalization and vulnerability to exploitation can also introduce further biases into the identification and treatment of trafficked people from marginalized communities; for example, impeding their access to housing, legal aid, and victim support services (Bryant-Davis and Tummala-Narra, 2017).

Third, attempts to tackle trafficking by using risk indicators often rests on the premise that identification of victims requires their 'rescue'. However, not only is 'rescue' a last resort at best, but trafficked people are also not necessarily best served by encounters with the police, government agencies, and other authorities. For example, identification as a potential trafficking victim can put people with irregular migration status at risk of deportation, and temporary residence permits (where available at all) can be contingent on cooperating with criminal justice responses (Brunovskis and Skilbrei,

2016). Paradoxically, people driven into trafficking out of economic need can find themselves in an even worse financial situation post-escape or 'rescue'. As an illustration, crackdowns and shutdowns of venues potentially hosting sex or labour trafficking have been associated with, for example, undue criminalization, seizure of earnings, and punitive immigration responses, and could therefore leave already marginalized groups in financially worse situations, especially when no victim services or alternative means of employment are offered (Smith and Mac, 2018; de Vries and Farrell, 2022).

Taking into account such considerations, the issue is not just that problem frames are highly selective but that they maintain and exacerbate power imbalances and inequalities along the lines of – at least – race, ethnicity, class, and gender in how they influence where resources are deployed and who is identified as a victim and deemed worthy of support. The resultant indicators oversimplify a complex problem and provide a false sense of accuracy through quantifications that camouflage structural biases in the ideological, political, and societal considerations behind these lists (Merry, 2016; Musto et al, 2020).

Empirical challenges in developing human trafficking indicators

In addition to the power imbalances and inequities in the production of indicator lists, attempts to define human trafficking indicators face a significant number of empirical challenges. Most notably, many established lists of indicators lack an empirical basis. For example, the International Labour Organization's widely used trafficking problem indicators (ILO, 2009) were developed through the Delphi method of expert consultation. This method treats all participants' expertise as equivalent, creating a false sense of consensus and limited generalizability (Hsu and Sandford, 2007). Such lists of trafficking indicators can acquire the veneer of 'truth' when publicized uncritically, repeated frequently and adapted to further purposes by influential figures and organizations – especially since they are often presented as stand-alone 'fact', stripped of information as to how they were derived and the associated limitations and biases (Straatman, 2019). Furthermore, these widely used indicators encourage citizen surveillance, yet with little thought as to the potential harms associated with its selectiveness and under-profiling – or over-profiling – of already marginalized groups such as people of colour, migrants, and sex workers (Andrijasevic and Anderson, 2009; O'Connell Davidson, 2015; Kenway, 2021).

Although lists of indicators need empirical substantiation, there are significant empirical challenges in trying to develop and validate trafficking indicators. The first and arguably most fundamental challenge comes back to the amorphous conceptual boundaries of human trafficking and shifting understandings of its meaning (Spencer and Broad, 2012; O'Connell Davidson, 2015). Despite a lengthy political and societal history of interest in human trafficking (Lammasniemi, this volume), its criminalization in international and national legislation is still relatively new (Gallagher, 2011). Furthermore, there is substantial variation between and within countries in terms of the specific foci and parameters of their laws (Farrell et al, 2010, 2014). For example, 'sex trafficking' is constituted very differently in different places – in part reflecting differences in regulatory approaches towards commercial sex – and many countries have only legislated against trafficking across national borders (Cockbain, 2018). As such, the legislative landscape provides few answers as to what exactly is specific to human trafficking, that could in turn underpin the production of indicators.

Second, as much as broad and a diverse set of definitions fail to determine what activity is specific to human trafficking, the limited number of prosecutions due to recent legislation or limited priority and capacity provide insufficient empirical ground to determine the commonalities in human trafficking events (Farrell et al, 2010, 2014). Using official records as the only empirical base for determining human trafficking indicators means immediately encountering major stumbling blocks around external validity (that is, generalizability) since they offer only a partial picture (Hundman et al, 2018; Cockbain and Bowers, 2019; Cockbain et al, 2020). Biased indicators are an inevitability when relying too heavily on data that can be skewed by so many factors, including levels of funding, awareness, differences in ease-of-prosecution, expertise, capacity, and the prioritization of certain facets of human trafficking (Cockbain et al, 2020; Farrell and de Vries, 2020).

Third, human trafficking is a 'hard-to-observe' problem (de Vries and Radford, 2021) as it is difficult to detect due to its partially hidden nature (Tyldum and Brunovskis, 2005). Without knowing the size and characteristics of the populations involved, it is impossible to establish a reliable sampling frame through which to gather generalizable data for the production of indicators (Farrell and de Vries, 2020).

Fourth, human trafficking is also hard to observe because it interconnects with various other activities in both the illicit and licit space. For example, human trafficking intersects with various crime and social issues such as organized crime, partner violence, sexual violence, wage theft, labour law violations, or racism and discrimination (Brennan, 2014; Bryant-Davis and Tummala-Narra, 2017). It is also socially and economically embedded in 'regular' society as it intersects with ordinary legitimate activity through social networks, supply chains, and/or shared geographies (de Vries, 2019; Kenway, 2021). Many of the commonly used indicators – such as underpayment, lack of protective equipment, or working excessive hours – may not be unique representations of 'trafficking' conditions but rather common features of a low-wage and devalued labour market at large. This difficulty in isolating human trafficking indicators from 'ordinary' and not necessarily better working arrangements is illustrated by Volodko et al (2019) in their exploratory study into trafficking indicators in online job advertisements (n=430) aimed at Lithuanians seeking work abroad. They found that 98.4 per cent of all advertisements in their sample contained at least one of the UNODC's trafficking indicators, throwing into question the utility and practical value of at least some of these indicators (most notably the provision of accommodation) in this context. If some element of coercion, fraud, or force is a common feature of labour markets worldwide, general trafficking indicators may add little value. The influence of the dominant criminal justice lens on the choice of trafficking indicators also translates into a routine neglect of factors that are informative from a broader labour rights perspective, such as 'a lack of freedom to organise collectively' or 'the compulsion to find wage labor' (Vandergeest and Marschke, 2020: 304).

There is a growing body of research and practice that examines the online footprint of human trafficking in internet classifieds, reviews, or recruitment advertisements (Latonero, 2011; Venkatesh, 2011; Dank et al, 2014; Latonero et al, 2015; de Vries and Radford, 2021). There has also been a notable proliferation of new software claiming to predict human trafficking in digitized data sources (Dubrawski et al, 2015; Portnoff et al, 2017). However, as much as neither the presence nor the absence of indicators is clear evidence for human trafficking in offline environments, concerns around skewness and bias in official records multiply in online environments, for two reasons in particular. First, biases and empirical limitations associated with indicator-based approaches can apply to a larger scale in online environments due to the scalable nature of automated searches for online indicators of human trafficking. Many of these automated searches rely on official records as a presumed accurate reflection of human trafficking (a 'ground truth') or use well-established indicator lists with little concern for validity (de Vries and Radford, 2021; Kjellgren, 2022). For example, researchers have applied automated searches purportedly to identify sex trafficking based on the presence of pre-established keywords from UNODC's human trafficking indicator lists (Latonero, 2011; Kennedy, 2012; Ibanez and Suthers, 2014), with little to no recognition that these indicators may insufficiently distinguish the extremes of exploitation (that is, 'trafficking') from commercial sex in general. Much of the screening of the online environment for traces of human trafficking occurs without critically evaluating the relevance and meaning of human trafficking indicators in a specific online context (Musto et al, 2020; de Vries and Radford, 2021; Kjellgren, 2022).

Second, in general, even less is known about what human trafficking victimizations look like online as opposed to offline (Hundman et al, 2018). More generally, the online and automated tools to detect human trafficking are too often perceived as 'objective' and 'unproblematic' while all data analytics carry their own 'implicit, generally unexamined, assumptions' (Chan and Bennett Moses, 2016: 33). Critical and nuanced assessments of the online manifestations of different forms of human trafficking are in their infancy, while the use of technology to detect human trafficking in online environments or to evaluate anti-trafficking efforts continues to accelerate (Kjellgren, 2022).

Problem frames and empirical challenges in the use of risk factors: the case of commercial sexual exploitation and trafficking of children in the US

The conceptual and empirical challenges in the production and use of trafficking indicators are particularly evident in the context of commercial child sexual exploitation and child trafficking. This section illustrates these concerns with a particular focus on the US, where any CSEC is viewed as a form of human trafficking. Considerable work exists on developing risk indicators profiles to identify precedents to CSEC, particularly highlighting childhood adversities such as abuse and neglect, poverty, unstable family settings, homelessness, and running away to increased risk of CSEC. These and various other risk factors populate most screening and assessment instruments used in the US (de Vries et al, 2020b).

Like problem and performance indicators, however, risk factors can be highly selective and reflect structural and political biases. Research has also begun to suggest that these generic lists of risk factors fail to reflect the empirical variety in CSEC risk profiles. Overall, they are either too broad, whereby nearly all minors could be labelled as 'at risk', or too selective, when they create narrow risk profiles that perpetuate an iconic victim profile (Reid et al, 2019; de Vries et al, 2020b; Gerasimov and Breuil, 2021). For example, Reid and colleagues (2019) identified that the common emphasis on running away as a key risk factor for CSEC marks a large group of minors referred to the child welfare system as 'at risk to CSEC' while it fails to identify a significant population of exploited young people who have experienced different childhood adversities, mental health concerns, or had no obvious histories of childhood adversities at all. Other empirical work has also challenged the focus on extreme childhood adversities as the key risk factors by highlighting their limited explanatory value: the prevalence of childhood abuse among sexually exploited young people does not make childhood abuse a risk factor unique to CSEC, nor indeed do all those abused in childhood go on to suffer CSEC. Such childhood adversities may increase a general risk to CSEC – *and other victimizations*. The specific risk factors that put youth at immediate or proximal risk to CSEC can look different. For example, de Vries et al (2020b) highlight that among a group of minors that all had experienced some type of childhood adversity, the most decisive signals for CSEC were not covered by most screening and assessment instruments. These included, for example, risk items that speak to social networks and interactions through which vulnerability to CSEC may be induced and maintained. Such research emphasizes the potentially crucial role of broader socio-ecological environments in creating 'risk'. Yet, the dominant focus on individual and/or family-based risk factors tends to overlook how broader social, geographical, and structural conditions structures can affect vulnerability and exposure to child sexual exploitation and trafficking (Cockbain and Olver, 2019; Firmin, 2020). Moreover, the definitions of 'safety' and 'risk' cannot simply be replicated across culturally and economically different societies where Western idealized views of childhood may have limited relevance, particularly amid harsh socio-economic constraints.

In addition to the empirical pushback on both broadly or narrowly defined risk profiles, it is critical to reflect upon the value-ladenness inherent to notions of 'risk', 'risk prevention', and 'risk control' (Musto, 2016). The Palermo Protocol – and consequently much national law – proceeds from the premise that children are incapable of giving informed consent to activities constituted as exploitation (Cockbain and Olver, 2019; Vaughn, 2019). Moreover, the omission of the means element in relation to children under the Palermo Protocol (in lay terms) means that a 'child does not need to prove that threats, fraud or coercion have been used as they cannot consent to be trafficked' (Faulkner, 2023: 308). Children are thus positioned as both uniquely vulnerable to trafficking and lacking in any agency. Relatedly, much international and national legislation requires a lower burden of proof around what constitutes child sex trafficking, which arguably facilitates the identification of children as victims and provision of support. Yet, there are valid concerns that an uncritical quantification of risk among children simply takes agency and broader societal structures and problems out of the equation (Oude Breuil, 2008; Breuil, 2021; Gerasimov and Breuil, 2021).

In particular, while legislation gives the impression that children are universally determined to be without agency in decision making, with assumed vulnerability to trafficking, research has noted how risk judgements around trafficking and exploitation in its various forms can be highly racialized and gendered (Faulkner and Nyamutata, 2020). As has been more broadly mentioned in research on risk assessments in relation to other topics such as radicalization, assessing risk can simultaneously 'infantilize' and 'adultify' racially and ethnically marginalized children (Vaughn, 2019: 65–6). Infantilization is the perspective that children are vulnerable and need to be 'protected' against risky behaviours, crime, and victimization through measures of control. 'Adultification' can broadly be understood as the treatment of children as adults through a victim-blaming process wherein victimization is primarily understood through involvement in illicit acts and met with harsher measures of control (Vaughn, 2019; Davis, 2022). Similarly, in the context of child sexual exploitation, institutionalized measures of control are deployed to address both the 'infantilization' and 'adultification' of risk, which can further marginalize young people by maintaining and exacerbating a disconnect from socio-economic opportunities, such as education. Against that background, risk measurements can be deeply problematic when they trigger risk control measures that maintain and exacerbate a disconnect from socio-economic opportunities such as education and, may not have a child's best interests at heart, nor address broader factors that increase resiliency and safety (Vaughn, 2019: 66).

This complex relationality between risk and control also speaks to the paradox in anti-trafficking efforts mentioned earlier. On the one hand, risk instruments can set an unrealistically high threshold for victim identification by maintaining and perpetuating an iconic and popular victim profile based on stereotypes of exceptional vulnerability and extreme harms (Christie, 1986; Elias, 1986; Srikantiah, 2007). Few victims meet this profile and can thus be excluded from access to victim services and social justice (Srikantiah, 2007; Reid et al, 2019). On the other hand, risk instruments can be – and sometimes have been – misused as discriminatory tools to identify 'risky groups' that need continued 'protection' through substantial means of control (Musto, 2016; Vaughn, 2019). The racialized and gendered framing of marginalized groups as 'at risk', 'vulnerable', and 'in need of control' is troublesome as these labels maintain, rearticulate, and exacerbate the systematic inequalities embedded in anti-trafficking discourse (Bryant-Davis and Tummala-Narra, 2017; Boukli and Renz, 2019; Vaughn, 2019; Fehrenbacher et al, 2020).

Implications for policy, interventions, and further research

Given the considerations of this chapter, indicator-based approaches to policy, practice, and research addressing human trafficking require greater scrutiny, transparency, refinement, testing, and improvement. As indicators underpin anti-trafficking efforts, interventions, and research, it is vital that they are approached more critically, the assumptions and data behind them interrogated robustly, and the potential unintended (or intended) consequences of their use given proper attention. To this end, there needs to be more discussion on how research, policy, and practice can move towards a more comprehensive and inclusive understanding of human trafficking. Five central thoughts may guide these discussions.

First, greater consideration needs to be given to what exactly success means – or should mean – in evaluations of anti-trafficking policy and practice (see further Francis, this volume). Recognizing the structural and social embeddedness of human trafficking, there is an obvious need to transition from a narrow criminal justice lens that defines success in terms of offenders prosecuted and victims 'rescued' towards a more inclusive, rights-based approach that also incorporates general improvements to labour-market conditions, safe migration routes, and so forth. The major challenge here is that this approach requires a fundamental reconceptualization of human trafficking from a binary issue of 'trafficking versus not trafficking' towards seeing trafficking as part of a broader problem on a continuum of exploitation (Skrivankova, 2010) which runs from decent work conditions to the extremes of forced labour. This continuum can be dynamic in nature, as individuals shift in and out of more or less exploitative situations (O'Connell Davidson, 2015). Such a reframing of the problem, and thus the risk and responses, shifts focus away from individual-based factors towards paying greater attention to the structures and systems that produce exploitation.

Second, and more modestly, even without this core reconceptualization of human trafficking, the development of problem, risk, and performance indicators could very usefully incorporate more local sources of knowledge – in particular from the Global South. Doing so could help mitigate the hegemonic influence of the US and Western European countries in shaping global anti-trafficking efforts (Merry, 2016; McGrath and Watson, 2018).

Third, there is a clear need for greater awareness and explicit recognition of how stereotypes and prejudice within anti-trafficking discourse – as articulated through some indicator lists – can exacerbate trauma and cause other tangible harms. Recognizing the dangers of 'risk profiling' – both in terms of under-profiling and over-profiling – is critical to prevent further institutional revictimization and broaden identification and access to victim care and justice (Bryant-Davis and Tummala-Narra, 2017). Before indicators are deployed – be it for research or intervention purposes – there really ought to be explicit consideration around who might be harmed due to under- or over-profiling and how these harms could be better mitigated. Obvious examples here include 'spot the signs' campaigns that effectively profile and further stigmatize certain groups such as irregular migrants or sex workers (Kjellgren, 2022).

Fourth, given the many different manifestations of human trafficking and their impact on various populations, it seems fundamentally misguided to seek to universalize either problem or risk indicators across different forms of human trafficking, demographic groups, or geographical contexts. As such, methodological approaches to the production of indicators would benefit from seeking inductively to identify what is and drives human trafficking victimizations while accounting for temporal and contextual variation in individual, family-based, and socio-ecological factors associated with human trafficking experiences. This shift requires greater investment in and prioritization of this sort of bottom-up, context-specific, deeply nuanced approaches, which seem to be undervalued currently compared with top-down global estimates of scale based on supposedly 'one size fits all' indicators. Yet while the latter may yield headline-grabbing statistics, as we have shown they are all too often simplistic and based on scant data. On a linked note, studies at both the micro and meso level can be valuable in teasing out useful insights into the immediate socio-ecological contexts within trafficking victimizations occur: for example, how people's social networks or geographical activity may affect exposure and risk (Cockbain, 2018; Firmin, 2020; de Vries et al, 2020a).

Fifth, while computational approaches have an obvious appeal in an increasingly digitized world, it is vital to acknowledge that they are no silver bullet for detecting human trafficking and come with their own (often unspecified) assumptions, biases, and other limitations and risks (Chan and Bennett Moses, 2016; Musto, 2016; Volodko et al, 2019; Kjellgren, 2022). Thus, both the development and the deployment of such computational tools needs to be approached critically and the implications for the privacy and welfare of potentially affected groups needs to be explicitly considered alongside the anticipated and actual benefits derived for genuine victims of abuse. Technological advancements undoubtedly help sift, sort, and prioritize otherwise unmanageably large volumes of information and compare and contradict pre-existing notions on human trafficking, as long as one recognizes that online data or computational tools are not neutral, generalizable, unambiguous, or unchanging: more work is needed to understand what the online manifestations of human trafficking can look like (de Vries and Radford, 2021; Kjellgren, 2022).

Conclusion

In conclusion, this chapter sought to elaborate on why it is important to recognize and act upon the empirical challenges and biases in the production and use of human trafficking indicators. Future work could extend this approach to integrate 'indicators', or broader descriptions of human trafficking, in research and policy that are not based on false dichotomies around victimhood but allows for the variability and empirical complexity of human trafficking.

References

Andrijasevic, R., and Anderson, B. (2009) 'Anti-trafficking campaigns: Decent? Honest? Truthful?', *Feminist Review*, 92(1): 151–5.

Aronowitz, A.A. (2001) 'Smuggling and trafficking in human beings: the phenomenon, the markets that drive it and the organisations that promote it', *European Journal on Criminal Policy and Research*, 9(2): 163–95.

Beale, M. (2011) 'The trafficking in persons report: who is the United Nations to judge?', *Council on Hemispheric Affairs*. Available from: www.coha.org/the-trafficking-in-persons-report-who-is-the-united-states-to-judge/#sthash.GUWhx4Zq.dpuf

Boukli, A. and Renz, F. (2019) 'Deconstructing the lesbian, gay, bisexual, transgender victim of sex trafficking: harm, exceptionality and religion–sexuality tensions', *International Review of Victimology*, 25(1): 71–90.

Brennan, D. (2014). *Life Interrupted: Trafficking into Forced Labor into the United States*, Durham, NC: Duke University Press.

Breuil, B.O. (2021) '"Little rascals" or not-so-ideal victims: dealing with minors trafficked for exploitation in criminal activities in the Netherlands', *Anti-Trafficking Review*, 16: 86–103.

Broad, R. (2015) '"A vile and violent thing": female traffickers and the criminal justice response', *British Journal of Criminology*, 55(6): 1058–75.

Brunovskis, A. and Skilbrei, M.-L. (2016) 'Two birds with one stone? Implications of conditional assistance in victim protection and prosecution of traffickers', *Anti-Trafficking Review*, 6: 13–30.

Bryant-Davis, T. and Tummala-Narra, P. (2017) 'Cultural oppression and human trafficking: exploring the role of racism and ethnic bias', *Women and Therapy*, 40(1–2): 152–69.

Butler, C.N. (2015) 'The racial roots of human trafficking', *UCLA Law Review*, 62(1464): 1464–513.

Carrabine, E. (2004) *Power, Discourse, and Resistance: A Genealogy of the Strangeways Prison Riot*, Farnham: Ashgate.

Chan, J. and Bennett Moses, L. (2016) 'Is big data challenging criminology?', *Theoretical Criminology*, 20(1): 21–39.

Charnysh, V., Lloyd, P., and Simmons, B.A. (2015) 'Frames and consensus formation in international relations: the case of trafficking in persons', *European Journal of International Relations*, 21(2): 323–51.

Choi, K.R. (2015) 'Risk factors for domestic minor sex trafficking in the United States: a literature review', *Journal of Forensic Nursing*, 11(2): 66–76.

Christie, N. (1986) 'The ideal victim', in E.A. Fattah (ed.) *From Crime Policy to Victim Policy: Reorienting the Justice System*, London: Palgrave Macmillan, pp 17–30.

Chuang, J. and Gallagher, A.T. (2012) 'The use of indicators to measure government responses to human trafficking', in J. Chuang and A.T. Gallagher (eds) *Governance by Indicators: Global Power through Qualification and Ranking*, Oxford: Oxford Scholarship Online.

Cockbain, E. (2018) *Offender and Victim Networks in Human Trafficking*, Abingdon: Routledge.

Cockbain, E. and Bowers, K. (2019) 'Human trafficking for sex, labour and domestic servitude: how do key trafficking types compare and what are their predictors?', *Crime, Law and Social Change*, 72(1): 9–34.

Cockbain, E. and Olver, K. (2019) 'Child trafficking: characteristics, complexities, and challenges', in I. Bryce, W. Petherick and Y. Robinson (eds) *Child Abuse and Neglect: Forensic Issues in Evidence, Impact and Management*, Amsterdam: Elsevier, pp 95–116.

Cockbain, E., Bowers, K., and Dimitrova, G. (2018) 'Human trafficking for labour exploitation: the results of a two-phase systematic review mapping the European evidence base and synthesising key scientific research evidence', *Journal of Experimental Criminology*, 14(3): 319–60.

Cockbain, E. Bowers, K., and Vernon, L. (2020) 'Using law enforcement data in trafficking research', in J. Winterdyk and J. Jones (eds) *The Palgrave International Handbook of Human Trafficking*, New York: Palgrave Macmillan, pp 1709–32.

Dai, X. (2007) *International Institutions and National Policies*, Cambridge: Cambridge University Press.

Dank, M.L. et al (2014) *Estimating the Size and Structure of the Underground Commercial Sex Economy in Eight Major US Cities*, Urban Institute: Washington, DC.

Davis, J. (2022) *Adultification Bias within Child Protection and Safeguarding*, London: Her Majesty's Inspectorate of Probation.

Davis, K.E., Kingsbury, B., and Merry, S.E. (2012) 'Indicators as a technology of global governance', *Law and Society Review*, 46(1): 71–104.

de Vries, I. (2019) 'Connected to crime: an exploration of the nesting of labour trafficking and exploitation in legitimate markets', *British Journal of Criminology*, 59(1): 209–30.

de Vries, I. and Dettmeijer-Vermeulen, C. (2015) 'Extremely wanted: human trafficking statistics. What to do with the hodgepodge of numbers?', *Forum on Crime and Society*, 8: 15–36.

de Vries, I. and Farrell, A. (2022) 'Explaining the use of traditional law enforcement responses to human trafficking concerns in illicit massage businesses', *Justice Quarterly*, 40(3): 337–62.

de Vries, I. and Goggin, K.E. (2020) 'The impact of childhood abuse on the commercial sexual exploitation of youth: a systematic review and meta-analysis', *Trauma, Violence, and Abuse*, 21(5): 886–903.

de Vries, I. and Radford, J. (2021) 'Identifying online risk markers of hard-to-observe crimes through semi-inductive triangulation: the case of human trafficking in the United States', *British Journal of Criminology*, 62(3): 639–58.

de Vries, I., Farrell, A., Bouché, V., and Wittmer-Wolfe, D.E. (2020a) 'Crime frames and gender differences in the activation of crime concern and crime responses', *Journal of Criminal Justice*, 66: 101651.

de Vries, I., Kafafian, M., Goggin, K., Bouchard, E., Goldfarb, S., and Farrell, A. (2020b) 'Enhancing the identification of commercial sexual exploitation among a population of high-risk youths using predictive regularization models', *Child Maltreatment*, 25(3): 318–27.

Doezema, D.J. (2010) *Sex Slaves and Discourse Masters: The Construction of Trafficking*, London: Zed Books.

Drakulich, K.M. (2015) 'Explicit and hidden racial bias in the framing of social problems', *Social Problems*, 62(3): 391–418.

Druckman, J.N. (2001) 'On the limits of framing effects: who can frame?', *Journal of Politics*, 63(4): 1041–66.

Dubrawski, A., Miller, K., Barnes, M., Boecking, B., and Kennedy, E. (2015) 'Leveraging publicly available data to discern patterns of human-trafficking activity', *Journal of Human Trafficking*, 1(1): 65–85.

Dunn, J.L. (2010) 'Vocabularies of victimization: toward explaining the deviant victim', *Deviant Behavior*, 31(2): 159–83.

Elias, R. (1986) 'The politics of victimization: victims, victimology, and human rights', *OUP Catalogue*, Oxford: Oxford University Press.

Farrell, A. and de Vries, I. (2020) 'Measuring the nature and prevalence of human trafficking', in J. Winterdyk and J. Jones (eds) *The Palgrave International Handbook of Human Trafficking*, New York: Palgrave Macmillan, pp 147–62.

Farrell, A. and Fahy, S. (2009) 'The problem of human trafficking in the US: public frames and policy responses', *Journal of Criminal Justice*, 37(6): 617–26.

Farrell, A., McDevitt, J., and Fahy, S. (2010) 'Where are all the victims?: understanding the determinants of official identification of human trafficking incidents', *Criminology and Public Policy*, 9(2): 201–33.

Farrell, A., Owens, C., and McDevitt, J. (2014) 'New laws but few cases: understanding the challenges to the investigation and prosecution of human trafficking cases', *Crime, Law and Social Change*, 61(2): 139–68.

Faulkner, E.A. (2023) *The Trafficking of Children: International Law, Modern Slavery, and the Anti-Trafficking Machine*, [Online] Cham: Springer.

Faulkner, E.A. and Nyamutata, C. (2020) 'The decolonisation of children's rights and the colonial contours of the Convention on the Rights of the Child', *International Journal of Children's Rights*, 28(1): 66–88.

Fehrenbacher, A.E. et al (2020) 'Transgender people and human trafficking: intersectional exclusion of transgender migrants and people of color from anti-trafficking protection in the United States', *Journal of Human Trafficking*, 6(2): 182–94.

Firmin, C. (2020) *Contextual Safeguarding and Child Protection: Rewriting the Rules*, Milton Park: Taylor & Francis.

Gallagher, A. (2001) 'Human rights and the new UN protocols on trafficking and migrant smuggling: a preliminary analysis', *Human Rights Quarterly*, 23: 975–1004.

Gallagher, A. (2011) 'Improving the effectiveness of the international law of human trafficking: a vision for the future of the US Trafficking in Persons reports', *Human Rights Review*, 12(3): 381–400.

Gallagher, A. (2012) 'Human rights and human trafficking: a reflection on the influence and evolution of the US Trafficking in Persons reports', in *From Human Trafficking to Human Rights*, Philadelphia, PA: University of Pennsylvania Press, pp 172–94.

Gerasimov, B. and Breuil, B.O. (2021) 'Trafficking in minors: confronting complex realities, structural inequalities, and agency', *Anti-Trafficking Review*, 16: 1–9.

Goffman, E. (1974) *Frame Analysis: An Essay on the Organization of Experience*, Cambridge, MA: Harvard University Press.

Goździak, E.M. and Vogel, K.M. (2020) 'Palermo at 20: a retrospective and prospective', *Journal of Human Trafficking*, 6(2): 109–18.

Gulati, G.J. (2011) 'News frames and story triggers in the media's coverage of human trafficking', *Human Rights Review*, 12(3): 363–79.

Hsu, C.-C. and Sandford, B.A. (2007) 'The Delphi technique: making sense of consensus', *Practical Assessment, Research, and Evaluation*, 12(1): 10.

Hundman, K., Gowda, T., Kejriwal, M., and Boecking, B. (2018) *Always Lurking: Understanding and Mitigating Bias in Online Human Trafficking Detection*. Proceedings of the 2018 AAAI/ACM Conference on AI, Ethics and Society, pp 137–43.

Ibanez, M. and Suthers, D.D. (2014) *Detection of Domestic Human Trafficking Indicators and Movement Trends Using Content Available on Open Internet Sources*, 2014 47th Hawaii International Conference on System Sciences, 1556–65.

ILO (International Labour Organization) (2009) *Operational Indicators of Trafficking in Human Beings*, Geneva: ILO.

Johnston, A., Friedman, B., and Sobel, M. (2015) 'Framing an emerging issue: how US print and broadcast news media covered sex trafficking, 2008–2012', *Journal of Human Trafficking*, 1(3): 235–54.

Kelley, J.G. and Simmons, B.A. (2015) 'Politics by number: indicators as social pressure in international relations', *American Journal of Political Science*, 59(1): 55–70.

Kempadoo, K. and Shih, E. (2022) *White Supremacy, Racism and the Coloniality of Anti-Trafficking*, New York: Routledge.

Kennedy, E. (2012) 'Predictive patterns of sex trafficking online', Dietrich College Honours Theses, Carnegie Mellon University. Available from: https://kilthub.cmu.edu/ndownloader/files/12212117 [Accessed 21 December 2023].

Kenway, E. (2021) *The Truth about Modern Slavery*, London: Pluto Press.

Kjellgren, R. (2022) 'Good tech, bad tech: policing sex trafficking with Big Data', *International Journal for Crime, Justice and Social Democracy*, 11(1): 149–66.

Latonero, M. (2011) *Human Trafficking Online: The Role of Social Networking Sites and Online Classifieds*, Research Series: September 2011, Los Angeles, CA: University of Southern California.

Latonero, M., Wex, B., and Dank, M. (2015) 'Technology and labor trafficking in a network society: general overview, emerging innovations, and Philippines case study', *Emerging Innovations, and Philippines Case Study* (6 March 2015).

Marchionni, D.M. (2012) 'International human trafficking: an agenda-building analysis of the US and British press', *International Communication Gazette*, 74(2): 145–58.

McGrath, S. and Watson, S. (2018) 'Anti-slavery as development: a global politics of rescue', *Geoforum*, 93: 22–31.

Merry, S.E. (2016) *The Seductions of Quantification: Measuring Human Rights, Gender Violence, and Sex Trafficking*, Chicago: University of Chicago Press

Merry, S.E. (2017) 'Counting the uncountable: constructing trafficking through measurement', in P. Kotiswaran (ed) *Revisiting the Law and Governance of Trafficking, Forced Labor and Modern Slavery*, Cambridge: Cambridge University Press.

Merry, S.E. and Conley, J.M. (2011) 'Measuring the world: indicators, human rights, and global governance', *Current Anthropology*, 52(S3).

Musto, J. (2009) 'What's in a name?: conflations and contradictions in contemporary US discourses of human trafficking', *Women's Studies International Forum*, 32(4): 281–7.

Musto, J. (2016) *Control and Protect: Collaboration, Carceral Protection, and Domestic Sex Trafficking in the United States*, Berkeley, CA: University of California Press.

Musto, J., Thakor, M., and Gerasimov, B. (2020) 'Between hope and hype: critical evaluations of technology's role in anti-trafficking', *Anti-Trafficking Review*, 14: 1–14.

O'Connell Davidson, J. (2015) *Modern Slavery: The Margins of Freedom*, Springer.

Oude Breuil, B.C. (2008) '"Precious children in a heartless world"? The complexities of child trafficking in Marseille', *Children and Society*, 22(3): 223–34.

Portnoff, R.S., Huang, D.Y., Doerfler, P., Afroz, S., and McCoy, D. (2017) *Backpage and Bitcoin: Uncovering Human Traffickers*, KDD '17: Proceedings of the 23rd ACM SIGKDD International Conference on Knowledge Discovery and Data Mining, pp 1595–604.

Reid, J.A., Baglivio, M.T., Piquero, A.R., Greenwald, M.A., and Epps, N. (2019) 'No youth left behind to human trafficking: exploring profiles of risk', *American Journal of Orthopsychiatry*, 89(6): 704.

Scarpa, S. (2020) 'UN Palermo trafficking protocol eighteen years on: a critique', in J. Winterdyk and J. Jones (eds) *The Palgrave International Handbook of Human Trafficking*, New York: Palgrave Macmillan, pp 623–40.

Skrivankova, K. (2010) *Between Decent Work and Forced Labour: Examining the Continuum of Exploitation*, York: Joseph Rowntree Foundation.

Smith, E. and Hattery, A.J. (2008) 'Incarceration: a tool for racial segregation and labor exploitation', *Race, Gender and Class*, 15(1/2): 79–97.

Smith, M. and Mac, J. (2018) *Revolting Prostitutes: The Fight for Sex Workers' Rights*, London: Verso.

Spencer, J. and Broad, R. (2012) 'The "groundhog day" of the human trafficking for sexual exploitation debate: new directions in criminological understanding', *European Journal on Criminal Policy and Research*, 18(3): 269–81.

Srikantiah, J. (2007) 'Perfect victims and real survivors: the iconic victim in domestic human trafficking law', *Immigration and Nationality Law Review*, 28: 741–98.

Straatman, J. (2019) 'European labour trafficking victims in the United Kingdom: a quantitative analysis of the indicators', MSc Dissertation, London: UCL.

Tyldum, G. and Brunovskis, A. (2005) 'Describing the unobserved: methodological challenges in empirical studies on human trafficking', *International Migration*, 43(1–2): 17–34.

UNODC (nd) *Human Trafficking Indicators*. Available from: www.unodc.org/pdf/HT_indicators_E_LOWRES.pdf [Accessed 21 December 2023].

US Department of State (2001) *Trafficking in Persons Report*. Available from: https://2009-2017.state.gov/j/tip/rls/tiprpt/2001/3929.htm [Accessed 21 December 2023].

Van Dijk, J. and Klerx-Van Mierlo, F. (2014) 'Quantitative indices for anti-human trafficking policies: based on reports of the US State Department and the Council of Europe', *Crime, Law and Social Change*, 61(2): 229–50.

Vandergeest, P. and Marschke, M. (2020) 'Modern slavery and freedom: exploring contradictions through labour scandals in the Thai fisheries', *Antipode*, 52(1): 291–315.

Vaughn, L. (2019) *'Doing Risk': Practitioner Interpretations of Risk of Childhood Radicalisation and the Implementation of the HM Government PREVENT Duty*. PhD Thesis, Liverpool: University of Liverpool.

Venkatesh, S. (2011) 'How tech tools transformed New York's sex trade', *Wired*, [online] 1 January. Available from: www.wired.com/2011/01/ff_sextrade/

Volodko, A., Cockbain, E., and Kleinberg, B. (2019). '"Spotting the signs" of trafficking recruitment online: exploring the characteristics of advertisements targeted at migrant job-seekers', *Trends in Organized Crime*, 23: 7–35.

Williamson, S.H. (2017) 'Globalization as a racial project: implications for human trafficking', *Journal of International Women's Studies*, 18(2): 74–88.

Wilson, M. and O'Brien, E. (2016) 'Constructing the ideal victim in the United States of America's annual trafficking in persons reports', *Crime, Law and Social Change*, 65(1–2): 29–45.

7

The Criminal Investigation of Human Trafficking Crimes in the UK: Benefits and Challenges of Police Collaboration During Police Investigations

Laura Pajón

Introduction

Human trafficking is a complex social problem with multiple embedded drivers, including socio-economic, political, and individual factors (Jurek and King, 2020; Tangen, 2020). Responses to the crime of human trafficking therefore need to be comprehensive and diverse, involving different tiers of actions and agencies (Rosenbaum, 2002; Dandurand, 2017; Gerassi et al, 2017; Gardner et al, 2021). This means that the response relies heavily upon law enforcement agencies and the prosecution of offenders (Matos et al, 2019; Jurek and King, 2020), which in the context of England and Wales sees the police operating as the leading agency in the operational response to human trafficking (HM Government, 2014).

During the last 20 years, a growing body of research has been published examining the detection, investigation, and prosecution of the offence of human trafficking with research conducted around the world (albeit predominately in the Global North) including the US, Portugal, Spain, Norway, the UK, Australia, the Netherlands, and Eastern European countries. The research incorporates a variety of methodologies, such as gathering views from practitioners (Farrell et al, 2008, 2010; Nichols and Heil, 2015) to empirical examinations of police files (Bjelland, 2016; Matos et al, 2019) or non-empirical explorations of policing responses (Gallagher and Holmes, 2008; Dandurand, 2017). The literature indicates that human trafficking is one of the most complex crimes to detect and investigate (Van der Watt and Van der Westhuizen, 2017), with numerous studies identifying the need and benefits of police collaboration with partner agencies to investigate human trafficking crimes (Kirby and Nailer, 2013; Farrell et al, 2014; Duijn et al, 2015; HMICFRS, 2017; Huff-Corzine et al, 2017).

The predominant focus of the research has been upon examining the challenges that police officers face when identifying and investigating human trafficking cases (Farrell et al, 2010; Barrick et al, 2014; Dandurand, 2017; Cockbain and Brayley-Morris, 2018). With fewer recent studies examining the factors that promote the prosecution of offenders, one notable contribution emerges through an empirical examination of factors associated with the conviction of offenders (Matos et al, 2019). The authors found that proactive investigations, gathering various sources of evidence, using different investigative strategies, and conducting transnational and multi-agency collaborations were some of the factors linked with a later conviction. Bjelland (2016) also examined factors correlated with the later prosecution of offenders, finding that police-initiated investigations were more likely to end in the prosecution of the offenders than when investigations were initiated by the report of a victim or a third party. While a large body of research illustrates the phenomenon of human trafficking and modern slavery and the complexity of investigations, much less research has been conducted concerning what occurs within criminal investigations of human trafficking cases (Friesendorf, 2009; Russell, 2018). This knowledge gap has begun to be addressed by focusing on and examining the investigation process rather than solely the outputs (Verhoeven and Van Gestel, 2011; Pajón and Walsh, 2020). The latter examined the investigative strategies used in four different police operations investigating sex trafficking criminality in Amsterdam, Holland, and observed that the investigative strategies chosen were (among others) dependent on the immediate circumstances and opportunities, and on the information available at the beginning of the investigation (Verhoeven and Van Gestel, 2011). While a recent examination identified core investigative actions that, according to substantially experienced human trafficking law enforcement professionals, should be undertaken during any human trafficking investigation, with multi-agency collaboration as a core component (Pajón and Walsh, 2020).

The aim of this chapter is to expand the current body of knowledge on the practice of police collaboration with partner agencies during human trafficking criminal investigations focusing within the jurisdiction of England and Wales. The chapter will examine two human trafficking police operations in three interconnected areas; namely, how the police collaborate with other agencies in practice during human trafficking investigations; the benefits and opportunities that collaboration offers to the police investigation; and, finally, the limitations and challenges when collaborating with partner agencies, such as NGOs (see further Francis, this volume) or European police forces. First, the chapter will scrutinize an investigation involving police collaboration with partner agencies (including law enforcement agencies and NGOs), and, secondly, a police operation involving a police collaboration with a European police force. I would like to note that the findings are indicative rather than conclusive. The primary purpose of this chapter is not to generalize results but to provide insight into the complexity of human trafficking police operations and police collaboration through a data-driven understanding of how police collaborations are undertaken in practice.

The chapter provides an overview of previous research on human trafficking investigation and multi-agency collaboration, prior to moving to examine two police operations, Operation Green and Blue[1] respectively, in accordance with the information provided by the lead investigators of the operations and the case files. The subsequent section will explore in detail the police collaboration in each investigation, looking at the benefits, limitations, and challenges experienced throughout the course of the investigation and discussing the findings.

Methodology

This chapter utilizes a case study methodology to examine the investigation process of two large human trafficking police operations, particularly the police collaboration undertaken during such investigations. I used a purposive sample selection strategy. The two police operations examined were conducted by the same police force to ensure that the differences identified between police operations were the result of differences between the examined trafficking cases rather than because of contextual and structural differences between police forces. After obtaining ethics authorization from the Faculty Research Ethics Committee, in addition to police vetting from the respective forces participating in the study, the Detective Chief Inspector of the Serious Organized Crime Unit (hereafter, SOCU) was asked to identify investigations after the implementation of the Modern Slavery Act, 2015 (hereafter, MSA 2015) that met the following criteria:

(i) that there was a trial date set up by the time data was collected (for those cases yet to involve a conviction);
(ii) the case involved adult exploitation and organized criminality; and

---

[1] The names of these operations have been changed and any identifying detail removed to ensure anonymity.

(iii) the researcher would be able to interview the investigators of the case and have access to police records considered relevant for the study.

Two operations were selected, Operation Green, which involved police collaboration with a wide range of partner agencies throughout the investigation, and Operation Blue, which consisted of an international police collaboration through forming a Joint Investigation Team (hereafter, JIT). After selecting the operations, face-to-face interviews were conducted with the investigators involved in each operation, with each interview lasting between two and three hours. Then the police files and official documents, such as policing decisions, meeting minutes, and court presentations, were analysed to complement the narratives and minimize potential limitations that the retrospective recalling of information of an event may have (Gabbert et al, 2018; Fisher and Geiselman, 1992). I also interviewed the Detective Chief Inspector of the SOCU and analysed police force records/statistics on human trafficking operations to gain a better understanding of the police organization, structure, and context. A thematic analysis was used to analyse the data, enabling the identification of the main benefits, challenges, and limitations that police faced when collaborating with other agencies in both police operations.

The selected operations: Operation Green and Operation Blue

Operation Green concerns the investigation of an Organized Criminal Group (OCG) which was involved in labour exploitation of Czech Republic nationals. The investigation starts using a multi-agency approach to gather intelligence and identify opportunities for prosecution and disruption. After two years of working in a multi-agency, a victim reported to a different police force to the one leading the investigation and included explanations as to his exploitation, in additional to identifying other exploited individuals. The victim gave information on the offenders' modus operandi to recruit, transport, and exploit victims, the specific locations and companies used, in addition to the control tactics used by the exploiters. After the victim's report, the focus of the investigation changed, shifting to corroborate the information provided by the victims. Undercover investigative strategies were used to gather intelligence on both the victims and offenders. After two months of gathering information on victims and the trafficking offence, a day of action involving different partner agencies was planned to rescue victims, arrest the main suspects, and collect further evidence. Of the total of 15 victims identified, 11 of them entered the National Referral Mechanism (hereafter, the NRM),[2] while seven suspects were arrested.

---

[2] NRM: the national framework for identifying victims of trafficking and ensuring that, once identified, victims are provided with adequate support.

Operation Blue consists of a joint investigation with Romanian police investigating another organized criminal gang involved in the sex trafficking of Romanian[3] nationals. Victims were targeted in their country of origin and transported to the UK to work as prostitutes.[4] The OCG was composed of 17 suspects (six of them operating in the UK), with the main leader in charge of the criminal network based in the UK. The investigation started after the report of a client in a brothel who maintained that he had been threatened. The name of the individual, who allegedly threatened the client, was flagged in the police database as a person of interest for the Romanian police as he was being prosecuted in Romania for sexual exploitation offences. Therefore, a JIT was established between the British police and the Romanian police to investigate and prosecute the case. The primary investigative strategy followed was to review intelligence previously gathered from phone calls from members of the public, reporting potential activity of prostitution within an area. Undercover investigative strategies and search warrants were used to gather evidence. Six suspects were identified operating in the UK (facing prosecution in Romania), but none of the victims identified engaged with the police.

Human trafficking: a complex crime

The United Nations Office of Drugs and Crime (hereafter, the UNODC) argues that human trafficking is 'better understood as a collection of crimes bundled together rather than a single offence; a criminal process rather than a criminal event', involving the recruitment, transportation, and exploitation of victims (UNODC, 2006; IOM, 2018). Trafficking is often depicted as a financially motivated crime (Belser, 2005; Leman and Janssens, 2008; OSCE, 2010, 2014; HM Government, 2019); thereby, to secure such profit, it is often committed alongside other offences, such as money laundering, immigration offences, fraudulent document offences, or investment in further criminal

---

[3] See further, All-Party Parliamentary Group on Prostitution and the Global Sex Trade (2018) 'Behind closed doors: organised sexual exploitation in England and Wales', which concluded that Romanian women were being trafficking on an industrial scale across the UK. Available from: www.appg-cse.uk/wp-content/uploads/2018/05/Behind-clo sed-doors-APPG-on-Prostitution.pdf [Accessed July 2023].

[4] Trafficking victim support specialist and Head of European operations at 'Justice and Care' Cristina Huddleston stated in 2020 that the 'agile, extraordinarily efficient model that has made the UK a primary destination for traffickers and pimps bringing women in from eastern Europe, particularly Romania' in addition to asserting that 'women often travel to the UK knowing that they are going to work in prostitution, but believe they will only do so for six months'. See further www.theguardian.com/global-development/ 2020/nov/30/silent-victims-the-hidden-romanian-women-exploited-in-the-uk-sex-trade [Accessed July 2023].

activities (Belser, 2005; Farrell et al, 2008; OSCE, 2010, 2014; Bouche et al, 2016; HM Government, 2019). Traffickers use legitimate businesses and mechanisms such as travel agencies, taxi drivers, or recruitment agencies to commit their offences (OSCE, 2010). Previous research has highlighted how traffickers can recruit and exploit multiple victims by working through flexible and adaptative networks to maximize profits and minimize risks (OSCE, 2010; Campana, 2016). The diversification and specialization of roles and the dynamic adaptation of the offenders when recruiting, transporting, and exploiting victims problematizes both the identification and arrest of those considered key players as well as the disruption of the crime (Salt, 2000; Viuhko and Jokinen, 2009; OSCE, 2010; Campana, 2016). By not targeting the right human trafficking offenders of the network could nurture the relationships between the remaining offenders subsequently creating stronger connections and the adoption of alternative mechanisms to prevent their identification (Duijn et al, 2015).

The identification of victims of human trafficking is neither easy nor straightforward (see further Hynes and Dottridge, Currie this volume). It is commonly said that victims are hidden in plain sight, referring to those who are being exploited via legitimate companies and industries. However, traffickers are known to use various techniques and strategies to minimize the chance of victims being identified (Viuhko and Jokinen, 2009; Jones et al, 2011; Ioannou and Oostinga, 2015). Traffickers use different forms of control over the victims to prevent them from escaping or asking for help. Standard control methods are using force, violence, or the threat of violence against the victims or their families. Such violence will vary from psychological coercion to physical violence (OSCE, 2010). For example, exploiters are known for taking possession of victims' passports, threatening violence to their families back home, creating drug dependence, depriving victims of food and water, or beating them, as examples of punishment to them and other victims, among many other forms (Viuhko and Jokinen, 2009; OSCE, 2010; Jones et al, 2011; Ioannou and Oostinga, 2015; IOM, 2018). Financial control methods, including controlling victims' bank accounts or holding wages, are commonly observed in trafficking offences (OSCE, 2010; Ioannou and Oostinga, 2015; IOM, 2018). Traffickers also minimize victims' opportunities for social interactions by continuously moving and relocating victims, as well as imposing rules including no access or use of personal mobile phones, restricting contact with their relatives, and preventing them from leaving their accommodation during daytime, or even advising them on how to interact with the police (Viuhko and Jokinen, 2009; Jones et al, 2011; Ioannou and Oostinga, 2015). Coupled with the victims' unfamiliarity with the place, potential language barriers or lack of understanding of their legal rights and the regulations of the country are also factors that prevent victims from either identifying or reporting their victimization (Farrell et al, 2008, 2012; Viuhko and Jokinen, 2009; OSCE, 2010). Other factors potentially include the shame or social stigma attached to the labels of trafficking victim/modern slave, to which some individuals object to the language operationalized (see further Hynes and Dottridge, this volume). As a result, many potential victims are not detected, or on occasions, they may be even misidentified as, for example, illegal immigrants or sex workers (Raphael et al, 2010; Farrell et al, 2012; Farrell and Pfeffer, 2014).

The deficits in knowledge and adequate training of frontline officers is another factor that can hinder, and even prevent, the identification of victims (Newton et al, 2008; Farrell et al, 2010; Farrell et al, 2014; Farrell and Pfeffer, 2014). Research had previously found that police officers held a number of misconceptions, including that victims of trafficking are foreign nationals only, or that the victims would present signs of physical injuries, for example. Other preconceptions, such as the fact that transportation or movement is a prerequisite for the commission of the crime and that sex trafficking is the only form of exploitation, were also identified (Farrell and Pfeffer, 2014; Farrell et al, 2015; Mapp et al, 2016). Yet, such misconceptions could also explain the under-identification of certain forms of exploitation, such as labour exploitation (see furher Currie and Weatherburn, this volume) or domestic servitude (Barrick et al, 2014; Farrell and Pfeffer, 2014).

The transnationality of the crime of human trafficking also makes it more difficult to identify and investigate. The Palermo Protocol explicitly constrained the definition of human trafficking in two interlinked ways; first, that for trafficking to have occurred a national border must have been crossed; and, second, that the perpetrators must be an organized criminal gang (see further, Table 1.1, this volume). As illustrated within this chapter, human trafficking does not necessarily involve crossing national borders. The Organization for Security and Co-operation in Europe (OSCE), for example, has identified that trafficking can occur within the same country, and it is suspected that most trafficking victims in England and Wales are recruited from countries other than the destination one (Cockbain and Bowers, 2019). The idealization of the Western world and the perceived attractive opportunities that those countries can offer in comparison with the options available in countries of origin make many individuals choose to take the risk and seek an alternative life in other countries (Viuhko and Jokinen, 2009). Human trafficking is a process; therefore, the crime can start and finish in different countries. As a result, to effectively investigate trafficking offences and gather evidence from the whole process (that is, recruitment, transportation, and exploitation), international collaboration and coordination between law enforcement agencies from two or more different countries is essential (Wheaton et al, 2010; IOM, 2018). However, cross-national police collaboration to investigate human trafficking crimes can be complicated due to several factors, including differences between criminal justice systems and legislation, police practices and procedures, states' capacity to respond to the crime, and the few effective mechanisms that are in place to facilitate international cooperation (Reichel, 2008; Dandurand, 2017).

As trafficking can involve both transnationality and organized criminal networks, it has been commonly assumed that measures to fight organized crime can also be applied to respond to human trafficking. For example, in the UK, the same strategic framework used to tackle Serious and Organized Crimes[5] has also been used to respond to human trafficking crimes. Nevertheless, the involvement of victims in human trafficking investigations rather than as the 'traditional' commodities used by criminals, such as drugs or weapons, presents greater and different challenges from an evidential point of view (Farrell et al, 2012). For instance, keeping track of the victims may be a challenging task that investigations into other organized criminality may not face. Victims' engagement is one of the most significant challenges faced by investigators, with many victims remaining reluctant to collaborate with the police and disclose their exploitative experiences (Farrell et al, 2008; Sheldon-Sherman, 2012; Andrevski et al, 2013; Cockbain and Brayley-Morris, 2018). They may fear retaliation by the traffickers against either themselves or their families (Farrell et al, 2008; Newton et al, 2008), or they many fears and/or mistrust the police due to erroneous perceptions based on stereotypes or previous experiences with the police either in the UK or elsewhere in the world, such as their country of origin (Clawson et al, 2006; Farrell et al, 2008; Farrell et al, 2012). Similarly, victims' involvement in criminal activities or illegal entry into the county may also promote victims' fear of being prosecuted or deported (Farrell et al, 2008, 2014). Finally, the trauma experienced, the debt bondage created by the exploiters, or the obliviousness of their own victimization and their legal rights have also been recognized as barriers to engaging (Farrell et al, 2008; Helfferich et al, 2011; Meshkovska et al, 2016).

Therefore while victims' accounts can be a rich source of information for the investigation, gathering information from victims can be a demanding task (Farrell et al, 2012). Interviewing victims of trafficking can be an opportunity for securing both the victims' engagement and obtaining more information about them and the offence; it may also re-traumatize victims, increase their anxiety, and, ultimately, impede the recalling of information and later engagement (Farrell et al, 2012; Meshkovska et al, 2016). Getting the account from a victim of trafficking takes time and, on occasions, police

---

[5] Serious and Organized Crime Strategy (2018). Available from: https://assets.publishing.service.gov.uk/government/uploads/system/uploads/attachment_data/file/752850/SOC-2018-web.pdf

officers can become frustrated due to changing accounts, inaccuracies, or victims failing to remember specific details (Clawson et al, 2006). Interviews with professionals and reviews of human trafficking cases conducted in the US, for example, found that, on occasions, police officers pressurized victims to provide an account or even arrested them to 'encourage' their collaboration (Farrell et al, 2012, 2016). Such practices are considered ineffective in obtaining the desired effect and can even achieve the contrary outcome, such as victims becoming increasingly uncooperative (Farrell et al, 2012).

While there is still little empirical evidence on 'best investigative strategies', there is full agreement that more innovative, victim-centred, and intelligence-led investigation practices are needed in the identification and investigation of human trafficking (David, 2007; Gallagher and Holmes, 2008; Verhoeven and Van Gestel, 2011; Farrell et al, 2012; UNODC, 2014; Matos et al, 2019). Intelligence-led strategies such as crime scripting, network analysis, open-sources data analysis, and proactive approaches such as multi-agency collaboration or parallel financial investigations have been argued to improve the investigation and detection of the crime (Gallagher and Holmes, 2008; Brayley et al, 2011; Cockbain et al, 2011; Brewster et al, 2014; Dandurand, 2017). Yet, most human trafficking cases come to the police's attention either through information given by the public, victim-service organizations, or other agencies such as health services (Clawson et al, 2006; Farrell et al, 2008, 2012, 2014; Bjelland, 2016). It is rare that investigations emerge proactively; for example, via data-scraping the internet (Farrell et al, 2012, 2014; Farrell and Pfeffer, 2014). This lack of proactive identification of cases is argued to involve the failure to identify many victims of trafficking (Farrell et al, 2012). The use of proactive strategies on the other hand, such as proactive monitoring of vulnerable and at-risk sectors or intelligence sharing through partnership work, are considered effective practices for identifying victims of trafficking (Gallagher and Holmes, 2008; Farrell et al, 2014).

Similarly, when it comes to police investigation, studies also show the still high reliance on victims of trafficking for evidence-gathering purposes (Gallagher and Holmes, 2008; Farrell et al, 2014), despite the evidential difficulties that they can present, such as difficulty in gathering an account of victims or their withdrawing from the criminal justice process – including disappearing (David, 2008; Farrell et al, 2008, 2014; Gallagher and Holmes, 2008; Brunovskis and Skilbrei, 2016). When examining Portuguese human trafficking investigations, Matos et al (2019) found that such a reactive approach correlated with the early disposal of the investigation due to the insufficient evidence found to prove the offence. However, one of the factors that correlated with securing the offender's conviction was, ironically, adopting proactive investigations (Matos et al, 2019). The authors observed that proactive investigations (which were notably fewer in occurrence) utilized planned, prompt, and timely strategies and were more comprehensive by collecting a wide range of evidence to prove the offence (Matos et al, 2019). Nevertheless, despite the benefits of adopting proactive and intelligence-led investigations, information sharing is one of the main challenges in the response to human trafficking even within and between police forces (HMICFRS, 2017; United States Department of State, 2019). As Farrell et al (2019) noted, trafficking cases were unlikely to be identified and referred to human trafficking units via ongoing investigations conducted in other police units. While different aspects contribute to this challenge, such as poor data-management practices or lack of standardization, one of the main ones is 'siloed' data; that is, data is only accessible to the agency collecting the data (United States Department of State, 2019). It has therefore been argued that working in partnership could help overcome barriers in information-sharing practices, promoting proactive and intelligence-led investigations, thereby reducing the need to rely on victims' testimony to ensure prosecution (Haughey, 2016; HMICFRS, 2017; ATMG, 2018). Moreover, that the benefits of multi-agency arrangements are also recognized for ensuring a more comprehensive response; meaning a response that ensures that the expertise of different stakeholders is shared and that powers and capabilities from various agencies are used to identify and safeguard victims of trafficking, as well as to disrupt human trafficking criminality (Farrell et al, 2008; Wilson and Dalton, 2008; Gerassi et al, 2017; Matos et al, 2018).

The role of multi-agency collaboration in human trafficking police investigations

Research on human trafficking investigations has found that when collaborating with other agencies, both the number of arrests, prosecutions, and convictions are higher, and the safeguarding of victims is promoted and improved due to the increased opportunities to share intelligence and resources, and the combined capabilities and expertise that different agencies bring (David, 2007; Farrell et al, 2008; Gerassi et al, 2017; Matos et al, 2019; Pajon and Walsh, 2022). In England and Wales, following academic and policy recommendations, there has been an increase in the number of police forces involved in anti-slavery partnerships[6] to maximize the opportunities to detect criminality proactively and safeguard victims. Similarly, police collaboration with partner agencies during human trafficking criminal investigations has also become common practice (HMICFRS, 2017; IASC and University of Nottingham, 2020). Yet, it has been identified that

---

[6] See further 'Partnerships for freedom: improving multi-agency collaboration on modern slavery' (2020). Available from: www.antislaverycommissioner.co.uk/media/1490/webtag_0920_gw_4428507_partnerships_for_freedom_v8_final.pdf [Accessed July 2023].

discrepancies exist in how police collaborate with partners (both nationally and internationally) (HMICFRS, 2017), recognizing the need to improve collaborative practices when responding to human trafficking (HMICFRS, 2017; ATMG 2018; College of Policing, 2022).

To improve the UK's law enforcement, responses to key investigative guidance, such as the Government's Modern Slavery strategy (HM Government, 2014) and the UK's College of Policing (2022), encourage investigators to collaborate with partner agencies. Indeed, multi-agency collaboration is well recognized by research, policy, and practice as beneficial, if not essential, to detecting and investigating human trafficking crimes (Kirby and Nailer, 2013; Farrell et al, 2014, 2019; Duijn et al, 2015; HMICFRS, 2017; Huff-Corzine et al, 2017). Despite the practice of police collaboration remaining inconsistent, police are increasingly engaging in different forms of collaboration with agencies and organizations to respond to human trafficking. Both globally and within the UK, we have seen examples of police forces engaging in anti-slavery partnerships and the creation of task forces to ensure a more comprehensive response to trafficking (Farrell et al, 2008; IASC and University of Nottingham, 2020). Similarly, examples also exist in forming JITs to investigate trafficking cases, including when undertaking both international and transnational investigations (Block, 2008; HMICFRS, 2017; Severns et al, 2020).

Agreement exists on the benefits of collaboration to overcome the limitations of single agencies and organizations when identifying and investigating trafficking crimes. Some of the most commonly identified benefits are the opportunities for intelligence sharing; enabling better mapping of the problem and identification of victims; the promotion of intelligence-led and victim-centred investigations; and the improved overall capacity of the police force to respond to human trafficking crimes (Fox and Butler, 2004; David, 2007; Farrell et al, 2008, 2019; Fischer et al, 2017; Gerassi et al, 2017; Matos et al, 2019). As previously alluded, police officers may hold misconceptions about trafficking offences, impacting their likelihood of detecting trafficking crimes. What research reveals is that the involvement of police forces in some form of multi-agency agreement promotes police officers' understanding of human trafficking, the perception of the issue as a serious problem in their community, and the recognition that other forms of exploitation (rather than sexual exploitation) are prevalent. While greater police understanding and acknowledgement of the risk that human trafficking poses for the community can promote both the identification of victims and an intelligence-led and victim-centred approach, research has revealed the critical role of non-law enforcement partners in identifying and providing information about trafficking victims. For instance, Farrell et al (2019) found that a large percentage of exploitation cases were identified by partners that engage with vulnerable members of society. These partners can provide relevant information about victims and locations that would unlikely be identified by police forces (Farrell et al, 2019).

Research has also identified the critical role of non-law enforcement organizations in providing adequate support for victims (David, 2007; Gerassi et al, 2017; Matos et al, 2019). Working in multi-agency teams helps better assess the psychological, social, emotional, and economic needs of the victims and, therefore, tailor responses accordingly (Matos et al, 2019). Police forces involved in multi-agency collaborations are more likely to support victims and meet victims' needs as part of their investigative approach when building human trafficking cases (Farrell et al, 2008: 87–8). As Farrell et al (2019) discuss, such connection with community partners provides victims with support and resources to facilitate their recovery and, ultimately, victims' engagement in the police investigation. Participation in multi-agency collaborations has also been found to improve the overall capacity of police forces to respond to trafficking crimes. Such forces were found to be more likely to have protocols, training, and specialized personnel in place. Most importantly, they had a better understanding of the services and capabilities of different agencies, which in turn allowed for better identification of opportunities for intelligence and support (Clawson et al, 2006; Farrell et al, 2008; Gerassi et al, 2017).

Previous research has found that police forces that have a close connection with partner agencies are more likely to conduct proactive, victim-centred, and intelligence-led and also more comprehensive investigations, using a wider variety of services, capabilities, and powers from different agencies (Clawson et al, 2006; Gerassi et al, 2017, Farrell et al, 2019). Yet, multi-agency collaboration is said to be more straightforward in theory than in practice (Harvey et al, 2015). Different barriers such as lack of trust, limited resources, different objectives and priorities, different procedures and policies, or a shortage of protocols for intelligence sharing, among others, have been found to problematize both the implementation and maintenance of police collaboration with partner agencies (Farrell et al, 2008; Dandurand, 2017; Gerassi et al, 2017). That is also the case when collaborating with other police forces, for instance, through the formation of JITs. While this type of collaboration allows more fluid and direct communication between police forces, the implementation of international collaboration is challenging in practice depending, among others, on factors related to the organizational culture, working practices, legal definitions, and personal relationships (Katona, 2020).

Within England and Wales, despite existing investigative guidelines and recommendations advising police forces to collaborate with partners in trafficking investigations, there is no standardized approach or protocols towards collaboration. Consequently, most police knowledge of collaborative practices and opportunities for cooperation results from past professional experiences and informal contacts (Wilson and Dalton, 2008; Gerassi et al, 2017). Such a lack of shared understanding may explain the limitations and uneven application of police collaboration across forces when investigating trafficking cases (Haughey, 2016; HMICFRS, 2017). For example, HMICFRS (2017) observed an absence of coordination and communication between police forces when a victim of trafficking was identified and/or safeguarded in a different police force area from where the exploitation occurred. In those cases, failures in communication between police forces when reporting the progress of the investigation and following up with victims were identified. This caused delays in the investigation and led to the poor provision of services to victims of trafficking. Moreover, while the report found evidence of international collaborations taking place, it also found that international checks were not always used (mainly at the initial stages of the investigation) (HMICFRS, 2017). As the HMICFRS (2017) noted, many investigators were not aware of how to conduct international intelligence checks through the National Crime Agency.

The benefits and challenges of police collaboration in human trafficking investigations

For both of the police operations (Operation Green and Operation Blue, respectively) scrutinized, multi-agency cooperation had an important role. Yet, differences exist between both operations. This section will examine each human trafficking operation, discussing the benefits, limitations, and challenges of the police collaboration.

Operation Green

In Operation Green, three main benefits were identified from the police collaboration with other agencies; namely, the opportunities to gather intelligence on the offender and the offence, in addition to the opportunity to disrupt criminality through the use of different agencies' powers and capabilities, and the capacity to engage with trafficked victims.

Operation Green adopted a multi-agency strategy at the very start of the investigation to get a better intelligence picture, and later on, after evidence of human trafficking was obtained, police collaborated with governmental and non-governmental agencies to support the prosecution of offenders and the safeguarding of victims. In the early stages, the multi-agency strategy consisted of having regular meetings with different partner agencies with enforcement powers, such as Her Majesty's Revenue and Customs, local government authorities, financial investigators, Fire and Rescue Services, and Environmental Health. This approach enabled them to gather extensive intelligence as about the OCG. As one of the lead investigators from

Operation Green pointed out: "We often have a small piece of the puzzle, and it is only by coming together that we finally get this complete picture, and we find out how each person feeds into the puzzle, and how we can deal with it." These multi-agency meetings enabled the investigators to build an intelligence picture of the OCG, including the different forms of criminality the offenders were involved in. The forms of criminality included benefit fraud, and the potential places and addresses where they operated, for example. The intelligence also provided multiple avenues to disrupt the offence. For instance, chances existed to arrest the suspects for other offences, such as benefit fraud, committed alongside the trafficking offence.

The second time a multi-agency strategy was implemented was when the investigation team had enough evidence to prove exploitation. This multi-agency strategy, involving agencies with enforcement powers and NGOs, focused upon the prosecution of the offenders and the engagement of victims. The benefits of the multi-agency collaboration were specially recognized in the planning and coordination of a reception centre as a safe place for the victim. The involvement of NGO members in the reception centre facilitated rapport-building with victims, thereby promoting their engagement (see further Francis, this volume). As the lead officer in the reception centred stated:

'I had my officers to step back and allow them [members of the NGO] to have a conversation, as opposed to me standing up and going "hiya, my name is such and such, and I am here for your best interest bla bla bla". You know, for them, I am just another cop, they don't know if they should trust me or not, whereas when I let them [members of the NGO] speak to the victims as individuals, you find the guys going out for a smoke and joining them, they kind of ended up with this kind of commonality, so when they say "right let's start doing the screening process", people were much more relaxed and more willing to speak freely about what happened.'

The use of interpreters for the duration of the police operation facilitated that both succinct and accurate explanations were given to the victims and ensured they were informed about what would happen next. The investigators interviewed also referred to a series of factors that facilitated victims' engagement. It was recognized that the intelligence obtained on victims helped plan the reception centre and build rapport. Additionally, giving both the time and space for NGO members to build rapport with victims and for victims in turn to understand what was happening was viewed as a facilitator of victim cooperation. The early allocation and clarification of roles and responsibilities of each partner agency and organization improved the implementation of a coordinated strategy.

However, investigators noted that factors the police had little control over also promoted rapport-building and, in turn, victims' engagement. An illustrative example relates to police officers speaking the same language as the victims or professionals from the NGO, in addition to having previous experience working with trafficked victims. The detective leading the reception centre from Operation Green, when reflecting upon the reasons for the high number of victims engaging with the police, stated: "I think we had the perfect storm, with all the ingredients of the people who were in the reception centre." He is referring to the fact that despite the strategies taken to promote victims' engagement through the involvement of NGOs to build rapport, the use of interpreters, and the coordination of a reception centre as a place of safety, there remained a series of other factors that played a role when engaging with victims. Some of theses factors included having a police officer who was a Czech national, with two members from the Salvation Army who were fluent in the language, and that the interpreter was someone with 'passion' for the job, in addition to having previous experience in human trafficking cases.

Despite the recognized benefits of the police collaboration, one significant limitation of the multi-agency collaboration implemented at the start of the investigation was the lack of evidence to prove exploitation and the limited intelligence on victims that they obtained. In Operation Green, it was not the intelligence obtained by the multi-agency but the report of one of the victims to a police station that provided further opportunities to gather intelligence on the offence and the victims. This promoted a change in the investigative approach, evolving from a disruptive multi-agency strategy to a police-focused and intelligence-led investigation with undercover tactics as the core investigative strategies to gather intelligence and evidence on victims and exploitation. The multi-agency disruptive operation was paused while the proactive police operation was ongoing. As the lead investigator explained, there was a risk that if suspects were prosecuted for other offences, they would destroy any remaining evidence, subsequently losing the opportunity to prosecute offenders for trafficking criminality. This links to the offenders being alerted to an ongoing police operation, leading to the increased risk of them moving victims to another location and causing the loss of the chance to identify and rescue any potential victim of exploitation. Such a change in the investigative approach created a challenge for the police investigators who had to manage, maintain, and balance partners' priorities and expectations while the undercover police operation was ongoing. As the lead investigators of the multi-agency strategy raised: "This was when it went interesting and frustrating at the same time because the investigation goes so slowly. We [that is, multi-agency] needed to wait till it was confirmed, or otherwise, the victim was related to our investigation and was interviewed, before we could take any action as a multi-agency."

Another challenge police officers experienced when engaging in collaboration with other agencies was the shortness of understanding as to with whom to collaborate, who to contact, and how to start such collaboration: "We didn't know who to invite. Who? Where do you start? So ok, I want to invite HMRC [that is, Her Majesty's Revenue and Customs], who do I write to? We don't know, would it be relevant? Would it be DWP [that is, Department for Work and Pensions]? We don't know. This was fresh. It was from scratch." The little knowledge about other agencies' capacities and capabilities prevented any quick and systematic contact with those agencies that could potentially support the investigation. Instead, agencies were contacted based on the presumption that they could support the police operation.

Operation Blue

In Operation Blue, police collaborated sporadically with agencies such as the National Crime Agency and Immigration and Enforcement for specific support. However, the primary collaboration was with the Romanian police force, as they were also investigating the same OCG. The main benefits identified included the opportunities to gather and share intelligence, the increased use of investigative strategies throughout the investigation, and the possibility of reducing the strain upon resources.

The formalization of a JIT that included investigators from both police forces allowed them to share all the intelligence they held on the OCG and the offence, identifying and deciding the best investigative approach to take to secure the prosecution and conviction of the offenders. One of the main benefits raised by investigators of such international police collaboration was the combination of investigative strategies. As both forces are regulated by different legal frameworks, differences between forces exist in the type of investigative strategies they could conduct to legally obtain evidence to prove the offence. Consequently, increasing the amount of intelligence to build a criminal intelligence picture on victims' movement and financial exploitation and the amount of evidence that could be used in court when proving exploitation. Another benefit of the international police collaboration was the resources saved in translation. Investigators made particular mention of the translation of old text messages that, without the support of the Romanian police, would have been costly and time-consuming: "They were able to translate what was being said and get the evidence as far back as 2015. Evidence about how they took advantage of these girls, how much money they got paid."

While recognizing the positives of international police collaboration in facilitating the prosecution of the offenders, interviewees considered the cornerstone for the collaboration's success to be the effective and constant communication between forces. Moreover, it highlighted the good level of English of the Romanian lead investigator as a critical facilitator for effective communication and cooperation. Yet, despite the benefits identified, a core limitation of such collaboration was its capability to engage with victims. Two Romanian officers participated in the police operation in the UK to be able to communicate with victims and overcome the language barriers. Yet, none of the victims identified in the different locations engaged with the police.

Challenges identified when conducting international police collaboration included the limited understanding of the procedures and regulations when forming a JIT, which was overcome with the support of the National Crime Agency and Europol. The lack of knowledge of the other police force's culture and legal framework was another aspect that caused difficulties. These difficulties included over agreeing on the investigative approach and strategies to undertake throughout the investigation. As the lead investigator reflected, it was particularly challenging "finding common ground, trying to achieve what they wanted evidentially in a way that we could do it and was lawful, so that took a bit of time, and there were conversations of 'but why you can't do that, or this', and 'this here is not legal', and it took a bit of time for understanding".

The practice of police collaboration to investigate human trafficking crimes

Multi-agency collaborations in the investigation of human trafficking have received support as the foundation of what has been termed as 'best' practices (GRETA 2016; Hyland 2016; ATMG 2018). The official police 'watchdog' in England and Wales found uneven practical application by the police forces during the criminal investigations of human trafficking offences (HMICFRS, 2017). Considering the current gap of evidence-based knowledge on the practice of police collaboration in this context, this chapter has sought to contextualize and exemplify how police collaboration is conducted in practice.

Research has indicated that police collaborating with partner agencies and other law-enforcement agencies has been beneficial within different aspects of the investigation. One of the main benefits identified in both operations was the opportunities that the alliance with other agencies generated to gather intelligence. While the challenges of getting a complete picture of trafficking criminality are well recognized, the collaboration with partners and discussion of the information each agency holds on the offence and the criminal group allowed the investigation team to build a criminal intelligence picture. This, in turn, created the chance to conduct intelligence-led approaches and, in the case of Operation

Green, opportunities for disruption. Moreover, it emphasized the potential of police collaboration with partner agencies to undertake a more comprehensive response to trafficking cases using the agencies' capacities, capabilities, knowledge, skills, and resources to meet the investigative objectives (Clawson et al, 2006; Gerassi et al, 2017, Farrell et al, 2019; Pajon and Walsh, 2022). Yet, differences between both operations existed in the opportunities that the multi-agency collaboration generated for the investigation. For example, in Operation Green, the multi-agency collaboration created opportunities for intelligence, disruption, and victims' engagement. While, in Operation Blue, the collaboration only created opportunities to promote the prosecution of offenders. Such differences are likely to be explained by the agencies and organizations involved in the collaboration (Pajon and Walsh, 2022). That is, differently from Operation Blue, Operation Green collaborated with non-law enforcement organizations. These agencies have the need of the victims and their long-term recovery as the core of their priorities, as opposed to police forces that, despite the increased use of a victim-centred approach when investigating human trafficking, the goals of arrest and prosecution very often overshadow meeting victims' need (Farrell et al, 2019). NGOs have the knowledge, skills, and capabilities to meet immediate needs, relating to things such as accommodation or support in the form of counselling. They can also effectively establish and support long-term needs, largely due to the fact that they are better equipped to build relationships of trust with victims, and ultimately facilitating their engagement with the criminal investigation (David, 2007; Farrell et al, 2019; Van Dyke and Brachou, 2021). As I have previously alluded to, one of the main differences between both respective operations was the number of victims that engaged with the police during the investigation.

The observations also indicate that the earlier intelligence is gathered on victims, in addition to the planning of a reception centre as a strategy to move victims from the situation of exploitation to a place of safety. These (among others) were relevant factors that facilitated the effective engagement with victims. Intelligence-led approaches conducted in Operation Green were effective in gathering evidence on the offence, and in planning a victim-centred investigative strategy (ATMG, 2018; Bjelland, 2018; Matos et al, 2019).

The lack of clarity on the roles and responsibilities of the members, unclear objectives, and unfamiliarity with partners' needs, culture, expertise, and priorities can all impact relationship and trust-building, therefore hindering the collaboration (McCreadie et al, 2008; Dandurand, 2017; Fischer et al, 2017; Katona, 2020). While data gathered did not allow for analysing aspects related to issues such as trust-building, or the lack of understanding of partners' capacities and capabilities, to differences in investigative priorities, and poor knowledge on how to start a collaboration both internationally and with partners based in the UK – were all challenges identified in both police operations evaluated. Through clarifying priorities, investigative objectives, roles, and responsibilities at the beginning of the operation facilitated the effective collaboration and the subsequent criminal investigation (Pajón and Walsh, 2020). Moreover, it was also found that factors related to personal characteristics (such as language skills) and expertise of the members involved in the collaboration, including previous experience working with human trafficking victims, facilitated the collaboration between agencies and helped secure the investigative objectives – namely, prosecution and victims' engagement.

Critical reflections

The case study methodology enables researchers to qualitatively examine and provide a better insights into complex issues such as human trafficking. Through examining the police operation via different data sources, including interviews and police files, permitted qualitative access to a rich amount of data and perspectives (Mason, 2002; Zainal, 2007). However, this methodology does not come without limitations; namely, relating to the generalization of results. Yet, the aim of this chapter is not to generalize the results but rather to provide a window to view the practice of police collaboration during human trafficking investigations. Ultimately, the aim of this research is to provide a better understanding of how human trafficking investigations are currently conducted, the challenges that exist, and the benefits of collaborating with other agencies.

Another important aspect to consider is that this chapter focuses exclusively on investigating human trafficking crimes from a policing perspective. Therefore, the research did not include the views of frontline police officers or views from other partner agencies, despite their core role in the investigation of trafficking crimes and the collaboration more generally. Only data from case files and the views from investigators were gathered to assess the police collaboration practice. Consequently, this chapter's findings cannot be considered isolated but need to be further addressed as part of a more comprehensive human trafficking response that includes other agencies and actors.

Conclusion

Human trafficking has been defined as a criminal justice issue (see further Table 1.1, this volume), with an expectation for law enforcement agencies to respond and even eradicate human trafficking criminality. Traditionally, police forces have focused on the identification and prosecution of offenders, and the need to adopt a victim-centred approach that meets the needs of the victims. This often means that police forces do not have the skills and resources to fulfil such requirements. Therefore, police collaboration with different law enforcement and non-law enforcement organizations has been considered critical when responding to and investigating trafficking offences. While studies have been published on multi-agency collaborations to respond to complex social problems, including multi-agency partnerships to respond to human trafficking crimes, little research has been conducted examining police collaboration during the criminal investigation of human trafficking crimes. Therefore, this chapter aims to provide insight into police collaborations during human trafficking investigations to better understand how such collaboration is conducted in practice, its benefits to the investigation, and the challenges officers face when engaging in such collaborations.

The observations align with previous research identifying police collaboration as beneficial for the criminal investigation of human trafficking crimes. In both operations, police collaboration with partner agencies allowed detectives to build a more comprehensive intelligence picture of the offence and gather evidence to prove exploitation. Findings also reveal the importance of collaborating with NGOs to secure a victim-centred approach that ensures that the immediate needs of the victims are met and, in turn, promotes victims' engagement. Nonetheless, engaging in collaboration proved to be challenging in practice. The lack of understanding of partner agencies and differences in organizations' priorities and working practices hindered the collaboration. Regardless of the identified challenges, data analysis revealed that aspects such as planning and clarification of roles of responsibilities supported and facilitated police collaboration and, in turn, promoted the prosecution of offenders and victims' engagement. While the findings of this chapter cannot be generalized, they highlight the importance of police collaboration during human trafficking investigations. Yet, further research needs to be conducted to examine the role of different agencies when investigating human trafficking crimes, what type of investigative practices promote victims' engagement, and ultimately what practices or mechanisms can be implemented to facilitate police collaboration with other agencies.

References

Andrevski, H., Larsen, J., and Lyneham, S. (2013) 'Barriers to trafficked persons' involvement in criminal justice proceedings: an Indonesian case study', *Trends and Issues in Crime and Criminal Justice*, 451. Canberra, Australia: Australian Institute of Criminology. Available from: www.aic.gov.au/publications/tandi/tandi451 [Accessed 21 December 2023].

Anti-Trafficking Monitoring Group (ATMG) (2018) *Before the Harm Is Done: Examining the UK's Response to the Prevention of Trafficking*. Available from: www.antislavery.org/wp-content/uploads/2018/09/Before-the-Harm-is-Done-report.pdf [Accessed 21 December 2023].

Barrick, K., Lattimore, P.K., Pitts, W.J., and Zhang, S.X. (2014) 'When farmworkers and advocates see trafficking, but law enforcement does not: challenges in identifying labor trafficking in North Carolina' *Crime, Law, and Social Change*, 61(2): 205–14.

Belser, P. (2005) *Forced Labour and Human Trafficking: Estimating the Profit*, Geneva: International Labour Organization. Available from: https://www.ilo.org/global/topics/forced-labour/publications/WCMS_081971/lang--en/index.htm [Accessed 21 December 2023].

Bjelland, H.F. (2016) 'Identifying human trafficking in Norway: a register-based study of cases, outcomes and police practices', *European Journal of Criminology*, 14(5): 522–42. doi: 10.1177/1477370816677619

Bjelland, H.F. (2018) 'Conceptions of success: understanding of successful policing of human trafficking', *Policing: A Journal of Police and Practice*. doi: 10.1093/police/pay073

Block, L. (2008) 'Combating organised crime in Europe: practicalities of police cooperation', *Policing: An International Journal of Police Strategies and Management*, 2(1): 74–81.

Bouche, V., Farrell, A., and Wittmer, D. (2016) *Identifying Effective Counter-Trafficking Programs and Practices in the U.S.: Legislative, Legal And Public Opinions Strategies that Work*. Available from: www.ncjrs.gov/pdffiles1/nij/grants/249670.pdf [Accessed 21 December 2023].

Brayley, H., Cockbain, E., and Laycock, G. (2011) 'The value of crime scripting: deconstructing internal child sex trafficking', *Policing: A Journal of Policy and Practice*, 5(2): 132–43.

Brewster, B., Polovina, S., Rankin, G., and Andrews, S. (2014) 'Knowledge management and human trafficking: using conceptual knowledge representation, text analytics and open-source data to combat organized crime', in N. Hernandez, R. Jäschke, and M. Croitoru (eds) *Graph-Based Representation and Reasoning*, Lecture Notes in Computer Science, vol 8577, Cham: Springer, pp 104–17. doi: https://doi.org/10.1007/978-3-319-08389-6_10

Brunovskis, A. and Skilbrei, M. (2016) 'Two birds with one stone? Implications of conditional assistance in victim protection and prosecution of traffickers', *Anti-Trafficking Review*, 6: 13–30. doi: https://doi.org/10.14197/atr.20121662

Campana, P. (2016) 'The structure of human trafficking: lifting the bonnet on a Nigerian transnational network', *British Journal of Criminology*, 56(1): 68–86.

Clawson, H., Dutch, N., and Cummings, M. (2006) *Law Enforcement Response to Human Trafficking and the Implications for Victims: Current Practices and Lessons Learned*. Available from: www.ncjrs.gov/pdffiles1/nij/grants/216547.pdf [Accessed 21 December 2023].

Cockbain, E. and Bowers, K. (2019) 'Human trafficking for sex, labour and domestic servitude: how do key trafficking types compare and what are their predictors?', *Crime, Law and Social Change*, 72(1): 9–34.

Cockbain, E. and Brayley-Morris, H. (2018) 'Human trafficking and labour exploitation in the casual construction industry: an analysis of three major investigations in the UK involving Irish Traveller offending groups', *Policing: A Journal of Policy and Practice*, 12(2): 129–49.

Cockbain, E., Brayley, H., and Laycock, G. (2011) 'Exploring internal child sex trafficking networks using social network analysis', *Policing: A Journal of Policy and Practice*, 5(2): 144–57.

College of Policing (2022) *Major Investigation and Public Protection: Modern Slavery*. Available from: www.app.college.police.uk/app-content/major-investigation-and-public-protection/modern-slavery/ [Accessed 21 December 2023].

Dandurand, Y. (2017) 'Human trafficking and police governance', *Police, Practice and Research: An International Journal*, 18(3): 322–36.

David, F. (2007) 'Law enforcement responses to trafficking in persons: challenges and emerging good practice', *Trends and Issues in Crime and Criminal Justice*, 347. Canberra, Australia: Australian Institute of Criminology. Available from: https://www.aic.gov.au/publications/tandi/tandi347 [Accessed 21 December 2023].

David, F. (2008) 'Trafficking of women for sexual purposes', *Research and Public Policy Series*, 95. Canberra, Australia: Australian Institute of Criminology. Available from: www.dss.gov.au/sites/default/files/documents/05_2012/rrp95_trafficking_of_women.pdf [Accessed 21 December 2023].

Duijn, P.A.C., Kashirin, V., and Sloot, P.M.A. (2015) 'The relative ineffectiveness of criminal network disruption', *Scientific Reports*, 4(4238): 1–15. doi: https://doi.org/10.1038/srep04238

Farrell, A. and Pfeffer, R. (2014) 'Policing human trafficking: cultural blinders and organizational barriers', *Annals of the American Academy of Political and Social Science*, 653(1): 46–64. doi: 10.1177/0002716213515835

Farrell, A., McDevitt, J., and Fahy, S. (2008) *Understanding and Improving Law Enforcement Responses to Human Trafficking*. Available from: www.ncjrs.gov/pdffiles1/nij/grants/222752.pdf [Accessed 21 December 2023].

Farrell, A., McDevitt, J., and Fahy, S. (2010) 'Where are all the victims? Understanding the determinants of official identification of human trafficking incidents', *Criminology and Public Policy*, 9(2): 201–33.

Farrell, A., Owens, C., and McDevitt, J. (2014) 'New laws but few cases: understanding the challenges to the investigation and prosecution of human trafficking cases', *Crime, Law and Social Change*, 61: 139–68.

Farrell, A., Pfeffer, R., and Brighuman, K. (2015) 'Police perceptions of human trafficking', *Journal of Crime and Justice*, 38(3): 315–33.

Farrell, A., DeLateur, M.J., Owens, C., and Fahy, S. (2016) 'The prosecution of state level human trafficking cases in the United States', *Anti-Trafficking Review*, 6: 48–70.

Farrell, A., Dank, M., de Vries, I., Kafafian, M., Hughes, A., and Lockwood, S. (2019) 'Falling victims? Challenges of the police response to human trafficking', *Criminology and Public Policy*, 18(3): 649–73.

Farrell, A. et al (2012) *Identifying Challenges to Improve the Investigation and Prosecution of State and Local Human Trafficking Cases*. Available from: https://www.ojp.gov/pdffiles1/nij/grants/238795.pdf [Accessed 21 December 2023].

Fischer, H., Vestby, A., and Bjelland, H. (2017) '"It's about using the full sanction catalogue": on boundary negotiations in a multi-agency organised crime investigation', *Policing and Society*, 27(6): 655–70.

Fisher, R.P. and Geiselman, R.E. (1992) 'The complexity of eyewitness memory', in F.R. Fisher and R.E. Geiselman (eds) *Memory Enhancing Techniques for Investigative Interviewing: The Cognitive Interview*, Springfield, IL: Charles C. Thomas, pp 11–16.

Fox, C. and Butler, G. (2004) 'Partnerships: where next?', *Safer Communities*, 3(3): 36–44.

Friesendorf, C. (2009) *Strategies Against Human Trafficking: The Role of the Security Sector*. Available from: https://documentation.lastradainternational.org/lsidocs/Trafficking+Complete[1].pdf [Accessed 21 December 2023].

Gabbert, F., Hope, L., and Confrey, M. (2018) 'Witness testimony', in A. Griffiths and R. Milne (eds) *The Psychology of Criminal Investigation: From Theory to Practice*, London: Routledge, pp 113–29.

Gallagher, A. and Holmes, P. (2008) 'Developing an effective criminal justice response to human trafficking: lessons from the front line', *International Criminal Justice Review*, 18(3): 318–43.

Gardner, A., Northall, P., and Brewster, B. (2021) 'Building slavery-free communities: a resilience framework', *Journal of Human Trafficking*, 7(3): 338–53.

Gerassi, L., Nichols, A., and Michelson, E. (2017) 'Lessons learned: benefits and challenges in interagency coalitions addressing sex trafficking and commercial sexual exploitation', *Journal of Human Trafficking*, 3(4): 285–302.

Group of Experts on Actions against Trafficking in Human Beings (GRETA) (2016) *6th General Report on GRETA's Activities*. Available from: https://rm.coe.int/1680706a42 [Accessed 21 December 2023].

Haughey, C. (2016) *The Modern Slavery Act Review*. Available from: www.gov.uk/government/publications/modern-slavery-act-2015-review-one-year-on [Accessed 21 December 2023].

Harvey, J.H., Hornsby, R.A., and Sattar, Z. (2015) 'Disjointed service: an English case study of multi-agency provision in tackling child trafficking', *British Journal of Criminology*, 55(3): 494–513.

Helfferich, C., Kavemann, B., and Rabe, H. (2011) 'Determinants of the willingness to make a statement of victims of human trafficking for the purpose of sexual exploitation in the triangle offender-police-victim', *Trends in Organised Crime*, 14(125). doi: https://doi.org/10.1007/s12117-011-9125-1

HM Government (2014) *The Modern Slavery Strategy*. Available from: https://assets.publishing.service.gov.uk/government/uploads/system/uploads/attachment_data/file/383764/Modern_Slavery_Strategy_FINAL_DEC2015.pdf [Accessed 21 December 2023].

HM Government (2019) *2019 UK Annual Report on Modern Slavery*. Available from: https://assets.publishing.service.gov.uk/government/uploads/system/uploads/attachment_data/file/840059/Modern_Slavery_Report_2019.pdf [Accessed 21 December 2023].

HM Inspectorate of Constabulary and Fire and Rescue Services (HMICFRS) (2017) *Stolen Freedom: The Policing Response to Modern Slavery and Human Trafficking*. Available from: www.justiceinspectorates.gov.uk/hmicfrs/wp-content/uploads/stolen-freedom-the-policing-response-to-modern-slavery-and-human-trafficking.pdf [Accessed 21 December 2023].

Huff-Corzine, L., Sacra, S.A., Corzine, J., and Rados, R. (2017) 'Florida's task force approach to combat human trafficking: an analysis of county-level data', *Police Practice and Research: An International Journal*, 18(3): 245–58.

Hyland, K. (2016) *Independent Anti-Slavery Commissioner: Annual Report 2015–2016*. Available from: https://assets.publishing.service.gov.uk/government/uploads/system/uploads/attachment_data/file/559571/IASC_Annual_Report_WebReadyFinal.pdf [Accessed 21 December 2023].

Independent Anti-Slavery Commissioner (IASC) and University of Nottingham (2020) *Partnership for Freedom: Improving Multi-Agency Collaboration on Modern Slavery*. Available from: https://iasctoolkit.nottingham.ac.uk/download/partnerships-for-freedom-improving-multi-agency-collaboration-on-modern-slavery/ [Accessed 21 December 2023].

International Organization for Migration (IOM) (2018) *Investigating Human Trafficking Cases Using a Victim-Centred Approach: A Trainer's Manual on Combating Trafficking in Persons for Capacity-Building of Law Enforcement Officers in Antigua and Barbuda, Belize, Jamaica, and Trinidad and Tobago*. Available from: https://publications.iom.int/books/investigating-human-trafficking-cases-using-victim-centred-approach-trainers-manual-combating [Accessed 21 December 2023].

Ioannou, M. and Oostinga, M.S.D. (2015) 'An empirical framework of control methods of victims of human trafficking for sexual exploitation', *Global Crime*, 16(1): 34–49.

Jones, L., Engstrom, D., Hilliard, P., and Sungakawan, D. (2011) 'Human trafficking between Thailand and Japan: lessons in recruitment, transport and control', *International Journal of Social Welfare*, 20(2): 203–11.

Jurek, L. and King, W.R. (2020) 'Structural responses to gendered social problems: police agency adaptations to human trafficking', *Police Quarterly*, 23(1): 25–54.

Katona, N. (2020) 'Combating trafficking of Hungarian women to Western Europe: a multi-level analysis of the international law enforcement cooperation', *Trends in Organized Crime*, 23(2): 115–42.

Kirby, S. and Nailer, L. (2013) *Using a Prevention and Disruption Model to Tackle a UK Organsied Crime Group*, London: Home Officer.

Leman, J., and Janssens, S. (2008) 'The Albanian and post-soviet business of trafficking women for prostitution: structural developments and financial modus operandi', *European Journal of Criminology*, 5(4): 433–51.

Mapp, S., Hornung, E., D'Almeida, M., and Juhnke, J. (2016) 'Local law enforcement officer's knowledge of human trafficking: ability to define, identify and assist', *Journal of Human Trafficking*, 2(4): 329–42.

Mason, J. (2002) *Qualitative Researching* (2nd edn), Thousand Oaks, CA: Sage.

Matos, M., Gonçalvez, M., and Maia, A. (2018) 'Human trafficking and criminal proceedings in Portugal: discourses of professionals in the justice system', *Trends in Organized Crime*, 21(4): 370–400.

Matos, M., Gonçalvez, M., and Maia, A. (2019) 'Understanding the criminal justice process in human trafficking cases in Portugal: factors associated with successful prosecutions', *Crime, Law and Social Change*, 72(5): 501–25. doi: https://doi.org/10.1007/s10611-019-09834-9

McCreadie, C., Mathew, D., Filinson, R., and Askham, J. (2008) 'Ambiguity and cooperation in the implementation of adult protection policy', *Social Policy and Administration*, 42(3): 248–66.

Meshkovska, B., Mickovski, N., Bos, A., and Siegel, M. (2016) 'Trafficking of women for sexual exploitation in Europe: prosecution, trials and their impact', *Anti-Trafficking Review*, 6: 71–90. doi: https://doi.org/10.14197/atr.20121665

Newton, P.J., Mulcahy, T.M., and Martin, S.E. (2008) *Finding Victims of Human Trafficking*. Available from: www.ncjrs.gov/pdffiles1/nij/grants/224393.pdf [Accessed 21 December 2023].

Nichols, A.J. and Heil, E. (2015) 'Challenges to identifying and prosecuting sex trafficking cases in the Midwest United States', *Feminist Criminology*, 10(1): 7–35.

Organization for Security and Co-operation in Europe (OSCE) (2010) *Analysing the Business Model of Trafficking in Human Beings to Better Prevent the Crime*. Available from: www.osce.org/secretariat/69028?download=true [Accessed 21 December 2023].

Organization for Security and Co-operation in Europe (OSCE) (2014) *Leveraging Anti-Money Laundering Regimes to Combat Trafficking in Human Beings*. Available from: www.osce.org/secretariat/121125?download=true [Accessed 21 December 2023].

Pajón, L. and Walsh, D. (2020) 'Proposing a theoretical framework for the criminal investigation of human trafficking crimes', *Policing: A Journal of Policy and Practice*, 14(2): 493–511.

Pajón, L. and Walsh, D. (2022) 'The importance of multi-agency collaborations during human trafficking criminal investigations', *Policing and Society*. doi: https://doi.org/10.1080/10439463.2022.2106984

Raphael, J., Reichert, J.A., and Powers, M. (2010) 'Pimp control and violence: domestic sex trafficking of Chicago women and girls', *Women and Criminal Justice*, 20(1–2): 89–104.

Reichel, P.L. (2008) *Cross-National Collaboration to Combat Human Trafficking. Learning from the Experience of Others*. Available from: https://pdfs.semanticscholar.org/1b6e/e65e0fe8a316508753c07a6b5975347e24d0.pdf [Accessed 21 December 2023].

Rosenbaum, D.P. (2002) 'Evaluating multi-agency anti-crime partnerships: theory, design and measurement issues', *Crime Prevention Studies*, 14: 171–225.

Russell, A. (2018) 'Human trafficking: a research synthesis on human-trafficking literature in academic journals from 2000–2014', *Journal of Human Trafficking*, 4(2): 114–36.

Salt, J. (2000) 'Trafficking and human smuggling: a European perspective' *International Migration*, 38(3): 31–56.

Serious and Organized Crime Strategy (2018). Available from: https://assets.publishing.service.gov.uk/government/uploads/system/uploads/attachment_data/file/752850/SOC-2018-web.pdf [Accessed 21 December 2023].

Severns, R., Paterson, C., and Brogan, S. (2020) 'The transnational investigation of organised modern slavery: a critical review of the use of joint investigation teams to investigate and disrupt transnational modern slavery in the United Kingdom', *International Journal of Crisis Communication*, 4: 11–22.

Sheldon-Sherman, J. (2012) 'The missing "P": prosecution, prevention, protection, and partnership in the Trafficking Victims Protection Act', *Penn State Law Review*, 117: 443–501.

Tangen, J. (2020) 'Timescapes in public policy – constructing the "victim of trafficking"', *Journal of Borderlands Studies*, 37(3): 475–92.

United Nations Office of Drugs and Crime (UNODC) (2006) *Toolkit to Combat Trafficking in Persons, Global Programme Against Trafficking in Human Beings*. Available from: www.unodc.org/documents/human-trafficking/HT-toolkit-en.pdf [Accessed 21 December 2023].

United Nations Office of Drugs and Crime (UNODC) (2014) *Global Report on Trafficking in Persons 2014.* Available from: www.unodc.org/documents/data-and-analysis/glotip/GLOTIP_2014_full_report.pdf [Accessed 21 December 2023].

United States Department of State (2019) *Trafficking in Persons Report, June 2019.* Available from: www.state.gov/wp-content/uploads/2019/06/2019-Trafficking-in-Persons-Report.pdf [Accessed 21 December 2023].

Van der Watt, M. and Van der Westhuizen, A. (2017) '(Re)configuring the criminal justice response to human trafficking: a complex-systems perspective', *Police Practice and Research: An International Journal*, 18(3): 218–99.

Van Dyck, R. and Brachou, A. (2021) *What Looks Promising for Tackling Modern Slavery: A Review of Practice-Based Research.* Available from: www.antislaverycommissioner.co.uk/media/1565/modern-slavery-report-what-looks-promising-a4-brochure-21-031-feb21-proof-2.pdf [Accessed 21 December 2023].

Verhoeven, M. and Van Gestel, B. (2011) 'Human trafficking and criminal investigation strategies in the Amsterdam Red Light District', *Trends in Organized Crimes*, 14(2/3): 148–64.

Viuhko, M. and Jokinen, A. (2009) *Human Trafficking and Organised Crime: Trafficking for Sexual Exploitation and Organised Procuring in Finland*, Publication Series no. 62, European Institute for Crime Prevention and Control (HEUNI).

Wheaton, E.M., Schauer, E.J., and Galli, T.V. (2010) 'Economics of human trafficking', *International Migration*, 48(4): 114–41.

Wilson, J. and Dalton, E. (2008) 'Human trafficking in the Heartland: variations in law enforcement awareness response', *Journal of Contemporary Criminal Justice*, 24(3): 296–313.

Zainal, Z. (2007) 'Case study as research method', *UTM Jurnal Kemanusiaan*, 5(1): 1–6.

PART III

Case Studies

8

Brexit-Precipitated or Free Movement-Facilitated? Labour Exploitation of EU Migrants in the UK

Samantha Currie

Introduction

The starting point for this chapter is the increased risk of labour exploitation for EU migrants in the UK following the UK's withdrawal from the EU. Commentators across different disciplinary perspectives have argued that changes to the legal framework prompted by Brexit[1] have heightened the likelihood of exploitative labour experiences among migrants from the EU (Anti-Trafficking Monitoring Group, 2017; French, 2018; Walsh et al, 2022). After setting out the current context around the position of EU migrants in the UK, the chapter will reflect on the position prior to the 2016 referendum in the UK on membership of the EU in which a majority (51.9 per cent) voted in favour of the UK leaving. It is argued that the free movement framework facilitated the exploitation of some – not all – EU migrants within the UK labour market. A particular focus of analysis is the experience of

---

[1] The UK's withdrawal from the EU, widely referred to as Brexit, was set in motion following the referendum in June 2016. The UK formally left on 31 January 2020 under the terms of the Withdrawal Agreement: Agreement on the withdrawal of the United Kingdom of Great Britain and Northern Ireland from the European Union and the European Atomic Energy Community [2019] OJ C 384 I/01.

those who moved to the UK from the Central and Eastern European (CEE) countries that acceded to the EU in 2004 (the 'EU8')[2] and 2007 (the 'EU2').[3] Migrants from both the EU8 and EU2 have been more heavily concentrated in sectors of the labour market in which slippage along the continuum from poor treatment in employment to more severe forms of labour exploitation is common (Fox et al, 2015; Fitzgerald and Smoczyński, 2017; Sumption and Fernández-Reino, 2018; see further Pajon, this volume). These migrants have had a higher visibility as victims of the types of exploitation deemed to constitute modern slavery than EU migrants from the older member states, such as the sexual exploitation of Romanian women (see further Pajon, this volume). Arguably, this can be traced back to the unequal way in which 'free' movement was extended to the new EU citizens at the time of EU enlargement. EU8 and EU2 migrants' access to the labour market was conditioned on their willingness to carry out low-skilled roles to plug gaps in the (pre-financial crash) labour market.

The chapter moves on to consider how the curtailed nature of the original access rights has ongoing implications for the treatment of migrants from the EU8 and EU2 states in the workplace. In addition, it shows that the restrictive trajectory of immigration policy generally, and the move towards limiting support for those identified as potential victims of modern slavery specifically – encapsulated in the Nationality and Borders Act 2022[4] and Illegal Migration Act 2023[5] – offers little solace for the future to *any* migrants experiencing labour exploitation in the UK. Throughout, this chapter relies on an understanding of exploitation as existing on a continuum (Skrivankova, 2010: 16) whereby 'labour exploitation involves a continuum of malpractices and legal infractions, many of which fall between its two extremes of "decent" work and "severe" exploitation' (Walsh et al, 2022: 2). The intention is not to insinuate that exploitation is an inevitable consequence of precarious work, but that precarious work makes exploitation more proximate. Migrant workers in low-skilled and insecure positions are therefore less able to render themselves invulnerable to the risk of exploitation.

---

[2] The EU8 comprises the 2004 CEE accession states: Czech Republic, Estonia, Hungary, Latvia, Lithuania, Poland, Slovakia, and Slovenia. Note that Malta and Cyprus also acceded in 2004 but were not subject to transitional limitations on the free movement rights of their citizens, purportedly as a result of their smaller population sizes.
[3] The EU2 comprises Romania and Bulgaria, the 2007 accession states.
[4] www.legislation.gov.uk/ukpga/2022/36/contents/enacted
[5] https://bills.parliament.uk/bills/3429

Brexit: a facilitator of labour exploitation

The loss of the currency of EU citizenship in the UK has had significant consequences for EU migrants already in the UK; for example, by necessitating navigation of the EU Settlement Scheme (hereafter, EUSS). For those wishing to move to the UK post-Brexit there is now a need to navigate the immigration system sans free movement; for example, through fulfilment of conditions in the Points-Based System (hereafter, the PBS). Underlying the premise that Brexit is a facilitator of exploitation is the idea that with such large-scale change to legal rights and increased insecurity of immigration status comes precariousness. Poorer working conditions become more likely and such conditions may encompass exploitation or become exploitative over time (Skrivankova, 2010; Lerche, 2011). This section first considers the position of EU migrants present in the UK before the end of free movement (31 December 2020) and, second, those who move in the aftermath of free movement to explain why Brexit is understood as having facilitated the potential for exploitation.

EU migrants already in the UK: navigating the EUSS

For those EU migrants in the UK prior to the end of free movement (31 December 2020), the EUSS has provided the means to retain residence rights. Settled status is available to those EU/EEA citizens and their family members who can evidence they have been continuously resident in the UK for five years by the time of their application. Such a grant allows them to remain in the UK indefinitely. Those who have not been continuously resident for five years are only eligible for pre-settled status; which enables them to stay until they have reached the five-year threshold, at which point they will need to apply for settled status. Following a grant of settled status, access to healthcare, pensions, and other benefits is relatively secure, and the right to reside in relation to accessing welfare benefits is considered as the default. A grant of pre-settled status, however, renders entitlement to welfare benefits dependent on the right to reside under the Immigration (EEA) Regulations 2016.[6] Therefore, the ability to access support is much more constrained under this status.

The deadline for EU migrants who were living in the UK before the 31 December 2020 deadline to apply to the EUSS to secure legal status was

---

[6] Note that this has been subject to legal challenge and a referral was made to the European Court of Justice (ECJ) for a preliminary ruling in Case C-709/20 *CG v Department for Communities in Northern Ireland* ECLI:EU:C: 2021:602. The ECJ held, however, that the UK was entitled to limit access to benefits for those with pre-settled status.

30 June 2021. While the EUSS represents a route to regularization, there are risks that the most vulnerable – such as those in precarious positions or subject to exploitation – will be outside of its reach (Barnard et al, 2022: 383). Several factors are significant in relation to this. For example, in terms of access, being unaware of the existence of the scheme or being unable to complete the necessary online forms and supply the necessary documentation electronically (Sumption and Fernández-Reino, 2020). In July 2021 the Home Office (2021) did agree to allow late applications to be made when there are 'reasonable grounds' for doing so. Moreover, the Home Office (2022) caseworker guidance specifies that such a reasonable ground for missing the deadline would normally include being a victim of modern slavery or not having the requisite digital or language skills. However, there are clear concerns that certain vulnerable groups of EU migrants are continuing to have difficulty in evidencing their continuous residence (Sumption and Fernández-Reino, 2020; Fernández-Reino and Sumption, 2022). The EUSS, therefore, while providing a route for regularization for those already in the UK, has in its operation excluded certain vulnerable migrants – while it is not possible to know the number of people who need to apply to the EUSS, or how many have not done so. This is concerning because it is the people who have likely not applied who are more vulnerable and without resources that stand to lose the most by virtue of not being able to evidence their security of status. Without the authority of a lawful EUSS status, such migrants exist in the UK irregularly, which brings increased risks of precariousness and potential for severe exploitation (Lewis and Waite, 2019: 221).

EU migrants in the UK post-free movement

Now that free movement no longer shapes the parameters of labour migration from EU states to the UK; all those who wish to migrate must do so under the terms of the UK'S PBS for immigration. The introduction of this system makes clear that highly skilled migration (although a more appropriate description might be 'highly valued') is prioritized.[7] Admission is granted under the Skilled Worker route on the basis of having secured a job offer from a licensed employer, educational qualification, English proficiency, and a salary that meets the set threshold, of which the general salary threshold is

---

[7] From January 2021, a points-based immigration system entered into effect under the Immigration Social Security Co-ordination (EU Withdrawal) Act 2020 (C. 20). See also www.gov.uk/government/publications/uk-points-based-immigration-system-employer-information/the-uks-points-based-immigration-system-an-introduction-for-employers [Accessed 27 January 2023].

£25,600 (Walsh et al, 2022: 1). There are currently very few lawful pathways to access work classified as low skilled in the UK. For example, there is a Temporary Seasonal Worker Visa Scheme within the agricultural sector, but this has a maximum capacity of 30,000 workers and the government has said it will seek to reduce reliance on the scheme further in 2023 with a view to it ending in 2024 (Home Office, 2021a; Walsh et al, 2022: 2). The absence of official routes to lower-skilled roles is likely to encourage reliance on informal routes (Simon et al, 2018).[8] As such there is a real possibility that those who seek to move to the UK in the future may be at increased risk of experiencing precarity and exploitation. Exclusion from work in the formal sector through restrictive immigration policy heightens vulnerability to exploitation with informality acting as a 'gateway to forced labour' (Allain et al, 2013: 5).

The former Independent Anti-Slavery Commissioner,[9] Dame Sara Thornton, highlighted the specific risks posed by the PBS for the facilitation of exploitation in her 2020/21 annual report (IASC, 2022: 50), specifically referring to the position of EU nationals in low-skilled sectors which have become reliant on EU migrant labour. This latter point brings the discussion to the next juncture; while the premise that Brexit, or more accurately changes to the law and policy framework prompted by Brexit, have facilitated the exploitation of migrants, the free movement framework itself has also facilitated exploitation, particularly in the case of certain groups of EU migrants.

Free movement as a facilitator of labour exploitation

The concept of free movement is associated with having created lawful pathways to migration.[10] The tabloid press has tended to take this association to the extreme, treating free movement as essentially equivalent to an open border for EU migrants (Morrison, 2019). This is despite EU law on free movement and citizenship having been on a restrictive trajectory for a

---

[8] The minimum salary threshold of £25,600 will be an effective bar in itself.
[9] In April 2022, after a term of three years, Dame Sara Thornton stood down from the position of Independent Anti-Slavery Commissioner. At the time of writing in March 2023 the government has still not appointed a new Commissioner, despite the office being a requirement of the Modern Slavery Act 2015 (s 40).
[10] Of course, the corollary of such lawful pathways for some is the closing down of lawful migration routes to others. The EU's privileging of intra-EU migration, on the one hand, and the exclusion of non-EU, 'third country' nationals on the other hand, has been subject to criticism by scholars. For example, see Kostakopoulou (2002, 2009). There is also a link that can be drawn here with the racialized nature of immigration controls – see further, Anderson (2013).

number of years, both as a consequence of more stringent conditions in EU secondary legislation[11] and case law of the European Court of Justice (hereafter, ECJ) interpreting the free movement of persons provisions in the EU treaties.[12] Yet it is true that EU law on the free movement of workers provided for open access to the labour market for EU nationals and that was not dependent on earning a certain salary or working a set number of hours.[13] This broadness of approach to defining EU migrant workers, and the lack of conditions attaching to the status, has – in stark contrast to the PBS – enabled free movement rights to be accessible to low-skilled workers. This ensured that 'over the past 15 years, free movement has been the main legal channel through which migrant workers have come to the UK to work low-skilled jobs' (Sumption and Fernández-Reino, 2018).

This section will first examine the disingenuously self-serving way the free movement framework originally applied to migrants from the CEE accession states. The post-EU enlargement transitional rules applicable to the EU8 and EU2 deliberately directed workers to jobs in low-skilled sectors, often characterized by precariousness. Second, it provides an overview of EU migrants' position in the labour market, emphasizing the role that EU8 and EU2 migrants have played in those sectors described as low skilled. Finally, it reflects on the extent to which EU8 and EU2 migrants have been visible as victims of modern slavery in the UK identification system (the National Referral Mechanism[14]), reflecting on how the original terms on which free movement was offered has increased migrants from the newer CEE member states' vulnerability to exploitation.

The terms of 'free' movement

In the early 2000s the approaching accession to the EU of several post-communist CEE states prompted much discussion. Some contributions were framed positively and emphasized the 'reunification' of European countries and peoples (Kengerlinsky, 2004).[15] However, even such prima facie welcoming implicitly prioritized the interests of the older, Western member states. Myslinska (2021: 271) has drawn attention to the 'western-centric

---

[11] Directive 2004/38 [2004] OJ L158/77.
[12] For example, Case C-333/13 *Dano* ECLI:EU:C: 2014:2358.
[13] Case 66/85 *Lawrie-Blum* ECLI:EU:C: 1986:284; Case 139/85 *Kempf* ECLI:EU:C: 1986:223.
[14] See further www.gov.uk/government/publications/human-trafficking-victims-referral-and-assessment-forms/guidance-on-the-national-referral-mechanism-for-potential-adult-victims-of-modern-slavery-england-and-wales [Accessed 15 July 2023].
[15] The EU15 refers to Austria, Belgium, Denmark, Finland, France, Germany, Greece, Ireland, Italy, Luxembourg, the Netherlands, Portugal, Spain, Sweden, and the UK, at this time.

inferiorisation of the CEE region' that was endemic in the enlargement process. The EU institutions, particularly the Commission, portrayed the CEE region in need of 'rescue' by older EU states to 'partake some of the achievement of western Europe' (2021: 273; see also Spanger, 2022). Accession states were required to satisfy the member states that several key criteria had been met, including stability of institutions guaranteeing democracy, the rule of law and human rights, and the functioning of a market economy. Other contributors to pre-enlargement debates were deliberately hostile to the idea of new EU citizens gaining rights to live and work in the EU15 (Migration Watch, 2003). The tone of debates from this time about migration have persisted in the UK. For example, controversy around the 2004 UK decision to allow EU8 nationals to access the labour market eventually fed into the climate in which the 2016 referendum on EU membership was held.

EU free movement rights were not automatically granted to the post-2004 EU citizens; they were phased in to align with the specific needs of the older member states through the transitional arrangements included in the Accession Treaties.[16] High wage differentials between the CEE accession states and the more established EU15 states, combined with high unemployment rates in some of the accession states (Paternoster, 2004), contributed to predictions of 'influxes' of arrivals should migration not be restricted. Transitional arrangements were introduced by the EU, authorizing national limitations on their exercise of free movement – the principal benefit bestowed by Union citizenship status and a key symbol of EU membership – for a period of up to seven years. Free movement per se was not subject to prohibition, but member states could lawfully derogate from the provisions in EU secondary legislation on one of the four freedoms of EU citizens: the free movement of *workers*.[17] The legal impact of the transitional arrangements, therefore, was that established member states were permitted to decide the conditions under which EU8 and EU2 nationals were able to access employment within their respective territories.

The approach taken by the UK in respect of EU8 nationals has been both extolled and bemoaned for its supposed generosity. The UK, along with Ireland and Sweden, formed part of the minority of EU15 states that allowed the free movement of EU8 workers, although this was subject to registration

---

[16] Treaty of Accession 2003 [2003] OJ L236/17; Treaty of Accession 2005 [2005] OJ L157/11.
[17] Then Articles 1–6, Regulation 1612/68 on free movement of workers within the Community [1968] OJ L257/2; now replaced by Regulation 492/2011 of the European Parliament and of the Council of 5 April 2011 on freedom of movement for workers within the Union [2011] OJ L141/1. Article 45 TFEU is the key primary law provision relating to free movement of workers.

on a Worker Registration Scheme (WRS). Yet, this decision was heavily influenced by economic and employment dynamics at the (pre-financial crisis) time. Skills shortages in 'hard-to-fill' jobs and certain sectors, tending to be low paid and deemed low skilled, were the primary motivation cited by the Labour government, which was also keen to promote the 'willingness to work' and 'flexibility' of EU8 migrants (Blunkett, 2004). The government simultaneously implemented rules restricting EU8 migrant workers' access to social welfare entitlement during the operation of the WRS, to the effect that even those lawfully in work in the UK were not able to access social benefits connected to employment in the same way that migrant workers from EU15 member states were. Due to these dual rules on labour market access and entitlement to social benefits, the UK's post-2004 enlargement system was one of the most disingenuous to emerge among the EU15. The UK was able to posit its approach as a liberal one, albeit in the interests of the economy, without significant scrutiny of the lawfulness or ethics of the system put in place (Currie, 2008).

If the rules on EU8 migration were surreptitiously deceitful, an overtly restrictive system was later implemented to limit the free movement rights of Romanian and Bulgarian (EU2) nationals.[18] The Labour government's approach in the aftermath of the 2007 enlargement was to impose labour market restrictions of the type envisaged by the transitional arrangements in the Accession Treaties. The decision to restrict EU2 migration was framed by the government as a response to some 'transitional impacts' of EU8 migration. When announcing that free movement to the UK would be curtailed for EU2 nationals, John Reid (Home Secretary at the time) reiterated that EU8 migration had been positive for the UK economy (Reid, 2006). He then went on to acknowledge the existence of some localized infrastructure-related effects, which included increased admissions for some schools coupled with increased demand for rental accommodation in certain areas. Romanians and Bulgarians were kept firmly within the remit of national immigration rules and were permitted to work in the UK only after obtaining a 'worker authorization card', essentially a work permit issued in relation to a specific job. This imposition of transitional restrictions was accompanied by the reservation of all places on the key 'low-skilled' migration schemes at the time – the Sectors Based Scheme and the Seasonal Agricultural Workers Scheme – for Romanians and Bulgarians. From a legal perspective this reflects the 'preference clause' in the Accession Treaties, which obliges member states implementing transitional arrangements to give preference to accession nationals over nationals of third countries. This framing of EU8

---

[18] Following Croatia's accession to the EU in 2013, the UK similarly implemented strict restrictions on Croatian nationals' access to the labour market (Home Office, 2012).

and EU2 migration as being principally to step into '3d' (dirty, dangerous, and demeaning) jobs (see ILO, 2010) evidences the government's expectation that the CEE accession nationals would essentially fulfil the role of a reserve army of labour (Pradella and Cillo, 2015: 44–56). Their presence would be welcome in so far as they were plugging gaps in parts of the labour market characterized by low pay and low status. Despite EU citizenship supposedly offering those who hold the status fundamental rights protection,[19] there is no doubt that economic considerations dominated decision making about the rights of the CEE accession migrants.

The curtailed way in which the free movement framework has been applied to EU8 and EU2 migrants has also influenced (and likely been influenced by) the racialization of CEE migrants. Spanger (2022: 158) in her research in the Danish context has explained how CEE migrants are positioned as 'other European'. In the UK context, critical race scholars have demonstrated how racialization of migrants from CEE countries is borne out through experiences of racism and xenophobia for individuals, and collectively through the normalization of stereotypes based on ethnicity and class (McDowell, 2008; Fox et al, 2012; Myslinska, 2021). This normalization of disadvantage and the idea that EU8 and EU2 migrants are distinct from other EU migrants has characterized their labour market experience, as the remaining discussion in this section will further explore.

EU migrants in the UK labour market

It is estimated that in 2018 3.6 million EU-born migrants lived in the UK, with Poland the country of origin with the largest number of EU migrants (832,000), followed by Romania (392,000), and then Ireland (369,000) (Vargas-Silva and Fernandez-Reino, 2019: 5). In terms of the wider picture, it is estimated that in 2018 the number of EU8 migrants in the UK was 1,323,000 (compared with 167,000 in 2004) and the number of EU2 migrants was 495,000 (compared with 42,000 in 2007) (Vargas-Silva and Fernandez-Reino, 2019: 4).

In the years following the 2004 and 2007 EU enlargements several studies have acknowledged the tendency of EU8 and EU2 migrants to occupy positions in the 'invisible but functional "secondary" part of the economy' within the EU15 member states (Iglicka, 2006; Favell, 2008). In the UK context this meant positions in cleaning, food processing, agriculture, hospitality, and catering were filled by EU8 and EU2 migrants in the years following the 2004 and 2007 accessions (Sumption and

---

[19] For example, Article 20 TFEU, Charter of Fundamental Rights of the European Union [2010] O.J. C83, vol 53, p 380.

Fernández-Reino, 2018). This underlines how 'certain business sectors within the UK have been heavily reliant on the recruitment of seasonal/ and or temporary' EU migrant labour (Walsh et al, 2022: 2). Working in low-skilled sectors obviously does not in and of itself equate to being in a position of exploitation. However, occupying low-paid and low-status positions undoubtedly renders people more vulnerable to precarious conditions of employment with an increased likelihood of exploitation. There is a body of evidence to support the view that EU8 and EU2 migrants in the UK have been exposed more to both disadvantageous and abusive labour conditions than migrants from EU14 member states (Fox et al, 2015). It is a well-established global trend that migrant workers are concentrated in the most 'precarious, unhealthy and dangerous jobs' (Pradella and Cillo, 2015: 48). The contention here is that EU8 and EU2 migrants have experienced a continuing differentiation from other EU migrants as regards to their labour market positioning and status, a trend which again links in with the racialization of CEE migrants (as discussed previously). A report from the Equality and Human Rights Commission (Kofman et al, 2009) picked up on the closer proximity of the cohort to precarity and the potential for this to spill over to exploitation:

> There is considerable research evidence of migrants from the eight Eastern European countries which joined the EU in 2004 [...] facing poor conditions, unfair treatment and workplace harassment. Exploitation may take the form of lower wages, payments in advance to secure jobs, and illegal or excessive deductions by gangmasters. Name-calling and racial harassment by supervisors and co-workers is common in some settings. Those employed by agencies, who are significant recruiters of labour in sectors such as cleaning, health, hospitality and manufacturing, may not even know who their employers are.[20]

This prompts reflection of whether CEE accession migrants from the EU8 and EU2, as a cohort of EU migrants particularly likely to be in low-skilled work in sectors with a high degree of precariousness, have been 'visible' as victims of labour exploitation in the UK. In other words, has there been official acknowledgment of EU8 and EU2 migrants' labour market positioning and vulnerability to exploitation?

---

[20] It is clear that recruitment agencies, based in the CEE region and UK, have played a role in directing some migrants into precarious and exploitative work. See Sporton (2013) and Currie (2008).

Visibility as victims of modern slavery

Modern slavery is the 'leading policy term used to refer to various forms of severe exploitation in the UK' (Lewis and Waite, 2019: 220) although as noted by others within this collection it remains as a contested term (see further Hynes and Dottridge, O'Connell, de Vries and Cockbain, and Bhagat, this volume). The aim of this part of the discussion is, to explore whether the experiences of EU migrants in the UK, with particular focus on CEE accession migrants who we know have been most present in low-skilled and precarious work, have been visible as victims of modern slavery in the UK. I assess this via a two-stage process; namely, whether the UK authorities (principally the system for identifying victims of modern slavery) have formally acknowledged EU8 and EU2 migrants as having experienced modern slavery. Second, consideration is given to whether any such recognition has prompted any action and/or remedy.

The differentiation that exists between EU14 migrants (that is, the 'old' pre-2004 member states), on the one hand, and EU8 and EU2 migrants, on the other hand holds a particular relevancy. A process of normalization has occurred about the 'rightful' role in the labour market of CEE accession migrants. Anderson (2015: 44) captures the difference in perception of CEE EU migrants that has persisted since the EU expansions of 2004 and 2007:

> [EU nationals] are no longer 'migrants' in that they are no longer subject to immigration controls. However, people from those states that have entered the EU since 2004 are, in political and public debate, still very strongly viewed as migrants. In the UK there are claims that they are both 'taking jobs' from British people, and claiming benefits to which they may be legally, but not morally, entitled.

The purposeful directing of CEE accession migrants through the application of legal rules to lower tiers of the labour market set in motion a long-term association between this group of migrants and low-status, more precarious forms of employment. This sentiment that EU8 and EU2 migrants do not have an equivalent status within the labour market as other EU migrants has been promulgated by parts of the media and some politicians. Overall, the more precarious labour market position of the migrants has been deemed acceptable, or even appropriate (O'Connell Davidson, 2010: 245), by virtue of the approach of the Accession Treaties, the national framework, and media/political and public discourse. Lewis and Waite (2019: 229) point to the vulnerabilizing role of the precarious legal status of EU8 and EU2 migrants who, although technically legally present in the UK, had conditions placed on their legality by the transitional mobility restrictions put in place by the UK – conditions which did not apply to other EU migrants. Lewis and Waite also point to the possibility of unscrupulous employers taking advantage of such vulnerability; for example, by making threats of denunciation to immigration authorities to migrants who may be uncertain about their own compatibility with immigration (or, here, free movement-related rules). Moreover, the findings of Burcu et al (2021) corroborate this; highlighting that both Romanian and Bulgarian workers had been threatened with being reported to the immigration authorities prior to the end of free movement when they were lawfully working within the UK labour market. The workers were also working without employment contracts and were not being paid the minimum wage.

While it seems that EU8 and EU2 migrants have had greater visibility as victims of labour exploitation than other EU migrants, it cannot be assumed that this has elevated their position in terms of allowing them to seek particular redress or have the actions of their employers challenged. The modern slavery terminology has contemporary currency and is the preferred language of the UK government and Parliament, encapsulated by the enactment of the Modern Slavery Act 2015. A point that is often ignored is the recognition that the often-lauded Modern Slavery Act is a central tool of the hostile environment, providing a component for the thrust of both anti-immigrant and anti-worker policies (see further Faulkner, this volume). However, the shortcomings of the UK's modern slavery frame and associated terminology that is favoured in law and policy arenas have been well examined in academic literature. For example, Mantouvalou (2018: 1045) has warned of the limiting effect of criminal law as a response to labour exploitation owing to the resulting focus on individual conduct and disregard of structural injustices. Labour law, or indeed a focus on protecting workers from labour abuse and exploitation, has not been part of the package of responses deemed appropriate to fight the 'scourge' of modern slavery.[21] O'Connell Davidson (2010: 245) has written persuasively that the language of modern slavery, especially in connection with human trafficking, 'divides[s] a small number of "deserving victims" from the masses that remain "undeserving" of rights and freedoms'. With Chuang (2014) emphasizing that by 'conflating trafficking and forced labour with the far more narrowly defined (and extreme) practice of "slavery" – however rhetorically effective – is not only legally inaccurate, but it also risks undermining effective application of the relevant legal regimes'.[22] The ultimate effect is that labour exploitation, viewed through the modern slavery prism, is a phenomenon that only happens exceptionally, and for

---

[21] Indeed, the term modern slavery has risen in prominence at a time when the government has been promoting repressive labour law measures, such as the Trade Union Act 2016.

[22] J.A. Chuang (2014) 'Exploitation creep and the unmaking of human trafficking law', *American Journal of International Law*, 108(4): 609–49.

which the state authorities have little responsibility or ability to influence (see Pavlou, 2018). The modern slavery frame does not tend to allow space for precarious employment per se, or 'non-extreme' exploitation, to be acknowledged or addressed.

An example of severe exploitation of post-accession CEE migrants is provided by the series of legal cases concerning the company DJ Houghton Catching Services, a supplier of labour to chicken farms.[23] Between 2008 and 2012 this gangmaster recruited[24] Lithuanian men who were required to catch chickens at night and load them on to trucks for distribution across the country. The catalogue of inadequate and abusive treatment amounted to a 'gruelling and exploitative work regime' in breach of the Agricultural Wages (England and Wales) Order 2010 and the Gangmasters (Licensing Conditions) Rules 2009.[25] This included withholding of wages, unlawful deduction of wages, not paying the minimum wage, breaching licensing standards concerning travel arrangements and safety at work, and providing inadequate, overcrowded accommodation. The claimants also reported limited access to toilet breaks and sleep deprivation, as well as being threatened and physically abused by supervisors. Such extensive poor treatment would clearly sit towards the more extreme end of the 'continuum of exploitation' (Skrivankova, 2010: 16) and the demarcation of this as exploitative would be uncontroversial. Indeed, although classifying forms of modern slavery is fraught with contention and the influence of (sometimes competing) political agendas (Quirk et al, 2020), this case could be considered an archetypal example of what 'counts' as modern slavery. It is important, however, not to overlook other less dramatic – or 'routine' (Murphy et al, 2020) – forms of exploitation which might typically go unchallenged or not obviously fall within a specific modern slavery category (for example, as trafficking or forced labour). Such undetected exploitation might include an individual being subject to one of the forms of mistreatment that the Lithuanian claimants in the previous case experienced – such as wage deduction – which would undoubtedly still have negative implications in terms of status and experience without, on its own, triggering the modern slavery paradigm. It is also the case that those in precarious forms of employment may initially be at the less extreme end of the continuum of exploitation, but later find that their conditions of employment deteriorate and level of exploitation increase. A link can be made here to Lerche's (2011) work on the continuum of labour relations.

---

[23] Including *G v DJ Houghton Catching Services Ltd* [2016] EWHC 1376 (QB) and *Antuzis v DJ Houghton Catching Services Ltd* [2019] EWHC 843 (QB).

[24] They were trafficked to the UK, with the assistance of a Lithuanian 'middleman'.

[25] As per Lane, J. in *Antuzis v DJ Houghton Catching Services Ltd* [2019] EWHC 843 (QB).

He has demonstrated how what tends to be termed 'low-end' un-decent work which does not fall within the formalized structures of recognized exploitation are still part of a 'continuum of measures deployed to disciple and cheapen labour' (2011: 23).

To anchor this discussion more firmly in the focus of the analysis here, EU8 and EU2 migrants' proximity to and experiences of labour exploitation have been part of media and public consciousness. Nevertheless, 'everyday abuses' (Quirk et al, 2020) of any workers will not usually be perceived as modern slavery. This points to the obfuscating impact of the modern slavery lens: by assessing exploitative experience through this prism, heavy with political connotation and a standard of exceptionalism. Only the more extreme examples of mistreatment have passed the modern slavery threshold and 'counted' as such, as in the *DJ Houghton* case. To this end: 'The concern to single out and stamp out "modern slavery" can mask, or even support, the legitimation of less extreme but still very real forms of exploitation of both migrant and local workers alike' (Freedland and Costello, 2014: 13).

Finally, Barnard and Ludlow (2016) have explored the enforcement of labour rights by EU8 migrants, finding that very few bring claims to Employment Tribunals in any event. These authors, writing with Fraser Butlin (2018), have also demonstrated that being in precarious employment that facilitates exploitation is the 'primary impediment to Tribunal enforcement'. This clearly indicates that employers' exploitative treatment of workers often goes unchallenged.

Now that the role of the free movement framework in facilitating labour exploitation has been considered, the discussion moves next to reflect on the relevance of the arguments expressed here for the future, as we move further into the post-Brexit and post-free movement era.

The aggravating impact of restrictive immigration policy

The chapter began with the premise that Brexit is facilitating labour exploitation of EU migrants and prior to arguing that labour exploitation was also part of the panoply of experiences of EU migrants under the operation of free movement. The conditionality of the version of free movement offered to CEE accession migrants and the deliberate directing to low-skilled sectors of the economy with higher levels of precariousness rendered these migrant workers more vulnerable to labour exploitation. The two previous substantive sections taken together substantiate the view that insecure immigration status *or* supposedly secure immigration status with ambiguity attached to it which, in turn, creates uncertainty as to the rights of the workers, increases the likelihood of labour exploitation. I note several concerning trends relating to the UK's position that seem likely to coalesce and entrench vulnerability of EU migrants to labour exploitation, consequently making it more difficult for those that are exploited to seek any protection.

First, the UK government has clearly signalled its intention to enforce the rules relating to the operation of the EUSS strictly, even to the extent that the refusal of rights to EU migrants appears to breach the terms of the Withdrawal Agreement signed between the EU and the UK in 2019. The Independent Monitoring Authority for the Citizens' Rights Agreements (hereafter, the IMA) was successful in a judicial review challenge against the Home Office on the basis that the stated position that citizens who fail to apply for settled status before the expiry of their pre-settled status automatically lose their rights.[26] The High Court held that the EUSS was operating unlawfully because a right to reside can only be removed in clearly defined circumstances set out in the Withdrawal Agreement. Despite this judgment, at the time of writing[27] no changes have been made to the EUSS and the Home Office is appealing the decision to the Court of Appeal. The broader immigration and asylum system is clearly also on a restrictive trajectory, as encapsulated in the Nationality and Borders Act 2022 and Illegal Migration Act 2023 both of which are wrapped in the rhetoric of 'stopping the boats'. The impact of this is that those who fall outside the scope of the EUSS will be within the remit of the standard immigration rules and thus, if deemed to be present illegally, subject to the 'hostile environment'-influenced enforcement (York, 2018). This includes potential prosecution for the offence of 'illegal working' under the Immigration Act 2016 which prohibits those without lawful status from working.

Second, there remains significant demand for staff in the sectors and roles that have in recent years been filled by EU8 and EU2 migrants. The summer of 2021 saw numerous reports of significant staff shortages across many of the sectors traditionally strongly associated with the presence of EU8 and EU2 migrants, including transport, hospitality, and construction (Partridge and Partington, 2021). The COVID-19 pandemic, and the travel restrictions in place since 2020 consequently, make it difficult to accurately assess the extent to which Brexit has contributed to the shortage of workers, although the absence of free movement rights has had an impact in reducing the available workforce from the EU (Thomas, 2021). As noted earlier in this piece, such positions will not be accessible through the

---

[26] *R (on the application of the Independent Monitoring Authority for the Citizens' Rights Agreements v Secretary of State for the Home Department* [2022] EWHC 3274 (Admin).
[27] March 2023.

post-Brexit PBS. Therefore, some workers will move irregularly and work within the shadow economy, with the clear risks this has for exploitation. In addition, staff shortages can be used to support the introduction of government- and employer-supported schemes to recruit EU8 and EU2 migrants to work in the sectors experiencing difficulties, as has been the case with the Temporary Seasonal Workers Visa Scheme for agricultural jobs. A temporary scheme was also implemented in 2021 in response to problems experienced in the road transport industry owing to a shortage of Heavy Goods Vehicle drivers. Temporary visas of up to three months' duration were available for 5,500 HGV drivers (Duncan, 2021). Offering time-limited entitlements to work in certain sectors to migrant workers, with conditions attached to residence and limited social entitlements, creates new risks. Temporary migration programmes are themselves criticized for being vehicles for exploitation (Consterdine and Samuk, 2018). Shipping workers in during times of particular economic need on the basis that they will leave after a short period, or else risk being illegally present in the UK – with the vulnerabilities that this status generates – itself represents a form of exploitative employment recruitment.

Third, even migrant workers formally identified as victims of modern slavery in the UK, based on having experienced (severe) labour exploitation, are not entitled to an automatic grant of leave to remain in order to secure their immigration status (Helen Bamber Foundation, 2020; Currie and Bezzano, 2021). This has considerable implications for the ability of those without a secure status to access appropriate support and protection to make progress towards recovery (British Red Cross, 2019). In turn, the inability to access support following identification as a victim of modern slavery can also, crucially, lead to re-exploitation (British Red Cross, 2019).[28] This affects those without secure status from within and outside the EU but is being experienced for the first time by many EU nationals who previously had an assumed automatic status in the UK under the EU Treaties. This point also links to the spilling over of the UK's restrictive approach to addressing 'illegal' immigration to the system for identifying and (supposedly) protecting victims of modern slavery. This can be seen in how Home Secretaries such as Priti Patel (2019–22) and Suella Braverman (6 September 2022–19 October 2022, and again 25 October 2022–13 November 2023), have insisted that the system for identifying victims of modern slavery – the National Referral Mechanism (NRM) – is being abused by criminals (Home Office, 2021b; Braverman, 2022). The current Conservative government's apparent desire to

---

[28] Although it is important to acknowledge that scholars have also drawn attention to the problematic nature of anti-trafficking-specific visas. For example, Raza (2022) links a US visa issued to victims of trafficking with a racialized immigration system with the consequential distinguishing between those worthy and protection and the undeserving.

prevent unlawful arrivals of migrants on small boats has also been presented prominently during 2022–23 as justification for sweeping changes to the immigration and asylum system that implicate victims of modern slavery.

The fusing of the political preoccupation with illegal immigration and the approach to addressing modern slavery is reflected in specific reforms across both the modern slavery and immigration frameworks. In November 2021 the Immigration Enforcement Competent Authority was set up to make NRM decisions in respect of suspected victims referred to the NRM who have a criminal conviction (a not uncommon situation seeing as it is well known that many victims are still to be prosecuted for crimes they have been compelled to commit) (Southwell and Roberts, 2017). It is further reflected in specific provisions of the Nationality and Borders Act 2022, such as the introduction of a new public order exemption to bar victims identified under the NRM from support if they have been given a prison sentence of 12 months or more, or if they have claimed to be a victim in 'bad faith'. The legislation also removes the right to 'further assistance' if an exploited person has already been through the NRM and, further, stipulates that a person's credibility is undermined as a consequence of 'late disclosure' of the exploitation they have experienced.[29] The Illegal Migration Act 2023 takes the conflation of the debates on 'illegal' immigration and modern slavery to a new level and, if enacted, will extend the reach of the public order exemption further to encompass anyone deemed to have entered the UK unlawfully. The implications of this for victims of modern slavery are far-reaching (Modern Slavery and Human Rights Policy and Evidence Centre, 2023). They include removing people from the UK who have already been issued with positive Reasonable Grounds (initial stage) NRM decisions, refusing access to support services, and ceasing the NRM process so that no Conclusive Grounds (final stage) NRM decision is made.[30] While those who have experienced modern slavery have never been immune from immigration enforcement, it is clear that the response to the 'problem' of illegal migration is now flagrantly striking right at the heart of the system put in place to support victims of modern slavery. Moreover, in the post-Brexit context, being deemed to be 'illegal' is relevant to the situation of considerably more migrants.

Conclusion

The discussion here has explored the vulnerability of EU migrants, particularly those from the CEE accession states, to labour exploitation.

---

[29] Part 5 of the Act deals with modern slavery.
[30] The modern slavery provisions are in clauses 21–8 of the Illegal Migration Bill 2023.

Brexit has precipitated conditions in which exploitation can occur. It has also been demonstrated, however, that the free movement framework – particularly the curtailed version extended to EU8 and EU2 migrants – has facilitated exploitation by deliberately directing workers to low-skilled and more precarious work in which slippage to exploitation can occur. The workers impacted by this framework, which extended a diluted version of free movement with attached conditionality and uncertainty, now also stand to be affected by the post-Brexit landscape in terms of the EUSS, which also operates based on similar conditionality, for example, as to length of residence as a qualifier for status. They therefore stand to be doubly disadvantaged by the combined impact of the post-EU enlargement free movement framework and the post-Brexit EUSS.

Insecure immigration status, and restrictive immigration policy generally, can enhance the vulnerability of people to labour exploitation. Moreover, immigration regimes tend to embody and reproduce inequalities of race, class, and gender, endemic within society at large. Immigration policy in the UK is interfering with the potential to protect and support victims of labour exploitation in the way that being classified as illegally present, and thus being subject to immigration enforcement, can trump the supposedly beneficial impact of being identified as a victim. The trend of immigration enforcement creeping further into the arena of modern slavery victim protection has become ever more established in recent years. Consequently, there is very little solace that can be offered to any migrants unable to demonstrate a lawful immigration status who experience labour exploitation in the UK.

References

Allain, J., Crane, A., LeBaron, G., and Behahani, L. (2013) *Forced Labour's Business Models and Supply Chains*, York: Joseph Rowntree Foundation.

Anderson, B. (2013) *Us and Them? The Dangerous Politics of Immigration Control*, Oxford: Oxford University Press.

Anderson, B. (2015) 'Precarious work, immigration and governance', in C. Schierup, R. Munck, B. Likiic-Brboricm, and A. Neergaard (eds) *Migration, Precarity and Global Governance: Challenges and Opportunities for Labour*, Oxford: Oxford University Press, pp 68–82.

Anti-Trafficking Monitoring Group (2017) *Brexit and the UK's Fight against Modern Slavery*, London: Anti-Trafficking Monitoring Group.

Barnard, C. and Ludlow, A. (2016) 'Enforcement of employment rights by EU-8 workers in Employment Tribunals', *Industrial Law Journal*, 45(1): 1.

Barnard, C., Ludlow, A., and Fraser Butlin, S. (2018) 'Beyond employment tribunals: enforcement of employment rights by EU-8 migrant workers', *Industrial Law Journal*, 47(2): 226–62.

Barnard, C., Fraser Butlin, S., and Costello, F. (2022) 'The changing status of European Union nationals in the United Kingdom following Brexit: the lived experience of the European Union Settlement Scheme', *Social & Legal Studies*, 31(3): 365–88.

Blunkett, D. (2004) Home Secretary, House of Commons: Hansard, HC Deb, vol 48, col 23, 23 February.

Braverman, S. (2022) 'Our plan for law and order', [speech at Conservative Party Conference] 4 October. Available from: www.conservatives.com/news/2022/our-plan-for-law-and-order [Accessed 27 January 2023].

British Red Cross (2019) 'Hope for the future: support for survivors of trafficking after the NRM', *British Red Cross*, [online]. Available from: https://trafficking-response.org/wp-content/uploads/2021/04/Hope-for-the-Future.pdf [Accessed 27 January 2023].

Burcu, O., Gardner, A., and Gray, C. (2021) *Understanding Risks of Exploitation for Vulnerable Migrant Workers in the UK During COVID-19*, Nottingham: University of Nottingham Rights Lab.

Chuang, Janie A. (2014) 'Exploitation creep and the unmaking of human trafficking law', *American Journal of International Law*, 108(4): 609–49.

Consterdine, E. and Samuk, S. (2018) 'Temporary migration programmes: the cause or antidote of migrant worker exploitation in UK agriculture', *Journal of International Migration and Integration*, 19(4): 1005–20.

Currie, S. (2008) *Migration, Work and Citizenship in the Enlarged European Union*, Farnham: Ashgate.

Currie, S. and Bezzano, J. (2021) *An Uphill Struggle: Securing Legal Status for Victims and Survivors of Trafficking*, University of Liverpool. Available from: www.liverpool.ac.uk/media/livacuk/law/2-research/An,Uphill,Struggle-Currie,and,Bezzano-Research,Report-Feb,2021.pdf [Accessed 27 January 2023].

Duncan, C. (2021) 'Fuel crisis: emergency visa scheme attracts just 27 tanker drivers from EU', *The Independent*, [online] 5 October. Available from: www.independent.co.uk/news/uk/home-news/fuel-crisis-eu-drivers-visa-b1932336.html [Accessed 27 January 2023].

Favell, A. (2008) 'The face of East-West migration in Europe', *Journal of Ethnic and Migration Studies*, 34(5): 701–16.

Fernández-Reino, M. and Sumption, M. (2022) *How Secure Is Pre-Settled Status for EU Citizens after Brexit?*, Oxford: The Migration Observatory, University of Oxford.

Fitzgerald, I. and Smoczyński, R. (2017) 'Central and Eastern European Accession: changing perspectives on migrant workers', *Social Policy and Society*, 16(4): 659–68.

Fox, J., Moroanu, L., and Szilassy, E. (2012) 'The racialization of the new European migration to the UK', *Sociology*, 46(4): 680–95.

Fox, J., Moroanu, L., and Szilassy, E. (2015) 'Denying discrimination: status, "race", and the whitening of Britain's new Europeans', *Journal of Ethnic and Migration Studies*, 41(5): 729–48.

Freedland, M. and Costello, C. (2014) 'Migrants at work and the division of labour law', in C. Costello and M. Freedland (eds) *Migrants at Work*, Oxford: Oxford University Press.

French, S. (2018) 'Between globalisation and Brexit: migration, pay and the road to modern slavery in the UK hospitality industry', *Research in Hospitality Management*, 8(1): 23–31.

Helen Bamber Foundation (2020) 'Urgent call for the UK Government to protect and safeguard survivors of modern slavery who have insecure immigration status', London: Helen Bamber Foundation. Available from: www.helenbamber.org/sites/default/files/2021-04/HBF-Urgent-Call-for-UK-Government-to-Protect-and-Safeguard-Survivors-of-Modern-Slavery-Final.pdf [Accessed 27 January 2023].

Home Office (2012) *Statement of Intent: Accession of Croatia to the European Union: Transitional Restrictions on Labour Market Access*. Available from: https://assets.publishing.service.gov.uk/government/uploads/system/uploads/attachment_data/file/117967/statement-of-intent.pdf [Accessed 27 January 2023].

Home Office (2021) *EU Settlement Scheme: Information for Community Groups* [promotional material] 1 July. Available from: www.gov.uk/government/publications/eu-settlement-scheme-introduction-for-community-groups/eu-settlement-scheme-information-for-community-groups#reasonable-grounds-for-late-applications [Accessed 27 January 2023].

Home Office (2021a) *Statement of Changes to the Immigration Rules*, 11 October. Available from: www.gov.uk/government/publications/statement-of-changes-to-the-immigration-rules-cp-542-11-october-2021 [Accessed 27 January 2023].

Home Office (2021b) *Press Release: Alarming Rise of Abuse within Modern Slavery System*, 20 March. Available from: www.gov.uk/government/news/alarming-rise-of-abuse-within-modern-slavery-system [Accessed 27 January 2023].

Home Office (2022) *EU Settlement Scheme: EU, other EEA and Swiss Citizens and their Family Members (version 17.0)*, 13 April. Available from: https://assets.publishing.service.gov.uk/government/uploads/system/uploads/attachment_data/file/1069096/EU_Settlement_Scheme_EU_other_EEA_Swiss_citizens_and_family_members.pdf [Accessed 27 January 2023].

Independent Anti-Slavery Commissioner, Annual Report (IASC) 2021–22 (2022), Presented to Parliament pursuant to Section 42 (10) (b) of the Modern Slavery Act 2015, London: Office of the Independent Anti-Slavery Commissioner. Available from: www.antislaverycommissioner.co.uk/media/1796/iasc-annual-report-2021-2022.pdf [Accessed 27 January 2023].

Iglicka, K. (2006) *Free Movement of Workers Two Years after Enlargement: Myths and Reality*, Warsaw: Centre for International Relations.

ILO (2010) *International Labour Migration: A Rights-Based Approach*, Geneva: ILO.

James, D. (2021) 'Migrant worker visa scheme needed to plug labour gap', *Farmers Weekly*, [online] 31 August. Available from: www.fwi.co.uk/news/eu-referendum/migrant-worker-visa-scheme-needed-to-plug-labour-gap [Accessed 27 January 2023].

Kengerlinsky, M. (2004) 'Restrictions in EU immigration policies towards new member states', *Journal of European Affairs*, 2(4): 12–13.

Kofman, E., Lukes, S., D'Angelo, A., and Montagna, N. (2009) *The Equality Implications of Being a Migrant in Britain*, London: EHRC Research Report, p 19.

Kostakopoulou, T. (2002) 'Long-term resident third-country nationals in the European Union: normative expectations and institutional openings', *Journal of Ethnic and Migration Studies*, 28(3): 443–62.

Kostakopoulou, T. (2009) *Citizenship, Identity and Immigration in the European Union: Between Past and Future*, Manchester: Manchester University Press.

Lerche, J. (2011) *The Unfree Labour Category and Unfree Labour Estimates: A Continuum within Low-End Labour Relations*, Manchester: Manchester Papers in Political Economy, CSPE.

Lewis, H. and Waite, L. (2019) 'Migrant illegality, slavery and exploitative work', in G. Craig, A. Balch, H. Lewis, and L. Waite (eds) *The Modern Slavery Agenda*, Bristol: Policy Press.

Mantouvalou, V. (2018) 'The UK Modern Slavery Act 2015 three years on', *Modern Law Review*, 81(6): 1017–45.

McDowell, L. (2008) 'Old and new European migrants: whiteness and managed migration policies', *Journal of Ethic and Migration Studies*, 35(1): 19–36.

Migration Watch (2003) *The Impact on Immigration of EU Expansion to Eastern Europe*, 27 July. Available from: www.migrationwatchuk.org/briefing-paper/33 [Accessed 27 January 2023].

Modern Slavery and Human Rights Policy and Evidence Centre (2023) *Explainer: The Illegal Migration Bill Modern Slavery Provisions*, v.1.1, 28 March. Available from: https://modernslaverypec.org/resources/migration-bill-explainer [Accessed 29 March 2023].

Morrison, J. (2019) 'Re-framing free movement in the countdown to Brexit? Shifting UK press portrayals of EU migrants in the wake of the referendum', *British Journal of Politics and International Relation*, 21(3): 594–611.

Murphy, C., Doyle, D.M., and Murphy, M. (2020) '"Still waiting" for justice: migrant workers' perspectives on labour exploitation in Ireland', *Industrial Law Journal*, 49(3): 318.

Myslinska, D. (2021) 'Not quite right: representations of Eastern Europeans in ECJ discourse', *International Journal of Politics, Culture, and Society*, 34(3): 271–307.

O'Carroll, L. (2020) 'Romanian fruit pickers flown to UK amid crisis in farming sector', *The Guardian*, [online] 15 April. Available from: www.theguardian.com/world/2020/apr/15/romanian-fruit-pickers-flown-uk-crisis-farming-sector-coronavirus [Accessed 27 January 2023].

O'Connell Davidson, J. (2010) 'New slavery, old binaries: human trafficking and the borders of "freedom"', *Global Networks*, 10(2): 244–61.

Partridge, J. and Partington, R. (2021) '"The anxiety is off the scale": UK farm sector worried by labour shortages', *The Guardian*, [online] 25 August. Available from: www.theguardian.com/business/2021/aug/25/the-anxiety-is-off-the-scale-uk-farm-sector-worried-by-labour-shortages [Accessed 27 January 2023].

Paternoster, A. (2004) 'Minimum wages: EU member states, candidate countries and the US 2004', *Statistics in Focus*, Brussels: Eurostat.

Pavlou, V. (2018) 'Where to look for change? A critique of the use of modern slavery and trafficking frameworks in the fight against migrant domestic workers' vulnerability', *European Journal of Migration and Law*, 20(1): 83–107.

Pradella, L. and Cillo, R. (2015) 'Labour, exploitation and migration in Western Europe: an international political economy perspective' in L. Waite, G. Craig, H. Lewis, and K. Skrivankova (eds) *Vulnerability, Exploitation and Migrants: Insecure Work in a Globalised Economy*, London: Palgrave, pp 44–56.

Quirk, J., Robinson, C., and Thibos, C. (2020) 'Editorial: from exceptional cases to everyday abuses: labour exploitation in the global economy', *Anti-Trafficking Review*, 15(1): 1–19.

Raza, A. (2022) 'Exploring the role of race and racial difference in the legislative intent of the Trafficking Victims Protection Act', in K. Kempadoo and E. Shih (eds) *White Supremacy, Racism and the Coloniality of Anti-Trafficking*, London: Routledge.

Reid, J. (2006) Home Secretary, Hansard, HC Deb, vol 450, col 84, 24 October.

Simon, M., Schwartz, C., Hudson, D., and Johnson, S.D. (2018) 'A data-driven computational model on the effects of immigration policies', *National Academy of Sciences Proceedings*, 115(34): 7914–23.

Skrivankova, K. (2010) *Between Decent Work and Forced Labour: Examining the Continuum of Exploitation*, York: Joseph Rowntree Foundation, p 16.

Southwell, P. and Roberts, P. (2017) *Modern Slavery Victims and the Criminal Justice System*, London: Hogan Lovells. Available from: https://athub.org.uk/wp-content/uploads/2017/07/Modern-slavery-victims-and-the-criminal-justice-system.pdf [Accessed 27 January 2023].

Spanger, M. (2022) 'Constructing victims and criminals through the racial figure of "the gypsy"', in K. Kempadoo and E. Shih (eds) *White Supremacy, Racism and the Coloniality of Anti-Trafficking*, London: Routledge.

Sporton, D. (2013) '"They control my life": the role of local recruitment agencies in East European migration to the UK', *Population, Space and Place*, 19(5): 443–58.

Sumption, M. and Fernández-Reino, M. (2018) *Exploiting the Opportunity? Low-Skilled Work Migration after Brexit*, Oxford: The Migration Observatory, University of Oxford.

Sumption, M. and Fernández-Reino, M. (2020) *Unsettled Status – 2020: Which EU Citizens Are at Risk of Failing to Secure their Rights after Brexit?*, Oxford: The Migration Observatory, University of Oxford.

Thomas, D. (2021) 'UK faces 2 years of labour shortages, CBI warns', *Financial Times*, [online] 6 September. Available from: www.ft.com/content/2ef7b9aa-4bfc-4c2f-8c66-13299ce4750f [Accessed 27 January 2023].

Vargas-Silva, C. and Fernandez-Reino, M. (2019) *Briefing: EU Migration to and from the UK*, Oxford: The Migration Observatory, University of Oxford.

Walsh, D., Pajón, L., Lawson, K., Hafeez, K., Heath, M., and Court, N. (2022) 'Increased risks of labour exploitation in the UK following Brexit and the COVID-19 pandemic: perspectives of the agri-food and construction sectors', *Journal of Human Trafficking*, 8(1): 1–16.

Waite, L., Craig, G., Lewis, H., and Skrivankova, K. (2015) *Vulnerability, Exploitation and Migrants: Insecure Work in a Globalised Economy*, London: Palgrave Macmillan.

York, S. (2018) 'The "hostile environment": how Home Office immigration policies and practices create and perpetuate illegality', *Journal of Immigration, Asylum and Nationality Law*, 32(4): 363–84.

9

The Modern Slavery Agenda in the UK: Labour Market Enforcement Perspectives on Law and Policy

Amy Weatherburn

Introduction

One of the stated aims of the Modern Slavery Act 2015 (hereafter, MSA 2015) was the consolidation of the legal framework prohibiting all criminal forms of labour exploitation. While the shift away from immigration law and the criminalization of the forced provision of work or services are both welcome developments, more efforts are required to ensure that the labour market is sufficiently equipped to tackle exploitation (Jones, 2019; Fudge, 2020; UN, 2020). A robust labour approach must account for the economic, social, and cultural disparities that foster the vulnerability and lack of choice very often encountered by potential victims of labour exploitation (Bravo, 2009). As such, scholars stress that a strong labour approach is needed to tackle issues such as the social construction of demand for cheap labour (Ollus and Jokinen, 2011; Shamir, 2012; Muskat-Gorska, 2017), as reinforced by Skrivankova who emphasizes that when we allow a labour market in which basic rights and laws are continually violated, we end up with 'a more general undermining of conditions of decent work' (2010: 4). Davies has further underscored the danger of focusing solely on severe forms of exploitation and overlooking the routine, more trivial and mundane practices of exploitation (2019). Taking this literature as a starting point, this chapter asserts that a strong, effective labour approach requires robust labour market enforcement mechanisms that are equipped to intercept and disrupt abusive working practices prior to them becoming severe enough to amount to modern slavery. Labour market enforcement in this chapter will focus on state-based mechanisms, institutions, and agencies that are mandated to tackle labour market non-compliance.

This chapter will consider the UK's modern slavery agenda from a labour market enforcement perspective by focusing upon the law and policy measures that have been introduced since the MSA 2015 and purport to protect workers from exploitation. I suggest that the UK's labour market enforcement perspective to tackling modern slavery presents a paradox. This paradox emerges because of labour market legislation being situated in immigration law – notably, a positive development of the MSA 2015 was the disconnect of anti-trafficking legislation from immigration law – and thus being granted the dual objective of (i) tackling illegal working, and (ii) cracking down on worker exploitation across all sectors (Department for Business, Innovation and Skills and Home Office 2015: 6). This chapter will demonstrate that the impact of this paradox leads to a skewed approach that is heavily weighted towards tackling illegal working, leading to a lapse in the protection of labour rights. Crucially, given the positioning of these changes in immigration law, the chapter will use illustrative examples related to the impact on migrant workers. However, it is critical to bear in mind that the implications of this policy approach are much more wide-ranging and can impact *all* workers who may be at an increased risk of labour market abuses or exploitative related practices.

In the first section will outline the measures that were introduced by subsequent legislative (notably the Immigration Act 2016[1]) and policy reform that seeks to contribute to disrupting modern slavery in the labour market. First, two institutional changes that sought to tackle labour market non-compliance will be outlined: (i) the establishment of the Director of Labour Market Enforcement (DLME); and (ii) the expansion of the remit of the Gangmasters Licensing Authority to create the Gangmasters and Labour Abuse Authority (GLAA), and the introduction of Labour Abuse Prevention Officers (LAPOs). Second, the introduction of new enforcement measures designed to complement existing sanctions and to be used to tackle deliberate and persistent non-compliance will be considered (Labour Market Enforcement Undertakings and Orders (LMEUs and LMEOs)). Third, a new policy development that has emerged from the efforts taken in recent years to further enhance the effectiveness of labour market enforcement will be briefly mentioned: the proposition for the creation of a single enforcement body.

In the second section, the emphasis will turn to consider the interconnectedness of the law and policy measures on labour market non-compliance that seek to tackle illegal working with the broader immigration law and policy framework that creates a 'hostile environment'

---

[1] www.legislation.gov.uk/ukpga/2016/19/contents/enacted [Accessed 3 July 2023].

and ultimately exacerbates the precarity of migrant workers. Here, I will illustrate how structural factors facilitate the precariousness and vulnerability of workers in today's labour market (Lewis et al, 2015; Mantouvalou, 2018). This paradoxical approach whereby the law gives and takes away has operational implications for labour market enforcement agencies who may not be able to truly deal with labour exploitation and abuses of employment law without having to also engage with immigration law enforcement.

Considering the paradoxical position between efforts to tackle labour market non-compliance and the structural factors that facilitate labour market precarity, I conclude by advocating for labour market enforcement mechanisms that focus on what Mantouvalou has coined the 'right to non-exploitative work' (2015a). Acknowledging the role of the state in facilitating such exploitative working conditions, the final section of this chapter emphasizes the need to ensure that all efforts must be made to minimize the risk of exploitation of workers in low-skilled sectors, including, inter alia the enforcement of the minimum wage, increased labour inspection, and ensuring that any migration channels do not tie workers to their employees. All of which are contributing factors to an increased risk of exploitation and precarity.

Where precarity in employment becomes the norm and is tolerated in society and in the law, the threshold for combating exploitation becomes unacceptably high. The role of the state in ensuring that the labour market landscape upholds the rights of workers is crucial to combating modern slavery. This will require improved efforts to ensure that measures tackling labour market non-compliance are well enforced and that the norm-setting role of the state does not create structural factors that contribute to abuse and exploitation.

Tackling labour market non-compliance: law and policy responses

From a law and policy perspective, several significant changes have been introduced since 2015 in the UK to address modern slavery. The introduction of expanded labour market compliance measures was intended to build on the modern slavery legislation by following the theoretical understanding of labour market compliance and deterrence (Metcalf, 2018: 32; Barnard and Butlin, 2020: 86). On the one hand, less serious violations of labour law by employers may be due to ignorance and incompetence requiring responses that assist and support employers to achieve compliance. On the other hand, severe labour exploitation requires stronger deterrence measures as employers are often deliberately breaching labour and criminal law standards for their own profit requiring more stringent sanctions. In this chapter, I will focus on deterrence measures as they are closely intertwined with cases of modern slavery.

The placing of these measures in the Immigration Act 2016, however, must be noted as it calls into question the ability of labour market enforcement agencies to truly deal with labour exploitation and abuses of labour law without having to first and foremost engage in immigration law enforcement (Fudge, 2018). This notion will be central to the presentation of the law and policy changes for tackling labour market non-compliance in this part, as the actions taken to tackle labour market non-compliance should not only be applicable to all workers in theory, but also in practice.

The establishment of the Director of Labour Market Enforcement

Following significant support in a public consultation (Department for Business, Innovation and Skills and Home Office, 2016: 10), the statutory mandate of a Director of Labour Market Enforcement (hereafter, DLME) was established under the Immigration Act 2016 (ss 1–9). The Director must develop a labour market enforcement strategy assessing the current and future scale and nature of non-compliance in the labour market (s 2), publish an annual report (s 3), and establish an information hub that gathers, stores, processes, analyses, and disseminates information relating to non-compliance in the labour market (s 8).

At the time of implementation, there were a few concerns regarding the lack of detail in statute of the exact functions of the Director when it comes to assessing the scale and nature of non-compliance in the labour market (s 2(2)), unlike comparable roles that have been created by statute such as the statutory basis of the functions of the Independent Anti-Slavery Commissioner in s 41 of the MSA 2015 (FLEX, 2016: 2). Similarly, there was a lack of understanding as to how exactly the Director's governance role when seeking to centralize and streamline the functions of the three main public enforcement bodies (the National Minimum Wage Inspectorate, the GLAA, and the Employment Agency Standards Inspectorate) responsible for enforcing these requirements would look like in practice (FLEX, 2016: 2).

For the first two years, the Office of the DLME – led by Sir David Metcalf former Chairman of the Migration Advisory Committee and a member of the Low Pay Commission (Department for Business, Energy and Industrial Strategy and Home Office, 2017) – saw several initiatives taken to ensure compliance with statutory functions. The shift from the political discourse that emphasized the need to 'clamp down on' and 'stamp out' illegal migration to a policy approach that demonstrates a clear and direct link with the anti-slavery efforts, including that of the Independent Anti-Slavery Commissioner (Barnard and Butlin, 2020: 86).

In addition to two comprehensive labour market enforcement strategies, the Office of the DLME consulted on several issues, including: sector-based research within warehouses, restaurants, hotel, cleaning, construction, care settings, in addition to scoping studies evaluating and assessing labour market non-compliance. Upon the retirement of Sir David Metcalf, Matthew Taylor was appointed as Interim DLME. Given the weight of the recommendations the Interim Director had outlined in his labour market review (Taylor, 2017) it would have been hoped that some would have seen the light of day, especially with progress towards the creation of a single enforcement body. However, progress has been stymied by the government's stalling of not only of the functioning of the Director but also of the implementation of the legislative reform of employment law that would enhance the protection of workers (Partington, 2021; Strauss, 2021).

Expansion: Gangmasters Labour Abuse Authority and Labour Abuse Prevention Officers

Sections 10 and 11 of the Immigration Act 2016 also reformed and renamed the Gangmasters Labour Abuse Authority (hereafter the GLAA – formerly the Gangmasters Licensing Authority). The remit of the GLAA was expanded to include enhanced enforcement powers to tackle labour exploitation and modern slavery offences across all sectors of the economy.[2] In order to accommodate this expanded remit, Labour Abuse Prevention Officers (hereafter, LAPOs) were introduced under s 12. LAPOs are specially trained officers who are authorized by the Home Secretary to use certain investigatory powers under s 114(b) of the Police and Criminal Evidence Act 1984 (PACE) with appropriate modifications in England and Wales for the purposes of investigating criminal labour market offences. LAPOs can take immediate and effective action against rogue employers operating in any sector.

The PACE powers ensure LAPOs have the requisite investigative powers to deal effectively with serious cases of worker exploitation. The powers enable LAPOs to:

(i) apply for a court search warrant to enter and search premises where there are grounds to believe that evidence likely to be of substantial value to the investigation of a labour market offence will be found;

---

[2] The GLAA is one of three enforcement bodies under the remit of the Director of Labour Market Enforcement, alongside the Employment Agency Standards Inspectorate (EAS) and His Majesty's Revenue and Customs National Minimum and Living Wage enforcement team (HMRC NMW/NLW team).

(ii) search a person on premises when executing a court search warrant, where there are reasonable grounds for suspecting that the person may have concealed on them material which might be evidence in relation to a labour market offence; and
(iii) arrest and search a person suspected of committing a labour market offence. (HM Government, 2019: 36)

Since the introduction of the new PACE powers, 36 LAPOs have been recruited, and put into post in the first year of operation (Taylor, 2020: 3). From May 2017 to October 2019, the GLAA LAPOs have conducted 747 inspections (Taylor, 2020: 26). The role and powers of LAPOs within the overarching framework of labour market enforcement initially were subject to scrutiny with a view to clarifying the scope of the new PACE powers with existing powers under s 17 of the Gangmasters (Licensing) Act 2004 that provided compliance officers with powers of inspection and entering premises for the sectors which they license. The practical implications of invoking these new powers have, however, come under the spotlight as, in practice, their scope and operationalization are not sufficiently clear and indeed do not account for the complexity of the factual circumstances that are under investigation:

> these powers are not able to be used interchangeably and that this is both inflexible and inefficient. [...] if a GLAA officer enters a premises under section 17 but then realises upon investigation that they may be encountering a criminal level issue, they cannot move to using their PACE powers but instead have to swap staff to then use those powers. This misunderstands the nature of offending by assuming that only one or other type will be present. (FLEX, 2019b: 27)

To address the lack of clarity the first DLME recommended further efforts to explore and clarify the LAPOs' powers and remit, a proposition accepted by the government (Department for Business, Energy and Industrial Strategy and Home Office, 2017: 26–7; Metcalf, 2018). Since then the memorandum of understanding that sets out the protocol for the circumstances in which the GLAA can tackle broader offending and when a case should be referred to the relevant body to pursue has been reviewed three times and 'no substantial or structural changes to the enforcement bodies' processes have been proposed' (Taylor, 2020: 23).

The first DLME stated that consulted stakeholders had raised concerns about too great a focus on the modern slavery remit of GLAA. The extent to which the attention on LAPOs will be measured is by an increase in prosecution for modern slavery, without putting aside continued efforts to ensure that risks in other regulated sectors (Metcalf, 2018: 6); namely, shellfish gathering and agriculture, where there are concerns about unlicensed activity taking place in these sectors, putting workers at risk of abuse and exploitation – for example, only 13 registered licence holders suggests incomplete coverage and unlicensed operations (Metcalf, 2018: 44–5).

Other concerns include the lack of licensing inspections being carried out and the under-utility of compliance officers, reduction in compliance inspections, and licence revocations over time (Taylor, 2020: 26). On the first Director warned that the current approach makes it easier for rogue gangmasters to evade the necessary scrutiny: '[E]ven where licenses are revoked there is often evidence of phoenixing. A more effective way of assessing compliance would be to undertake unannounced visits' (Metcalf, 2019: 42).[3]

New enforcement powers: Labour Market Enforcement Orders and Labour Market Enforcement Undertakings

The extended institutional remit has been complemented with new enforcement powers, as a tool to tackle and disrupt labour exploitation. The new regime of Labour Market Enforcement Undertakings (LMEUs) and Labour Market Enforcement Orders (LMEOs) was designed to complement existing sanctions and to be used to tackle deliberate and persistent non-compliance across all areas of state enforcement.

LMEUs and LMEOs were introduced in the Immigration Act 2016 and are available in England, Scotland, and Wales.[4] Where there is a reasonable belief that a trigger labour market offence has been, or is being, committed (such as using an unlicensed gangmaster), the enforcement bodies can request a business enter an undertaking to take steps to prevent further offending. When an undertaking is refused or not complied with the enforcement bodies may seek an LMEO from the courts. An order can also be granted on conviction for a trigger offence. Breach of an order can lead to a prison term of up to two years and/or an unlimited fine. Previously, such offences would have only attracted a civil penalty or criminal fine. The new system was designed to complement existing sanctions already available to the enforcement bodies, to be used where appropriate to prevent further labour market offences.

These undertakings and orders are intended to tackle the middle ground of non-compliance and are an additional tool in more serious and persistent

---

[3] Accepted by government (Department for Business, Energy and Industrial Strategy, 2020: 11).
[4] An equivalent tool is used in criminal law under the MSA 2015 with Slavery Trafficking Prevention Orders (ss 14–22).

cases, where the enforcing authority is of the view that existing civil sanctions will not prevent or stop the non-compliance and prosecution is not yet proportionate. Each of the enforcement bodies has the power to use these undertakings and orders for breaches within their own remit (HM Government, 2019).

Since their introduction in 2016, 62 LMEUs have been served on businesses by the three main labour market enforcement bodies: the Employment Agency Standards Inspectorate (EAS), the Gangmasters and Labour Abuse Authority (GLAA), and His Majesty's Revenue and Customs – National Minimum Wage Team (HMRC-NMW) (Taylor, 2020: 19–20).[5] The first ever LMEO was served by the GLAA in October 2018 to a man and woman convicted of supplying illegal workers to food factories (GLAA, 2018; Taylor, 2020: 20). Initial use of these enforcement measures was predominantly restricted to the GLAA; however, the HMRC-NMW team have increasingly employed them with a view to disrupt serious and persistent offending and to gain compliance in the worst cases (Taylor, 2020: 19–20) (see Table 9.1). It was reported that:

> HMRC Serious Non-Compliance teams (SNC) have conducted 166 joint working operations. Operations have taken place in sectors that have been identified by the Director as being high risk, including car washes, nail bars, textiles and construction. In all cases the intelligence received has pointed to National Minimum Wage risks existing alongside a range of other labour market abuse risks, including modern slavery and people trafficking. (Department for Business, Energy and Industrial Strategy, 2020: 10–11)

As the number of undertakings and orders increase, the next step will be to ensure that there is sufficient monitoring to ensure compliance with the orders and their effectiveness and increased collaboration between enforcement bodies, including information sharing on their experiences and best practice and successes affecting ongoing compliance (Department for Business, Energy and Industrial Strategy, 2020: 12; Taylor, 2020: 20). Despite the increased use of the measures, the Interim Director expressed concern that the low number of prosecutions for labour market offences is detrimental to their objective as an effective deterrent (Taylor, 2020: vi). This was also an issue raised by the previous Director who also highlighted that non-compliance was due to a lack of incentive as 'the chances of being

---

[5] Parliamentary Question – Labour market enforcement undertakings Date: 4 June 2019. Ref: 260093. Asked by: Stephanie Peacock (Barnsley East). Available from: www.gla.gov.uk/media/6080/peacock-040619-lmeus.pdf [Accessed 3 June 2021].

Table 9.1: Number of LMEUs and LMEOs issued by the enforcement bodies

	2017/18		2018/19		2019/20	
	LMEU	**LMEO**	**LMEU**	**LMEO**	**LMEU**	**LMEO**
EAS	4		4		3	
HMRC-NMW			7		21	
GLAA	2		15	2	6	
Total	**6**		**26**	**2**	**30**	

Source: Department for Business, Energy and Industrial Strategy and Employment Agency Standards Inspectorate, 2021: 14

investigated by enforcement officers and the scale of financial penalties [...] are too low' and, in some instances, 'employers are actively including these costs as part of their wider business model' (Taylor, 2020: 16).

Looking to the future: single enforcement body

A recommended best practice by the International Labour Organization (ILO) is that inspection be placed under the supervision and control of a central authority, in accordance with ILO Labour Inspection Convention, 1947 (No 81). The introduction of the Immigration Act 2016 included the aim of establishing a single enforcement body. The government took this suggestion forward by conducting a public consultation. The proposal was supported by the DLME subject to thorough consideration (Metcalf, 2019: 20). As FLEX raise in their response to the consultation for a single enforcement body, it is important to consider those changes that could be made under the existing framework (FLEX, 2019a: 1). However, the future of the single enforcement body is not bright, as it has been hampered by the government's lack of response to the consultation and the delay to the introduction of the Employment Bill 2019–2020 (Partington, 2021).

The paradox of a labour market enforcement perspective: the 'hostile environment' trumps labour market security

The continued non-implementation and/or the lack of political will to fully embed the plethora of reforms I discussed in the first section of this chapter and the political emphasis on illegal working has resulted in a lapse in safeguarding the rights of (potentially exploited) workers. Given the worsening situation, in this section I will demonstrate that structural factors can contribute and are intricately linked to the slippery slope towards labour market abuse and, in the most serious of cases, modern slavery. The creation of a 'hostile environment' and the impact on migrant workers' precarity and vulnerability to potential exploitation and abuse will be considered. Crucially, given the implications of a post-Brexit world on the maintenance of a level playing field for workers' rights (see further Currie, this volume), a focus will be placed on the structural composition of immigration law and policy that in fact contributes to exploitation and abuse of migrant workers who have a right to work. The example of temporary migration programmes that impose restrictions on migrant workers will illustrate the diminished positioning of labour market enforcement when faced with an overwhelming emphasis on immigration enforcement.

Despite the inclusion of labour market non-compliance measures in the Immigration Act 2016 that arguably seek to protect workers from exploitation, the overall immigration law and policy framework is premised upon positing a 'hostile environment' that subsequently creates precarity. For workers to be truly protected from exploitation, there needs to be a complete disassociation with immigration law enforcement that fails to prioritize first and foremost the rights of exploited migrants (FLEX, 2016: 2). For instance, the Immigration Act 2016 sought the confiscation of wages as proceeds of crime for illegal employment offences, whereas the emphasis on the worker overlooks the possibility of their exploitation and abuse by a non-compliant employer. Aliverti also highlights that such punitive measures were not just isolated to 'workplace penalties and sanctions [but] were supplemented with a myriad of restrictions on vital areas of modern life (to rent a house, to open a bank account, to drive, etc)' (Aliverti, 2020: 339). Indeed, these examples illustrate the 'carceral and punitive approach to stamping out labour market exploitation' (Fudge, 2018: 568) that leads to protective measures that are designed to assist victims of exploitation (regardless of their migration status) being overlooked.

While anti-trafficking scholars and activists are aware of this blind spot, the state-based mechanisms that prioritize immigration enforcement and adopt a heavy-handed criminal justice approach fail to appreciate the nexus between forced criminality and exploitation. The 2021 judgment of the European Court of Human Rights in *V.C.L. & A.N. v the United Kingdom* [2021] Applications nos 74603/12 and 77587/12 underlines the continued emphasis on illegality of workers rather than the possibility that they are exploited and in need of protection. The case involved two Vietnamese children who were identified by authorities in cannabis cultivation farms and were sanctioned under criminal law rather than offered protection as victims of human trafficking for forced criminality (Faulkner, 2023, 299). Admittedly, the facts of the case pre-dates the introduction of the MSA 2015; however, it is telling that the day after the Strasbourg judgment in

February 2021, a Crown Court judge handed down a 26-month sentence to an undocumented cannabis gardener who had been put to work to pay off debts owed to his traffickers (Brassingonot, 2021).

The disregard for the rights of victims illustrates that framing provisions under immigration legislation fails to recognize the heightened vulnerability of migrant workers to labour exploitation (Shamir, 2012) and further reinforces the need to pivot labour market enforcement mechanisms towards a worker-centred approach, that guarantees the rights of workers, regardless of migration status.

Importantly, the contribution of the structures of immigration law and policy to exploitative working practices is not restricted to illegal working, with the MSA operationalized as part of the hostile environment. The focus on immigration is also problematic in the sense that, one of the most significant, and yet

> least understood features of forced labour in the UK is that most suspected victims have the right to work [as EU nationals]. Yet the stigma migrants increasingly face in the UK often means that people believe their migration status is more precarious than it is. Threats to report migrants to immigration authorities are used by traffickers to control victims and to silence those who complain. (Robinson, 2015)

The power imbalance between unscrupulous employers/traffickers and employees/victims will only be heightened in the post-Brexit context as a cohort of workers who previously had the freedom of movement and right to work find themselves working in heightened precarity as third-country nationals. This precarity will be further entrenched if the handling of labour shortages in low-skilled sectors focuses primarily only on temporary migration programmes that seek to stem the number of permanent migrants (FLEX, 2019b: 16).

The use of restrictive visa regimes as a catalyst for exploitation is well known and, in the UK, this is particularly the case for the Overseas Domestic Workers (ODW) visa regime (Mullally and Murphy, 2014; Demetriou, 2015; Mantouvalou, 2015b; Weatherburn and Muraskiewicz, 2016). While the regime no longer ties workers to their employers since changes introduced by the Immigration Act 2016, it does exacerbate the dependency of workers on their employers, placing significant conditions on their entry and stay in the UK. In particular, the poor regulation and monitoring of the ODW visa in fact leaves migrant domestic workers faced with several issues that facilitate their labour insecurity maintaining them in a position of precarity. Primarily this is the result of a lack of a realistic window to find a new employer within the scope of a non-renewable, six-month visa and the inability to effectively report abusive and exploitative employment. Even when detected as potential victims of modern slavery, research has delved into the inability of migrant domestic workers to survive on destitution-based levels of subsistence because of their denial of the right to work during the National Referral Mechanism (NRM) process (Kalayaan, 2019: 28). The implications of which leads to risk of re-victimization due to their failure to repay debts and support their families who rely on them for subsistence needs.

Considering this, Kalayaan recommends that all migrant domestic workers referred to the NRM, irrespective of their visa status, must be granted permission to work. This would prevent them falling into destitution and at risk of further exploitation, enable them to support themselves and their families, improve their mental health, and assist in their recovery. Further, it would also ensure workers are not pressurized in to having to exit support services under the NRM and enter exploitative work in order to meet the requirement to be self-sufficient should they have to apply for further leave to remain (Kalayaan, 2019: 33). Here the proposals for reform place a clear emphasis on a labour approach and the interests of migrant workers to gain access to the labour market and have their labour rights protected. The issue of reform was further raised in a collective Communication from the UN Special Rapporteurs on contemporary forms of slavery, the human rights of migrants, and trafficking in persons (OHCHR, 2021) who called for a timely reassessment of the immigration rules governing the ODW visa. Unfortunately, the UK government, failing to recognize the above-mentioned concerns emanating from evidence-based research, does not yet see the need for urgent reform (Permanent Mission of the United Kingdom of Great Britain and Northern Ireland, 2021).

The lessons learned from the deficiencies of the ODW visa regime should inform the development of immigration policy when seeking to facilitate and regulate labour mobility post-Brexit. Unfortunately, the use of restrictive visa regimes continues to be the preferred direction for immigration policy in low-skilled sectors. Such measures are counterintuitive to the 'modern slavery' ethos and should be carefully considered in policy measures that are developed to address the inevitable shortage of labour caused by the end of free movement of EU workers. Emphasis should be placed on compliance and enforcement efforts on economic sectors where there is a need for low-paid, low-skilled workers. For example, unscrupulous employers are already using the uncertainty of Brexit to impose or perpetuate abusive working conditions on workers (FLEX, 2019b: 7).

In this regard, the introduction of a seasonal workers programme premised upon a tied visa regime and sponsoring operator company is disappointing (HM Government, 2018). Following a two-year pilot that granted 2,500 visas to limited horticultural roles, the seasonal workers visa scheme was expanded in February 2020, with an increased quota year on year, with 30,000 visas available in 2023. The current scheme, in place until 2024, grants licences to 'scheme operators' consisting of four recruitment agencies that sponsor workers who, once they have applied for a visa, are then placed with agricultural businesses who have identified a business need. The seasonal worker can work up to six months out of a 12-month period and does not have the opportunity to renew or extend their visa. The workers are placed with the business that requested the provision of seasonal workers; however, it is possible to request a transfer – yet, the request may be declined by the operator.

Advocates for tackling modern slavery highlight the extent to which such migrant workers, with limited stays and restricted access to rights, may be subject to exploitative working conditions. The findings from a study of the seasonal workers pilot in Scotland's agriculture sector demonstrated that a restrictive visa regime heightens the risk of forced labour (Robinson and Fife Migrants Forum, 2021). The lived experience of migrant workers who are subject to such restrictions portrays a world where they are vulnerable to exploitation and do not have their labour rights protected or enforced. Instead, workers had encountered deception about the nature of the work, degrading living conditions, excessive dependency on employers, and lack of freedom to change employer. The extent to which these concerns are not sufficiently addressed through regulation and monitoring is even more alarming. The lack of proactive labour market enforcement, including on-site workplace inspections and the lack of awareness among migrant workers of their ability to access their rights, illustrates the urgent need for an emphasis on regulation.

Despite the evidence-based research findings from the implementation of the pilot, very few changes in the design and oversight of the seasonal worker scheme were made before it was expanded. Therefore, it is not unsurprising then that several concerns around the welfare of seasonal workers have been identified following compliance visits by the Home Office. Issues raised by workers related to poor standard of accommodation, not being paid correctly for hours worked, non-provision of personal protective equipment (PPE), ill-treatment and discrimination, and denial of access to healthcare (Independent Chief Inspector of Borders and Immigration 2022: 44–5). While the direct contact with seasonal workers is to be welcomed, the lack of follow-up or rectification of concerns raised following compliance visits requires further urgent attention.

Additional issues of concern relate to the debt bondage of workers, who are required to pay recruitment fees (even though this is illegal) and additional expenses connected to the migratory pathway, such as the visa fee and the travel costs; importantly, post-Brexit, given the loss of European seasonal workers, the distance travelled and, by consequence, the cost borne by temporary seasonal workers has increased tenfold, with a significant increase in number of applicants from Central Asian countries. Although, in principle the latter expenses are to be paid for by the employer, the reality is that the migrant workers often bear the financial burden. Contrary to their expectations, the financial situation of the workers does not improve upon arrival, with several seasonal workers finding themselves working on zero-hour contracts with restricted working hours. These circumstances, exacerbated by the short, non-renewable duration of the visa, merely exacerbate the debt levels. However, a couple of recent developments demonstrate that the regulation and enforcement of the seasonal workers visa are beginning to tighten up, with a recent announcement that a minimum of 32 hours a week will be guaranteed to all seasonal workers (Department for Environment, Food and Rural Affairs, 2023) and the revocation of a scheme operator's licence (an Indonesian recruitment agency) due to concerns over the debt levels of workers upon arrival (up to £5,000) and the lack of work leading to some workers being sent home a few weeks after their arrival in the UK (Dugan, 2023).

Conclusion

Labour market enforcement legislation and policy measures are of paramount importance to any efforts to tackling modern slavery, as is the crucial role of enforcement bodies to securing the 'right to non-exploitative work' (Mantouvalou, 2015a). However, by positioning labour market enforcement measures within immigration law we must also consider the role of the state in potentially facilitating exploitative working conditions thus creating a paradoxical labour market–immigration enforcement nexus. The paradox may only be overcome by decoupling efforts that seek to minimize the risk of exploitation of workers in low-skilled sectors from immigration enforcement. Moreover, structural factors such as tied, restrictive visa regimes that increase the risk of exploitation and precarity must be dismantled, with a shift in focus on tackling labour market non-compliance through enhanced enforcement, monitoring, and oversight.

The ability of labour market enforcement agencies to address a wide range of non-compliance – from recklessness to deliberate efforts to profit from labour market abuses – offers a window of opportunity to prevent severe labour exploitation that may amount to modern slavery. The spectrum of non-compliance in labour market enforcement mirrors the continuums that have been evoked in scholarship that place an emphasis on the workers' perspective; namely, their own situation of vulnerability (Shamir, 2012) and exploitation (Skrivankova, 2010). Undertaking innovative and creative enforcement measures midway along the spectrum can be mutually reinforcing as they will have a significant impact on the individual circumstances of workers whose situation makes them vulnerable to exploitative and abusive working practices.

Given the prevalence of issues related to wage theft and abuse (Migrant Justice Institute, 2021), the restitution of back pay – where the rate of recuperation remains low – can be used as an example to illustrate how enforcement mechanisms can adopt a multi-pronged approach targeting different points of the spectrum of non-compliance. In England and Wales, non-payment of the National Minimum Wage (NMW) and the national living wage is a criminal offence under s 31 of the National Minimum Wage Act 1998 and the National Minimum Wage Regulations 2015, No 621. However, it is generally not included on the indictment of trafficking prosecutions (Weatherburn, 2021: 228). The DLME raised a similar concern that efforts to recuperate the NMW are focusing on 'lower hanging fruit' with record levels of arrears identified and numbers of workers assisted reached record levels in 2017/18; this was primarily due to ten 'big' cases where average arrears per worker was only £64, suggesting more 'technical' NMW breaches were being picked up' (Metcalf, 2019: 26fn8). The Director recommended that future efforts should focus further along the spectrum of non-compliance (Metcalf, 2018: 6). To fully engage with the full spectrum of non-compliance, Paoli and Greenfield, however, assert that the 'low-hanging fruit' should not be disregarded (2015) as this contributes to the normalization of routine exploitative practices that 'can, collectively at least, result in harm to (migrant) workers and the reputation of industries associated with hazardous work' (Davies, 2019: 297).

Since the introduction of the MSA 2015 subsequent law and policy reforms have been introduced to tackle illegal working and labour exploitation; however, delays to their timely implementation and a lack of political will to pursue reforms that will further strengthen employment rights in post-Brexit Britain jeopardizes the possibility for meaningful change and will further heighten the insecurity and precarity that is currently a key. Consequently, the knock-on effect of such inertia will be a further heightening of the insecurity and precarity that currently waylays the UK labour market, whereby a large proportion of the workforce experiencing in work poverty and not able to secure a minimum level of income that provides for a dignified and stable livelihood.

A point of particular concern is that the current labour market is on course for further insecurity and precarity given the positioning of key labour market enforcement measures in immigration law and policy wherein the prioritization of maintaining a 'hostile environment' for migrant workers overlooks the necessity of enforcing employment law for all workers. Within this chapter I have sought to illustrate how structural factors resulting from the state's political agenda lead to a paradox with the modern slavery law and policy; ultimately, putting into question the real possibility for workers in the UK to fully realize their 'right to non-exploitative work'.

Overall, the role of the state in ensuring that the labour market landscape upholds the right to non-exploitative work is crucial to combating labour exploitation. Where precarity in employment becomes the norm and is tolerated in society and in law, the threshold for combating exploitation becomes unacceptably high. It is necessary to continue to fight against such a situation and continue to improve efforts to ensure that the labour market non-compliance is well enforced, and the norm-setting role of the state does not create structural factors that contribute to exploitation and abuse.

References

Aliverti, A. (2020) 'Doing the dirty job', in A. Bogg, J. Collins, M. Freedland, and J. Herring (eds) *Criminality at Work*, Oxford: Oxford University Press.

Anti-Trafficking Monitoring Group (2018) *Before the Harm Is Done: Examining the UK's Response to the Prevention of Trafficking*.

Barnard, C. and Butlin, S.F. (2020) 'Where criminal law meets labour law: the effectiveness of criminal sanctions to enforce labour rights', in A. Bogg, J. Collins, M. Freedland, and J. Herring (eds) *Criminality at Work*, Oxford: Oxford University Press.

Brassington, J. (2021) 'Jail for Black Country cannabis farmer put to work to pay back traffickers', *Express and Star*, [online] 17 February. Available from: www.expressandstar.com/news/crime/2021/02/17/jail-for-black-country-cannabis-farmer-put-to-work-to-pay-back-traffickers/ [Accessed 3 June 2021].

Bravo, K. (2009) 'Free labour! A labour liberalization solution to modern trafficking human beings', *Transnational Law and Contemporary Problems*, 18: 545–615.

Chuang, J. (2006) 'Beyond a snapshot: preventing human trafficking in the global economy', *Indiana Journal of Global Legal Studies*, 13(1): 137–63.

Davies, J. (2019) 'From severe to routine labour exploitation: the case of migrant workers in the UK food industry', *Criminology and Criminal Justice*, 19(3): 294–310.

Demetriou, D. (2015) '"Tied visas" and inadequate labour protections: a formula for abuse and exploitation of migrant domestic workers in the United Kingdom', *Anti-trafficking Review*, 5: 69–88.

Department for Business, Energy and Industrial Strategy (2020), *UK Labour Market Enforcement Strategy 2019/20 – Government Response*, 9 October. Available from: https://assets.publishing.service.gov.uk/government/uploads/system/uploads/attachment_data/file/925523/director-labour-market-enforcement-strategy-2019-2020-govt-response.pdf [Accessed 3 June 2021].

Department for Business, Innovation and Skills and Home Office (2015), *Tackling Exploitation in the Labour Market, Public Consultation*, October. Available from: www.gov.uk/government/uploads/system/uploads/attachment_data/file/471048/BIS-15-549-tackling-exploitation-in-the-labour-market.pdf [Accessed 3 June 2021].

Department for Business, Innovation and Skills and Home Office (2016), *Tackling Exploitation in the Labour Market, Government Response*, January. Available from: www.gov.uk/government/uploads/system/uploads/attachment_data/file/491260/BIS-16-11-government-response-to-tackling-exploitation-in-the-labour-market.pdf [Accessed 3 June 2021].

Department for Business, Energy and Industrial Strategy and Home Office (2017), *Sir David Metcalf Named as the First Director of Labour Market Enforcement*, 5 January. Available from: www.gov.uk/government/news/sir-david-metcalf-named-as-the-first-director-of-labour-market-enforcement [Accessed 3 June 2021].

Department for Business, Energy and Industrial Strategy and Employment Agency Standards Inspectorate (2021) *Employment Agency Standards (EAS) Inspectorate: Annual Report, 2018 to 2019* (12 January).

Department for Environment, Food and Rural Affairs and the Rt Hon Mark Spencer MP (2023) Speech Farming Minister Mark Spencer: National Farmers Union Conference, 21 February. Available from: www.gov.uk/government/speeches/farming-minister-mark-spencer-national-farmers-union-conference [Accessed 27 February 2023].

Dugan, E. (2023) 'UK recruiter of debt-hit Indonesians loses seasonal workers licence', *The Guardian News*, [online] 9 February. Available from: www.theguardian.com/uk-news/2023/feb/09/uk-recruiter-debt-hit-indonesians-loses-seasonal-workers-licence [Accessed 27 February 2023].

FAIRWORK Belgium (2019) *Travailleurs sans papiers: Rapport annuel 2018*.

Faulkner, E.A. (2023) *The Trafficking of Children: International Law, Modern Slavery, and the Anti-Trafficking Machine*. 1st edition, [Online]. Cham: Springer International Publishing AG.

FLEX (2016) *Briefing: Immigration Bill Part One – January 2016*. Available from: www.labourexploitation.org/publications [Accessed 3 June 2021].

FLEX (2019a) *Good Work Plan: Establishing a New Single Enforcement Body for Employment Rights – Submission to the Department for Business, Energy and Industrial Strategy by Focus on Labour Exploitation* (FLEX), Consultation, 2 October.

FLEX (2019b) *The Risks of Exploitation in Temporary Migration Programmes: A FLEX Response to the 2018 Immigration White Paper*, May.

Fudge, J. (2018) 'Illegal working, migrants and labour exploitation in the UK', *Oxford Journal of Legal Studies*, 38(3): 557.

Fudge, J. (2020) 'Twenty years after Palermo, can we stop discussing labour exploitation and start fixing it?', *Open Democracy*, [online] 19 November. Available from: www.opendemocracy.net/en/beyond-trafficking-and-slavery/twenty-years-after-palermo-can-we-stop-discussing-labour-exploitation-and-start-fixing-it/ [Accessed 3 June 2021].

GLAA (2018) 'Couple convicted of labour exploitation', Press Release, 26 October. Available from: www.gla.gov.uk/whats-new/press-release-archive/25102018-couple-convicted-of-labourexploitation/ [Accessed 3 June 2021].

Goodin, R. (1987) 'Exploiting a situation and exploiting a person', in S. Reeves (ed) *Modern Theories of Exploitation*, London: SAGE.

Harvey, M. (2020) 'Coronavirus exposes Britain's bogus self-employment problem', *The Conversation*, 14 May. Available from: https://theconversation.com/coronavirus-exposes-britains-bogus-self-employment-problem-138459 [Accessed 3 June 2021].

HM Government (2018) *The UK's Future Skills-Based Immigration System*. Available from: https://assets.publishing.service.gov.uk/government/uploads/system/uploads/attachment_data/file/766465/The-UKs-future-skills-based-immigration-system-print-ready.pdf [Accessed 3 June 2021].

HM Government (2019) *Good Work Plan: Establishing a New Single Enforcement Body for Employment Rights*, Consultation, July. Available from: https://assets.publishing.service.gov.uk/government/uploads/system/uploads/attachment_data/file/817359/single-enforcement-body-employment-rights-consultation.pdf [Accessed 3 June 2021].

Independent Chief Inspector of Borders and Migration (2022) *An Inspection of the Immigration System as it Relates to the Agricultural Sector, May–August 2022*. Available from: www.gov.uk/government/publications/an-inspection-of-the-immigration-system-as-it-relates-to-the-agricultural-sector-may-to-august-2022 [Accessed 27 February 2023].

Jones, J. (2019) 'Is it time to open a conversation about a new United Nations treaty to fight human trafficking that focuses on victim protection and human rights?', in J. Winterdyk and J. Jones (eds) *The Palgrave International Handbook of Human Trafficking*, Cham Switzerland: Palgrave Macmillan, pp 1803–17.

Kalayaan (2019) *Dignity Not Destitution: The Impact of Differential Rights of Work for Migrant Domestic Workers in the National Referral Mechanism*, October. Available from: www.kalayaan.org.uk/wp-content/uploads/2019/10/Kalayaan_report_October2019.pdf [Accessed 3 June 2021].

Lewis, H., Dwyer, P., Hodkinson, S., and Waite, L. (eds) (2015) *Precarious Lives: Forced Labour, Exploitation and Asylum*, Bristol: Policy Press.

Mantouvalou, V. (2015a) 'The right to non-exploitative work', in V. Mantouvalou (ed) *The Right to Work: Legal and Philosophical Perspectives*, Oxford: Hart Publishing.

Mantouvalou, V. (2015b) '"Am I free now?" Overseas domestic workers in slavery', *Journal of Law and Society*, 42(3): 329–57.

Mantouvalou, V. (2018) 'Legal construction of structures of exploitation', in H. Collins et al (eds) *Philosophical Foundations of Labour Law*, Oxford: Oxford University Press.

Mantouvalou, V. (2020) 'Welfare-to-work, structural injustice and human rights', *Modern Law Review*, 83 (5): 929–54.

Metcalf, D. (2018) *United Kingdom Labour Market Enforcement Strategy 2018/19, Presented to Parliament Pursuant to Section 5(1) of the Immigration Act 2016*, (HM Government, May). Available from: https://assets.publishing.service.gov.uk/government/uploads/system/uploads/attachment_data/file/705503/labour-market-enforcement-strategy-2018-2019-full-report.pdf [Accessed 3 June 2021].

Metcalf, D. (2019) *United Kingdom Labour Market Enforcement Strategy 2019/20. Presented to Parliament Pursuant to Section 5(1) of the Immigration Act 2016* (HM Government, July). Available from: https://assets.publishing.service.gov.uk/government/uploads/system/uploads/attachment_data/file/819014/UK_Labour_Market_Enforcement_Strategy_2019_to_2020-full_report.pdf [Accessed 3 June 2021].

Migrant Justice Institute (2021) 'Migrant workers' access to justice for wage theft: a global study of promising initiatives'. Available from: www.migrantjustice.org/wagethefta2j [Accessed 23 February 2023].

Mohamed, E. (2021) 'Review of UK workers' rights post-Brexit is axed in sudden U-turn', *The Guardian*, [online] 27 January. Available from: www.theguardian.com/politics/2021/jan/27/review-of-uk-workers-rights-post-brexit-is-axed-in-sudden-u-turn [Accessed 3 June 2021].

Mullally, S. and Murphy, C. (2014) 'Migrant domestic workers in the UK: enacting exclusions, exemptions, and rights', *Human Rights Quarterly*, 36(2): 397–427.

Muskat-Gorska, Z. (2017) 'Can labour make an effective contribution to legal strategies against human trafficking?', in R. Piotrowicz et al (eds) *Routledge Handbook of Human Trafficking*, London: Routledge.

Office of the United Nations High Commissioner for Human Rights (OHCHR) (2021) *Special Procedures Communication AL GBR 6/2021*, Mandates of the Special Rapporteur on contemporary forms of slavery, including its causes and consequences; the Special Rapporteur on the human rights of migrants; and the Special Rapporteur on trafficking in persons, especially women and children, 27 May. Available from: https://spcommreports.ohchr.org/TMResultsBase/DownLoadPublicCommunicationFile?gId=26423 [Accessed 11 August 2021].

Ollus, N. and Jokinen, A. (2011) 'Trafficking for forced labour and labour exploitation – setting the scene', in N. Ollus, A. Jokinen, and K. Aromaa (eds) *Trafficking for Forced Labour and Labour Exploitation in Finland*, Poland and Estonia: FLEX-HEUNI.

Paoli, L. and Greenfield, V.A. (2015) 'Starting from the end: a plea for focusing on the consequences of crime', *European Journal of Crime, Criminal Law and Criminal Justice*, 23(2): 87–100.

Partington, R. (2021) '"Deafening silence": UK government blasted over delays to employment reforms', *The Guardian*, [online] 17 February. Available from: www.theguardian.com/business/2021/feb/18/deafening-silence-uk-government-delays-covid-employment-reforms-legislation [Accessed 3 June 2021].

Permanent Mission of the United Kingdom of Great Britain and Northern Ireland (2021) *Response United Kingdom of Great Britain and Northern Ireland to Special Procedures Communication AL GBR 6/2021*, 28 July. Available from: https://spcommreports.ohchr.org/TMResultsBase/DownLoadFile?gId=36472 [Accessed 11 August 2021].

PICUM (2015) *Position Paper, Employers' Sanctions: Impacts on Undocumented Migrant Workers' Rights in Four EU Countries* (April).

PICUM (2017) *Summary of Findings in Belgium and the Czech Republic on the Implementation of the Employers' Sanctions Directive*.

Robinson, C. (2015) 'The UK's new immigration bill creates perfect conditions for slavery to thrive', *The Guardian*, [online] 28 August. Available from: www.theguardian.com/global-development/2015/aug/28/slavery-uk-immigration-act-2014-hostile-environment-undocumented-migrants-focus-on-labour-exploitation-flex [Accessed 3 June 2021].

Robinson, C. and Fife Migrants Forum (2021) *Assessment of the Risks of Human Trafficking for Forced Labour on the UK Seasonal Workers Pilot (FLEX, 2021)*. Available from: https://labourexploitation.org/publications/assessment-risks-human-trafficking-forced-labour-uk-seasonal-workers-pilot [Accessed 3 June 2021].

Shamir, H. (2012) 'A labor paradigm for human trafficking', *UCLA Law Review*, 60(1).

Skrivankova, K. (2010) 'Between decent work and forced labour: examining the continuum of exploitation', JRF Programme Paper (November).

Strauss, D. (2021) 'UK government position on labour market abuse to fall vacant' *Financial Times*, [online] 26 January. Available from: www.ft.com/content/4b5c4dbb-5638-4ff3-b9fb-ff7b8cf8dd10 [Accessed 3 June 2021].

Taylor, M. (2017) *Good Work: The Taylor Review of Modern Working Practices*. Available from: https://www.gov.uk/government/publications/good-work-the-taylor-review-of-modern-working-practices [Accessed 3 June 2021].

Taylor, M. (2020) *United Kingdom Labour Market Enforcement Annual Report 2018/19, Presented to Parliament Pursuant to Section 5(1)(b) of the Immigration Act 2016* (HM Government, July). Available from: https://assets.publishing.service.gov.uk/government/uploads/system/uploads/attachment_data/file/898213/United_Kingdom_Labour_Market_Enforcement_Annual_Report_2018-19.pdf [Accessed 3 June 2021].

United Nations (2020) *Report of the Special Rapporteur on Trafficking in Persons, Especially Women and Children, 20 Years After: Implementing and Going Beyond the Palermo Protocol Towards a Human Rights Centred Approach*, Doc. A/75/169.

Weatherburn, A. (2021) *Labour Exploitation in Human Trafficking Law*, Cambridge: Intersentia.

Weatherburn, A. and Muraskiewicz, J. (2016) 'The impact of the 2012 Domestic Workers in a Private Household Visa on human trafficking for domestic servitude', *Journal of Immigration, Asylum and Nationality Law*, 30(3): 204–21.

Wintermayr, I. and Weatherburn, A. (2021) *Access to Protection and Remedy for Victims of Human Trafficking for the Purpose of Labour Exploitation in Belgium and the Netherlands* (ILO, April).

10

Insights from Uganda: Wartime Sexual Violence, Knowledge Production, and Power

Allen Kiconco

Content warning: this chapter contains discussion of violence and sexual violence.

Introduction

The Rome Statute of the International Criminal Court (ICC) recognized sexual slavery as a war crime as recently as 1998.[1] The Court that pioneered the recognition of the practice was the Special Court for Sierra Leone, with Trial Chamber I of the Court holding that three high-ranking members of the Revolutionary United Front[2] (RUF) were guilty of crimes against humanity – namely, rape, sexual slavery, and forced marriage – under the category of 'other inhumane acts' in 2009 (Oosterveld, 2011). The decision marked the first time an international criminal tribunal convicted the crime of forced marriage. The Trial Chamber confirmed Sierra Leone's Truth and

---

[1] As per Article 7(g): 'Rape, sexual slavery, enforced prostitution, forced pregnancy, enforced sterilization, or any other form of sexual violence of comparable gravity.' See further: https://legal.un.org/icc/statute/99_corr/cstatute.htm [Accessed 15 July 2023].

[2] The Revolutionary United Front was formed in 1991 in Sierra Leone, playing a significant role in the 11-year civil war. The UN Special Court for Sierra Leone was established in 2002 and indicted five leading members of the RUF – Sankoh, Sam Bockarie, Issa Hassan Sesay, Morris Kallon, and Augustine Bgao – for war crimes. For more context on the RUF, see further I. Abdullah (1998) 'Bush path to destruction: the origin and character of the Revolutionary United Front/Sierra Leone', *Journal of Modern African Studies*, 36(2): 203–35.

Reconciliation Commission's findings that girls and women were subjected to sexual and gender-based violence during the war in Sierra Leone (Truth and Reconciliation Commission, 2004). These legal developments have had a direct impact in Uganda.

On 8 July 2005, the ICC prosecutor officially issued arrest warrants for Joseph Kony, the Lord's Resistance Army[3] (LRA) leader and his top four commanders for war crimes and crimes against humanity (Allen, 2006). On 6 December 2016, Trial Chamber IX of the ICC commenced its trial against Dominic Ongwen, one of the five LRA commanders indicted.[4] At the time of the trial, the other three commanders were dead, and only Kony was at large. Ongwen was accused of 70 counts of war crimes and crimes against humanity. The Trial Chamber IX found Ongwen guilty of all 19 sexual and gender-based violence charges, including sexual slavery, forced marriage, rape, enslavement, and forced pregnancy in February 2021,[5] with the Court sentencing Ongwen to 25 years' imprisonment in May 2021.[6] The trial was the first in which the ICC convicted a rebel commander for forced pregnancy as a war crime and a crime against humanity. Additionally, it was the first time that the ICC convicted forced marriage, which was charged under the category of 'other inhumane acts', constituting a crime against humanity.

While the charging, prosecution, and conviction of sexual violence in international criminal law are subject to divergent opinions, these developments in international law have drawn attention to sexual violence as core, not peripheral, wartime experiences. The issue that I perceive arises is that international law draws upon research into sexual violence. Yet, knowledge focusing on how sexual violence research is undertaken, documented, and communicated in different forums remains limited, with concrete materials examining the politics and dynamics of researching conflict societies remaining scarce.

Political polarization, the heavy presence of armed actors, international intervention, precarious security, mistrust, and individual and collective trauma intensify the ethical research imperative 'do no harm' (see further Hynes and Dottridge, this volume). However, conflict studies researchers

---

[3] See further R. Doom and K. Vlassenroot (1999) 'Kony's message: a new Koine? The Lord's Resistance Army in northern Uganda', *African Affairs (London)*, 98(390): 5–36; T. Allen and K. Vlassenroot (eds) (2010) *The Lord's Resistance Army: Myth and Reality*, London and New York: Zed Books.

[4] Case available: www.icc-cpi.int/CaseInformationSheets/OngwenEng.pdf [Accessed 21 December 2023].

[5] Trial judgment available from: www.icc-cpi.int/CourtRecords/CR2021_01026.PDF and https://bit.ly/33rpsW9

[6] Sentencing available from: www.icc-cpi.int/CourtRecords/CR2021_04230.PDF

often do not necessarily make their own field experiences and dilemmas a primary focal point when writing up their findings. In most cases, the final product overshadows what happened behind the scenes that enabled the creation of said final product. Questions of methodologies, methods, ethics, and politics of knowledge production are usually briefly addressed, suggesting successful and smooth research. Consequently, less is known about how researchers and policy makers concerned with the harms experienced by survivors of wartime sexual violence and their communities can participate in meaningful knowledge production without exacerbating their situations.

In 2012 and 2013, approximately six years after the conflict between the government of Uganda and the LRA ended in northern Uganda in 2006, I conducted six months of ethnographic research in four Acholi region districts; namely, Kitgum, Lamwo, Pader, and Gulu. I undertook this research as part of my doctoral research at the University of Birmingham, UK. During this research I collaborated with 57 formerly abducted women. During rebel captivity, these women experienced sexual violence, forced marriage, sexual slavery, and torture (Kiconco, 2021). Because of experienced personal and collective distress, they were not always comfortable talking about their experiences, fearing potential risk retribution and trauma by sharing what they experienced. In attempts to gain insight into and documenting their experiences, I faced several challenges, including gaining access, negotiating consent, and successfully conducting interviews with them – characterized by trauma, profound distrust, and social fragmentation.[7]

There is no recipe for safe, ethical, and balanced fieldwork, but researchers can learn from each other's experiences, including mistakes that have been made. Within this chapter I will discuss some of the chaotic realities of fieldwork in post-conflict societies like northern Uganda. I argue that it is possible and necessary to conduct sound, rigorous, and reflexive research in challenging post-war contexts. However, research methods, ethics, and fieldwork practices need to be adapted in culturally and experientially sensitive ways to keep the research subjects safe and the research on ethically solid ground (see further Hynes and Dottridge, this volume). One successful example of this is how I gained access, negotiated consent, and interviewed formerly abducted women in northern Uganda. Through a reflective and self-critiquing analysis of power relations, I discuss the steps taken to address power distribution questions and navigate fieldwork challenges.

The chapter briefly discusses some power dynamics that confront field researchers working with war survivors and their communities. It then summarizes the general methodology adopted for the study, followed by a discussion of my positionalities and implications on fieldwork practice. The

---

[7] To protect the participants' identities, names and places have been anonymized.

chapter then shifts to the procedures followed in the study to implement the 'do no harm' principle, including procedures for access, negotiating consent, and ensuring the interviewees' confidentiality. Throughout, I discuss the dilemmas that emerged when undertaking the research.

'The field': power and feminist methodology

The field is an interesting concept, understood in contrast with a location described as 'home'. Traditionally, fieldwork involves journeying to 'the field,' in most cases, a small rural community inhabited by people seen as bearing little relation to the researcher's home society. This entails a researcher travelling to 'the field', asking locals questions about their opinions/ experiences, and observing how and why they live differently. The purpose of fieldwork is to collect information to enable the researcher to critique, deconstruct, and reconstruct /accounts of experiences or phenomena (Mitchell, 2013; Nhemachena, Mlambo, and Kaundjua, 2016). However, the common use of 'the field' is a shorthand for power relations, which cannot be separated from hierarchies underpinned by power structures in knowledge production. Often, researchers have several privileges that their research subjects may not have, making travelling to 'the field' meaning leaving a privileged home environment to research a less privileged location and people. These dynamics are intensified if 'the field' is a conflict-affected society.

Experience shows that the basic requirements of undertaking fieldwork in conflict contexts range from minute preparations to the ethics of interacting with host communities, state authorities, and fighting parties. The process involves honing and adapting research methodologies to suit people's lifestyles and cultures. All of this might sound straightforward, but experience shows that accessing, negotiating 'the field', and collecting appropriate data is not (Wood, 2006; Eriksson Baaz and Stern, 2016; Cronin-Furman and Lake, 2018; Krause, 2021; see also Hynes and Dottridge, this volume).

Often, conflict societies cannot provide scientific and technical guidance and monitor research ethics. They face war-induced poverty, attracting negative media coverage and extraction characterizing negotiation with outsiders, including researchers. The local population is often hesitant, distrustful, and suspicious when sharing information with non-local researchers (see further Bhagat, this volume). People are secretive because they are embedded in highly threatening contexts (Chakravarty, 2012). The historical context of lack of trust, weak states, and extraction makes conducting rigorous research present a range of methodological, ethical, logistical, and security challenges not usually confronted in non-war field contexts.

Often, arriving in 'the field', a researcher can feel confident that with approval from their home institution's Institutional Review Board (IRB), certification from the host country's national ethics committee, and perhaps a prearranged partnership agreement with a local or international organization, they are clear to begin their research. However, arriving in and navigating the field can be a different story. The researcher finds that the IRB's regulatory structures have less relevance (Cramer, Hammond, and Pottier, 2011; Basini, 2016). Indeed, 'the basic ethical principles established to guide research on human subjects are necessary but insufficient in conflict and post-conflict environments' (Campbell, 2017: 89). It is within these environments that international development agencies and non-governmental organizations (NGOs) dominate (see further Bhagat and Francis, this volume). The researcher might find it challenging to separate themselves from the institutions that local populations are accustomed to interacting with and expecting assistance (Wood, 2006; Cronin-Furman and Lake, 2018). Power relations emerge as an issue instantly, including those within individual and institutional relationships (Cramer et al, 2021; Dodsworth and Cheeseman, 2018; Lewis et al, 2019). Besides research subjects, the researcher has to address power relations in collaboration with such gatekeepers, research brokers, and assistants (Mwambari, 2019; Parashar, 2019; Bunting, Kiconco, and Quirk, 2020; Bukavu series[8]).

There is increasing attention and focus on the lived experiences of women in conflict contexts within the continent of Africa. Yet, focusing and privileging their experience/perspectives in scholarship does not guarantee power in the research process. The research participants and the researcher do not belong to the same power hierarchy, and power relations are continuously perpetuated, both implicitly and explicitly. Thus, the relationship between them remains the most unequal and potentially damaging. This made researching women's lives and lived experiences complicated, fraught with challenges, politics, and dilemmas, necessitating flexibility in approach. A series of questions arise, such as: how do the backgrounds of both I (the researcher) and the women influence the research? How can I ensure that the research is not extractive and harmful? How do I ensure the research is a positive experience and mutually beneficial for everyone involved? These are questions that the researcher must grapple with before, during, and after fieldwork.

There is consensus among feminist scholars in conflict-related sexual violence that research should acknowledge and disrupt the power imbalances, including minimizing power hierarchies between the researcher and the researched women. An effective way to address this is through centring the women and their voices in the research. The research should develop a non-hierarchical relationship with the women, making the research a

---

[8] Available from: www.gicnetwork.be/silent-voices-blog-bukavu-series-eng/

meaningful partnership that turns them into co-creators of knowledge. This relationship should be developed respectably and valuably, including building trust, empathy, and ensuring reciprocity (Mackenzie, McDowell, and Pittaway, 2007; Thomson, Ansoms, and Murison, 2013). Ultimately, the research should prioritize power, collaboration, and inclusivity, which involves valuing relationships, reflecting on own practice, learning with the research subjects, and developing horizontal collaborations.

Power dynamics and ethics associated with my research in northern Uganda were complex. I relied upon a feminist approach to reduce the hierarchy between the formerly abducted women and I, including keeping trust and inclusiveness at the centre of our encounter. Researching them meant not working with data but with the fabrics of their lives. Therefore, to humanize the interactions with the participants, I had to be more interested in ethical storytelling rather than the data collected.

Reflections on positionality

What comes out clearly in feminist conflict-related sexual violence research is that all considerations of power and ethics vary with the researcher's positionality (Wibben, 2016; Bunting, Kiconco, and Quirk, 2020; Bukavu series). According to feminist research, reflexivity is self-criticism and self-conscious scrutiny of the self as a researcher (Ackerly and True, 2008). Remaining reflexive throughout the research means acknowledging positionalities and their influence on its substantive and practical aspects, including design, methods, and dissemination. Reflexivity allows the researcher to become aware of their multiple positionalities, including race, nationality, gender, age, class, ethnicity, social status, and religious beliefs (Ergun and Erdemir, 2010; Carling, Erdal, and Ezzati, 2014). Ultimately, this enables the researcher to see where they are located upon the 'grids of power relations and how those influences methods, interpretations, and knowledge production' (Sultana, 2015: 376). Consequently, they become sensible of the risk of constructing or reinforcing power imbalances in the field (Bott, 2010; Bouka, 2015).

Yet, positionality is often approached as a technical problem and less political, reducing positionality to insider-outsider dichotomy (Bilgen, Nasir, and Schöneberg, 2021). Indeed, African scholars choose to research in their home communities, hoping their insider identity (especially ethnicity) would afford them more access to the field and research subjects. However, this approach has its version of complications; for example, studies reveal layers of challenges scholars must negotiate to conduct fieldwork in home societies (Mandiyanike, 2009; Jok, 2013; Keikelame, 2018; Yacob-Haliso, 2018). What is often missed within these studies is an acknowledgement that most African researchers enjoy a high standing within their communities, especially if they went to the best national universities or studied abroad. Additionally, these researchers come from privileged class backgrounds, further creating layers to their positionality that influence how they experience the field. Numerous social, institutional, and economic layers separate African researchers from respondents, even with common geographical backgrounds and ethnicities.

While I was returning to Uganda to conduct fieldwork on my fellow Ugandan women, I was not returning home to Uganda to research as an insider in the Acholi region. I was an outsider because I did not share cultural, linguistic, and ethnic heritage with the research subjects. I was born and raised in the rural Ankole region, western Uganda. As an adolescent, I relocated to the capital, Kampala, in the central region. With this ethnic background and internal migration, I speak many Bantu languages spoken in Uganda's central and western parts, different from the Luo language spoken in the Acholi region. As a Munyankole (person from Ankole) woman working in the Acholi area for the first time, my project's success depended on recruiting an interpreter and transcriber to help with the research.

Based on Ugandan standards, I come from an affluent family, with parents depending on ranching for livelihood. This background afforded our (my siblings and I) education in some of the best high schools in Uganda, setting the course for me to attend the country's most prestigious university before travelling abroad for postgraduate studies. During fieldwork in the Acholi region, this class background placed me in a contrasting position of difference. Coming from a higher learned class of urban elites that rural Ugandans highly respect made the class difference between the research subjects and me explicit. Moreover, there was a possibility that I could be associated with President Museveni's regime, dominated by people from Ankole (my ethnicity).

In the early stages of my privately funded doctoral research in the UK, I reflected on these positionalities and pondered how to navigate them. At some point, I contemplated researching sexual violence within my community and ethnicity. I was, however, aware of how difficult it would be to ask people to talk about such a sensitive subject with non-family members. While sexual violence is also a private/domestic matter in the Acholi region, the war opened an investigation avenue. However, during fieldwork, I found the theoretical understanding of 'the field' limiting. As a Ugandan, I struggled with the language of the Acholi region as a site of otherness and isolation – Acholi was not different from the Ankole region, my home. While the protracted conflict devastated and impoverished the Acholi region, life in towns and villages were not unusual in their difficulties. I did not find life fundamentally separate from home or any other part of Uganda. Continuing to view Acholi as a different and unusual place, I risked a disservice to both the research subjects and the knowledge generated. Therefore, I stopped viewing the Acholi region and people based on their differences from home, but I approached fieldwork with humanity, curiosity, and in full acknowledgement of my limited knowledge. This also involved treating the women as people with their entire lives bigger and beyond my project's lifespan, with my study dependent on their busy lives and their generosity.

The success of my project would depend on the development of meaningful rapport and trust between these women and myself that would inspire them to work with me. Sharing nationality, gender, and rural background with the women in the research afforded me some degree of social proximity: a Ugandan woman interested in the lives of Ugandan women was a considerable advantage. Throughout the study, I felt that these women were my fellow Ugandan people and did not feel a significant distance between us. I did not want to harm them. However, as the following pages show, it was much easier to wish than adhere to the 'do no harm' principle. As I reflect on how I grappled with ethical and practical challenges of accessing, negotiating consent, and interviews, I elaborate on the reasons for the difficulty of adhering to the ethical imperative.

Navigating risk, access, and collaboration

Fieldwork usually necessitates reliance on local contacts, gatekeepers, and fixers. Like any other researcher preparing for the field, I established connections with local contacts to navigate the Acholi terrain and access formerly abducted women. The experience involved working around gatekeepers (see further Bhagat, this volume) and the complex layers of the local authority and shifting-risk dynamics. I collaborated with rehabilitation organizations because of my interest in the local context of the conflict, but more importantly, how they addressed formerly abducted women when they returned home from rebel captivity.

Negotiation for collaboration with organizations involved facing research fatigue with some project managers, who often lamented that many (foreign) researchers worked with their organizations but 'forgot them' upon returning to their home countries/institutions. One hinted that "… for you, it is different. This is our [Ugandan] achievement (PhD) … you will bring it back home [Uganda]". Ultimately, my nationality made access to some organizations possible. I kept truth at the centre of negotiations for collaboration with organizations. I made it clear to the managers that I was conducting privately funded research purely for my academic qualification. I would not return to them with money or projects at the end of the study but would share my findings with them. Although I needed their help to access formerly abducted women and their communities, I remained an independent researcher as the managers did not control field activities or the final findings. Throughout the fieldwork, the organizations served as primary gatekeepers for the research, facilitating access to most formerly abducted women encountered in the study, in addition to the arrangement including the offer of psychological support to interviewees. However, the collaboration involved power dynamics that I did not immediately find apparent. Failure to identify and address them earlier in the research might have influenced gaining access to the women. International and local organizations wielded power and influence in the Acholi region at the time of the study, as people did not question their work or recommendations. I was now part of these organizations, and I appreciated the bond we shared of working with formerly abducted women. I did not want to jeopardize the rapport and trust created with them. Yet, I knew that the research subjects associated certain organizations with power and influence, which in turn I relied upon to access them. I subsequently distanced my study from organizational projects to develop rapport with the research subjects.

Besides organizational partnership, I collaborated with non-abducted locals to help with the study and hired two interpreters, Diana Angom and Kenneth Onen, both residents of Kitgum town. Additionally, I worked with two transcribers, Francis Onekalit and Peter Labeja, from Kitgum and Gulu town, to help with the data collection. As university graduates, I recruited all of them based on their previous data-collection and transcription expertise. Playing these critical roles shaped my knowledge of what transpired during and post-war in the Acholi region. Therefore, the research team included five people, with the management of the fieldwork and collected data undertaken by me. My field research occurred six years after the conflict ended and the Acholi region was relatively peaceful; sharply contrasting the brutal and indiscriminate violence in the earlier years. However, independent access by non-locals remained challenging due to mistrust and research and/or intervention fatigue. This further entrenched the importance of trust in local individuals and organizations relating to both my academic career and personal security.

Fieldwork: the obstacle course

Demographic information varied among the women that participated in my research, which also dictated how they related to me and communicated their experiences. Their age at the time of the study ranged from 18 to 43 years. The majority were abducted as adolescents and teenagers, with ages at abduction ranging between 6 and 30 years. They lived with the rebels for varying periods, ranging between one and 12 years, with some participants being back home (at the time of the study) for six years or more.

While I had the support of the rehabilitation organization, accessing these women was difficult with obstacles appearing throughout the study. Several years of recovery and reintegration had already passed for most of them. Their history compelled them to keep low profiles, and some were reluctant to talk about their past, fearing re-stigmatization or research fatigue. Consider these two experiences:

> 'I no longer want to be associated with NGOs pretending to profile formerly abducted women (and former abductees) in view of finding help (assistance) for them. I am saying this because I have been profiled too many times that those NGOs must be very rich right now out of my stories. Since 2005, when I returned, different NGOs came to interview me, but none has returned to give me feedback or bring me proceeds. They are not helping us in any way.'[9]

> 'I want to caution you about revealing our stories and identities to the public. This is what is increasing stigma among us. We have come to this conclusion because whenever researchers come to us, we later learn that the story is on Radio Mega FM and Radio King. Moreover, we get nothing out of them. This is so bad. We feel that those who collect information from us when they use them to generate income (wealth) that we do not share are abusing our generosity. If they are going to use the information to set up NGOs or organizations, it should be used on the mutual understanding that the activity will develop us. This is my appeal to you. I am saying this because different NGOs that came to profile us vanished for good without bringing us feedback or proceeds.'[10]

I documented several considerations, particularly from interviewees in town areas. I understand such statements to indicate experiences of research fatigue among formerly abducted persons in northern Uganda. They also highlight the extractive tendencies by outsiders, including researchers such as me and international organizations (Bunting, Kiconco, and Quirk, 2020). To limit research fatigue, I sought to work with women with less exposure to researchers and organizations. I relied on my collaboration with rehabilitation centres to access women in more remote communities. As the research progressed, I employed a chain referral strategy with interviewed women, mostly in towns. Unlike in rural communities, many town interviewees kept their past secrets, making it difficult to access them. Therefore, I accessed most of them through their colleagues, remaining

---

[9] Interview 58: 36 years old, abducted at age 15 for ten years. Gulu town, 6 February 2013.
[10] Interview 49: 38 years old, abducted aged 15 for 12 years. Gulu town, 6 February 2013.

alert to the fact that asking already interviewed women to 'recruit' others would be against research ethics; I asked them to 'encourage' women in their circles to come forward.

Owing to the sensitivity of the research topic, I initially planned to work with a female interpreter as I believed using a man would hinder the women's participation. However, this was not my experience. I briefly worked with the rehabilitation centre staff to follow up on their projects and beneficiaries in rural communities. During these visits, I observed how difficult it could be for two young women to negotiate access in contexts where older men served as final gatekeepers to women as community elders, fathers, and husbands. I, therefore, relied on Kenneth to lead the research team during encounters with district, community, and family heads, who were, in most cases, men. The research protocol included approaching the chief administrative officer (CAO) to present research clearance from my university, the governing ethics body in the country, the Uganda National Council for Science and Technology, and an introduction letter from a rehabilitation centre. With the district CAO's clearance, we then approached the government leader, Local Council One, for an introduction and clearance to do research in his community. We proceeded to meet the family head, father, or husband to ask permission to speak with their relative, such as their wife, daughter, or niece. In most of these encounters with family heads, I did not say much, as Kenneth presented my credentials and explained the purpose of our visit and the kinds of people we were interested in talking to. After such regulated encounters at district, community, and family levels, we accessed formerly abducted women and negotiated their participation in the study.

I encountered ethical dilemmas at the family level, particularly stigmatization and intimidation by husbands/in-laws for participating. An illustrative example can be drawn from our first visit to Lamunu's family. Kenneth, Diana, and I engaged her husband, mother, and father-in-law about the purpose of our visit and the research project. When the 21-year-old Lamunu returned from fetching water, we spoke to her privately under a compound tree. On the following day, as Diana and I conversed with her in the sitting room of her marital home, Lamunu went silent. Like many women in the sample, the LRA rebels had abducted her at the age of 10 from her family home in the night. After three years in captivity, she returned as an orphan following the death of her parents. She moved in with well-wishers in an Internally Displaced person's camp. She later moved in with the first man who offered her marriage. After what seemed like a very long pause, Lamunu rested her hands from fiddling with her soiled fingernails and clothes. Seated on an old mat facing me, she raised her shy and tired face to look at my face. In a low tone, Lamunu said "… because you came here yesterday, today, in the morning, they [husband and in-laws] quarrelled, saying that if you people are thinking of taking me back to school, then

I should know that no one will do my garden work".[11] We had arranged to engage the husband and in-laws in a family discussion that afternoon; however, Lamunu requested that this was cancelled.

I interpreted such experiences to reflect these women's vulnerable positions in their communities, characterized by tension, stigma, intimidation, and abuse (Kiconco, 2021). These women's interaction with NGOs exacerbated tensions between them and both their families and communities. Most families saw their women as having access to NGO support. Lamunu's family members understood my language when I told them that I was not compensating her participation financially, materialistically, or via skill training. However, with the research team arriving in their compounds in a four-wheel-drive branded with an NGO name and logo, they sought to push for a different dialogue, for money. I found it difficult to minimize such experiences of intimidation as without engaging their families accessing the women would not have been feasible. Moreover, some locations were difficult to access on foot or by motorbike, so I had to use an appropriate vehicle, but this risked misrepresenting my position as a doctoral researcher. Consequently, I relied upon the interviewees to forewarn or alert me to tendencies of intimidation, and as I did with Lamunu, I restricted my engagement with families. To avoid retributive domestic violence, I limited the information that I shared with family members, in order to not reveal the true nature of the study. The interview contents were not discussed with anyone in the interviewees' immediate surroundings. However, given the closely knitted nature of communities in Acholi, some people might have imagined the content shared in the interview.

Negotiating for informed consent

The permission of organizations or the gatekeepers was indispensable in accessing interviewees. Yet, there was a real possibility that some women would feel pressured to participate because of the support provided by these organizations in addition to permission given for the research by them. Therefore, I treated this possibility sensitively. After identifying and accessing interviewees through organization collaboration, I talked to them privately and directly to seek their permission to participate. Protection required them to sign a formal statement (informed consent) documenting ethical considerations for their participation; these included safeguarding their anonymity, ensuring freedom to refuse consent (voluntary participation), physical safety, and minimizing distress and/or risks for interviewees.

---

[11] Interview 20: 20 years old, abducted at 6 years for three years, Omiya Anyima, Kitgum district, 8 November 2012.

Accordingly, I designed a detailed form, translated from English to the local language, to explain participation terms. Consent covered not just participation but also audio recordings of interviews. However, several challenges implementing the terms and conditions of informed consent arose. Their abduction cut short the women's formal education, and therefore many were illiterate during the interviews and did not pay much attention to the written informed consent. Moreover, signing the documents constituted evidence of their participation, in contradiction to the promise of confidentiality. As such, it was difficult to explain how signing a formal document could protect them from harm.

The procedure of signing forms violated local norms and systems of addressing harm, consenting to something, or feeling protected from harm. From a Ugandan woman's perspective, the procedure breached the interpersonal custom practised in many contexts of Ugandan culture. It questioned the trust that must underlie interpersonal relations and arrangements in the Acholi region, particularly in rural areas where engagements remain informal. Signing a form to consent to their participation contrasted the women's known way of giving consent, including non-formalized procedure and intimacy of their involvement in the project. With signing consent forms having the potential to impede interviews and data collected, I resorted to seeking informed consent orally. This included relying upon unwritten and non-formalized verbal consent, renewed each time I interacted with interviewees. In the first meeting with the women, Diana and Kenneth explained who I was, the purpose of the research, voluntary participation, and confidentiality. The women were informed that they could choose what to discuss and whether the information provided was acceptable for publication or simply informative for me. The interpreters explained that the benefit of the study was the exploration of lived experiences of formerly abducted women in northern Uganda. No other benefits were available. The ethical considerations were communicated conversationally, which involved spending considerable time with the women in the initial encounters. However, the informal approach humanized the process of seeking consent for the study. Throughout the interview, the women were asked to provide verbal confirmation of continued consent and periodic reminders of the right of withdrawal. Although I was aware that verbal guarantees of confidentiality carried very little weight, I believe the interviewees accepted mine on trust.

I had the impression that the interviewees appreciated the terms of the informed consent, which they interpreted as acknowledging them as experts of their experience and worlds. Some women demonstrated a clear understanding of informed consent, taking advantage of the different levels of confidentiality. Here I will identify four illustrative examples.

First, as consent negotiations happened via informal conversations, many women asked multiple questions about their participation. Second, a woman who had previously agreed to participate requested a cancellation 20 minutes into the interview. Third, three women refused to be recorded but accepted notes being taken. Fourth, a woman asked for the recorder to be turned off before discussing a family business she shared with the husband. Subsequently, the recorder was switched on after narrating what she considered sensitive information.

Negotiating consent directly with the women put them in control of participating in the study and sharing information. To ensure safety, comfort, and privacy, they selected the interview site and convenient time. All conversations were held in private, usually at home when their husbands were either away or on church premises. After agreeing on the interview site, we warned the women at the beginning of the interview of some diversionary tactics if someone showed up abruptly, including switching entirely to an unrelated set of questions. While questions of privacy and confidentiality differed from interviewee to interviewee, the options remained entirely up to them.

"I cannot tell you everything": navigating ethics and in-depth interviews

Despite my best efforts, re-traumatization made some women distance themselves from my project. The rebels had abducted now 29-year-old Akello on her way to school at the age of 16. After six years of captivity, she returned home with two children fathered by her captor-commander. Like most participants in town areas, she kept her past a secret. We met this single mother through a rehabilitation centre. While negotiating participation in a room provided by the centre, she turned to me and said, in English, "… my sister; I cannot tell you everything that happened to me while in abduction, it is tough". She then asked to look at the questions that I had formulated to direct the conversations. With a fading smile, Akello said, "… the questions are moderate".[12] She granted me an interview, but I did not comprehend what Akello meant by 'hard'. Did she consider her experience too sensitive and unexplainable? Did she not want to tell it in detail, or did she not know how to tell it to a stranger such as me? Akello's experience reminded me of Julian Murchison's (2010) observation about conducting ethnographic research:

---

[12] Interview 57: 29 years old, abducted at age 16 for six years, Gulu town, Gulu district. 5 February 2013.

when you record the words of an informant, you may wonder about the degree to which the informant's description matches what happened, what she experienced, or what she thinks. ... Interviewees may consciously and unconsciously censor, emphasise, deceive, misremember, or provide a partial account for a variety of reasons. (2010: 104)

Indeed, as I read their transcribed stories post-fieldwork, I noted that some women held back on some experiences and expounded on other aspects of their own account without probing. It was clear that many of the women based in towns had narrated their stories many times before; I was thus getting a formal narrative of victimhood. Studies suggest that such women might present a victim narrative in research interviews to conceal actual war experiences or access support (Utas, 2005). I sensed that the women were only interested in talking about their experiences of violence during captivity and their current struggles. They gave detailed accounts of the day of their abduction, sexual violence, and physical torture during captivity. It was only after probing that they talked about other experiences, such as their roles in captivity, their pre-captivity lives, their coping mechanisms, their progress over the years, and their life plans, which did not seem to matter much. This was in contrast with their rural counterparts, many of whom were narrating their stories for the first time and were more likely to give detailed accounts of their childhood, family/kinship relations, current challenges, and prospects. Although I appreciated this variance in the data, it raised questions about the reliability and validity of the data. On the other hand, I interpreted this experience as how women such as Akello exercised control over their stories. Knowingly or unknowingly, they asserted themselves as the most important people in this storytelling process – some maintained detachment from interviews by withholding information or refusing to share certain content. However, balancing power within interviews depended largely on the woman's perceptions, status in captivity, and their status back home. Women who held prominent leadership positions in the rebel group or served as commanders' wives, such as Akello, seemed to exercise more power on what they wanted to say, in addition to how and where to say it. This also included women who viewed themselves as having made significant progress with their reintegration into their communities, including good marriages or livelihoods. They told stories that did not damage their social standing or versions that were available in their communities. I noted that women in rural areas were the most vulnerable in the study, with limited power to exercise during interviews.

I found that space and the method of telling the story are essential. Fear and distrust towards researchers are common among such vulnerable women in conflict situations; an experience further compounded by more 'formal' research methods and spaces often pursued by researchers. These include controlling the woman by imposing time limits, questions, and interruptions for follow-up questions or clarifications. All the stories documented in my research demonstrated that narrating stories via interviews connected formerly abducted women to their past and guided them to imagine the future they desired. However, because of their formal nature, interviews sometimes posed a significant limitation for the study. I sensed specific nuances associated with the women and their lived experiences might not have been accessible via 'formal' interviews that ran for one or two hours with interpreters. As Baines and Stewart (2011) demonstrate in northern Uganda, there is more to learn from less formal storytelling methods and spaces. The approach could reveal contextual factors and highlight deep dynamics and complex issues surrounding rebel abduction and reintegration.

As a Ugandan woman researcher, I am mindful of how difficult it is for people to talk about issues related to sexual violence both in times of peace and conflict. People hardly talk about these taboo subjects within families, let alone to outsiders, and I was acutely aware that the interviews could open doors to trauma. After the interviews, the women returned to their families and communities without a support system to help deal with the relived trauma that followed our discussion. Thus, I recognize that while these women agreed to participate in the study, I could not fully access their experiences, yet that was fine by me, as far as the research was concerned. The significant factor for me, was to be loyal to the relationships formed with the women, the information that they shared, and the knowledge that was produced, however partial. I humanized the interview process through negotiations, informality, empathy, listening, and respect to the best of my capacity. To allow the women greater control over the interview situation, I used autobiographical and personal narrative strategies to encourage them to tell their stories. While all these strategies worked well for the research, I would be naive to assume that the relationships I formed with the women were equal or that I became an 'insider'.

Overall, the fieldwork was possible mainly because my enquiries met with the enthusiastic collaboration of formerly abducted women and many residents of the Acholi region. Irrespective of our different backgrounds, the women were willing to discuss their experiences. Their desire for their stories to be documented became my motivation to write the book that emerged from this research, within which I tried to the best of my ability to present the varying experiences of these Acholi women, which should be read as representing a much larger group of war participants in northern Uganda. That group predominately remain invisible in the scholarship and policies on conflict, gender, and reintegration.

Conclusion

The concept of 'the field' cannot be separated from several hierarchies underpinned by the long history of power structures in knowledge production. Researchers have several privileges that their research subjects might not have; such power dynamics intensify if 'the field' is a conflict situation. The purpose of informed consent is to ensure that fieldwork in such contexts 'does no harm' to those involved in the research, particularly research subjects. However, executing informed consent in conflict situations can present a researcher with enormous challenging dilemmas.

The chapter has reflected upon my experience of conducting ethnographic research in northern Uganda centralized upon the lived experiences of formerly abducted women in the Acholi region. The research practice discussed appears to have sufficiently addressed the ethical challenges encountered. I have used my experience to show that research methods, ethics, and fieldwork practices need to be adapted in culturally and experientially sensitive ways to keep the research subjects safe and the research on ethically solid ground.

The starting point is to think critically about positionalities, asking how they could be negotiated and implications on issues associated with ethical research practice. Many dilemmas emerge, change, and develop throughout the research process in ways that sometimes are unpredictable. However, keeping trust at the centre of negotiations, interactions, and reconciliation of dilemmas with research participants and other collaborators is helpful, ethical, and shifts power towards the research subjects. Researchers must acknowledge their knowledge limitations, and forces them to be sensitive to contextual ethical issues sometimes drawn upon to solve ethical dilemmas. This requires a flexible approach; one that works against traditional methodologies that adhere to top-down procedures of fieldwork advocated by institutional ethical committees, such as paternalism. Ultimately, a researcher must apply a transparent approach that acknowledges the continuing negotiation of positionalities and pieces of knowledge with different collaborators in the field.

References

Ackerly, B. and True, J. (2008) 'Reflexivity in practice: power and ethics in feminist research on international relations', *International Studies Review*, 10(4): 693–707.

Allen, T. (2006) *Trial Justice: The International Criminal Court and the Lord's Resistance Army*, London: Zed Books.

Ayça, E. and Erdemir, A. (2010) 'Negotiating insider and outsider identities in the field: "insider" in a foreign land; "outsider" in one's own land', *Field Methods*, 22(1): 16–38.

Baines, E. and Stewart, B. (2011) '"I cannot accept what I have not done": storytelling, gender and transitional justice', *Journal of Human Rights Practice*, 3(3): 245 –63.

Basini, H. (2016) '"Doing no harm": methodological and ethical challenges of working with women associated with fighting forces/ex-combatants in Liberia', in A.T.R. Wibben (ed) *Researching War: Feminist Methods, Ethics and Politics*, New York: Routledge, pp 163–84.

Bilgen, A., Nasir, A., and Schöneberg, J. (2021) 'Why positionalities matter: reflections on power, hierarchy, and knowledges in "development" research', *Canadian Journal of Development Studies*, 42(4): 519–36.

Bott, E. (2010) 'Favourites and others: reflexivity and the shaping of subjectivities and data in qualitative research', *Qualitative Research*, 10(2): 159–73. https://doi.org/10.1177/1468794109356736

Bouka, Y. (2015) 'Researcher positionality', *Conflict Field Research*, [online]. Available from: http://conflictfieldresearch.colgate.edu/working-papers/%20researcher-positionality/ [Accessed 21 December 2023].

Bunting, A., Kiconco, A., and Quirk, J. (eds) (2020) *Research as more than extraction? Knowledge production and sexual violence in post conflict African societies*, Beyond Trafficking and Slavery, Open Democracy, London

Campbell, S.P. (2017) 'Ethics of research in conflict environments', *Journal of Global Security Studies*, 2(1): 89–101.

Chakravarty, A. (2012) '"Partially trusting": field relationships opportunities and constraints of fieldwork in Rwanda's post-conflict setting', *Field Methods*, 24(3): 251–71.

Cramer, C., Hammond, L., and Pottier, J. (eds) (2011) *Researching Violence in Africa: Ethical and Methodological Challenges*, Leiden and Boston: Brill.

Cramer, C., Johnston, D., Oya, C., and Sender, J. (2021) 'Mistakes, crises, and research independence: the perils of fieldwork as a form of evidence', *African Affairs*, 115(458): 145–60.

Cronin-Furman, K. and Lake, M. (2018) 'Ethics abroad: fieldwork in fragile and violent contexts', *Political Science and* Politics, 51(3): 607–14.

Dodsworth, S. and Cheeseman N. (2018) 'The potential and pitfalls of collaborating with development organisations and policymakers in Africa', *African Affairs*, 117(466): 130–45.

Eriksson Baaz, M. and Stern, M. (2016) 'Researching wartime rape in the Democratic Republic of Congo', in A.T.R. Wibben (ed) *Researching War: Feminist Methods, Ethics and Politics*, New York: Routledge, pp 117–40.

Jørgen, C., Bivane Erdal, M., and Ezzati, R. (2014) 'Beyond the insider–outsider divide in migration research', *Migration Studies*, 2(1): 36–54.

Keikelame, M.J. (2018) '"The tortoise under the couch": an African woman's reflections on negotiating insider-outsider positionalities and issues of serendipity on conducting a qualitative research project in Cape Town', *International Journal of Social Research Methodology*, 21: 219–30.

Kiconco, A. (2021) *Gender, Conflict and Reintegration in Uganda: Abducted Girls, Returning Women*, London: Routledge.

Krause, J. (2021) 'The ethics of ethnographic methods in conflict zones', *Journal of Peace Research*, 58(3): 329–41.

Lewis, C. et al (2019) 'Walking the line: brokering humanitarian identities in conflict research', *Civil Wars*, 21(2): 200–27.

Mackenzie, C., McDowell, C., & Pittaway, E. (2007) 'Beyond "do no harm": the challenge of constructing ethical relationships in refugee research', *Journal of Refugee Studies*, 20(2): 299–319. doi: https://doi.org/10.1093/jrs/fem008

Mandiyanike, D. (2009) 'The dilemma of conducting research back in your own country as a returning student: reflections of research fieldwork in Zimbabwe', *Area*, 41: 64–71.

Mitchell, A. (2013) 'Escaping the "field trap": exploitation and the global politics of educational fieldwork in "conflict zones"', *Third World Quarterly*, 34(7): 1247–64.

Murchison, J. (2010) *Ethnography Essentials: Designing, Conducting, and Presenting Your Research*, Hoboken, NJ: Wiley.

Mwambari, D. (2019) 'Local positionality in the production of knowledge in northern Uganda', *International Journal of Qualitative Methods*, 18: 1–12.

Nhemachena, A., Mlambo, N., and Kaundjua, M. (2016) 'The notion of the "field" and the practices of researching and writing Africa: towards decolonial praxis', *Africology: The Journal of Pan African Studies*, 9(7): 15–36.

Ojok, M.J. (2013) 'Power dynamics and the politics of fieldwork under Sudan's prolonged conflict', in D. Mazurana, K. Jacobsen, and L.A. Gale (eds) *Research Methods in Conflict Settings: A View from Below*, New York: Cambridge University Press, pp 149–65.

Oosterveld, V. (2011) 'The gender jurisprudence of the Special Court for Sierra Leone: progress in the Revolutionary United Front judgments', *Cornell International Law Journal*, 44: 49–74.

Parashar, S. (2019) 'Research brokers, researcher identities and affective performances: the insider/outsider conundrum', *Civil Wars*, 21(2): 249–70.

Sultana, F. (2015) 'Reflexivity, positionality and participatory ethics: negotiating fieldwork dilemmas in international research', *ACME: An International Journal for Critical Geographies*, 6(3): 374–85. Available from: https://acme-journal.org/index.php/acme/article/view/786 [Accessed 15 December 2023].

Thomson, S., Ansoms, A., and Murison, J. (eds) (2013) *Emotional and Ethical Challenges for Field Research in Africa: The Story Behind the Findings*, Basingstoke: Palgrave Macmillan.

Truth and Reconciliation Commission (2004) *Witness to Truth: Report of the Sierra Leone Truth and Reconciliation Commission*, Vol 3B. Available from: www.sierra-leone.org/Other-Conflict/TRCVolume3B.pdf [Accessed 15 December 2023].

Utas, M. (2005) 'Victimcy, girlfriending, soldiering: tactic agency in a young woman's social navigation of the Liberian war zone', *Anthropological quarterly*, 78(2): 403–30.

Wibben, A.T.R. (ed) (2016) *Researching War: Feminist Methods, Ethics and Politics*, New York: Routledge.

Wood, E. (2006) 'The ethical challenges of field research in conflict zones', *Qualitative Sociology*, 29(3): 373–86.

Yacob-Haliso, O. (2018) 'Intersectionalities and access in fieldwork in post-conflict Liberia: motherland, motherhood, and minefields', *African Affairs*, 118(470): 168–81.

11

Beyond Victim-Centric Research: Participatory Action Research in a Trafficking 'Hotspot' of Nepal

Ayushman Bhagat

Introduction: reimagining the political epistemology of victim-centric anti-trafficking research

'Human trafficking' represents an emotionally charged global concern spanning over a century (Kempadoo and Shih, 2022; Dolinsek and Hearne, 2023; Faulkner, 2023; Pinto, 2023; Lammasniemi, this volume). The term was legally defined in 2000 via Article 3 (see further Table 1.1, this volume) of the Protocol to Prevent, Suppress and Punish Trafficking in Persons, Especially Women and Children (hereafter, the Palermo Protocol).

In wake of the Palermo Protocol, trafficking research has offered several insights into legal and policy frameworks (Gallagher, 2010), enforcement of domestic anti-trafficking laws (Kaye et al, 2019), emerging trends of trafficking (Sweileh, 2018), demand/supply of trafficking (Aronowitz, 2014), victims' identification, experiences and services (Palombi et al, 2019), and stakeholders' perceptions (Hounmenou, 2020). The Protocol subsequently extended the scope of trafficking research beyond the prevailing focus on sex work to encompass other sectors such as domestic, agricultural, construction, and fishing, thereby facilitating an expansion in trafficking literature (Goździak and Graveline, 2015; Russell, 2018), thereby attempting to address 'the full spectrum of issues related to human trafficking' (Bossard, 2022: 1). The transferability of trafficking research to influence policy formulation, practical applications, and ideological interpretations serves as a political epistemology, contributing to the sustenance of what Faulkner describes as an 'Anti-trafficking Machine' (Faulkner, 2023). This political epistemology multiplies 'contemporary abolitionism' (McGrath, Rogaly, and Waite, 2022), which, in turn, leads to unintended adverse consequences for the very individuals this machine aims to safeguard, often referred to as 'collateral damage' (Dottridge, 2017; see further Hynes and Dottridge, this volume).

For example, following the recommendations of survey-based research which found widespread exploitation of Nepalese citizens in several Gulf countries, the government of Nepal imposed total migration bans on domestic work in 2017 (Shivakoti, 2020; Bhagat, 2022a). Yet, due to the lack of alternative employment opportunities in Nepal, this restrictive migration policy forces citizens to rely upon unlicensed agents to facilitate their migration journeys. Coupled with the proliferation of anti-trafficking measures, which creates the potential to criminalize citizens as 'traffickers' (Bhagat, 2022b, 2023b). Despite well-established critical scholarship which interrogates and problematizes the anti-trafficking discourse, anti-trafficking measures continue to increase (Brennan, 2005; Kelly, 2005; Snajdr, 2013; Chuang, 2014; Chapman-Schmidt, 2019; Feingold, 2019; Esson, 2020; Yea, 2020b; Beutin, 2023). Arguably this is due to the uncritical mobilization of the term 'trafficking' by politicians, media personnel, government officials, UN experts, lobby groups, activists, lawyers, celebrities, religious leaders, consultants, and even some academics to further their political and economic projects (Quirk, 2011; Strauss, 2017). These actors mobilize the term 'trafficking' in policy reports, newspaper articles, magazines, blogs, academic journals, podcasts, social media posts, films, and documentaries in a manner which suits their ideologies the best (Kempadoo, 2015); subsequently, justifying the growth of anti-trafficking measures. Critical scholars not only interrogate the assumptions, politics, and impacts of such measures (Chuang, 2014; Kempadoo, 2016; Faulkner, 2018; McGrath and Watson, 2018; Bernstein, 2019; Laurie and Richardson, 2020), but also probe the limitations of the methodology used to generate knowledge of trafficking and anti-trafficking measures (Kelly, 2005; Tyldum and Brunovskis, 2005; di Nicola, 2007; Brunovskis and Surtees, 2010; Tyldum, 2010; Molland, 2013). They dismiss the premises and promises of such research, which is frequently characterized by stereotypical portrayals of violence, extrapolated quantification, and emotionally charged public appeals, which serve to validate harmful anti-trafficking measures (Broome and Quirk, 2015; Gallagher, 2017; Feingold, 2019; Quirk et al, 2020). By doing so, they challenge the grand narrative of anti-trafficking and its 'best practices', which often fail to align with the actual lived experiences of impacted individuals.

Despite a long-standing demand for micro-level empirical investigations, trafficking research predominately indicates a relative absence of robust research with 'trafficking victims' (Russell, 2018; Sweileh, 2018). While

Tyldum (2010) makes a strong ethical case against researching people before trafficking happens, she argues for more trafficking research upon post-trafficking; most empirical research (from the Global South) falls under this criterion (Locke, 2010; Laurie et al, 2015; Musto, 2016; Molland, 2018; Yea, 2020a; Parmanand, 2021; Kiconco, this volume; Hynes and Dottridge, this volume). This research is often facilitated by a few local anti-trafficking NGOs (see further Kiconco, this volume) which creates a 'golden middle' by not only granting researchers access to victims but also ensuring their safety and privacy (Brennan, 2005; Laczko and Gozdziak, 2005: 38). These NGO-assisted research interventions are assumed to lay the groundwork for the examination of victims' experiences and the institutional support to assure their welfare, with the knowledge generated often feeding into the development of new anti-trafficking strategies. Subsequently, this political epistemology of trafficking helps in the justification of 'old' initiatives, in addition to the formulation of 'new' initiatives which have the potential to reproduce conservative ideologies of race, sex, gender, mobility, and labour.

I argue that the 'golden middle' approach privileges people who are labelled as 'trafficked victims', which is a legally defined category that demarcates them (but not all) as deserving subjects of knowledge and protection. This epistemic privileging of trafficking victims excludes a wide range of people as 'underserving' subjects of trafficking research. While I understand the significance of amplifying the voices of individuals who hold legal recognition as 'trafficked victims' or 'survivors', it often results in excluding the voices of those who endure extreme exploitation in their labour employments, but either do not meet the criteria to be labelled as 'victims' or 'survivors' (O'Connell Davidson, 2010; Strauss, 2017) or do not want to expose themselves as a 'victims' due to underlying stigma (Laurie and Richardson, 2020; see further Hynes and Dottridge, this volume). This often well-intended research attempts to engage survivors with the help of politically charged and funding dependent anti-trafficking NGOs, which could dismantle the space in which both 'victims' and 'non-victims' reside (Bhagat, 2023b). The issue that arises is that the outcomes of such geographically blind research tend to reproduce the existing tropes of trafficking but exacerbate the problematic boundaries between 'victims' and 'non-victims'.

This chapter illustrates an epistemic framework for trafficking research grounded in people's mobility and labour struggles. I present a comprehensive account of an academic Participatory Action Research (PAR), conducted in 2017–18 in a region stigmatized as a 'hotspot' of trafficking in Nepal (Bhagat, 2022c, 2023a). I aim to address the concern of lack of transparency in trafficking research, in addition to addressing some of the methodological questions in qualitative research raised by Hitchings and Latham (2019, 2020, 2021). The chapter begins with a brief overview of the research's inception, within which I argue the necessity of shifting the focus from trafficking victims to the mobility struggles of people in certain contexts. I present a step-by-step account of a grounded trafficking research study that utilized a PAR approach – an approach that holds considerable value for both anti-trafficking researchers and practitioners alike.

Placing mobility before political categories

The Institute of Hazard, Risk, and Resilience (IHRR) at Durham University, UK, supported my doctoral research through the Christopher Moyes Memorial Foundation studentship. Building upon my policy[1] and grassroots-level experiences in India, I pitched the idea of examining 'risk and resilience of human trafficking in Nepal' in a post-disaster context.[2] I emphasized that comprehending and combatting the issue of 'human trafficking' necessitated understanding the perspectives of those directly impacted by it. The conviction arose from my policy and grassroots frustrations while assisting the implementation of the International Labour Organization (ILO) projects on 'bonded labour', and 'labour trafficking' in India. The interactions with the actors of the ILO, trade unions, government departments, recruitment agencies, and NGOs provided valuable insights; however, my preference for participatory approaches to development clashed with the imposition of top-down imperialistic approaches to 'trafficking'. Subsequently, through this research, I made a sincere effort to engage with and bring to fore the voices, experiences, and insights of individuals directly affected by the discourse of trafficking.

During the research design phase of my doctoral research, I was introduced to the politics of the dominant and counter approaches to anti-trafficking. The critical anti-trafficking literature spoke to my conflicted experiences of the policy world and cautioned me against the normalization of unethical research practices. This includes, but is not limited to, the uncritical utilization of the stigma-bearing term 'trafficking' in the field, the post-research consequences of exclusively interviewing 'trafficked victims' in a community space shared by labour migrants with diverse subjectivities, the selection of the most horrific stories while disregarding narratives that question the state and anti-trafficking interventions, and the tampering and fabrication of data for political purposes. My previous experiences compelled me to question the credibility of certain

---

[1] I assisted implementation of ILO-DFID-funded Anti-trafficking programme as a consultant. The opportunity helped me to work with various actors – the UN, NGOs, government departments, placement agencies, and trade unions.
[2] I am a rural development professional with a grassroots-level experience of living and working with communities living in and around wildlife sanctuaries of India.

anti-trafficking research influenced by the 'collaborating' NGOs, which at times controlled (whether directly or indirectly) the research process. This control risked turning research into a mere performance and inadvertently stigmatizing 'specific bodies, people, groups, and places' (Laurie and Richardson, 2020: 121; see further Kiconco, this volume) by associating them with trafficking.

I decided to distance myself from the exclusive, if not stigmatizing, political category of trafficking victims. Instead, following Urry (2007), I adopted mobility as a starting point to explore the lives of people on the move directly impacted by the discourse of anti-trafficking. This shift has significant epistemological implications for trafficking research, by presenting an opportunity to engage with both individual and collective mobility, and labour experiences of people on the move without succumbing to the limiting dichotomy of 'trafficked' and 'non-trafficked'. Moreover, this shift is attuned to the political exclusions of those whose labour and mobility experiences are sometimes more arduous than those categorized as 'trafficked victims', thereby ethically transgressing the political boundary between trafficked and non-trafficked people during the research process. To facilitate inclusive engagement, I adopted a PAR approach and relied upon continuous action and reflection with people throughout and beyond the research process.

Ethical reflections

Assuring the 'ethical' in anti-trafficking research should commence with an enquiry into the categories of trafficking and the practical repercussions of their political translations. One noteworthy effort in this direction is Siegel and de Wildt's (2016) edited volume, *Ethical Concerns in Research on Human Trafficking*, where authors delve into four categories of human trafficking – 'sex', 'labour', 'organ', and 'child'. The book delves into complexities related to researching 'victims', 'vulnerable', 'pimps', 'criminals', and 'saviours' in the context of human trafficking, but seldom reflects on the ethics of engaging with the political category of trafficking, and its possible translations. On the contrary, some authors emphasized labelling people as 'slaves' as an ethical endeavour to save them from exploitative practices (Boyd and Bales, 2016). The assumption here is that all translations of the term trafficking are positive. Although I cannot proclaim that these researchers have not reflected on how the use of 'slave' or 'trafficked victim' increases the privileged distance between them and their research participants, prima facie they seem to have overlooked the geographically specific political translations of the term 'trafficking'.

The ethics of translation demands an examination of all the possible intrepretations of the term 'trafficking' and measures to mitigate its harmful effects. Considering the sensitivity and the stigma attached to the term in the village, I refrained from its use unless my research companions and participants used it during our interactions. Moreover, I argue that research employing the term 'human trafficking' to construct or reinforce political subjectivities of victims and criminals to gain immediate political traction must not be geographically blind. For example, Laurie and Richardson (2020) have recently shown how deliberatly producing political subjectivities of 'victims' and 'perpetrators' not only stigmatizes prospective and returnee migrants, but also the places where they reside, thereby producing 'Hot-Spots' (Bhagat, 2023a). Hence, geography matters when it comes to navigating the effects of translation.

Even if the research adheres to high 'ethical' standards, the issue of distance and translation between the researcher and the researched persists when the vantage point of the enquiry is the term 'human trafficking'. To address this concern and taking into account the arguments made by critical scholars regarding the seductions of the political discourse of human trafficking, I changed the epistemological focus to mobility and positioned it as a motor of all the political subjectivities – an autonomy of migration viewpoint (Scheel, 2019).

The next question is how to ensure the demand of being ethical in the political process of researching trafficking and anti-trafficking. Here, I followed the University Ethics Committee's prescribed ethical codes to ensure a foundation of research ethics. These codes revolve around principles of confidentiality, informed consent, and anonymity, with the aim to prevent harm, and if possible, would also do some good to the research participants. Both my research companions and I ensured the university-prescribed ethical clauses at every level of intervention – interpersonal, household, group, community, and national. Each participatory activity including training, action and reflection meetings, focused groups, and interviews started with a thorough discussion on anonymity, confidentiality, and informed consent. Consequently, some participants initially rejected the anonymity clause, while others requested specific portions of the discussion to be anonymized. With some even leaving the conversation and withdrawing their consent midway (see further Kiconco, this volume).

The limits of the university-prescribed ethical codes were made bare while living in the community, shedding light on the intricate necessity of maintaining the 'ethical' during everyday encounters with the community members. My research companions and I remained highly vigilant in these encounters, engaging in thorough reflections on 'everyday ethics' during our action and reflection meetings. Overall, the demand was to ensure every encounter was ethical with agents, household members, community members, NGO members, disaster victims, those vulnerable to human trafficking, and other Nepali citizens. This care towards ethics in each encounter resulted in a geography of ethics that was differentially negotiated by the participants at various intervention sites.

To ensure 'everyday ethics of encounter', I found PAR literature on participatory ethics helpful (Cahill, 2007a). Manzo and Brightbill (2007) position participatory ethics as ethics of representation, accountability, social responsiveness, agency, reflexivity, and constant concern for the participants. Since the process of PAR attempts to blur the differences between the researcher and participants, the ethical codes used in this research were contextually grounded and iterative. For example, during the fieldwork, I spent considerable time developing and maintaining a trusting relationship with my research participants. Once the fieldwork was over, I sustained the relationship with my research participants via social media and, finally, I strengthened it by physically returning to the research site. The ethics of reflexivity were particularly helpful as every informed action we took during the research was a result of reflection on the output of often-uncomfortable actions. For example, the continuous action and reflection during the entire research process raised some doubts in the community regarding the planned intervention (that is, migrant information centre) in the community. After weighing and discussing the 'collateral damage' of my research, I failed to continue with the planned intervention and anonymized the research site. Upon my return, most of the community members suggested that anonymizing was perhaps the best idea to avoid the anti-trafficking gaze in the community. Hence, failure to intervene was an ethical necessity, and the failure to represent the community was an ethical demand. Perhaps, the most ethical impact of this PAR was not to create any impact.

Methodology, knowledge production, and unravelling power dynamics

PAR is a research approach rooted in the struggles of communities trying to break free from the tyranny of limiting structures (Glassman and Erdem, 2014). As a hybrid research orientation, PAR encompasses various research traditions historically unfolded worldwide, including action research in Columbia, popular research in India, and participatory research in Brazil and Chile (Freire, 1970; Borda, 2006). Through embracing the ethos of emancipatory movements, PAR views research, education, and action as an interconnected reflexive process, offering critical responses to positivist, hierarchical, and damaging research approaches (Khanlou and Peter, 2005; Borda, 2006; Mazzei, 2007; Armstrong et al, 2011). This hybrid research approach can be viewed as an endeavour to 'study, reframe, and reconstruct social practices' (Kemmis and McTaggart, 2007: 277). By drawing on the capabilities and resources of researchers and participants, this approach seeks to transform the existing situation through a bottom-up approach (Kindon et al, 2007). While some argue that this bottom-up research approach draws its strength from a rigorous self-reflective cycle of action-reflection where both researcher and participants reflect on and learn from each other to address the pressing issues (Kinpaisby-hill, 2011). Subsequently, academics chose this research approach, with the ultimate aim of advancing the interests of the participants (Kesby, 2005) while upholding the highest ethical standards (Cahill et al, 2007; Cahill, 2007a; Elwood, 2007; Manzo and Brightbill, 2007; Pain, 2008; Butcher, 2020).

However, the intersection of PAR and human trafficking simultaneously transforms the research approach to encompass methodology, political epistemology, funding category, development project, and bordering technique. Due to the high 'impact' possibilities offered by the PAR, anti-trafficking scholars, activists, and NGOs often adopt this research approach as a quick-fix method to support the 'trafficked victims' as well as to generate the knowledge for improving anti-trafficking interventions (Dharel, Rai, and Thapa, 2015; Laurie et al, 2015; Twis and Preble, 2020; Dhungel, 2021; Miller et al, 2022). The growing popularity of PAR in anti-trafficking circles underscores the commodification of anti-trafficking research, where primary beneficiaries are limited to those labelled as 'victims'. This commodification reinforces the selective marginalization of 'non-victims' as undeserving and unworthy subjects of knowledge and protection. The approach not only legitimizes the political divide between accepted and non-accepted 'victimhood' (Christie, 1986) but also effectively suppresses the possibility of collective and inclusive action.

Critical scholars have shown that the 'victimhood' in the discourse of trafficking has a long ideological history (Lammasniemi, this volume; Doezema, 2010). Consequently, the complex and ideologically charged agenda of anti-trafficking (often reinforced by the anti-trafficking NGOs) reverses the foundation of PAR. When such research is NGO led it often perpetuates the imperialistic top-down approach, seeking to reinforce 'old' and develop convenient 'new' knowledge to align with specific abolitionist ideologies and donor requirements. As a result, NGO-led PAR on human trafficking tends to legitimize all the dismissive criticisms of PAR made by post-structural scholars (Cooke and Kothari, 2001; Cameron and Gibson, 2005). On the other hand, academic-led PAR attempts to address some of these critiques (Laurie et al, 2015). Yet, it is often conducted under the auspices of the organizing anti-trafficking NGO – the discourse masters.

The challenge that emerged was whether to forsake PAR as a research approach or forge ahead with a determination to build upon its existing critiques. Abandoning the approach would forfeit the radical potentialities that PAR holds in terms of 'dialogic engagement with co-researchers, and the development and implementation of context-appropriate strategies oriented towards empowerment and transformation' (Kindon, Pain, and

Kesby, 2007: 3). To relinquish the power of the critical cycle of action and reflection throughout the research process would mean forsaking the very nexus between theory, politics, and practice which PAR offers (Pain et al, 2007; Pain and Kindon, 2010). Such abandonment would have signified surrendering my own value system – which is not an option. Therefore, taking inspiration from Cahill (2007b), Kindon, Pain, and Kesby (2007), Armstrong, Aznarez, and Banks (2011), and Laurie and Richardson (2020), I decided to adopt PAR as the approach to conduct this research.

PAR involves co-identification of pressing issues by participants and researcher, followed by a collective action and reflection process to co-develop solutions. This process has significant social and political ramifications (Khanlou and Peter, 2005), such as the production of the alternative power structure in the intervened space (Cooke and Kothari, 2001). Therefore, ensuring fair selection of research sites and participants is critical. Much has been written about biases in participant selection (Brunovskis and Surtees, 2010; Tyldum, 2010; Merry, 2021); I argue that 'where' we conduct our research matters. Drawing on my subjectivity as an anti-trafficker, I decided to conduct a scoping study in Nepal and after receiving the university's ethics approval, I arrived in Kathmandu, Nepal, in July 2017.

Scoping study: participatory project mapping

I devised participatory project mapping, as a research tool to both locate the site and map the project. This enabled me to situate the objectives of academic participatory research in line with the objectives of various Nepalese actors working on issues such as migration, anti-trafficking, livelihood, and labour, without creating dependence upon such actors.

Initially, I developed a live database of actors in Nepal working on anti-trafficking, migration, gender, and labour issues before contacting them. I arranged meetings with the actors who responded to my request and were using either English or Hindi to communicate.[3] Within each meeting, I used a snowballing technique to meet and network with other anti-trafficking actors and subsequently met with more than ten organizations, including – anti-trafficking networks, NGOs, INGOs, government departments, and UN agencies – in Kathmandu. To map the current state of trafficking and anti-trafficking research in Nepal I asked these five questions during each meeting:

---

[3] Later, I used my positionality as an ex-ILO consultant and sought help from the ILO to establish contact with other actors.

1. What is your understanding of human trafficking?[4]
2. What is the magnitude of the problem in Nepal?
3. What kind of research has already been done in Nepal?
4. What research would you like to do?
5. Where would you like to conduct the research?

I attended a research dissemination workshop organized by UN Women on human trafficking, illegality, and migration-related issues, which provided networking opportunities in addition to scheduling meetings with other NGOs working in this field. The iterative process of snowballing led me to the administrative headquarter of the Sindhupalchok district of Nepal. Here, I encountered language issues, as most of the government and non-government officials spoke in Nepali, and this barrier changed my mapping strategy. Once I encountered language barriers, the research transformed into a mapping process, driven by political maps. During one of the meetings, a government official brought along two, old, district political maps, as due to language barriers we were unable to communicate effectively. A local engineer pointed out the earthquake-impacted sites where female migration was high and I used the maps to interview several district-level anti-trafficking NGOs and government departments to locate villages based on two criteria: first, high female migration and, second, that it was impacted by the 2015 Gorkha earthquake.

Subsequently, I identified the top-three villages, which numerous actors asked me to avoid due to language issues,[5] inaccessibility during the rainy season,[6] and the hostility of the community members against anti-trafficking NGOs. For example, one HIV/AIDS-based NGO manager advised that interviewing people in these areas would be difficult as generally people do not reveal information to outsiders due to trust issues. Moreover, most of the researchers do not live within the community, and no one has ever returned to the villages after the data collection.

Nevertheless, I then went to the nearest municipality of these three sites and met with an anti-trafficking NGO manager to conduct the same mapping exercise. The manager prioritized the same three sites and put me in touch with a local female political leader from the Communist Party of Nepal via telephone. After our conversation about the project, I requested

---

[4] In Kathmandu I used the term 'trafficking' only to understand the actors' viewpoints, and their implementation strategies. I tried to avoid the term 'trafficking' as much as I could in the district, and at village level.
[5] The language used by the mountain-dwelling indigenous community is Tamang, which is difficult to understand.
[6] The bus services are put on halt during rainy seasons due to a lack of bridges and roads, and the dangers of landslides.

her assistance in facilitating my preliminary visit to these villages. The next day, a local engineer took me to some of these villages on his motorbike. We went near some of these sites, only to realize the difficulties of accessing these villages on a motorbike, due to the rainy season and non-existent Himalayan roads. After a few unsuccessful attempts, I contacted the political leader, explaining the situation to which she responded by requesting that I trek up the Himalayan mountain as she had arranged accommodation at a teacher's house in one of the villages upon my arrival. I realized that the village was divided into two wards upon my arrival, as per the new administrative shuffling in Nepal.

Over the next few days, I met with individuals, women's groups, NGO members, and a trafficked survivor[7] – the most powerful woman in the village. Additionally, I met with other actors such as teachers, community leaders, social workers, and trafficking victims/survivor group leaders as identified by the teacher with whom I was staying. I observed that information about female mobility was not revealed, as the emerging concern was focused upon the exploitation of males in Malaysia and Qatar. I highlighted that I wished to understand the mobilities of both men and women who go to work for foreign employment. Many of them gave their consent; however, in retrospect, I feel the consent was given only under the influence of the communist political leader, who shared a complex relationship with the community. While I acknowledge a classic critique of the PAR approach, where existing power structures in the community are exploited (Cooke and Kothari, 2001), the only alternative option I had was to navigate a hard-to-reach research site with the help of the anti-trafficking NGO and a local political leader. Before I left the community, the teacher, whom I was living with, revealed that she was leaving her teaching duties soon and planned to depart for Dubai to work as a cleaner. She also told me that there were so many truths in the community, and people would reveal details once I become familiar with them.

The stay in Nepal

I conducted the research in a post-disaster site recuperating from a tremendous loss of life, infrastructure, and livelihood. At the same time in November 2017, events such as a scheduled assembly election in Nepal and state-imposed financial incentive deadlines on the post-disaster housing construction transformed the research site into a politically charged arena. I lived in the community for a period exceeding a hundred days, in an

---

[7] The victim identifies herself as the political subject category of the victim and is a leading member of the local trafficking victims support group.

attempt to understand multiple realities of mobility from a visually immobile and devastated place.

Project construction: steering committee, research companions, safe space, and training

Initially, some participants asked me to engage with leaders of all three political parties[8] in the village. They cautioned me against the political animosity within the community and the forthcoming assembly elections in Nepal, which could disrupt my research process. I again adopted a snowballing technique to identify key actors in the community. Starting with some participants, I asked everyone to nominate (with reasons) at least three people I should meet. The snowballing took me to the people with whom I discussed the participatory project. The process helped members of the community become accustomed to my presence, the proposed project, and my intentions. I stopped the process once the chain became repetitive and called a general meeting.

Community members such as the president of the ward, community leaders, political group leaders, teachers, health workers, educators, women's group leaders, and the sex trafficking survivor group leader all participated in the general meeting, in addition to with more than 25 participants. We started our discussion by trying to make sense of the nature of the previous research conducted in the community. Discussing the meaning of participation in research and the formation of a steering committee – a common practice adopted by several NGOs in the community. PAR generally begins with the constitution of a steering committee or an advisory body (Blake, 2007), which operates to ensure the supervision of ethical procedures and create a troubleshooting forum of influential community members.

Prior to nominating, the participants reflected on the number, constitution, gender mix, and roles of the committee. After nominations, we then discussed the selection criteria of 'peer' researchers, the compensation(s), the selection of an interpreter, a safe space of action and reflection, meeting dates, in addition to community-level compensation. Finally, we reflected upon issues of representation, anonymity, confidentiality, accountability, and the risk-benefit of the research at the community level.

Several qualitative researchers often employ peer researchers to assist in fieldwork (Ryan et al, 2010; Edwards and Alexander, 2011; Marlowe et al, 2015) and the next step of the project was the recruitment of 'peer'

---

[8] Communist Party of Nepal (Unified Maoist-Leninist); Communist Party of Nepal (Maoist Centre) Nepali Congress Party; Rashtriya Prajatantra Party of Nepal.

researchers.[9] Due to conceptual, political, and ethical difficulties in executing the project, scholars often employ peer researchers, on the assumption that cultural capital would 'enable [them] to identify and access exploited workers across the groups' (Siegel and de Wildt, 2016). Their insider status privileges them with the capacity to connect with their peers, a form of 'cultural capital', which enriches the research process.

I recruited a few people with the help of the steering committee and called them 'peer researchers', while they identified themselves as *'sathi anusandhankarta'* – a combination of two Nepali words in which *'Sathi'* denotes a 'friend' and 'companion' and *'anusandhankarta'* is 'researcher'. The signifier and signified produced here are unique and the essence of the term cannot be captured by any another popular terms (especially peer researchers) in the literature.

I argue that the word 'peer'[10] is often uncritically celebrated in participatory approaches. The Oxford English Dictionary considers peer as a verb, meaning 'be just visible' and as a noun meaning 'a person of the same age, status, or ability as another specified person'. While the first talks about visibility, the second gives us a sense of equality which is central to the PAR. The first meaning reveals an ethical tension between the individual desire of visibility and their vulnerability to the forces which often capitalize on their visibility. The second meaning reveals a conceptual fallacy between the impossibility of intersubjectivity between researcher and researched, despite an unwavering awareness of positionality and reflexivity (Noxolo, 2017). A false sense of equality could potentially mask the bargaining power of 'peer' researchers, who could end up researching in an exploitative labour relationship in some of the most 'ethical' research.

Initially, some of the people I engaged with doubted the entire process and subsequently there were instances when we experienced guarded responses, negotiated the disagreements, and in some cases, they simply refused to cooperate. I argue that the term 'research companion' transcends the allure of the term 'peer', which can falsely imply a flat hierarchy among individuals despite their distinct positionalities. Research companions in this research included a youth leader (initially, a sex trafficking survivor/victim consented to this but who later dropped out because her husband did not want his wife to work with a male Indian researcher), an HIV patient, a middle-aged social worker (whom I later learnt used to take women to Indian brothels),

---

[9] 'People who live within, and have everyday experiences as a member of, a particular geographical or social "community", and who use their contacts and detailed lay knowledge in a mediating role, helping to gather and understand information from and about their peers for research purposes' (Edwards and Alexander, 2011: 269).

[10] Oxford English Dictionary Online.

a women's group leader, and a health professional. The local assistant, who worked as an interpreter, provided invaluable support throughout the process. Indubitably, the insider status of my research companions served the research process well but given the sensitivity of the topic, they became outsiders to the project when it came to interacting with the agents, and the ownership of the project outcome. Research companions negotiated many aspects of the research – for example, they negotiated the decision-making power given to the steering committee members during the general meeting, and the compensation amount. One such negotiation was the negotiation of a safe space for the community members for planning, action, reflection, and negotiation during the research process.

Due to the sensitivity of the research topic, I requested a safe space where we could sit periodically, reflect on our actions, and plan new ones on a regular basis. Some advisory board members suggested a post-earthquake infrastructure '*Mahila Chalfal chautari*' (Women's Discussion Centre). The centre was anchored by an NGO working on land rights, managed by a committee, and presided over by a research companion. When I asked for his support, the research companion was reluctant to offer the place, fearing the 'wrath' of the NGO. Upon my request and in my presence, he rang the NGO leader who denied access to the space.[11] I was later assigned a room by the steering committee, in a post-earthquake, dilapidated, and deserted school.

Initially my interpreter emphasized the need for training as various community members encountered difficulties understanding my research intentions. Recognizing the potential benefits of training to learn more about the community's history, issues, and way of life, we opted for a participatory training session, adopting a cross-cultural participatory training process (Kwan and Walsh, 2018), due to the fact that training programmes enhance research skills among participants and create a platform for discussing and negotiating research ethics (Pain, 2004, 2008). During the training, we addressed the ethics of functioning within the community and the needs of the research companions, in addition to my own requirements for cultural understanding.[12]

---

[11] Later, I went to Kathmandu to talk to the same NGO leader who had been denied access. After hearing about the project, the NGO leader allowed me to use 'their' infrastructure for research purposes. That site became our meeting space throughout the fieldwork in the community, where we met over seven times to critically reflect, and reflectively plan out field activities.

[12] During the training session we discussed and reflected on topics and issues – such as past, current, and future problems, language and translation, participation, research and ethics, collective action and reflection, and agents; reflecting on our positionalities and negotiated roles, and responsibilities in addition to issues which community members have historically

The approach

Within one of our reflection meetings, we decided that each research companion would mobilize and organize groups based on criteria such as geographical locations, personal contacts, gender, age, and mobility experience. Subsequently, five groups were formed – one mixed group (with the majority women), one all-Gulf group (only women), one mixed group, one youth group (all men), and one mixed group (relatively immobile). The group formations not only helped us to increase the reach of the research (with ten focus-group discussions taking place) but also to bring people into the conversation.

In the first round of focused group discussion, a research companion facilitated the meeting of their group in the native Tamang language, within which we discussed challenges and opportunities (source, transit, and destination) in the mobility of foreign employment and different forms and degrees of exploitation.

Upon reflection, we decided that it is important to have a rights-based (namely, focusing upon human/labour) awareness-generation session.[13]

This stage of the project saw three types of interviews taking place; namely: (1) interviews with participants occupying different political subject positions – trafficking victims, illegal immigrants, and illegal migrants, to understand mobility patterns; (2) interviews with influential people – teachers, political leaders, and community development workers – of the village, to understand the history of mobility in the community; and (3) interviews with stakeholders who influence and facilitate the mobility of the community – for example, household members and unlicensed agents.

I discussed ethical choices – informed consent, confidentiality, and anonymity – with each of them and the interviews were recorded with permission. I did not include any of the research companions in these interviews, especially when interacting with (unlicensed) agents, ensuring their safety and avoiding social stigma.

---

faced. We also conducted several participatory exercises, including problem prioritization, pre- and post-disaster village mapping, migration history and trends, gendered mobility mapping, and a project timeline.

[13] I went to Kathmandu to collect different awareness-generating materials (in the Nepali Language) from organizations such as the ILO and GEFONT (General Federation of Nepalese Trade Union). We synthesized the information and decided that the research companion would conduct the awareness-generation activity in their language (Tamang). It was an interactive process where we discussed the meanings and forms of freedom and unfreedom faced by the community members.

The research companions maintained a register with the names of people living outside the community. During action-reflection meetings, we discussed their names before selecting them for interviews. Upon selection, research companions organized these interviews. I conducted most of the interviews, using the services of the interpreter in only a few cases when the interviewee could not speak in Hindi at a time and location preferred by the interviewees. We captured mobility stories which the participants thought were the most interesting, both by drawing maps (in a notebook) and through recording their viewpoints. Subsequently, we discussed these maps while depicting journeys without names and debated over the names of people whose mobility stories would further enrich the project. These reflections frequently changed the criteria of the interviews – including people who had only been to India, those who were planning to leave soon, or had recently returned from labour relations, in addition to those who were immobile and those who were classified as sex trafficking victims but did not identify with that label.

Finally, I conducted interviews with stakeholders during my stay within the community, as this need emerged within the action-reflection meetings. During both the focused group discussions and interviews, numerous questions were directed at me, including questions relating to the government mobility ban, the operations of NGOs and their funding, for example.[14] These questions were subsequently blended with some of my own and fed into the interviews conducted with some anti-trafficking actors.

Analysis, reflection, and the pause

The analysis of this PAR project was an ongoing iterative process of organizing, describing, classifying, interpreting, and representing data before, during ,and after the fieldwork. Several issues were raised during this process; for example, regarding an information centre which was initially discussed by the community (and suggested by some of the stakeholders such as the ILO) as a form of community-level compensation. Throughout the village stay (more than 100 days), the discussion regarding an information resource centre (which was predetermined during the start

---

[14] Specific questions included – why were some people allowed, and some people not allowed to cross the borders? Why are anti-trafficking NGOs sympathetic to the agents who support their political parties? Why has the government implemented a mobility ban? Why do anti-trafficking NGOs support only a few selective people in the community? What are the sources of their funds? Why are they not at all transparent in terms of their functioning?

of the research process) generated a positive response from the participants and companions. Yet, some were highly sceptical and/or maintained silence about it. I noted that many anti-traffickers supported the idea of a migrant resource cell or information resource centre as a soft approach for dealing with 'labour trafficking'.

The information centre encapsulated the most difficult aspect of the fieldwork, as asserted by Klocker (2015) that there is no guarantee that the impact of the research will be positive. Klocker, when faced with a similar situation while conducting research relating to domestic workers in Tanzania, commented that:

> There were many days when it all felt too difficult: I cried about this project, I got angry, I had nightmares, I experienced anxiety attacks and heart palpitations, sleepless nights and as a PhD student and novice researcher an overwhelming sense of being utterly out of my depth. I experienced a 'maelstrom of emotions'. (Klocker, 2015: 39)

I regularly visited Kathmandu and remained in touch with NGO members to try and ensure that we effectively collaborated to establish the information centre. I underwent a series of discussions and negotiations with the steering committee members, research companions, and most importantly, with myself, regarding both the positive and negative aspects of establishing an information centre – the creation of a potentially stigmatized place that was visible within the community and subsequently highlighted the movement of people through illegal channels. Moreover, there was the risk of making the mobility facilitators visible to the state, which had imposed the mobility ban. Coupled with comments within interviews with agents that if the state identifies agents who facilitate mobility through illegal channels, they could be charged with trafficking. This subsequently informed my decision after a period of intense reflection to leave the community to avoid the damage of this intervention (in the form of an information centre) which could have the potential to unleash damage upon the community. Prior to departing, I called another general meeting and discussed both the positive and negative aspects of the information centre with everyone. The group asked for some time to think and reflect on the issue with other members. Given the sensitivity of the activity, I suggested that the research companions should organize a general meeting, record the proceedings in a register, and take the signatures of more than two thirds of the population, before we could commence the activity. The aim here was clear – to democratically legitimize the decision and ensure community ownership. After the conclusion of the research, I have remained in touch with my research companions and several participants, all of which do not favour the idea of an information centre.

The next steps

During action-reflection meetings the routes that people take from the community to their labour employment were discussed. Subsequently, these routes were discussed with important stakeholders, including the National Human Rights Commissions, Nepal, government departments, trade union members, and anti-trafficking and migration NGOs. Together we formulated different questions and discussed participatory observation methods; this change in methodological approach required university approval.

I traced checkpoints that included four Indo-Nepal borders, a landing site in New Delhi, and four airports – Kathmandu, New Delhi, Colombo, and Kuwait. I contacted,[15] interacted with, and interviewed a range actors during the process, such as border guards, NGO members patrolling the borders and/or the checkpoints, rehabilitation centre staff, local people living on the borderlands, commuters, and rickshaw/auto-rickshaw/taxi drivers. I created an electronic research diary to capture day-to-day encounters, self-reflection, and participant observation. This engagement with hundreds of actors in multiple sites revealed the diverse nature of mobility experiences, and heterogeneity of mobility struggles of individuals before they enter into their labour relation.

After completing the fieldwork, I returned to my university to analyse the data, presented my findings to scholars and activists, wrote, and defended my doctoral thesis. Throughout my lectures, seminars, and conference papers, I channelled my feelings of guilt, pain, frustration, and failure. I emphasized to my research methods students that I was the greatest beneficiary of the research undertaken. The discomfort of feeling powerless in addressing the rightlessness, oppression, and exploitation experienced by my research participants, coupled with the guilt and shame of building a career from their suffering, still lingers within me.

I stayed connected with my research companions and several community members via social media. Upon securing a permanent post in the UK, I mobilized internal funds and began planning my return to the community. Initially, I reached out to the communist leader, expressing my eagerness to return to the community and engage in discussions about the research findings. Additionally, I reached out to several research companions and community members conveying my interest in returning to the community. Everyone welcomed the idea and ensured their support.

---

[15] Some of these contacts were provided by community members, agents, government officials, trade union members, and NGO officials.

I reached the research site after a 7-hour bus ride from Kathmandu in June 2022, some five years after my initial arrival in 2017. I was accommodated in the newly constructed house of one of my research companions, and subsequently we met with most of the research companions. I learned that several participants, including research companions and some 'trafficking survivors', had already left the community for employment. Yet, we managed to organize a meeting, bringing together 25 community members,[16] in a newly constructed communal space.

I began by recounting everything I had done since my previous field visit, with the interpreter translating into the local language. Subsequently, I presented the thesis and a draft policy brief in Nepalese to the community members. A youth leader read the policy brief aloud, and then the floor was opened for a Q&A session, within which I was asked questions such as why the thesis had not been translated into Nepalese and how did I portray the community within the research.[17]

I felt more nervous than during my PhD viva, feeling a mix of helplessness, awkwardness, and scared. I struggled to provide satisfactory responses, and some community members accepted them while others rejected them, highlighting the shortcomings in the research. I came to the realization that I failed to consult them adequately during the writing phase of my doctoral thesis, in addition to failing to address the human rights violations caused by migration bans, which were enacted to protect them.

The community members emphasized the importance of maintaining anonymity for the research site and creating a resource centre, asserting that unless there is a migration ban in Nepal, any 'awareness generation' intervention would reveal the spectrum of mobility strategies adopted by the community members to both the state and anti-traffickers. They thoroughly examined the policy brief, suggested several changes, and offered insights to make the policy recommendations more effective. Consequently, I edited

---

[16] The meeting saw the presence of several community members, including an elected ward member, the president of the steering committee, research companions, and various research participants.

[17] Questions included – we congratulate you on your thesis, but how have you represented our community? We do not want you to portray us negatively. What is the impact of the research? We cannot see any changes in our village since you left. Why did you choose to focus on one specific issue? Seasonal labor migration in India is a far more important and neglected issue compared with countries such as Qatar and Malaysia. You should have highlighted the harassment and bullying that community members face in India, especially by the Indian border police. Why have you not translated the entire thesis into Nepalese? How do you plan to approach the Nepalese authorities, and what do you intend to communicate to them? When are you planning to conduct research in the community again? Last time, we were occupied with constructing our houses, but now we have more time to focus on addressing various other issues effectively.

the brief before presenting it to the policy makers of Nepal (Bhagat, 2022b). Finally, we concluded the meeting, and before leaving, Heidi, an anti-trafficking survivor, said: "You have proved me wrong. I never expected that you would ever return to the community, and nobody here did either." Establishing a trusting relationship is the most important aspect of every research process and this point of knowledge extraction without return is also illustrated within this volume (see further Kiconco).

Conclusion

'Human trafficking' research necessitates clear definitional boundaries concerning the embodied experiences of mobility and labour to determine which incidents qualify as human trafficking. Conceptually, the subjective nature of these two elemennts makes it difficult, if not impossible, to trace definitive boundaries. Hence, attempts to ethically rationalize the temporal categories of research – 'pre-trafficking', 'during trafficking', and 'post-trafficking' – uncritically categorize research participants within a range of political labels. These categories, including victims, vulnerable peoples, and perpetrators, carry political implications of exclusion, potentially resulting in a biased enquiry. However, most researchers start with one political category with an assumption that these exclusions, contradictions, complications, and stigmatizations will not harm the participants, especially after they leave the research site. Therefore, the selection of research participants is a critical political moment, and one that demands the burden of ethical responsibility.

Moving beyond the critical scholars' position (which stresses the importance of adopting a temporal frame of 'post-trafficking' research to highlight and fight exploitative practices and structural injustices), I made the choice to focus on the mobility experiences of individuals from a specific site in Nepal. The research took place in an area where, in wake of the 2015 earthquake relief interventions elevated the reliance on NGOs. Simultaneously, there was a substantial increase in mistrust towards anti-trafficking NGOs. The latter group either supported victims/survivors support groups, raised awareness about the risks of illegality, or intercepted people at the India–Nepal borders. While navigating this space, I encountered a complicated web of tensions, failures, absences, confusion, and moments where translations produced intense feelings. Some examples include some people exercising their right to withdraw during an interview; a total reluctance of research companions to include agents in the research; or people calling me a spy or a corrupt NGO representative in the middle of a focused group discussion; the entire community using silences as a political tool to guard information; or the refusal of some of the community members to run the information centre. While these political moments made this research emotionally and intellectually challenging, unpacking them offered new ways of seeing, disrupting, analysing, knowing, and changing long-held views on trafficking and anti-trafficking.

This translation and interpretation of words and silences took a heavy toll on me. During the fieldwork, there were numerous instances when I became angry, shed tears out of helplessness, wanted to quit everything, got frustrated and anxious, was physically sick, and burned out. I experienced all these emotions to translate words and silences so that I could ethically and justifiably represent the struggles of community members; this remains something that no one can fully represent. The process of data analysis demanded a constant awareness of my ever-shifting subjectivity, and simultaneously, capturing spaces where the words and silences of the participants arrive without being fully aware of their subjectivity. For example, during my field visit, I interacted with several people – some of them thought I might be able to change their world; some of them thought I had a lot of money; some of them thought I was a spy; some of them thought I was a researcher; and others placed me into of all these positions. Participants were categorizing me into these different positions, of which I was unaware, which further questioned the translation and interpretation of the words and silences. I wonder whether human geography researchers have no control over the meaning; are there ways to be open to the otherness of the other?

The continuous action and reflection of PAR allow a way to have some control over the meaning of the research findings. Continuous analysis of the people's mobility experiences showed a critical world view of simultaneity of conflicts, bordering, waiting, and subversions and heterogeneity of differential ways of being, doing, and navigating international mobility. This relationship of simultaneity and heterogeneity between everyday practices of the anti-trafficking actors of the Global South and the diverse mobility experiences of the people on the move is one of the central findings of the research. Empirical material suggests that both people on the move and actors and institutions following the discourse of trafficking were trying to subjugate each other through their mobility and control practices. Unearthing the encounters between these two was an intense, emotionally taxing process, which allowed me to map the mess and make it visible through this research. While there was no intention to drastically change the lives of my research participants or to support the anti-trafficking cause, the endeavour to understand messiness gave rigour to the research process. This research does not follow a neat model, nor do I intend to make it neat. However, following Noxolo (2017), I still ask three questions: (1) how much had I been able to perceive the intersection of dense power relations? (2) How much had I been able to interpret and translate whatever I claim to have perceived? And, finally, (3) in what ways is the knowledge produced amid this multiplicity interesting and important for both the researcher and the researched?

References

Armstrong, A., Aznarez, M., and Banks, S. (2011) *Connected Communities Participatory Research: Ethical Challenges Research: Ethical Challenges*. Centre for Social Justice and Community Action, Durham University. https://www.dur.ac.uk/resources/beacon/CCDiscussionPapertemplateCBPRBanksetal7Nov2011.pdf

Aronowitz, A.A. (2014) 'Understanding human trafficking as a market system: addressing the demand side of trafficking for sexual exploitation', *Revue Internationale de Droit Penal*, 85(3): 669–96. https://doi.org/10.3917/ridp.853.0669

Bernstein, E. (2019) *Brokered Subjects: Sex, Trafficking, and the Politics of Freedom*, Chicago, IL: University of Chicago Press.

Beutin, L.P. (2023) *Trafficking in Antiblackness: Modern-Day Slavery, White Indemnity, and Racial Justice*, Durham, NC: Duke University Press.

Bhagat, A. (2022a) 'Entrapment processes in the emigration regime: the presence of migration bans and the absence of bilateral labor agreements in domestic work in Nepal', *Theoretical Inquiries in Law*, 23(2): 222–45.

Bhagat, A. (2022b) *The Impact of Migration Bans on Female Nepalese Citizens*. Available from: www.trafflab.org/_files/ugd/11e1f0_8ac111427f244f4cb460b415d5de2a9d.pdf [Accessed 21 December 2023]

Bhagat, A. (2022c) 'Trafficking borders', *Political Geography*, 95: 102598 https://doi.org/10.1016/j.polgeo.2022.102598

Bhagat, A. (2023a) '"Who is not an agent here?": the collateral damage of anti-trafficking in Nepal', *Antipode*, 55(1). https://doi.org/10.1111/ANTI.12882

Bhagat, A. (2023b) *Forgotten Survivor Initiatives: The Zombie Projects of Anti-Trafficking*, London: OpenDemocracy: Beyond Trafficking and Slavery.

Blake, M.K. (2007) 'Formality and friendship: research ethics review and participatory action research', *Acme*, 6(3): 411–21.

Borda, O.F. (2006) 'The North–South convergence: a 30-year first-person assessment of PAR', *Action Research*, 4(3): 351–8. https://doi.org/10.1177/1476750306066806

Bossard, J. (2022) 'The field of human trafficking: expanding on the present state of research', *Journal of Human Trafficking*, 8(1): 1–3. https://doi.org/10.1080/23322705.2021.2019527

Boyd, Z. and Bales, K. (2016) *Getting What We Want: Experience and Impact in Research with Survivors of Slavery*, Cham: Springer, pp 173–90. https://doi.org/10.1007/978-3-319-21521-1_11

Brennan, D. (2005) 'Methodological challenges in research with trafficked persons: tales from the field', *International Migration*, 43(1/2): 35–54.

Broome, A. and Quirk, J. (2015) 'The politics of numbers: the normative agendas of global benchmarking', *Review of International Studies*, 41(5): 813–18. https://doi.org/10.1017/S0260210515000339

Brunovskis, A. and Surtees, R. (2010) 'Untold stories: biases and selection effects in research with victims of trafficking for sexual exploitation', *International Migration*, 48(4): 1–37. https://doi.org/10.1111/j.1468-2435.2010.00628.x

Butcher, S. (2020) 'Research solidarity? Navigating feminist ethics in participatory action research in Kathmandu, Nepal', *Gender, Place and Culture*, 28(4): 497–518. https://doi.org/10.1080/0966369X.2020.1751087

Cahill, C. (2007a) 'Repositioning ethical commitments: participatory action research as a relational praxis of social change', *Acme*, 6(3): 360–73.

Cahill, C. (2007b) 'The personal is political: developing new subjectivities through participatory action research', in *Gender, Place and Culture*, 14(3). https://doi.org/10.1080/09663690701324904

Cahill, C., Sultana, F., Pain, R., and Farhana, F. (2007) 'Participatory ethics: politics, practices, institutions', *Acme*, 6(3): 304–18. Available from: https://collections.lib.utah.edu/dl_files/09/ef/09efbe4465e161dcba2e4913509244e775c3458e.pdf [Accessed 21 December 2023].

Cameron, J. and Gibson, K. (2005) 'Participatory action research in a poststructuralist vein', *Geoforum*, 36(3): 315–31. https://doi.org/10.1016/j.geoforum.2004.06.006

Chapman-Schmidt, B. (2019) ' "Sex trafficking" as epistemic violence', *Anti-Trafficking Review*, 12(12): 172–87. https://doi.org/10.14197/ATR.2012191211

Christie, N. (1986) 'The ideal victim', in E.A. Fattah (ed), *From Crime Policy to Victim Policy*, London: Palgrave Macmillan.

Chuang, J.A. (2014) 'Exploitation creep and the unmaking of human trafficking law', *The American Journal of International Law*, 108(4): 609–49. https://www.jstor.org/stable/10.5305/amerjintelaw.108.4.0609

Cockbain, E., Bowers, K., and Hutt, O. (2022) 'Examining the geographies of human trafficking: methodological challenges in mapping trafficking's complexities and connectivities', *Applied Geography*, 139: 102643. https://doi.org/10.1016/J.APGEOG.2022.102643

Cooke, B. and Kothari, U. (2001) *Participation: The New Tyranny?* London: Zed Books.

Cornwall, A. and Jewkes, R. (1995) 'What is participatory research?', *Social Science and Medicine*, 41(12): 1667–76. https://doi.org/10.1016/0277-9536(95)00127-s

Dharel, M., Rai, W.B., and Thapa, N. (2015) 'Understanding vulnerabilities and strengthening response', University of Sydney. Available from: https://resourcecentre.savethechildren.net/pdf/understanding-vulnerabilities-and-strengthening-response-march-7-2016.pdf/ [Accessed 4 January 2024].

Dhungel, R. (2021) 'Unpacking human trafficking from neoliberalism and neoconservatism paradigms in Nepal: a critical review', *Molung Educational Frontier*, 11: 188–211. https://doi.org/10.3126/MEF.V11I0.37854

di Nicola, A. (2007) 'Researching into human trafficking: issues and problems', in M. Lee (ed) *Human Trafficking*, London: Willan Publishing, pp 49–72.

Doezema, J. (2010) *Sex Slaves and Discourse Masters: The Construction of Trafficking*, London: Zed Books.

Dolinsek, S. and Hearne, S. (2023) *Prostitution in Twentieth Century Europe*, London: Routledge. https://doi.org/10.1080/13507486.2022.2029361

Dottridge, M. (2017) 'Collateral damage provoked by anti-trafficking measures', in R. Piotrowicz, C. Rijken, and B. Heide (eds) *Routledge Handbook of Human Trafficking*, London: Routledge, pp 342–54. https://doi.org/10.4324/9781315709352-27

Edwards, R. and Alexander, C. (2011) 'Researching with peer/community researchers ambivalences and tensions', in M. Williams and W.P. Vogt (eds) *The SAGE Handbook of Innovation in Social Research Methods*, London: SAGE, pp 269–92. https://doi.org/10.4135/9781446268261.n17

Elwood, S. (2007) 'Negotiating participatory ethics in the midst of institutional ethics', *Acme*, 6(3): 329–38.

Esson, J. (2020) 'Playing the victim? Human trafficking, African youth, and geographies of structural inequality', *Population, Space and Place*, Wiley Online Library. https://doi.org/10.1002/psp.2309

Faulkner, E.A. (2018) 'The victim, the villain and the rescuer: the trafficking of women and contemporary abolition', *Law, Social Justice and Global Development Journal*, 21: 1–15. https://go.gale.com/ps/i.do?p=AONE&sw=w&issn=14670437&v=2.1&it=r&id=GALE%7CA560926615&sid=googleScholarlinkaccess=fulltext

Faulkner, E.A. (2023) *The Trafficking of Children: International Law, Modern Slavery, and the Anti-Trafficking Machine*, Cham: Springer Nature. https://doi.org/10.1007/978-3-031-23566-5

Feingold, D. (2019) 'Trafficking in numbers: the social construction of human trafficking data', in P. Andreas and K. Greenhill (eds) *Sex, Drugs, and Body Counts*, Ithaca, NY: Cornell University Press, pp 46–74. https://doi.org/10.7591/9780801458309-005/HTML

Freire, P. (1970) *Pedagogy of the Oppressed*, London; New York: Continuum.

Frost, N. and Jones, C. (1998) 'Video for recording and training in participatory development', *Development in Practice*, 8(1): 90–4. https://doi.org/10.1080/09614529854043

GAATW (2007) *Collateral Damage: The Impact of Anti-Trafficking Measures on Human Rights around the World*, Global Alliance Against Traffic in Women (GAATW).

Gallagher, A.T. (2010) 'The international law of human trafficking', in *The International Law of Human Trafficking*, Cambridge: Cambridge University Press. https://doi.org/10.1017/CBO9780511761065

Gallagher, A.T. (2017) 'What's wrong with the Global Slavery Index?', *Anti-Trafficking Review*, issue 8, 2017, pp. 90–112. https://doi.org/10.14197/ATR.20121786

Glassman, M. and Erdem, G. (2014) 'Participatory action research and its meanings: vivencia, praxis, conscientization', *Adult Education Quarterly*, 64(3): 206–21. https://doi.org/10.1177/0741713614523667

Goździak, E.M. and Graveline, S (Eds) (2015) *In Search Data and Research of Human Trafficking: Analysis of Research Based Literature (2008–2014)*, Institute for the Study of International Migration. https://www.researchgate.net/publication/280567558_In_search_of_data_and_research_on_human_trafficking_Analysis_of_research-based_literature_2008-2014

Guillemin, M. and Gillam, L. (2004) 'Ethics, reflexivity, and ethically important moments in research', *Qualitative Inquiry*, 10(2): 261–80. https://doi.org/10.1177/1077800403262360

Hitchings, R. and Latham, A. (2019) 'Qualitative methods I: on current conventions in interview research', *Progress in Human Geography*, 44(2): 389–98. https://doi.org/10.1177/0309132519856412

Hitchings, R. and Latham, A. (2020) 'Qualitative methods II: on the presentation of "geographical ethnography"', *Progress in Human Geography*, 44(5): 972–80. https://doi.org/10.1177/0309132519879986

Hitchings, R., and Latham, A. (2021) 'Qualitative methods III: on different ways of describing our work', *Progress in Human Geography*, 45(2): 394–403. https://doi.org/10.1177/0309132520901753

Hounmenou, C. (2020) 'Engaging anti-human trafficking stakeholders in the research process', *Journal of Human Trafficking*, 6(1): 30–49. https://doi.org/10.1080/23322705.2018.1512284

Kaye, J., Millar, H., and O'Doherty, T. (2019), 'Exploring human rights in the context of enforcement-based anti-trafficking in persons responses', *The Palgrave International Handbook of Human Trafficking*, 1: 601–21. https://doi.org/10.1007/978-3-319-63058-8_36/COVER

Kelly, L. (2005) '"You can find anything you want": a critical reflection on research on trafficking in persons within and into Europe', *International Migration*, 43(1–2): 235–65. https://doi.org/10.1111/j.0020-7985.2005.00319.x

Kemmis, S. and McTaggart, R. (2007) 'Participatory action research: communicative action and the public sphere', in N.K. Denzin and Y.S. Lincoln (eds) *The Sage Handbook of Qualitative Research*, New York: SAGE, pp 271–330. http://citeseerx.ist.psu.edu/viewdoc/download?doi=10.1.1.473.4759&rep=rep1&type=pdf

Kempadoo, K. (2015) 'The modern-day white (wo)man's burden: trends in anti-trafficking and anti-slavery campaigns', *Journal of Human Trafficking*, 1(1): 8–20. https://doi.org/10.1080/23322705.2015.1006120

Kempadoo, K. (2016) 'Revitalizing imperialism: contemporary campaigns against sex trafficking and modern slavery', *Cadernos Pagu*, 47. https://doi.org/10.1590/18094449201600470008

Kempadoo, K. and Shih, E. (2022) *White Supremacy, Racism and the Coloniality of Anti-Trafficking*, New York: Routledge.

Kesby, M. (2005) 'Retheorizing empowerment-through-participation as a performance in space: beyond tyranny to transformation', *Signs: New Feminist Approaches to Social Science*, 30(4): 2037–65. https://www.jstor.org/stable/pdf/10.1086/428422.pdf?refreqid=excelsior%3A9a277a31cc0ef43ed6fe729cc598ce0d

Khanlou, N. and Peter, E. (2005) 'Participatory action research: considerations for ethical review', *Social Science and Medicine*, 60: 2333–40. https://doi.org/10.1016/j.socscimed.2004.10.004

Kindon, S., Pain, R., and Kesby, M. (2007) 'Participatory action research: origins, approaches and methods', in *Participatory Action Research Approaches and Methods: Connecting People, Participation and Place*, London: Routledge, p 260.

Kinpaisby-hill, M. c (2011) 'Participatory praxis and social Justice', in V.J. Del Casino, M.E. Thomas, P. Cloke, and R. Panelli et al (eds), *A Companion to Social Geography*, West Sussex: Blackwell Publishing Ltd, pp 214–34.

Klocker, N. (2015) 'Participatory action research: the distress of (not) making a difference', *Emotion, Space and Society*, 17: 37–44. https://doi.org/10.1016/j.emospa.2015.06.006

Kwan, C. and Walsh, C.A. (2018) 'Ethical issues in conducting community-based participatory research: a narrative review of the literature', *The Qualitative Report*, 23(2): 369–86. https://nsuworks.nova.edu/tqr/vol23/iss2/6

Laczko, F. and Gozdziak, E. (2005) 'Data and research on human trafficking', *International Organization for Migration*, 43(1-2): 5–16. https://doi.org/10.1111/j.0020-7985.2005.00309.x

Laurie, N. and Richardson, D. (2020) 'Geographies of stigma: post-trafficking experiences', *Transactions of the Institute of British Geographers*, 46(1): 120–134. https://doi.org/10.1111/tran.12402

Laurie, N., Richardson, D., Poudel, M., Samuha, S., and Townsend, J. (2015) 'Co-producing a post-trafficking agenda: collaborating on transforming citizenship in Nepal', *Development in Practice*, 25(3): 465–77. https://doi.org/10.1080/09614524.2015.1029436

LeBaron, G., Pliley, J.R., and Blight, D.W. (2021) 'Fighting modern slavery and human trafficking: history and contemporary policy', in G. LeBaron, J.R. Pliley, and D.W. Blight (eds) *Fighting Modern Slavery and Human Trafficking*, Cambridge: Cambridge University Press.

Locke, R.A. (2010) 'Rescued, rehabilitated, returned: institutional approaches to the rehabilitation of survivors of sex trafficking in India and Nepal', Master's thesis, University of Denver. https://digitalcommons.du.edu/etd

Manzo, L.C. and Brightbill, N. (2007) 'Toward a participatory ethics', in S. Kindon, R. Pain, and M. Kesby (eds) *Participatory Action Research Approaches and Methods*, London: Routledge, pp 33–40.

Marlowe, J.M., Lou, L., Osman, M., and Alam, Z.Z. (2015) 'Conducting post-disaster research with refugee background peer researchers and their communities', *Qualitative Social Work*, 14(3): 383–98. https://doi.org/10.1177/1473325014547252

Mazzei, L.A. (2007) 'Toward a problematic of silence in action research', *Educational Action Research*, 15(4): 631–42. https://doi.org/10.1080/09650790701664054

McGrath, S. and Watson, S. (2018) 'Anti-slavery as development: a global politics of rescue', *Geoforum*, 93: 22–31. https://doi.org/10.1016/j.geoforum.2018.04.013

McGrath, S. and Mieres, F. (2021) 'The business of abolition: marketizing "anti-slavery"', *Development and Change*, 53(1): 3–30. https://doi.org/10.1111/DECH.12701

McGrath, S., Rogaly, B., and Waite, L. (2022) 'Unfreedom in labour relations: from a politics of rescue to a politics of solidarity?', *Globalizations*, 19(6): 911–21. https://doi.org/10.1080/14747731.2022.2095119

McIntyre, A. (2009) *Participatory Action Research*, Los Angeles: SAGE.

Merry, S.E. (2021) 'The seductions of quantification: measuring human rights, gender violence, and sex trafficking', in *The Seductions of Quantification*, Chicago, IL: University of Chicago Press. https://doi.org/10.7208/9780226261317

Miller, A., Alejano-Steele, A.R., Finger, A., and Napolitano, K. (2022) 'The Colorado project to comprehensively combat human trafficking: community-based participatory research in action', *Journal of Human Trafficking*, 8(1): 59–81. https://doi.org/10.1080/23322705.2021.2019532

Molland, S. (2013) 'Tandem ethnography: on researching "trafficking" and "anti-trafficking"', *Ethnography*, 14(3): 300–23. https://doi.org/10.1177/1466138113491671

Molland, S. (2018) '"Humanitarianized" development? Anti-trafficking reconfigured', *Development and Change*, 0(0): 1–23. https://doi.org/10.1111/dech.12459

Musto, J. (2016) *Control and Protect: Collaboration, Carceral Protection, and Domestic Sex Trafficking in the United States*, Berkeley, CA: University of California Press.

Noxolo, P. (2017) 'Subjectivity', in *International Encyclopedia of Geography: People, the Earth, Environment and Technology*, Hoboken, NJ: John Wiley & Sons, pp 1–5. https://doi.org/10.1002/9781118786352.wbieg0621

O'Connell Davidson, J. (2010) 'New slavery, old binaries: human trafficking and the borders of "freedom"', *Global Networks*, 10(2): 244–61. https://doi.org/10.1111/j.1471-0374.2010.00284.x

O'Connell Davidson, J. (2015) *The Margins of Freedom: Morden Slavery*, Basingstoke: Palgrave Macmillan.

Pain, R. (2004) 'Social geography: participatory research', *Progress in Human Geography*, 28(5): 652–63. https://doi.org/10.1191/0309132504ph511

Pain, R. (2008) 'Ethical possibilities – towards participatory ethics', *Children's Geographies*, 6(1): 104–8. https://doi.org/10.1080/14733280701791975

Pain, R. and Kindon, S. (2010) 'Participatory geographies', *Environment and Planning A*, 39(12): 2807–12. https://doi.org/10.1068/a39347

Pain, R., Kindon, S., and Kesby, M. (2007) 'Participatory action research: making a difference to theory, practice and action', in *Participatory Action Research Approaches and Methods: Connecting People, Participation and Place*, London: Taylor & Francis, p 287.

Palombi, L.C., Van Ochten, H., and Patz, C. (2019) 'The pharmacists' role in identifying and supporting victims of human trafficking', *Journal of Human Trafficking*, 5(3): 255–66. https://doi.org/10.1080/23322705.2018.1494486

Parmanand, S. (2021) 'Salvation as violence: anti-trafficking and the rehabilitation of rescued Filipino women into moral subjects', *Journal of International Women's Studies*, 22(2): 78–91. https://vc.bridgew.edu/jiws/vol22/iss2/8

Pinto, M. (2023) 'Discursive alignment of trafficking, rights and crime control', *International Journal of Law in Context*, 19(2): 122–42. https://doi.org/10.1017/S1744552322000209

Quirk, J. (2011) *The Anti-Slavery Project: From the Slave Trade to Human Trafficking*, Philadelphia, PA: University of Pennsylvania Press.

Quirk, J., Robinson, C., and Thibos, C. (2020) 'Editorial: from exceptional cases to everyday abuses: labour exploitation in the global economy', *Anti-Trafficking Review*, 2020(15): 1–19. https://doi.org/10.14197/ATR.201220151

Russell, A. (2018) 'Human trafficking: a research synthesis on human-trafficking literature in academic journals from 2000–2014', *Journal of Human Trafficking*, 4(2): 114–36. https://doi.org/10.1080/23322705.2017.1292377

Ryan, L., Kofman, E., and Aaron, P. (2010) 'Insiders and outsiders: working with peer researchers in researching Muslim communities', *International Journal of Social Research Methodology*, 14(1): 49–60. https://doi.org/10.1080/13645579.2010.481835

Scheel, S. (2019) *Autonomy of Migration? Appropriating Mobility within Biometric Regimes*, London: Routledge.

Scheibelhofer, E. (2015) 'Ethnic and racial studies insider research on migration and mobility: international perspectives on researcher positioning', *Ethnic and Racial Studies*, 39(3): 543–45. https://doi.org/10.1080/01419870.2015.1093157org/10.1080/01419870.2015.1093157

Shivakoti, R. (2020) 'Protection or discrimination? The case of Nepal's policy banning female migrant workers', in D. Upadhyaya Joshi and C. Brassard (eds) *Urban Spaces and Gender in Asia: Sustainable Development Goals Series*, Cham: Springer, pp 17–34. https://doi.org/10.1007/978-3-030-36494-6_2

Siegel, D. and de Wildt, R. (2016) *Ethical Concerns in Research on Human Trafficking*, Cham: Springer. https://doi.org/10.1007/978-3-319-21521-1

Sijapati, B. et al (2015) *Migration and Resilience: Experiences from Nepal's 2015 Earthquake* (Research Paper VII). Available from: https://www.ilo.org/kathmandu/whatwedo/publications/WCMS_379082/lang--en/index.htm [Accessed 4 January 2024].

Snajdr, E. (2013) 'Beneath the master narrative: human trafficking, myths of sexual slavery and ethnographic realities', *Dialectical Anthropol*, 37: 229–56. https://doi.org/10.1007/s10624-013-9292-3

Strauss, K. (2017) 'Sorting victims from workers: forced labour, trafficking, and the process of jurisdiction', *Progress in Human Geography*, 41(2): 140–58. https://doi.org/10.1177/0309132516629002

Sweileh, W.M. (2018) 'Research trends on human trafficking: a bibliometric analysis using Scopus database', *Global Health*, 14: 106. https://doi.org/10.1186/s12992-018-0427-9

Twis, M.K. and Preble, K. (2020) 'Intersectional standpoint methodology: toward theory-driven participatory research on human trafficking', *Violence and Victims*, 35(3): 418–39. https://doi.org/10.1891/VV-D-18-00208

Tyldum, G. (2010) 'Limitations in research on human trafficking', *International Migration*, 48(5): 1–13. https://doi.org/10.1111/j.1468-2435.2009.00597.x

Tyldum, G. and Brunovskis, A. (2005) 'Describing the unobserved: methodological challenges in empirical studies on human trafficking', *International Migration*, 43(1–2): 17–34. https://doi.org/10.1111/j.0020-7985.2005.00310.x

Urry, J. (2007) *Mobilities*, Cambridge: Polity Press.

Urry, J. (2012a) *Mobile Lives*, Universitat de Girona, Càtedra Ferrater Mora de Pensament Contemporani.

Urry, J. (2012b) *The New Mobilities Paradigm*, Universitat de Girona, Càtedra Ferrater Mora de Pensament Contemporani.

Wilson, E., Kenny, A., and Dickson-Swift, V. (2018) 'Ethical challenges of community-based participatory research: exploring researchers' experience', *International Journal of Social Research Methodology*, 21(1): 7–24. https://doi.org/10.1080/13645579.2017.1296714

Yea, S. (2020a) 'Prefiguring stigma in post-trafficking lives: relational geographies of return and reintegration', *Area*, 52: 558–65, [online] 1–8 February. Available from: https://doi.org/10.1111/area.12620

Yea, S. (2020b) 'Towards critical geographies of anti-human trafficking: producing and precluding victimhood through discourses, practices and institutions', *Progress in Human Geography*, 45(3): 513–30. https://doi.org/10.1177/0309132520923136

12

Saviours or Disrupters? The Role of Non-State Actors in the Government-Centric Realm of Anti-Trafficking in Belize

Cherisse Francis

Introduction

Anti-trafficking is traditionally seen as an international law matter concerning national governments. Yet, non-state actors (NSAs) have been involved in the movement from its inception (Meriläinen and Vos, 2015) and hoped that the Protocol to Prevent, Suppress and Punish Trafficking in Persons, Especially Women and Children (Palermo Protocol) would be a watershed providing them with a recognized role in combatting trafficking in persons (Gallagher, 2001). Unprecedented numbers of non-governmental organizations (NGOs) were represented at Protocol negotiations and the final document mentions cooperation with civil society (United Nations Protocol to Prevent, Suppress and Punish Trafficking in Persons, Especially Women and Children, art 6(3), art 9(3), art 10(2); Ditmore and Wijers, 2003; Gallagher, 2015). However, national anti-trafficking policies are still arranged and evaluated according to state action (Chuang, 2014; International Organization for Migration, 2005; *Global Report on Trafficking in Persons*, 2018). This means that any state/non-state collaborations are ad hoc and subsequently leaves unanswered questions about the roles of NSAs and 'strategies to enable us to take full advantage of their contributions' (Bruderlein, 2000: 3).

The tensions between NSAs and governments are a microcosm of wider societal issues. With shifting global political and economic conditions over the last 20 years, the disquiet has intensified as national governments struggle to maintain their citizens. Especially in smaller, resource-constrained nations such as Belize, which lack significant political power or economic leverage with such national governments accused of compromising their sovereignty to attract foreign aid (Kempadoo, 2016). NSAs attempt to close the gap, by acting where national governments cannot or will not (Jidovu, 2019). This has resulted in critiques that NSAs are overinvolved and use inappropriate interventions (Kamler, 2013; Haynes, 2014; Limoncelli, 2016; Dottridge, 2021; see further Kiconco and Bhagat, this volume). Without the national government's approval to legitimize their work, NSAs' access to some resources, stakeholders, and programmes is limited (Segrave and Milivojević, 2010; Jidovu, 2019; Grono, 2021).

This chapter utilizes Belize as a lens for other developing countries and illustrates how such framing promotes the often hierarchical and segregated responses to trafficking of both states and NSAs. This exacerbates vulnerabilities and inequalities, which stagnates progress. Moreover, it does not holistically represent both the positive and negative impacts that such actors have upon anti-trafficking. Unfortunately, this status quo means that NSA interventions go unchecked by official sources, are sporadic in multiple cases, and fail to address the real issues with human trafficking. The prominent North–South divide, sovereignty versus the global good, and economics affect actors' interactions with each other and the system of anti-trafficking. These tensions can only be mitigated by better understanding the role of NSAs and the effects of colonialism.

This chapter therefore argues that NSAs are integral to anti-trafficking policies but are frequently misunderstood and under-utilized. Moreover, it suggests that state-NSA cooperation is required for mitigating trafficking, as neither government nor NSAs can solve the world's problems in isolation. The United Nations (UN) and others have proposed public-private partnerships as a means for collaboration (Wang and Ma, 2021). With this 'hybrid type of governance' NSAs co-govern with state actors and 'adopt governance functions that have formerly been the sole authority of sovereign nation states' (Schaferhoff et al, 2009: 451–2). Effectively, public-private partnerships facilitate opportunities for needed interactions with the aim of combatting trafficking (Schaferhoff et al, 2009).

The scaffolding: knowledge, methods, and terminology

There are inherent dangers in using generic and oversimplified terminology such as 'non-state actors' to lump seemingly unrelated entities together (Bruderlein, 2000; Josselin and Wallace, 2001; Stubbs, 2003). This chapter intentionally utilizes 'non-state actors' (NSAs) to avoid the wider definitional issues and convolution often encountered when categorizing actors (Stubbs, 2003; Bieler et al, 2004). Additionally, as Josselin and Wallace (2001) suggest, this gives the 'reader a sense of the diversity and complexity' of NSAs which now constitute global society (Josselin and Wallace, 2001: 4). Within this work NSA means any entity involved in anti-trafficking which is not a national government; more specifically, the government of Belize in the latter parts of the chapter.

The first half of this chapter will explain and situate partnerships within wider development literature, moving to apply that literature to anti-trafficking to contextualize the Belize case study. Public-private partnerships have become a central research topic in International Relations and among other disciplines, yet remain difficult to delineate (Schaferhoff et al, 2009). Subsequently, scholars have created frameworks for understanding and implementation related to various security and crime control issues (Stubbs, 2003). Although writers such as Lagon (2015) have identified and categorized some of the 'most crucial partnerships' between states and NSAs since the inception of the Palermo Protocol, there is no dedicated public-private partnerships framework for anti-trafficking (Lagon, 2015).[1]

Generally, evaluations like this do not account for the 'highly context specific' nature of public-private partnerships implementation that depends on the actors involved (de Koning, 2018: 172). Neither do they assess the power relationships between actors, the 'nature and history of both the public-private sectors and their geographic locations' (de Koning, 2018: 172). To offset that absence, the second half of this chapter will adopt Lindsey, Chapman, and Dudfield's (2020) six-part configuration for partnerships. This framework (albeit not an infallible system) was originally applied to sports and development, but it offers the most suitable opportunity to interrogate the minutia of anti-trafficking, including various hierarchies. Through utilizing this framework as a lens for analysis, this case study will interrogate how public-private partnerships have operated in the Belizean anti-trafficking field. I will illustrate how simple but creative methods can resolve some frictions between state and NSAs (particularly foreign entities) while benefitting the anti-trafficking community.

This work was influenced by my ongoing empirical research as a part of my doctoral research which focuses on the framing of anti-trafficking efforts in the Caribbean. It involved 12 in-depth semi-structured interviews with government officials, NGOs, intergovernmental organizations (IGOs), and individuals who were currently or had previously worked in Belize.[2] These are broad source materials which will be utilized together with reports from international bodies such as the US government which track anti-trafficking efforts both in Belize and globally via the Trafficking in Persons Reports

---

[1] For example, Lagon (2015: 22) employed the Protocol's mandates to label relationships according to their purposes (protection, prosecution, prevention) and the outlier, resources.

[2] The sample reflects the size of the network in Belize where individuals play multiple roles.

(Boukli et al, this volume) and coupled with the literature to both explain and critique the different relationships in Belize.

The rise of NSAs

NSAs are not new phenomena and have contributed to social processes since the 1850s when organizations such as the International Red Cross and the World Wildlife Fund began responding to specific causes in Europe (Boli and Thomas, 1997). They expanded relatively quickly, subsequently spreading European Imperialist thought across the globe and later engaging in Global South 'development' by the 1940s (Boli and Thomas, 1999). Since then, the quantity of active such actors' ebbs and flows reflecting 'the general state of the world', rising in periods of growth and declining sharply in times of crisis (Boli and Thomas, 1997; Josselin and Wallace, 2001: 5; Stubbs, 2003).

These changes are often precipitated by global economic and social conditions. Various studies reveal that since the 2000s multiple national governments face difficulties maintaining their social responsibilities in health, welfare, and citizen security (Jidovu, 2019). Based on evidence detailing the impact of NSAs in resolving other social issues, governments could benefit from the additional funding, technical support, and international attention that comes with such actors (Keck and Sinnink, 2014). However, many governments remain tied to traditional notions that power and authority are reserved for politicians who determine the most appropriate actions (Boli and Thomas, 1997; Bieler et al, 2004). Therefore, rather than supporting collaboration some governments undermine NSAs by employing coercive powers, political forces, and limiting resources (Josselin and Wallace, 2001).

This conservative position contrasts with the contemporary perspective shared by development scholars and practitioners who recognize that many important initiatives in global social governance erode the public/private dichotomy (Stubbs, 2003). With globalization as well as technological improvements, literature and practice have grown beyond the one-dimensional government-centric approach (Boli and Thomas, 1997; Brinkerhoff and Brinkerhoff, 2002; Bernstein, 2010; Jidovu, 2019). Though not specifically labelled as public-private partnerships the establishment of the International Criminal Court[3] and advancements in tackling the small arms trade signify what can be achieved when NSAs collaborate meaningfully with governments, IGOs, and private bodies (Jidovu, 2019; Bruderlein, 2000). These examples helped to shift the predominant question from whether NSAs play a role to how they play a role (Josselin and Wallace, 2001; Brinkerhoff and Brinkerhoff, 2002; Bernstein, 2010; Jidovu, 2019).

---

[3] See further https://legal.un.org/icc/statute/99_corr/cstatute.htm [Accessed 15 July 2023].

Yet, controversies in defining and negotiating partnerships inhibit their advancement (Jidovu, 2019).

Theoretically, healthy partnerships should include mutual respect, balanced participation, and respective autonomy (Jidovu, 2019). These characteristics would enable the private sector to retain efficiency and competitiveness, and uphold public sector accountability to society (Brinkerhoff, 2002). NSAs offer better relatability and capacity building than traditional actors; however, their work is more effective with government credibility and close involvement with local stakeholders (Bruderlein, 2000). Often, these nuances are overlooked, and the individualized, often conflicting objectives of different actors lead scholars to conclude that there is no definitive form of partnerships but rather a loose application of concepts improperly applied to a broad range of overlapping relationships (Brinkerhoff and Brinkerhoff, 2002; Lindsey, Chapman, and Dudfield, 2020). Currently, most public-private partnerships result from necessity rather than willingness. In this context it is governments (usually those in developing countries) who are unable to ignore the usefulness of NSAs and consequently reticently tolerate them. Quite often pseudo-partnerships like this will achieve initial objectives but also cause NSAs to be critiqued on grounds of legitimacy, trust, and sustainability. Within the field of anti-trafficking, partnerships are even more complicated (Josselin and Wallace, 2001); and depending upon the operative narrative, NSAs are viewed differently, as 'heroes or villains' by enthusiasts, realists, and idealists.

Public-private partnerships have been presented as a viable solution offering better cost efficacy, faster project implementation, and improved social services (Jidovu, 2019). Furthermore, they represent 'the ongoing reconfiguration of authority in world politics and reflect the fact that nonstate actors ... are increasingly engaged in authoritative decision making' (Schaferhoff et al, 2009: 452).

Partnerships and development in anti-trafficking

Anti-trafficking in its current formulation is relatively recent but retains many of the challenges previously outlined in state/non-state relationships coupled with additional intricacies from its transnational and interdisciplinary nature. Both states and NSAs have been involved in anti-trafficking since the 19th century when the concept emerged and it has not always been a harmonious existence (Barrows, 2017). Early actors from liberal societies in Europe and the US were driven by their own agendas. Some feminists lobbied against government policies using anti-prostitution rhetoric (Doezema, 2010; Gallagher, 2010; Schmitt, 2017). Other groups ventured abroad 'rescuing victims' across Africa, Asia, and Latin America from what they considered an immoral and uncivilized existence (Josselin and Wallace,

2001; Lammasniemi, 2017, 2020, this volume). On the other side of the spectrum, larger organizations, such as the International Bureau, functioned as de facto government agents collaborating to enforce legislation such as the English Aliens Act of 1905 (Limoncelli, 2017). This Act was primarily aimed at limiting the movement of poor Eastern European Jews into England but indirectly affected anti-trafficking efforts due to the resulting national security concerns about 'white slavery' and the associated border security implications (Lammasniemi, 2017). For groups and activists that were more speculative about government action there was little room for teamwork.

Throughout the latter half of the 20th century, government attention towards trafficking in persons waned but civil society continued working, eventually influencing norms and policy (Limoncelli, 2017). Arguably, feminist organizations have remained at the forefront sustaining anti-trafficking in persons (hereafter, ATIPs) campaigns worldwide and contributing to the most widely used definition of Trafficking in Persons (hereafter, TIP) (Sharma, 2003). When global interest returned in the 1990s and the Palermo Protocol was enacted the involvement of NSAs also rose (Sharma, 2020). History has a tendency to repeat itself, as neatly highlighted through a wide range of actors and responses. Governments favoured criminal justice, border security, and immigration control strategies to address trafficking and used legislation as ammunition. Yet, many lacked the capacity and finances for implementation. Concurrently, resources emanating from the Global North, directed towards the Global South, surged under the guise of 'humanitarianism', 'development aid', and with 'UN organisations, national governments, civil society organisations and philanthrocapitalist groups jumped onto the anti-trafficking bandwagon' (Kotiswaran, 2019). Both have continued to use anti-trafficking to further their own purposes and challenge government action through critique.

Almost immediately, local governments raised concerns about such interventions and the impacts on their sovereignty (Josselin and Wallace, 2001). Two decades later, it is customary for Global North nations, international organizations, and philanthropists to intervene in developing countries.[4] Many non-governmental stakeholders (including those interviewed) attribute improved victim support services and rehabilitation among other things to this external intervention. These improvements are tempered by scathing reports outlining how foreign entities commenced operations without obtaining national government approval or consulting with local partners to ensure cultural relativity, responsiveness to needs, and sustainability (Klees, 2002; Kapoor, 2012; Haynes, 2014; Limoncelli, 2016).

---

[4] See further S. Okyere (2017) '"Shock and awe": a critique of the Ghana-centric child trafficking discourse', *Anti-Trafficking Review*, (9): 92–105.

Few intervenors possess the specialized knowledge and training that anti-trafficking requires. Instead, many operate on 'best intentions' and 'good faith' (Barrows, 2017: 284–9). From media records and research, the projects they implement either target the wrong populations or are ineffective resulting in further exploitation, corruption, improper allocation of resources and re-traumatization of victims (Kempadoo, 2016 ;Barrows, 2017; Merlan and Marchman, 2020a, 2021b). Such negative reports have made national governments even more wary of embracing NSAs for fear of losing their credibility, independence, and moral positions (Alidu and Asare, 2014; Foot et al, 2019). Scholars criticize these intercessions as displays of soft politics and economically driven decisions rather than having altruistic motives (Quirk, 2020). Emerging literature from anti-trafficking scholars such as Limoncelli (2016) reflects these contradictions questioning how the actions of NSAs foster development, reinforce, or hinder state power and social change. Through querying how these actions affect the inequalities 'within and between countries in the Global North and South' as far as combatting trafficking is concerned (Limoncelli, 2016: 317).

The historical and practical nuances of human trafficking such as conflations with transatlantic slavery and prostitution present a challenge in both balancing what roles NSAs should play and the extent to which states or international entities should regulate them. Thus, states and NSAs have long been framed as 'broad, opposing categories' with contrasting roles rather than potential bedfellows (Josselin and Wallace, 2001: 2). Given the range of complexities identified when defining and applying state and NSA partnerships, the simplest method of dissecting these dynamic relationships in anti-trafficking and proposing improvements is through the lens of a framework. The following case study of Belize will shed light on how these state/non-state relationships manifest differently based on surrounding political and economic situations, as well as the local culture and the involved stakeholders (Lindsey et al, 2020).

Belize: the good, the bad, and the ugly

Belize (formerly British Honduras) became independent in 1981 after more than 100 years (Hanson et al, 2004). The former British colony has been politically stable, but the high crime rate is a function of the civil wars and insurrections in their Central American neighbours, porous borders, and immigration concerns (Hanson et al, 2004). Additionally, Belize's economy like those of its Caribbean relatives is volatile, relying on agriculture and textile trade along with tourism predominately from the Global North (Hanson et al, 2004). In this context the Belizean government has found it challenging to combat trafficking in persons (Ezeilo, 2014). According to one former anti-trafficking stakeholder in Belize 'a government that doesn't

Figure 12.1: Partnerships in Belize's anti-trafficking field

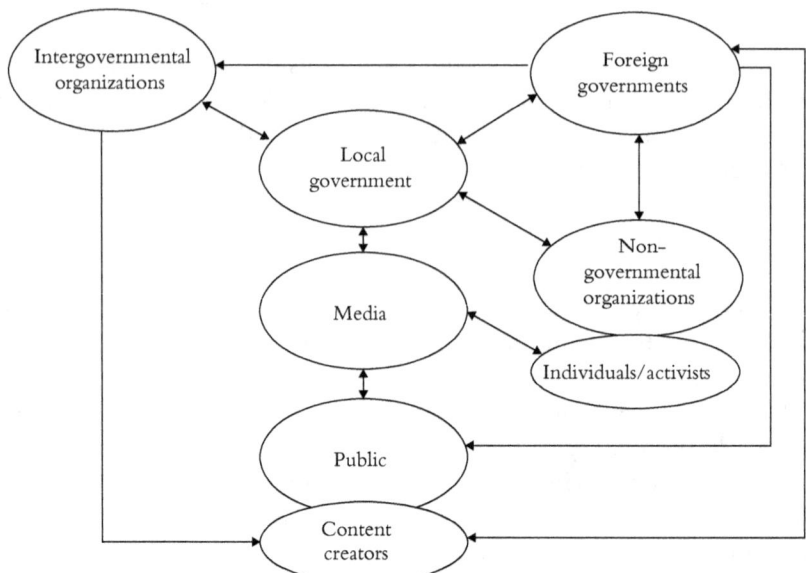

necessarily have a lot in terms of resources or there's a lot of competing priorities … it's sometimes difficult I think convincing the government in terms of devoting appropriate resources to all those issues'. Consequently, their anti-trafficking sector comprises a series of multi-levelled state and NSAs which are difficult to compartmentalize due to their interconnectedness (Figure 12.1 illustrates a simplified version of these interactions).

At any given time, numerous relationships are shaping the framing of trafficking and anti-trafficking in Belize. The power dynamics, levels of success, and influence differ but each interaction can be described as a 'partnership' exerting distinct stressors between the parties and requiring specific considerations to be 'transformative'. Lagon (2015: 23) opines those transformative partnerships 'reduce the incidence and resulting dehumanization of human trafficking and meaningfully contribute toward the crime's eventual elimination'. In Belize, trafficking exists but the collaboration between various entities has enabled more awareness and capacity building as well as victim assistance efforts. Each relationship in Figure 12.1 will be examined to indicate its impact and potential areas for improvement.

Lindsey et al (2020) have built upon the works of Sansom (2006), Zafar Ullah et al (2006), and Batley and Mcloughlin (2010) to provide a framework explaining the nature of state/non-state relationships. Their categories of 'state-centred implementation, complementary implementation, co-produced implementation, non-state-centred implementation, state-led regulation, and non-state-led adversarial advocacy' are not mutually exclusive but have all been utilized to varying degrees in anti-trafficking as will be explored in the following section (Lindsey et al, 2020: 131–6). Notably, some of the relationships discussed do not fit into these six categories and therefore will be considered as outliers because they supersede the government of Belize as the state.

'Overseer partnership'

The first level of state/non-state relationships in Belize is the 'overseer partnership' through which external entities influence Belizean policy and practice by holding the country ransom over funding opportunities or international obligations. The two biggest overseer relationships are the government of Belize and the UN vis-à-vis the Palermo Protocol and between governments of Belize and the US. In both instances government of Belize officials have repeatedly defended their country and anti-trafficking efforts against critiques but have also had to cede control (Channel 5 Belize, 2013; Channel 5 Belize, 2017).

After acceding to the Palermo Protocol in 2003 the government has created domestic legislation and undertaken other UN obligations. However, the Palermo Protocol is an unenforceable document relying on government action (Gallagher, 2010; Massey and Rankin, 2020). Unprompted government anti-trafficking efforts remain minimal raising questions about the applicability of the Protocol in local contexts (Thibos, 2020). Furthermore, despite adopting the Palermo Protocol's system, the Caribbean (including Belize) is often absent from global anti-trafficking discussions and omitted from measurement indices such as the UN Office on Drugs and Crime (UNODC) Global Trafficking Report (Kempadoo, 2016; Nixon, 2016). Therefore, the UN becomes a passive overseer unable to hold the government of Belize accountable (Shoaps, 2013; Allain, 2014; Langer, 2018). Thus, the relationship between the UN anti-trafficking approach and developing nations is stagnant (Gallagher, 2015; Wijers, 2015; Wylie, 2016; Okyere, 2020). Having recognized the consequences of this lacuna on their international reputation the government has commenced discussions over the last few years to amend their legislation to fit their realities.

In contrast, the US government is much more visible in Belizean anti-trafficking efforts (Kempadoo, 2016). The US emerged as a powerhouse in anti-trafficking and some aspects of the Protocol were even drawn from US policies (Chuang, 2014). As the self-appointed 'global sheriff' on trafficking in persons they began ranking countries in their annual Report from 2000 according to prevention, prosecution, and (victim) protection (Chuang, 2014: 612; see further Boukli et al and de Vries and Cockbain, this volume). Between 2004 when Belize first appeared in the Report and 2015, they dropped from Tier 2 Watch List to Tier 3 (United States of America Department of State, 2015). This low ranking from the second lowest to the lowest tier prompted the US to escalate their critiques threatening in 2018 to cut all US non-humanitarian, non-trade assistance for the next fiscal year (Amandala Newspaper, 2015; Belize Breaking News, 2018). Government officials responded acknowledging the value of the TIP Report for informing their anti-trafficking actions while simultaneously rejecting many of the assertions.

This careful balance is essential because not only is the Report the most renowned of the few international monitoring mechanisms but Belize's government actors including law enforcement also depend on foreign aid and investment from wealthy benefactors to fund actions (Hanson et al, 2004). According to one of the Belizean NGOs interviewed, "they [the US government] hold currency because they give governments money". For this reason, US recommendations to Belize must be considered. Though the US' overseer partnership with the government of Belize keeps the latter accountable this relationship is not mutually beneficial or reciprocal.

The TIP Report focuses heavily on convictions and prosecutions while ignoring significant strides made in prevention, public awareness, and personnel changes to accommodate investigations and cases (Humes, 2021). This is somewhat unfair given that the Belizean criminal justice system is not yet equipped for high numbers of prosecutions or convictions. One prominent government official lamented that these 'are the end of a long process and are not as easy to acquire as believed' (Belize Breaking News, 2015). Since 2004, the government continuously states that trafficking occurrences in Belize are low and they have done everything within their limited capacity to address the issues (Channel 5 Belize, 2013a; Channel 5 Belize, 2017b; Belize Breaking News, 2018).

Moreover, the methods and indices used for the TIP Report have been decried as an exercise to export US foreign policy and promote their unilateral sanctions regime (Chuang, 2005). Purportedly, data for the Report are gathered from local stakeholders including the government, local and international NGOs, international organizations, journalists, academics, and survivors, as well as 'published reports, news articles, academic studies, research trips to every region of the world' (United States of America Department of State, 2020: 38). Interviewees questioned the veracity of these sources and methodologies viewing them as "unverifiable", "unfair", and "inaccurate". The uncertainty of Belizean stakeholders, both governmental and NSAs, suggests that US processes fall short of being inclusive or systematic in a way that incites increased prosecutions or protects victims.

Government-led partnerships

Despite the influence 'from above', the government is the primary actor responsible for national anti-trafficking efforts. This dominance is asserted in many of their relationships aligning with 'state-centred implementation' and 'state-led regulation' (Lindsey et al, 2020).

State-centred implementation is the most common configuration throughout anti-trafficking relationships in Belize though not the most effective. With this arrangement, state institutions sanctioned by local legislation control the execution of projects and are the main change-agents (Danziger et al, 2009; Lindsey et al, 2020). The Anti-trafficking in Persons (Prevention) Act of Belize, 2013[5] specifies that government entities are responsible for returning victims to their 'country of citizenship or lawful residency' (s 34), data collection (s 48), and public awareness (s 50) (Anti-trafficking in Persons (Prevention) Act of Belize 2013). The Act establishes the Anti-Trafficking in Persons Council[6] (hereafter, the Council) to guide and coordinate the national anti-trafficking activities (ss 5–11). Interestingly, s 2(c) provides for the presence of some civil society organizations with 'appropriate experience, knowledge and expertise'. However, the government of Belize deliberately outnumbers these NSAs who have little decision-making or coercive powers. An overabundance of state-centred implementation brings with it the bureaucracy and financial constraints which characterize state interventions (Vance, 2011). It also removes the ability of NSAs to counterbalance unfettered governmental discretion (Danziger et al, 2009). From the perspective of at least two of the NSA stakeholders interviewed (a grassroots NGO and a former government of Belize employee), civil society organizations' inclusion in the Council is a 'political box-checking exercise'. It maintains the perception that engages the NSA community but realistically government cooperation with civil society organizations 'remains at its infant stage' (Ezeilo, 2014: 9). Understandably, national governments utilize this to reinforce their legislative sovereignty supporting the traditional view that anti-trafficking is a state concern (Lindsey et al, 2020).

A completely unregulated NSA sector has the potential to interfere with the government's authority, creating space for actors to create their own narratives and misconceptions about human trafficking (Kidd, 2008). Consequently, a strong sense of authority and discretion is paramount for developing countries that in the past have been railroaded by developed nations. This is also the case for Belize based on its experience with the TIP

---

[5] See further www.belizejudiciary.org/download/LAWS-of-Belize-rev2011/Laws-of-Belize-Update-2011/VOLUME%206B_2/Cap%20108.01%20Trafficking%20in%20Persons%20(Prohibition)%20Act.pdf [Accessed 15 July 2023].

[6] See further http://humandevelopment.gov.bz/index.php/atips/ [Accessed 15 July 2023].

Report. Foreign entities far outnumber local organizations and the former have been accused of advancing their own mandates without regard for the local anti-trafficking community or government efforts. This 'othering' and apprehension creates barriers to governments and NSAs working together. According to one of the 'foreign' NGOs interviewed:

> 'Sometimes the relationships with outsiders like us can take really years to build and I think one of the adjustments that we've had to make is just to make more investments and building and fostering good relationships, rapport and trust. Showing up, doing what we say we're going to do, investing in those foundational elements before really pushing on things that have to do with creating policy changes, programmatic changes you know, wide scale, systemic changes.'

Thus, state-centred implementation does not work well in this field, which is targeted towards upholding human rights. An approach which minimizes misunderstandings is necessary.

By comparison, state-led regulation has been used to temper the harshness of state-centred implementation. In state-led regulation NSAs are governed by state legal frameworks but it focuses mainly on operational matters such as NGO registration requirements (Lindsey et al, 2020). Presently, the main regulatory mechanism for NSAs in Belize is legislation such as the Anti-trafficking in Persons (Prevention) Act and the Non-Governmental Organizations (NGO) Act, Revised Edition, 2011 which allows state bodies to determine when to partner with NSAs and police how NSAs operate.

Objectively, this is a positive practice bringing external NSAs within national parameters of control but is often long-winded and complicated. Resultantly, it runs the risk of under-including civil society organizations and segueing into state-centred implementation (Lindsey et al, 2020). Belizean policy stipulates that foreign entities should be registered before operating in-country. The process of setting up an NGO in Belize is listed as taking 6–8 weeks but takes significantly longer (International Services Limited, nb). Consequently, only a few organizations complete the process. Others leave in frustration or circumvent these procedures using loopholes (Kidd, 2008; Heiss and Kelley, 2017).

OEWM, a US-based, Christian anti-trafficking charity officially registered as a non-profit organization in 2014 (Financial Intelligence Unit Belize, nd; On Eagles Wings, nd; The San Pedro Sun, 2015). After registration, OEWM Belize started community work with other NGOs and state departments (Belize Vineyard Ministries, nd; Nunez, 2015; The San Pedro Sun, 2015; Graniel, 2017). Though OEWM Belize registered as an anti-trafficking organization their work in Belize focused on abolishing prostitution and assisting migrants. This is not uncommon in anti-trafficking which frequently gets conflated or 'conveniently conflated' (O'Connell Davidson, 2015) with anti-prostitution or migration mandates. However, in Belize this conflation reinforces harmful discourses and misplaced resource allocation. Irregular migration is a much bigger problem requiring its own resources and approaches. As state-led regulation does not include substantive matters national governments do not influence the activities of NSAs beyond their compliance with the national framework (Lindsey et al, 2020). Thus, entities such as OEWM that fail to maintain their specified objectives simultaneously are rarely reprimanded. NSAs do not see governments as influential in ATIPs. Instead, as one NGO participant indicated: "They [governments] know there's NGOs so they just leave it to the NGOs." NSAs therefore depend on each other to "spread the word" rather than government entities such as the police and they also indicate that "in Belize we don't take our laws seriously". While state-led regulation allows NSAs more control it does not cement the active and participatory partnerships with local governments needed for increased prosecutions and better victim support. Instead, as one of the NGO representatives interviewed postulated, the government of Belize and NGOs operate as separate entities with neither being aware of what the other is doing. After a few years of sporadic, non-trafficking specific work, OEWM separated from their Belizean chapter and left the country. OEWM is not the only organization that has used 'anti-trafficking' as a means to enter Belize, gain support, funding, or media attention and then pursue its own interests. In most cases the result is the same; a failure to address the root causes of trafficking, a transient or temporary presence, and conflict with the local population. Therefore, it is important for states to retain some power in regulating NGOs and other entities operating within their borders (Lindsey et al, 2020).

One observation is that state-led regulation in anti-trafficking mostly concerns non-Belizean operations as the government tends to vilify commentary from international agencies including Human Rights Watch and Transparency International. Government representatives insist that comments about the lack of progress are inaccurate and out of touch (Holmes, 2009). On her 2013 mission to Belize, the former Special Rapporteur on Trafficking in Persons mentioned that independent institutions are required for monitoring and evaluation as government watchdogs are not failsafe, particularly in developing world contexts where corruption is rife (Holmes, 2009; Ezeilo, 2014).

Between a state and non-state focus

Even where focus shifts from dominant governments acting as dictators, governments have found loopholes to propel their interests. Developing countries over-utilize the flexibility of international law requiring countries to only put measures in place 'as necessary', 'in appropriate cases', and 'to the extent possible'. This has become a justification for not fully meeting their international obligations which Belize has repeatedly cited resource constraints in response to US and UN reports (Amandala, 18 June 2010). Despite the government being economically disadvantaged, stakeholders say that the government receives all the funding and then decides what to do with it. Furthermore, local NSAs are responsible for challenging state action through 'non-state led adversarial advocacy' (Lindsey et al, 2020). This configuration works because as Keck and Sinnink (2014) argue, NSAs provide an important check and balance of governmental power by critiquing state policies and practices with the goal of improving them (Keck and Sinnink, 2014). As local NSAs are key to resolving social issues including anti-trafficking as they interact with wide audiences producing intelligence and establishing relationships of trust that governments cannot access. This practice-based knowledge is harder for governments to ignore and refute because local groups as a part of the community are invested in the country. Government of Belize representatives reported that local NGOs have "stayed on their backs" demanding change often appearing in the media when situations arise.

Interviewees from local NGOs indicated that attempts to directly alert the government of their shortcomings or initiate partnerships have been dismissed as "trouble making". Whereas in jurisdictions such as the UK, the US, and elsewhere, NSAs such as Anti-Slavery International have had significant leeway and success in openly critiquing government policies and practices, the same is not true in Belize. The government of Belize is reluctant to work with NSAs unless said entities are willing to conform to governmental mandates and discourses. Due partially to the relatively small size of the country and the lack of accountability mechanisms opposing the government could result in ramifications for the operation of the organization in country. Even more alarming is the fact that some activists have left the country after government officials were sabotaging their reputations or forbidding government employees from collaborating. Therefore, despite their own reservations with the US TIP Report, NSAs choose to provide information because the 'overseers' get results. In the past, data provided to the US by Belizean NGOs have unearthed allegations of government collusion, which led to investigations and changes to internal procedures (US Department of State TIP Report, 2021).

In Belize, local NSAs also enhance anti-trafficking efforts through more public-facing roles which have borne fruitful relationships with the government and provide a different perspective on how non-state-led adversarial advocacy could be amended. The media is a major information source that influences the public understanding of human trafficking. As argued by Chouliaraki (2008), 'the media do not simply address a pre-existing audience that awaits to engage in social action, but that they have the power to constitute this audience as a body of action in the process of narrating and visualizing distant events' (Chouliaraki, 2008: 832, cited in Sharapov and Mendel, 2018: 543). Customarily, media personnel were not thought of as ATIPs front-lined stakeholders and received no training about proper reporting etiquette, although this is addressed in the Anti-trafficking in Persons (Prevention) Act. After a few instances of inaccurate and insensitive reporting about operations and cases up to 2020 and backlash from activists, treatment of media personnel has changed (Sutherland, 2020; 7 News Belize, 2020). Recognizing that they have the potential to affect public perceptions of TIP, compromise victim and perpetrator security, and further jeopardize the US TIP Report, the Council has begun exploring training for media officials. This would provide an opportunity for the press to fulfil their obligations to the public while respecting the sensitivities of human trafficking protected within legislative frameworks.

Overall, the state and NSAs hold significantly different interpretations of what achieving 'development aspirations' may involve, which prevents successful partnerships (Lindsey et al, 2020: 136). As mentioned, local grassroots organizations can provide a wealth of knowledge and aid in comprehensive public awareness (Keck and Sinnink, 2014). Data collection is one lacuna in Belize's anti-trafficking efforts which organizations and activists working with vulnerable populations could address if utilized correctly rather than being excluded. A significant portion of the human trafficking cases discovered or reported in Belize have been instances of sex trafficking connected to migrants from neighbouring territories. This would suggest that the migrant community and sex workers are prime partners for the government to disseminate and gather necessary information. However, the steady anti-migrant, anti-prostitution undertone of governments creates hesitancy to work together.

Non-state-led methods

McGrath and Watson (2018) argue that 'trafficking is routinely presented as a problem of and for development'. NSAs have repurposed their involvement in anti-trafficking to establish a foothold in countries, often developing nations, and advance their own objectives. This has been seen with several UN agencies, most pointedly the UNODC and other intergovernmental organizations. Funding is often the main tool that they use to accomplish this. Arguably, money is the biggest determinant of anti-trafficking efforts and comes from multiple private donors and governmental agencies – predominantly from the Global North (Schmitt, 2017). The US government has been the largest and most consistent donor since the early 2000s providing billions of dollars to NGOs and international organizations for anti-trafficking efforts in the developing world (Rosen and Weber, 2019; Dottridge, 2021). As a part of their extended remit 'to spur change', the US Office to Monitor and Combat Trafficking (J/TIP) specifically funds projects in countries which rank poorly in the Report (Lagon, 2015). Since Belize ranked poorly in the 2004 Report there has been a flurry of NGOs and foreign governments responding to the needs, resource constraints, and perceived lack of political will in-country. Initially, the response was mostly local but with the external funding sources came foreign NSAs as implementing partners, also called grantees.

As anti-trafficking support moves through the system in the form of money or other necessary resources, it connects multiple stakeholders often creating a tripartite relationship between donors, grantees, and the local government. NGO interviewees opined that donors provide funding to national governments and though better suited, they, the local NGOs, are omitted because they lack the technical and social capital to handle large disbursements of funds. They also cautioned that funders should revisit this approach as it lacks accountability for states. This perspective reinforces earlier suggestions that trust between the government and NSAs is low. However, after tracking funding patterns in the Caribbean, funding is rarely disbursed directly to local governments and instead filters through grantees (US Embassy Belmopan, 2017; IOM, 2020).

Implementing partners are selected to mobilize resources through tender processes. Successful grantees tend to emanate from the Global North with political or religious views that align with or at the very least do not oppose those of the funders (Schmitt, 2017; Klees, 2002; Quirk, 2020). Though not explicitly stated, this ideological connection enables a small number of larger entities to generate millions of dollars per year while excluding smaller, in some instances more qualified, organizations (Hoff, 2014). Moreover, with implementing partners retaining Global North philosophies, the prevalent discourse in Belize resonates with this in effect colonizing the anti-trafficking space. Based on previous experiences, donors have increased monitoring and evaluation mechanisms to make contributions meaningful for the local community. Many external funders attempt to ensure local engagement by requiring letters from local governments or implementing partners to support funding bids. Beyond this, the government is perfunctory to the design and implementation of projects as grantees report directly to their donors. This does not alleviate the concern of Belizean stakeholders about the self-serving and exploitative motives of foreign entities as well as a lack of cultural nuance. At least one grantee reported that they were met with a level of scepticism by representatives of the government of Belize and the local population because of their affiliation with the US government.

Notwithstanding the challenges, some of the relationships configured between donors, grantees, and local governments have produced tangible results through complementary implementation and co-produced implementation (Lindsey et al, 2020). Complementary implementation requires states and NSAs to work closely together with as much creativity and formality as the situation necessitates (Lindsey et al, 2020). On the positive side this avoids 'unnecessary or unwieldy legal, contractual or procedural' obligations (Brinkerhoff, 2002, 21; Batley and Mcloughlin, 2010: 136). Co-produced implementation is more evolved, and each actor becomes either 'source, recipients or conduits' of resources (Lindsey et al, 2020: 134). Deciding between the two approaches depends on the context. Holmes (2009) postulates that both are structured to allow external entities to fill gaps left by governments in a way that governments can embrace. When properly utilized, either methodology can resolve the usual tensions and create efforts that promote change.

Complementary and co-produced implementation

The Council has frequently received funding from and partnered with IGOs such as the IOM, international NGOs, and foreign governments (OIM, 2020; Caribbean News Global Contributor, 2021). These relationships often take the form of complementary implementation where the implementing partner provides materials and resources while the government covers logistics and participants. Such transient interactions bring vital funding to Belize and provide training and public awareness. However, their open-ended and sporadic nature has been used for the benefit of the partnering organizations for publicity and fund-raising (Sansom, 2006; Ulla et al, 2006; San Pedro Sun, 2018). This works well for shared short-term objectives but is ill-suited for sustainable progress (Batley, 2006; Lindsey et al, 2020). At the end of funding terms these NSA partners typically withdraw leaving the government without a plan for continuity. This parasitic interaction is not one-sided and the government has been accused of 'piggy-backing' on pre-existing entities to 'appear active' (Anonymous Belize Social Justice Advocate, 2019). Thus, developing countries often require a little more formality than complementary relationships support to provide all parties with clear expectations and responsibilities (Batley and Mcloughlin, 2010).

For Belize, co-produced implementation is more suited for grantee–local government partnerships. It is more risky than complementary relationships and offers less individual autonomy but accommodates for the constantly shifting climate surrounding ATIPs (Lindsey et al, 2020). State institutions have a track record for low levels of political will and some reluctance to external criticisms (Ezeilo, 2014). On the other hand, non-governmental institutions have displayed very low levels of loyalty to governmental objectives and have pulled out of projects when funds have finished, or they have grown tired (Channel 5 Belize, 2006).

Co-produced implementation partnerships perform better within 'agreed and fixed timescales' between less actors and with greater commitments to accommodate for these challenges (Sansom, 2006: 211; Lindsey et al, 2020: 134). Thus, it often manifests in anti-trafficking when international donors provide funds for specific programmes which are then stewarded by implementing partners to provide parameters of operation (Lindsey et al, 2020). Co-produced implementation has fuelled some of the most sustained and transformational partnerships between grantees and the government such as the relationship between the government and the Human Trafficking Institute (HTI). The HTI is a US anti-trafficking NGO which started an informal relationship with the government of Belize in 2017 and has worked since then through consistent action and engagement to break down initial barriers and misconceptions (Love FM, 2017; Roberts, 2017; Wicker, 2018).

This partnership now resembles a co-produced implementation model. Since 2018 the HTI has been taking steps to formalize the partnership through written agreements and memorandums of understanding with the Commissioner of Police (COP) and the Chief Justice of the Supreme Court (CJ) (Ross and King, 2018; MenaFM, 2021). Although these documents are not legally binding they include the agreed objectives, practices, and accountability mechanisms for each party as well as timelines on engagement and cost-sharing (Mayhew, 2005; Sansom, 2006). Memorandums of understanding are a common trend in co-produced implementation which has been used from broad-based victim researcher-practitioner research to engagements with indigenous communities in Canada but had not previously been used to address trafficking in Belize (Alcock et al, 2017; Murray, 2019).

With these guidelines in place, the HTI continues to build the government's anti-trafficking capacity, providing physical and human resources that the government could not otherwise afford. This partnership differs from others involving NSAs in Belize, where previously the resources emanated from one source and the autonomy of both partners was limited (Batley, 2006; Lindsey et al, 2020). Development studies literature suggests that this restriction can result in either NSAs ceding to government agendas or international donors exerting dominance over government missions, leading to power struggles and dependency (Soublière and Cloutier, 2015). The latter usually prevails reducing the effectiveness of these partnerships which depend on trust and mutual confidence (Soublière and Cloutier, 2015).

Instead, the HTI works in tandem with the government allowing the needs of the country to inform the process (Barrachina and Monjaraz, 2013). This correlative collaboration enables the government to retain sovereignty and take responsibility for assets but provides the needed initial revenue, training, and strategies for success (Ross and King, 2018). As a testament to the effectiveness of this approach, the HTI was able to renew and expand their agreements with new appointees after both the COP and

CJ changed. This is uncommon in Belize where political interference in the civil service often arises.

This partnership and others like it are not infallible and in fact elevate larger political issues such as neo-colonialism and the self-serving motives of donors. This is especially pertinent with Global North actors seeking to impact the Global South (Murdie and Bhasin, 2011; Lindsey et al, 2020). As an observation, most of the anti-trafficking entities which have consciously imbedded in Belize and communicated with the government are still represented by the stereotypical white, middle-class, male 'saviour'. This contradicts with the diverse and multi-ethnic population of Belize meaning that even the most well-intentioned efforts will lack cultural nuance and efforts are inappropriately allocated. The vestiges of slavery and colonization in Belize further exacerbate the hesitance of the government and wider populations of Belize to accept these actors. Nevertheless, this approach solidifies that effective anti-trafficking strategies require multiple stakeholders at different levels for sustainable improvements.

Working outside the state: the other side

Another type of cross-tier partnership which requires consideration is the 'international facilitator–local entity relationship' and it is like the grantee–local government relationship but involves 'foreign' grantees and other individuals or groups working with local partners through programming, advocacy, or even as service providers. Banks and Hulme (2012) and McLoughlin (2011) agree that placing NSAs in a central role is beneficial because civil society is better equipped to implement participatory, grassroots development than state entities (McLoughlin, 2011; Banks and Hulme, 2012; Lindsey et al, 2020). However, as best practice, grantees and other foreign groups should liaise with local stakeholders to execute effective projects.

These interactions most often arise in Belize as a form of 'non-state centred implementation' but are not sustainable (Lindsey et al, 2020: 133–4). Interviewees recalled several foreign-based or international organizations coming into Belize to "combat trafficking" and corresponding with local NGOs as an entry point to the country. Those coming as grantees are often subjected to stipulations and reporting points determined by the grantors so that they retain a level of control (Berkovitch and Gordon, 2008; Quirk, 2020). In other partnership models, this has led to NSAs sacrificing their authenticity and local relevance out of desperation to preserve their organizations and the work (Lindsey, 2017: 806). Within the last five years and especially since COVID-19 the number of sources and amounts of anti-trafficking resources have been steadily decreasing. This means that they frequently replicate state or donor and language and modalities. This misplaced loyalty is toxic for grantees when establishing and maintaining relationships with local governments who might have other priorities. Fear of losing funding leads many well-meaning grantees down the slippery slope of being donor pawns rather than partners.

Though not within the last five years, the example of OEWM Belize also displays the detrimental impacts of this type of approach. While OEWM Belize was working in Belize its policies and practices conformed with the mandates of its parent organization more than with the local contexts and development needs of Belize (Banks and Hulme, 2012). As a faith-based organization OEWM supported the abolitionist approach to anti-trafficking. This contrasts with the reputation of San Pedro as a hotspot for 'romance tourism' where it is legal to provide consensual adult sexual activities in exchange for commercial gain (van Wijk, 2006). Therefore, not all sex-workers are victims of exploitation or trafficking as the abolitionist view would suggest (Rudon, 2014). OEWM came into Belize to 'rescue victims' but often ended up mislabelling irregular migrants as victims of trafficking and exploitation. The 'evangelical humanitarianism' often practised by groups such as OEWM could be considered a conflict of interests and objectives between them and the Belizean population (Bernstein, 2010).

Sex worker-led advocates in the country have lamented that these kinds of approaches also infringe on their rights as autonomous sex workers due to the conflation between sex work and sex trafficking. This discourse then paints an inaccurate picture for the international audience that human trafficking in Belize is not out of hand but concentrated in the sex work sector leading to resources again being funnelled into the wrong places. The autonomous Belizean sex workers are of the view that they need to be treated as a part of the solution rather than a part of the problem. If international facilitators took the time to orientate themselves with local entities and minority groups such as this, progress could be much swifter. Once OEWM severed ties with its local chapter, the local organization changed its name and rebranded aligning with another international NGO with anti-trafficking as a part of its mandate. Though still religious, the new organization does not advocate using abolitionist perspectives. Instead, it articulates its mandate as providing a voluntary restoration programme and creating a 'sustainable survivor-centred model that will include trauma informed counselling, group therapy, mentoring, employment and vocational training, health and medical assistance' (Est/Her, nd). This reconstituted approach has reduced some of the tensions with the local entities and the government has even donated to their efforts (Nunez, 2021).

On the other hand, this wider scope introduces another form of international facilitators; self-funded, 'volun-tourists' from the US and the UK visit Belize for a few days or weeks at a time. The volun-tourists suggest that their primary objective is to offer their services with local NGOs. Many of these individuals have no training or specialized knowledge in anti-trafficking but are motivated by 'doing good' to support their own moral or religious persuasions. Although they offer financial value as well as technical and human support to constrained local entities their 'help' stimulates humanitarianism and the white saviour complex. It has been noted that foreign individuals and entities alike view these Global South countries as backward and animalistic, in need of saving. Thus, when weighed against the potential damage, the benefits are dubious. Many reports have named and shamed well-known international entities for their methods and actions (Mensah and Okyere, 2019).

Conclusion

Partnerships have been heralded as an important concept to be embraced within the anti-trafficking schemata. If we end where we began, a partnership is 'a dynamic relationship among diverse actors, based on mutually agreed objectives, pursued through a shared understanding of the most rational division of labour based on the respective comparative advantages of each partner' (Brinkerhoff, 2002: 21). NSAs are invaluable to address lacunae left by governments providing important capacity and financial resources. The roots of the global NSA sector are, certainly, 'Northern and Western, while also being also complex and contradictory' (Boli and Thomas, 1999; Stubbs, 2003). Their involvement in anti-trafficking, however, must fit with the local conditions and development needs of the country requiring creativity and flexibility. As expected, examining these relationships through the lens of these frameworks also reveals that the most significant challenges in these relationships include power imbalances and a lack of consistency (Lindsey et al, 2020).

In a developing country such as Belize even the flexible typology of co-produced implementation requires some adaptations to achieve more prosecutions, increased public awareness on TIP, and survivors who can reintegrate into society. What has become clear is that it is possible for the state and NSAs to work together in a feasible way. While there is no empirical data to measure the effective of state/non-state partnerships in Belize, participants have reported that the resources provided through these partnerships have exponentially increased the investigative powers of police and allowed them to conduct training sessions for other governmental stakeholders, thereby increasing the number of reports. The court system has also seen improvements as the number of human trafficking cases increased and the designated trafficking in persons judge was able to complete her first human trafficking trial, the second in the country since 2016 in March 2020 (Wicker, 2020). As an additional clue as to the impact of these relationships, Belize was upgraded to Tier 2 Watch List on the US State Department Report in 2019 after four years on Tier 3 (Breaking Belize News, 2019b).

Following that, the Report as well as government officials have credited partnerships as one reason for the improvements (Breaking Belize News, 2019a; The San Pedro Sun, 2019; Channel 5 Belize, nd).

Collaboration between state and NSAs does not necessarily require states to cede their sovereignty or control to NSAs. However, there is a need for egalitarian partnerships that consider local conditions and include respect. In the past, governments and national stakeholders around the world have complained that foreign and international anti-trafficking entities invaded their territories and began programmes or projects without their knowledge or approval. This subsequently led to damage which the government has to repair (Channel 5 Belize, 2013a). Despite this, there is scope and need for collaboration. Creative solutions could increase the effectiveness of outputs, reduce re-traumatization and victimization, and benefit everyone involved.

References

Alcock, D., Elgie, J., Richmond, C., and White, J. (2017) 'Developing ethical research practices between institutional and community partners: a look at the current base of literature surrounding memorandums of understanding in Canada', *International Indigenous Policy Journal*, 8(4): 1–37.

Alidu, S.M. and Asare, B.E. (2014) 'Challenges of civil society networks in Ghana: a comparative study of four networks', *Journal of Economics, Management and Trade*, 4(7): 1143–58.

Allain, J. (2014) 'No effective trafficking definition exists: domestic implementation of the Palermo Protocol', *Albany Government Law Review*, 7(1): 111–42.

Amandala Newspaper (2010) 'Child sex tourism "an emerging trend in Belize"', *Amandala Newspaper*, [online] 18 June. Available from: https://amandala.com.bz/news/child-sex-tourism-an-emerging-trend-in-belize [Accessed 22 May 2022].

Amandala Newspaper (2015) 'Belize hits rock-bottom on TIP scale', *Amandala Newspaper*, [online] 28 July. Available from: https://amandala.com.bz/news/belize-hits-rock-bottom-trafficking-persons-scale/ [Accessed 15 August 2021].

Anonymous Belize Social Justice Advocate (2019) 'Belize a human trafficking nightmare!', *Belize News and Opinion*, [online] 5 January. Available from: www.breakingbelizenews.com/2019/01/05/belize-a-human-trafficking-nightmare/ [Accessed 15 August 2021].

Banks, N. and Hulme, D. (2012) *The Role of NGOs and Civil Society in Development and Poverty Reduction*, Brooks World Poverty Institute Working Paper No. 171.

Barrachina, C. and Monjaraz, A. (2013) 'Belize: reflections on police training and professionalization', *Journal of Arts and Humanities*, 2(2): 53–63.

Barrows, J. (2017) 'The role of faith-based organizations in the US anti-trafficking movement', in M. Chisolm-Straker and H. Stoklosa (eds) *Human Trafficking Is a Public Health Issue: A Paradigm Expansion in the United States*, Switzerland: Springer, pp 277–91.

Batley, R. (2006) 'Engaged or divorced? Cross-service findings on government relations with non-state service-providers', *Public Administration and Development*, 26(3): 241–51.

Batley, R. and Mcloughlin, C. (2010) 'Engagement with non-state service providers in fragile states: reconciling state-building and service delivery', *Development Policy Review*, 28(2): 131–54.

Berkovitch, N. and Gordon, N. (2008) 'The political economy of transnational regimes: the case of human rights', *International Studies Quarterly*, 52(4): 881–904.

Bernstein, E. (2010) 'Militarized humanitarianism meets carceral feminism: the politics of sex, rights, and freedom in contemporary anti-trafficking campaigns', *Signs: Journal of Women in Culture and Society*, 36(1): 45–71.

Bieler, A., Higgott, R., and Underhill, G. (2004) *Non-State Actors and Authority in the Global System*, London: Routledge.

Boli, J. and Thomas, G. (1997) 'World culture in the world polity: a century of international non-governmental organization', *American Sociological Review*, 62(2): 171–90.

Boli, J. and Thomas, G. (eds) (1999) *Constructing World Culture: International Nongovernmental Organizations since 1875*, California: Stanford University Press

Breaking Belize News (2015) 'Human trafficking report overvalues convictions: BATC Chair', *Breaking Belize News*, [online] 29 July. Available from: www.breakingbelizenews.com/2015/07/29/human-trafficking-report-overvalues-convictions-batc-chair/ [Accessed 22 May 2022].

Breaking Belize News (2018) 'US cuts aid to Belize over Human Trafficking Tier 3 ranking', Breaking Belize News, [online] 30 November. Available from: https://www.breakingbelizenews.com/2018/11/30/us-cuts-aid-to-belize-over-human-trafficking-tier-3-ranking/ [Accessed 15 August 2021].

Breaking Belize News (2019) 'Belize a human trafficking nightmare!', Breaking Belize News, [online] 05 January. Available from: https://www.breakingbelizenews.com/2019/01/05/belize-a-human-trafficking-nightmare/ [Accessed 15 August 2021].

Breaking Belize News (2019) '"Belize's upgrade on Trafficking in Persons Report is just the beginning," says Charge d'Affaires', Breaking Belize News, [online] 03 July. Available from: https://www.breakingbelizenews.com/2019/07/03/belize-upgrade-on-trafficking-in-persons-report-is-just-the-beginning-says-charge-d-affaires/ [Accessed 15 August 2021].

Brinkerhoff, J.M. (2002) 'Government–nonprofit partnership: a defining framework', *Public Administration and Development*, 22(1): 19–30.

Brinkerhoff, J.M. and Brinkerhoff, D.W. (2002) 'Government–nonprofit relations in comparative perspective: evolution, themes and new directions', *Public Administration and Development*, 22(1): 3–18.

Bruderlein, C. (2000) 'The role of non-state actors in building human security: the case of armed groups in intra-state wars', Centre for Humanitarian Dialogue [*Geneva*]. Available from: https://www.files.ethz.ch/isn/7284/doc_7302_290_en.pdf [Accessed 17 November 2021].

Caribbean News Global Contributor (2021) 'IOM Belize signs agreement in fight against human trafficking …', *MENAFM*, [online] 11 March. Available from: https://menafn.com/1101739947/IOM-Belize-signs-agreement-in-fight-against-human-trafficking [Accessed 15 August 2021].

Channel 5 Belize (2006) 'Belize joins anti human trafficking network', *Channel 5 Belize*, [online] 26 April. Available from: https://edition.channel5belize.com/archives/9445 [Accessed 15 August 2021].

Channel 5 Belize (2013) 'C.E.O. Judith Alpuche disagrees with some aspects of preliminary report', *Channel 5 Belize*, [online] 16 December. Available from: https://edition.channel5belize.com/archives/93430 [Accessed 15 August 2021].

Channel 5 Belize (2017) 'P.M. Barrow: "I don't accept" U.S. claim of gov't complicity in human trafficking', *Channel 5 Belize*, [online] 30 June. Available from: https://edition.channel5belize.com/archives/148890 [Accessed 15 August 2021].

Channel 5 Belize (2017) 'Belize refocuses efforts to address human trafficking', *Channel 5 Belize*, [online] 25 August. Available from: https://edition.channel5belize.com/archives/151761 [Accessed 5 June 2022.]

Channel 5 Belize (2019) 'Belize upgrade to Tier 2 in U.S. Department of State's 2019 TIP Report', *Channel 5 Belize*, [online] 20 June. Available from: https://edition.channel5belize.com/archives/186722 [Accessed 30 August 2021]

Chouliaraki, L. (2008) 'The media as moral education: mediation and action', *Media, Culture and Society*, 30(6): 831–52.

Chuang, J. (2005) 'The United States as global sheriff: using unilateral sanctions to combat human trafficking', *Michigan Journal of International Law*, 27(2): 437–94.

Chuang, J.A. (2014) 'Exploitation creep and the unmaking of human trafficking law', *American Journal of International Law*, 108(4): 609–49.

Cruz, K., O'Connell Davidson, J., and Sanchez Taylor, J. (2019) 'Tourism and sexual violence and exploitation in Jamaica: contesting the "trafficking and modern slavery" frame', *Journal of the British Academy*, 7(1): 191–216.

Danziger, R., Martens, J., and Guajardo, M. (2009) 'Human trafficking & migration management', in C. Friesendorf (ed) *Strategies Against Human Trafficking: The Role of the Security Sector*, Vienna: Reprocenter Vienna (Study group information).

De Koning, M., (2018) 'Public-private partnerships in education assessed through the lens of human rights', in G. Steiner-Khamsi and A. Draxler (eds) *The State, Business and Education: Public-Private Partnerships Revisited*, Cheltenham: Edward Elgar. Available from: www.elgaronline.com/view/edcoll/9781788970327/9781788970327.00015.xml [Accessed 19 April 2022].

Dempsey, M.M., Hoyle, C., and Bosworth, M. (2012) 'Defining sex trafficking in international and domestic law: mind the gaps', *Emory International Law Review*, 26(1): 137–62.

Ditmore, M. and Wijers, M. (2003) 'The negotiations on the UN Protocol on Trafficking in Persons', *Nemesis*, 4: 79–88.

Doezema, D.J. (2010) *Sex Slaves and Discourse Masters: The Construction of Trafficking*, New York: Zed Books.

Dottridge, M. (2021) *Private Donors: The Pied Pipers of 'Modern Slavery'? openDemocracy*. Available from: www.opendemocracy.net/en/beyond-trafficking-and-slavery/private-donors-the-pied-pipers-of-modern-slavery/ [Accessed 30 August 2021].

Ezeilo, J.N. (2014) *Report of the Special Rapporteur on Trafficking in Persons, Especially Women and Children, Joy Ngozi Ezeilo*, Geneva: United Nations Human Rights Council. Available from: https://digitallibrary.un.org/record/773720 [Accessed 15 August 2021].

Financial Intelligence Unit Belize (nd). Available from: https://fiubelize.org/wp-content/uploads/2021/08/npo.pdf [Accessed 11 April 2022].

Foot, K., Sworn, H., and Alejano-Steele, A. (2019) 'Structures and practices of cross-sector engagement in counter-human trafficking coalitions in the Global South', *Cosmopolitan Civil Societies: An Interdisciplinary Journal*, 11(1): 27–45.

Gallagher, A. (2001) 'Human rights and the new UN protocols on trafficking and migrant smuggling: a preliminary analysis', *Human Rights Quarterly*, 23(4): 975–1004.

Gallagher, A.T. (2010) *The International Law of Human Trafficking*. Cambridge: Cambridge University Press.

Gallagher, A.T. (2015) 'Two cheers for the trafficking protocol', *Anti-Trafficking Review*, 4: 14–32. Available from: www.antitraffickingreview.org/index.php/atrjournal/article/view/88/109 [Accessed 5 June 2022].

Graniel, S. (2017) '$1,500 donated to Hope Heaven, San Pedro's first children's home', *Ambergris Today*, [online] 7 February. Available from: www.ambergristoday.com/content/stories/2017/02/07/1500-donated-hope-heaven-san-pedros-first-childrens-home [Accessed 15 August 2021].

Grono, N. (2021) 'The catalysing power of philanthropy in anti-trafficking', *openDemocracy*, [online] 3 February 2021. Available from: https://www.opendemocracy.net/en/beyond-trafficking-and-slavery/catalysing-power-philanthropy-anti-trafficking/ [Accessed 30 August 2021].

Hanson, R., Warchol, G., and Zupan L. (2004) 'Policing paradise: law and disorder in Belize', *Police Practice and Research: An International Journal*, 5(3): 241–57.

Haynes, D.F. (2014) 'The celebritization of human trafficking', *The Annals of the American Academy of Political and Social Science*, 653(1): 25–45.

Heiss, A. and Kelley, J.G. (2017) 'From the trenches: a global survey of anti-TIP NGOs and their views of U.S. Efforts', *Journal of Human Trafficking*, 3(3): 231–54.

Hoff, S. (2014) 'Where is the funding for anti-trafficking work? A look at donor funds, policies and practices in Europe', *Anti-Trafficking Review*, 3: 109–32. Available from: https://gaatw.org/ATR/AntiTraffickingReview_Issue3.2014.Following_the_Money.pdf [Accessed 5 June 2022].

Holmes, L. (2009). 'Human trafficking & corruption: triple victimisation?' in C. Friesendorf (ed), *Strategies Against Human Trafficking: The Role of the Security Sector*. Geneva: National Defence Academy and Austrian Ministry of Defence and Sport and Geneva Centre for the Democratic Control of Armed Forces.

Humes, A. (2021) 'Cabinet adds funding to address trafficking in persons', *Breaking Belize News*, [online] 21 July. Available from: www.breakingbelizenews.com/2021/07/21/cabinet-adds-funding-to-address-trafficking-in-persons/ [Accessed 5 June 2022].

International Organization for Migration (2005) *Exploratory Assessment of Trafficking in Persons in the Caribbean Region*, Geneva: International Organization for Migration (IOM). Available from: https://publications.iom.int/system/files/pdf/exploratory_assessment2.pdf [Accessed 5 June 2022].

International Organization for Migration (2020) 'IOM strengthens Belize's tourism sector against trafficking in persons', *IOM*, [online] 5 June. Available from: https://programamesoamerica.iom.int/en/news/iom-strengthens-belizes-tourism-sector-against-trafficking-persons [Accessed 5 June 2022].

Jidovu, A. (2019) 'The role of public–private partnership in community development', *Revista Universitară de Sociologie*, XV(2): 194–203.

Josselin, D. and Wallace, W. (eds) (2001) *Non-State Actors in World Politics*, London: Palgrave Macmillan.

Kamler, E.M. (2013) 'Negotiating narratives of human trafficking: NGOs, communication and the power of culture', *Journal of Intercultural Communication Research*, 42(1): 73–90.

Kapoor, I. (2012) *Celebrity Humanitarianism: The Ideology of Global Charity*, London: Routledge.

Keck, M.E. and Sikkink, K. (2014) 'Transnational advocacy networks in international politics: introduction', in M. Keck and K. Sikkink (eds), *Activists Beyond Borders: Transnational Advocacy Networks in International Politics*, Ithaca, NY: Cornell University Press.

Kempadoo, K. (2016) 'The war on humans: anti-trafficking in the Caribbean', *Social and Economic Studies*, 65(4): 5–32.

Kidd, B. (2008) 'A new social movement: sport for development and peace', *Sport in Society*, 11(4): 370–80.

Klees, S.J. (2002) 'NGOs: progressive force or neo-liberal tool?', *Current Issues in Comparative Education*, 1(1): 49–54.

Kortiswaran, P. (2019) 'Trafficking: a development approach', *Current Legal Problems*, 72(1): 375–416.

Lagon, M. (2015) 'Traits of transformative anti-trafficking partnerships', *Journal of Human Trafficking*, 1(1): 21–38.

Lammasniemi, L. (2017) 'Anti-white slavery legislation and its legacies in England', *Anti-Trafficking Review*, 9: 64–76. Available from: https://antitraffickingreview.gaatw.org/index.php/atrjournal/article/view/264 [Accessed 5 June 2022].

Lammasniemi, L. (2020) 'International legislation on white slavery and anti-trafficking in the early twentieth century', in J. Winterdyk and J. Jones (eds) *The Palgrave International Handbook of Human Trafficking*, Switzerland: Palgrave Macmillan Cham.

Langer, S. (2018) 'Inconsistent trafficking obligations and how Guyana got caught in the middle', *Washington University Global Studies Law Review*, 17(2): 559–87 Available from: https://openscholarship.wustl.edu/law_globalstudies/vol17/iss2/12/ [Accessed 5 June 2022].

Limoncelli, S.A. (2016) 'What in the world are anti-trafficking NGOs doing? Findings from a global study', *Journal of Human Trafficking*, 2(4): 316–28.

Limoncelli, S.A. (2017) 'The global development of contemporary anti-human trafficking advocacy', *International Sociology*, 32(6): 814–34.

Lindsey, I. (2017). 'Governance in sport-for-development: problems and possibilities of (not) learning from international development', *International Review for the Sociology of Sport*, 52(7): 801–18.

Lindsey, I., Chapman, T., and Dudfield, O. (2020) 'Configuring relationships between state and non-state actors: a new conceptual approach for sport and development', *International Journal of Sport Policy and Politics*, 12(1): 127–46. Available from: www.tandfonline.com/doi/abs/10.1080/19406940.2019.1676812?journalCode=risp20 [Accessed 5 January 2021].

Massey, S and Rankin, G. (2020) *Exploiting People for Profit*, London: Palgrave Macmillan.

Mayhew, S.H. (2005) 'Hegemony, politics and ideology: the role of legislation in NGO–government relations in Asia', *Journal of Development Studies*, 41(5): 727–58.

McGrath, S. and Watson, S. (2018) 'Anti-slavery as development: a global politics of rescue', *Geoforum*, 93: 22–31.

Mcloughlin, C. (2011) 'Factors affecting state-non-governmental organisation relations in service provision: key themes from the literature', *Public Administration and Development*, 31(4): 240–51.

Mensah, B. and Okyere, S. (2019) *How CNN Reported on 'Child Slaves' Who Were Not Really Enslaved*. Available from: www.aljazeera.com/opinions/2019/3/18/how-cnn-reported-on-child-slaves-who-were-not-really-enslaved [Accessed 15 August 2021].

Meriläinen, N. and Vos, M. (2015) 'Public discourse on human trafficking in international issue arenas', *Societies*, 5(1): 14–42.

Merlan, A. and Marchman, T. (2020) 'A famed anti-sex trafficking group has a problem with the truth', VICE News. Available from: https://www.vice.com/en/article/k7a3qw/a-famed-anti-sex-trafficking-group-has-a-problem-with-the-truth [Accessed 15 August 2021].

Merlan, A. and Marchman, T. (2021) 'Inside a massive anti-trafficking charity's blundering overseas missions', VICE News. Available from: https://www.vice.com/en/article/bvxev5/inside-a-massive-anti-trafficking-charitys-blundering-overseas-missions [Accessed 15 August 2021].

Murdie, A. and Bhasin, T. (2011) 'Aiding and abetting: human rights INGOs and domestic protest', *Journal of Conflict Resolution*, 55(2): 163–91.

Murray, C. (2019) 'Quick reference: memorandum of understanding (MOU) for victim researcher-practitioner collaborations' (Centre for Victim Research). Available from: https://ncvc.dspacedirect.org/bitstream/handle/20.500.11990/1065/CVR%20Quick%20Reference_MOU%20Victim%20Researcher-Practitioner%20Collaborations_508.pdf?sequence=5&isAllowed=y [Accessed 5 June 2022].

Nixon, A.V. (2016) 'Sex/trade/work in the Caribbean: challenging discourses of human trafficking', *Social and Economic Studies*, 65(4): 113–22.

Nunez, D. (2015) 'San Pedro Social Service Office renovated by On Eagles Wings Ministries', *Ambergris Today*, [online] 19 January. Available from: www.ambergristoday.com/content/stories/2015/january/19/san-pedro-social-service-office-renovated-eagles-wings-ministries [Accessed 15 August 2021].

Nunez, D. (2021) 'Est/Her receives donations of sewing machines', *Ambergris Today Online*, [online] 11 May. Available from: www.ambergristoday.com/news/2021/05/11/esther-donation-sewing-machines [Accessed 5 June 2022].

O'Connell Davidson, J. (2015) *Modern Slavery: The Margins of Freedom*, London: Palgrave Macmillan.

OIM, P.M. (2020) *IOM Strengthens Belize's Tourism Sector Against Trafficking in Persons, Western Hemisphere Program*, International Organization for Migration (IOM). Available from: https://programamesocaribe.iom.int/en/news/iom-strengthens-belizes-tourism-sector-against-trafficking-persons [Accessed 30 August 2021].

Okyere, S. (2017) '"Shock and awe": a critique of the Ghana-centric child trafficking discourse', *Anti-Trafficking Review*, (9): 92–105.

Okyere, S. (2020) *The Master's Tools Will Never Dismantle the Master's House: Time to Rethink the Palermo Protocol, openDemocracy*. Available from: www.opendemocracy.net/en/beyond-trafficking-and-slavery/the-masters-tools-will-never-dismantle-the-masters-house-time-to-rethink-the-palermo-protocol/ [Accessed 31 August 2021].

Quirk, J. (2020) *Are We Better Off on the Inside? Modern Slavery and Human Trafficking as Platforms for Political Mobilisation, openDemocracy*. Available from: www.opendemocracy.net/en/beyond-trafficking-and-slavery/are-we-better-inside-modern-slavery-and-human-trafficking-platforms-political-mobilisation/ [Accessed 30 August 2021].

Roberts, J. (2017) 'Belize officials seek victim-centered approach to anti-trafficking work', Human Trafficking Institute. Available from: https://www.traffickinginstitute.org/belize-officials-seek-victim-centered-approach-to-anti-trafficking-work/ [Accessed 15 August 2021].

Rosen, L.W. and Weber, M.A. (2019) 'Human trafficking and foreign policy: an introduction', *Congressional Research Service*, [online] 7 January. Available from: https://sgp.fas.org/crs/row/IF10587.pdf [Accessed 7 May 2021].

Ross, K.L. and King, T. (2018) *Belize Enters Agreement with the Institute to Enhance the Capacity of Belize's Specialized Human Trafficking Unit – Human Trafficking Institute, Human Trafficking Institute*. Available from: www.traffickinginstitute.org/belize-enters-agreement-with-the-institute-to-enhance-the-capacity-of-belizes-specialized-human-trafficking-unit/ [Accessed 15 August 2021].

Rudon, M. (2014) 'U.S. embassy sponsors human trafficking workshop', *Channel 5 Belize*, [online] 20 October. Available from: https://edition.channel5belize.com/archives/105164 [Accessed 15 August 2021].

Sansom, K. (2006) 'Government engagement with non-state providers of water and sanitation services', *Public Administration and Development*, 26(3): 207–17.

Schaferhoff, M., Campe, S., and Kaan, C. (2009) 'Transnational public-private partnerships in international relations: making sense of concepts, research frameworks, and results', *International Studies Review*, 11(3): 451–74. [Accessed 11 April 2022].

Schmitt, V. (2017) 'NGOs and the anti-trafficking movement: advocacy and service', in M. Chisolm-Straker and H. Stoklosa (eds) *Human Trafficking Is a Public Health Issue: A Paradigm Expansion in the United States*, Switzerland: Springer, pp 263–76.

Segrave, M. and Milivojević, S. (2010) 'Auditing the Australian response to trafficking', *Current Issues in Criminal Justice*, 22(1): 63–80.

Sharapov, K. and Mendel, J. (2018) 'Trafficking in human beings: made and cut to measure? Anti-trafficking docufictions and the production of anti-trafficking truths', *Cultural Sociology*, 12(4): 540–60.

Sharma, N. (2003) 'Travel agency: a critique of anti-trafficking campaigns', *Refuge*, 21(3): 53–65.

Sharma, N. (2020) 'Anti-trafficking is an inside job', *openDemocracy*, [online] 18 December 2020. Available from: https://www.opendemocracy.net/en/beyond-trafficking-and-slavery/anti-trafficking-inside-job/ [Accessed 31 August 2021].

Shoaps, L.L. (2013) 'Room for improvement: Palermo Protocol and the Trafficking Victims Protection Act', *Lewis and Clark Law Review*, 17: 931.

Soublière, J.-F. and Cloutier, C. (2015) 'Explaining levels of local government involvement in service delivery: the dynamics of cross-sector partnerships in Malawi', *Public Administration and Development*, 35(3): 192–205.

Staff, B.B.N. (2018) 'US cuts aid to Belize over Human Trafficking Tier 3 ranking', *Breaking Belize New*, [online] 30 November. Available from: www.breakingbelizenews.com/2018/11/30/us-cuts-aid-to-belize-over-human-trafficking-tier-3-ranking/ [Accessed 15 August 2021].

Staff, B.B.N. (2019) '"Belize's upgrade on Trafficking in Persons Report is just the beginning," says Charge d' Affaires', *Breaking Belize News*, [online] 3 July. Available from: www.breakingbelizenews.com/2019/07/03/belize-upgrade-on-trafficking-in-persons-report-is-just-the-beginning-says-charge-d-affaires/ [Accessed 15 August 2021].

Stubbs, P. (2003) 'International non-state actors and social development policy', *Global Social Policy*, 3(3): 319–48.

Sutherland, M. (2020) 'Former bar owner convicted of human trafficking', *The Reporter*, 12 March, p 4.

The San Pedro Sun (2015) 'On Eagles Wings Ministries Belize chapter officially launched', *The San Pedro Sun*, [online] 21 January. Available from: www.sanpedrosun.com/community-and-society/2015/01/21/eagles-wings-ministries-belize-chapter-officially-launched/ (Accessed 15 August 2021).

The San Pedro Sun (2018) 'Human trafficking continues to pose a challenge in Belize', *The San Pedro Sun*, [online] 24 March. Available from: www.sanpedrosun.com/crime-and-violence/2018/03/24/human-trafficking-continues-pose-challenge-belize/ [Accessed 15 August 2021].

The San Pedro Sun (2019) 'Belize upgraded to Tier 2 Watch List in the 2019 Trafficking in Persons Report', *The San Pedro Sun*, [online] 20 June. Available from: www.sanpedrosun.com/government/2019/06/20/belize-upgraded-to-tier-2-watch-list-in-the-2019-trafficking-in-persons-report/ [Accessed 30 August 2021].

Thibos, C. (2020) *Twenty Years of Trafficking: Taking Stock of the World the Palermo Protocol Built*, openDemocracy. Available from: www.opendemocracy.net/en/beyond-trafficking-and-slavery/twenty-years-trafficking-taking-stock-world-palermo-protocol-built/ [Accessed 31 August 2021].

Touzenis, K. (2010) *Trafficking in Human Beings – N° 3 – Human Rights and Transnational Criminal Law, Developments in Law and Practices*, Paris: UNESCO.

United Nations Office on Drugs and Crime (2018) *Global Report on Trafficking in Persons (2018)*, Vienna: UNODC. Available from: www.unodc.org/e4j/data/_university_uni_/global_report_on_trafficking_in_persons_2018.html [Accessed 30 August 2021].

United Nations Treaty Collection (nd) Available from: https://treaties.un.org/pages/ViewDetails.aspx?src=TREATY&mtdsg_no=XVIII-12-a&chapter=18&clang=_en [Accessed 31 August 2021].

United States of America Department of State (2015) *Trafficking in Persons Report*, United States of America Department of State. Available from: https://2009-2017.state.gov/documents/organization/245365.pdf [Accessed 22 May 2022].

United States of America Department of State (2020) *2020 Trafficking in Persons Report 20th Edition*, United States of America Department of State. Available from: www.state.gov/wp-content/uploads/2020/06/2020-TIP-Report-Complete-062420-FINAL.pdf [Accessed 22 May 2022].

United States of America Department of State (2021) *2021 Trafficking in Persons Report*, United States of America Department of State. Available from: https://www.state.gov/reports/2021-trafficking-in-persons-report/ [Accessed 22 May 2022].

United States Embassy Belmopan (2017) 'U.S. government funds RET international project to combat gender-based violence and trafficking in persons', *US Embassy Belmopan*, [online] 6 December. Available from: https://bz.usembassy.gov/u-s-government-funds-ret-international-project-combat-gender-based-violence-andtrafficking-persons/ [Accessed 5 June 2022].

van Wijk, J. (2006) 'Romance tourism on Ambergris Caye, Belize: the entanglement of love and prostitution', *Etnofoor*, 19(1): 71–89.

Vineyard Missions (nd) *Vineyard Missions*. Available from: http://www.vineyardmissions.org/belize [Accessed 15 August 2021].

Wang, N. and Ma, M. (2021) 'Public-private partnership as a tool for sustainable development – what literatures say?', *Sustainable Development*, 29(1): 243–58. Available from: https://onlinelibrary.wiley.com/doi/abs/10.1002/sd.2127 [Accessed 25 August 2021].

Wicker, M. (2018) '2018 Global Human Trafficking Academy – Human Trafficking Institute'. Available from: https://www.traffickinginstitute.org/tag/2018-global-human-trafficking-academy/ [Accessed 15 August 2021].

Wicker, M. (2020) *Belize Celebrates Second Conviction Ever Under 2013 TIP Act – Human Trafficking Institute*. Available from: www.traffickinginstitute.org/belize-celebrates-second-conviction-ever-under-2013-tip-act/ [Accessed 30 August 2021].

Wijers, M. (2015) 'Purity, victimhood and agency: fifteen years of the UN trafficking protocol', *Anti-Trafficking Review*, 4: 56–79. Available from: https://gaatw.org/ATR/AntiTraffickingReview_Issue4.pdf [Accessed 30 August 2021].

Wylie, G. (2016) *The International Politics of Human Trafficking*, London: Palgrave Macmillan.

Zafar Ullah, A.N., Newell, J.N., Uddin Ahmed, J., Hyder M.K.A., and Islam A. (2006) 'Government–NGO collaboration: the case of tuberculosis control in Bangladesh', *Health Policy and Planning*, 21(2): 143–55.

Index

A

abolitionism 16, 57
 unintended consequences 262
action-reflection meetings 276, 278
action research 267
 see also participatory action research
activism xxv–xxvi, 6
Africa *see* Ethiopia; Gabon; Liberia; Nigeria; Sierra Leone; Tanzania; Uganda
African researchers 256–7
agribusiness 72, 73
Albania 115, 118–19, 120, 125, 126, 129, 130, 131–2, 133
Aliverti, A. 229
Anderson, B. 116, 207
Anthias, P. 68, 69, 72, 73
Anthony, T. 96
anti-immigration policies xxvi, xxix, 21, 40, 47
 'hostile environment' 228–33, 234
Anti-Slavery International 304
anti-trafficking campaigns 31
 collateral damage 113–14, 262
 commodification of anti-trafficking research 268
 criticisms 82, 262
 NSAs *see* non-state actors
 top-down imperialistic approaches 264
anti-trafficking enforcement xxvii–xxiv, 291
Arana, Julio Cesar 65, 66
Argentina 8
Armstrong, A. 269
Association for Moral and Social Hygiene (AMSH) 33
Australia 96
 Modern Slavery Acts 5
awareness-generation 275
'awareness raising' xxvi, xxviii, xxix
Aznarez, M. 269

B

back pay 234
Baines, E. 256
Bales, Kevin 56, 58, 62
Banbury, Sir Frederick 45

Banks, S. 269, 309
Barnard, C. 210
Batley, R. 298
Beales, Edmond 37
Belize 23–4
 NGOs 300, 302, 303, 304, 305, 306, 308, 309, 310
 non-state actors (NSAs) 292, 293, 297–9, 311–12
 between state and non-state focus 303–5
 complementary and co-produced implementation 307–9
 government-led partnerships 301–3
 non-state-led methods 305–9
 'overseer partnership' 299–300
 working outside the state 309–11
 OEWM 302M 310
 sex trafficking 305, 310
 US anti-trafficking efforts 299–300, 311–12
 US TIP Report 300, 301–2, 304, 305, 311
Bellagio-Harvard Guidelines 53
Beutin, L.P. 3, 56
Bhagat, A. 6
bias 269
Bjelland, H.F. 169
Blanchette, T.G. 57
Bland, Lucy 33
blind spots 57
Boatcă, M. 62
Bolivia 55, 62, 63, 94
 agribusiness 72, 73
 coca farming 72
 decolonization and modern slavery 67–73
 Indigenous people 67–73
 Morales government 67, 69, 70, 71, 72, 75
 resource extraction 72, 73
border control 9
Braverman, Suella 212
Bravo, K.E. 58
Brazil 60, 62, 267
 data on modern slavery 57
 racialized discrimination 57
Brexit 21, 197
 facilitating labour exploitation 199–201
 see also EU migrants in the UK

Brightbill, N. 267
Bristow, Edward 42
British Sociological Association 122
Bronfenbrenner, U. 119
Bryant-Davis, T. 153
Bryman, A. 114
Bulgaria 204, 208
Bunting, A. 58
Butler, Josephine 34, 36–9, 41–2
Butlin, Fraser 210

C

Cahill, C. 269
Canada 87, 93, 95–6, 96–7
capitalism 60, 62, 64, 73, 74, 84, 86
case studies 15, 20–4
Casement, Roger 66, 67
Castilla, Ramon 64
Castles, S. 116
Castro-Gómez, S. 85
Chapman, T. 293
chattel slavery 7
children 124
  commercial sexual exploitation and trafficking (CSEC) in the US 146, 157–9
  idealized views of 158
  'infantilization' vs 'adultification' 158–9
Chile 267
Chinese labourers 64
Chirif, A. 67
Chuang, J.A. 124, 208
civil society organizations 16, 132, 291, 309
coca farming 72
Cockbain, E. 6
Colombia 65, 66, 95, 267
colonial laws 86
colonial matrix of power 84–5
colonial violence 86, 87
  structural violence 24
coloniality xxiv, xxix, 5, 7, 14–17, 73–4
  'civilizing mission' 74, 98
  epistemic violence 83–5, 86, 103
  forced labour 86
  Latin America *see* Belize; Bolivia; Brazil; Colombia; Ecuador; Guatemala; Mexico; Panama; Peru; Venezuela
  legacies 83
  politics of 'rescue' 149, 153, 154
  self-centred economic exploitation 21
  TIPRs and 82, 102–3
Coloniality/Modernity School 61
'coloniality of power' 54, 55, 60–3
  labour in post-independence Peru 63–7
commercial sexual exploitation of children (CSEC) 146, 157–9
commodification of labour 61, 84
community migration norms 118
comparative case study approach 55
confidentiality 254, 266

conflict contexts 243, 244, 255
conflict studies 242–3
consent 126, 127, 128, 129, 252–4, 257
Contagious Diseases Acts (CDAs) 31–2, 34, 36, 37, 38, 39, 47
Coote, William A. 34, 40–1, 42, 43, 44, 46
corporate pressure 58–9
corporate social responsibility xxviii, xxix
COVID-19 pandemic 211
Creoles 62, 63
criminal investigation process 19–20
  complexity 169
  see also police investigations
criminal justice models xxvii–xxix, 149, 150–1, 153–4, 155–6
criminalization 40, 47, 48, 149, 153
critical anti-trafficking scholarship 262
critical race scholarship 205
Cugoano, Ottabah 61, 62
cultural imperialism 19
Cunneen, C. 87
customary international law 4

D

Da Silva, A.P. 57
data analysis 120
data protection 129
data silos 177
de Ayala, Waman Puma 61
de Vries, I. 6, 157
de Wildt, R. 265
debt bondage 64, 68, 232
decolonization 54, 75, 84
  Bolivia 67–73
dependency theorists 60
Determinants of Migrant Vulnerability (DoMV) 117, 120, 121
development discourses 74
digitization of information 145, 147
Diptée, A.A. 57, 58
DoCarmo, T.E. 125, 128
Doezema, Jo 32
domestic workers 230, 231
  Nepalese migration bans 262, 276
Dudfield, O. 293
Dussel, E. 61
Dyer, Alfred 34, 39

E

ecological models 117–18, 119
Economic and Social Research Council 122
economic underdevelopment 57
Ecuador 95
Elmy, Elizabeth Wolstenholme 36, 39, 41
emancipation 64
emancipatory movements 267
empirical challenges 154–7
  commercial sexual exploitation and trafficking of children in the US 157–9

INDEX

enforcement *see* UK: labour market enforcement
England
  Contagious Diseases Acts (CDAs) 31–2, 34, 36, 37, 38, 39, 47
  Public Morality Council (PMC) 41
  trade with Peru 63–4, 65, 66
  trafficking in women 31–3
    legal and social landscape of the mid-19th century 34–9
    legal framework on anti-trafficking 39–47
    women's rights activism 31, 32, 33, 34, 36–9
  see also UK
epistemic violence 83–5, 86
  TIPRs 88–90, 91, 103
ethical dilemmas 129–30, 138
ethical investment and consumption xxviii
ethical research 22, 23
  academic standards 114
  age limits 119
  anonymity 266
  beneficiaries 134–5
  children 124, 129
  Community of Practice (CoP) 130
  conceptual approaches
    avoiding methodological nationalism 116–7, 135
    beyond harm minimization 131–5, 138, 139
    consent and wider considerations 135–8
    country-specific considerations 130–1
    ecological models 117–18, 119
    ethics in practice 126
    methodology 118–22
    pre-identified ethical considerations 126–30
    procedural ethics and ethical guidelines 122–5
    situation-specific analysis 117
  confidentiality 266
  data analysis 120
  data protection 129
  debriefing 129
  developing a 'living' Ethical Protocol 115–16, 119–20, 139
  informed consent 126, 127, 128, 129, 252–4, 266
  participatory action research (PAR) 265–7
  payment for taking part 128–9
  policy impacts 135–7
  post-conflict societies 244, 246, 255
  potential harms 115
  power imbalances 124, 128, 139, 244–8
  qualitative data 120
  recruitment 251
  responsibility towards participants 114
  re-traumatization 254
  risks and benefits of participating 126

'sensitive' research 125
Shared Learning Events (SLEs) 118–19, 120, 126, 129, 130, 131, 132, 133
Ethical Research Involving Children (ERIC) 124
ethics
  distance and translation 265–6
  participatory ethics 267
  see also ethical research
Ethiopia 7
ethnographic research xxviii–xxiv, 22
EU: GRETA 149
EU migrants in the UK 21
  Accession Treaties and 204, 207
  Brexit 21, 197, 199
  chicken farms 209
  continuum of exploitation 209–10
  EU Settlement Scheme (EUSS) 199–200, 211, 214
  EU8 and EU2 migrants 198, 203–8, 210, 211, 212, 214
  free movement as a facilitation of labour exploitation 201–2
    terms of 'free' movement 202–5
    UK labour market 205–6
    visibility as victims of modern slavery 207–10
  'hostile environment' trumps labour market security 229, 230, 234
  low-skilled work 198, 201, 204, 206
  minimum wage 208, 209
  post-Brexit Points-Based System (PBS) 199, 200, 201, 212
  precarious work and exploitation 198, 206, 207, 214
    aggravating impact of restrictive immigration policy 210–13
    prior to the end of free movement 199–200
  racism and xenophobia 205
  Seasonal Agricultural Workers Scheme 204, 232
  Sectors Based Scheme 204
  Skilled Worker route 200
  Temporary Seasonal Visa Scheme 201, 212
  Worker Registration Scheme (WRS) 204
European imperialism xxiv, 7, 10, 14, 294
Europol 184
exploitation 12, 14
  commercial sexual exploitation and trafficking of children (CSEC) in the US 146, 157–9
  EU migrants in the UK 201–10
  extractive industries 72, 73

F

Farrell, A. 177, 178, 179
Faulkner, E.A. 261–2
feminist campaigns 295, 296
feminist research approaches 118, 244–8
  see also women's rights

feudalism 60, 74
fieldwork 243
  navigating risk, access, and collaboration 248–52
  negotiating for informed consent 252–4, 257
  positionality 246–8, 257
  power and feminist methodology 244–8
Firmin, C. 117
FLEX 228
forced labour 86
forced marriage 241, 243
France: 'duty of vigilance' laws 5
Francis, C. 6
free movement *see* EU migrants in the UK

G

Gabon 97
Gaiman, Neil 2
Gallagher, A.T. 135, 136
Gangmasters and Labour Abuse Authority (GLAA) 221, 224–6, 227
gender-based violence 242
  see also wartime sexual violence
Gilligan, C. 124
Global Alliance Against Traffic in Women (GAATW) 114
global benchmarking frameworks 13
Global North 296, 305, 306, 309
Global South 3, 10, 160, 281, 294, 296, 309, 311
globalization xxiv, 58, 59, 74, 294
Greenfield, V.A. 234
Gross Domestic Product (GDP) 147
Group of Experts on Action against Human Trafficking (GRETA) 149
guano 63–5
Guatemala 94, 99
Gustafson, B. 71

H

Hay, I. 114
hierarchies of knowledge 84
Hitchings, R. 263
Holmes, L. 307
'hostile environment' 228–33, 234
Hulme, D. 309
human rights
  hypocrisies 12
  legal regimes 10–12
Human Rights Watch 303
human trafficking
  chronology xxiv
  complexity 172–4
  definition 148, 280
  empirical challenges 154–7
  indicators *see* indicator-based approaches
  investigation *see* police collaboration
  'law and order' interventions xxvii–xxix
  see also crime and national security perspectives
  legal regimes 4–5, 8–10
  modern slavery and 2, 5
  'newness' xxiv–xxvi, xxix
  online footprint 156–7
  post-trafficking 263
  prioritization of certain facets 155
  research scope and unintended consequences 261–2
  socially and economically embedded 155–6, 160
  socio-ecological factors 160–1
  top-down imperialistic approaches 264, 268
Human Trafficking Institute (HTI) 308
humanitarianism xxix, 296, 311
Humphreys Bebbington, D. 73
hydrocarbon interests 72, 73

I

immigration 5
immigration law xxvi, xxix, 21, 40, 47
imperialism xxiv, 7
  top-down approaches to 'trafficking' 264, 268
  US 150
  TIPRs 89, 90, 91, 99, 103, 149
  see also colonialism
India 60, 267
Indian Penal Code 86
indicator-based approaches 18–19, 145–7
  aetiology 147–50
  crime and national security perspectives 149, 150–1, 153–4, 155–6
  disproportionate focus on sex trafficking 150, 151
  empirical challenges 154–7
  commercial sexual exploitation and trafficking of children in the US 157–9
  implications for policy, interventions, and further research 159–61
  performance indicators 146–7, 149
  problem indicators 145–6, 149
  quantifiable information 147–50
  risk indicators 146
  victim narratives and hierarchies of victimhood 147, 152–4
  vocabulary of victimization within human trafficking discourse 150–4
Indigenous peoples 16, 17, 56
  Bolivia 67–73, 94
  Canada 87, 93, 95–6, 96–7
  deaths 86
  enslavement 86
  Peru 63–7, 94
  sexual exploitation of Indigenous women 87
  stereotypes 83, 85, 94–6
  TIPR categories 82
  TIPR construction of 'Indigenous victims' of human trafficking 92, 103

equivocality of indigeneity 92–4
geographical clusters 99–102
moral anxieties 96–7
norm-setters and norm-followers 99
reproducing stereotypes of vulnerability 94–6
socio-economic factors 98–9
state mechanisms 97–8
TIPR search terms 91
information-sharing 177
informed consent 126, 127, 128, 129, 252–4, 257, 266
Inter-American Commission on Human Rights 69
intergovernmental organizations (IGOs) 293
International Abolitionist Federation (IAF) 31, 33
International Association for the Study of Forced Migration (IASFM) 123–4
International Bureau 296
International Criminal Court (ICC) 241, 242, 294
International Labour Organization (ILO) 56, 154, 228, 264
international law as tool of oppression 14
International Organization for Migration (IOM) 117, 118, 119, 120, 130, 307
data protection 129
International Red Cross 294
interpreters 249, 253, 274
investigations *see* police investigations
Ireland 203, 205
Israel, M. 114
Italy 86

J
Jacobsen, K. 114
Jessop, B. 59
Josselin, D. 292

K
Kalayaan 231
Kaye, J. 87
Kelley, J.G. 149
Kempadoo, K. 56, 57
Kesby, M. 269
Kindon, S. 269
Klocker, N. 277
knowledge extraction 280
Kony, Joseph 242

L
labour exploitation 21, 32, 84
labour market enforcement *see* UK: labour market enforcement
Ladies National Association for the Repeal of the Contagious Diseases Acts (LNA) 36–7
Lagon, M. 293, 298
Laite, Julia 33

Landau, L.B. 114
language barriers 270
Latham, A. 263
Latin America
'coloniality of power' 60–7
Creoles 62, 63
state autonomy 59, 60
Wars of Independence 62
Western conquest 84
see also Belize; Bolivia; Brazil; Colombia; Ecuador; Guatemala; Mexico; Panama; Peru; Venezuela
Laurie, N. 266, 269
Lauterpacht, H. 12
'law and order' interventions xxvii–xxix
see also crime and national security perspectives
League of Nations 6–7, 8
LeBaron, G. 59
legal regimes 4–5
human trafficking 8–10
slavery 5–8
Lerche, J. 209
Levy, N. 136
Lewis, H. 207–8
LGBTQ victims of trafficking 152, 153
Liberia 7
Lindsey, I. 293, 298
Lithuania 209
Lock Hospitals 36
Lord's Resistance Army (LRA) 242, 243
low-skilled work 198, 201, 204, 207, 210
Ludlow, A. 210

M
Malaysia 96
Mantouvalu, V. 208, 222
Manzo, L.C. 267
Mariategui, Jose Carlos 64
Matos, M. 176
Maurice, Gregory 43
Mcloughlin, C. 298, 309
Merry, Sally Engle 87
Metcalf, Sir David 223, 224
methodology
comparative case study approach 55
methodological nationalism 19, 116–17, 135
Mexico 94, 95
Mignolo, W.D. 61, 62, 75
migration norms 118
migration studies 135–6
minimum wage 208, 209, 234
mobility 265, 275, 276, 281
modern slavery 82
appeals to altruism 3
chronology xxiv
coloniality and 54, 55, 73
legacies 83
see also coloniality; 'coloniality of power'

definitions 4–5, 6
emotional responses to 3, 6, 13
EU migrants in the UK 207–10
exclusion from global markets 53–4
global context 3
human trafficking and 2, 5
key legislation xxiv
legal regimes 4–5
  human rights 10–12
  human trafficking 8–10
  slavery 5–8
locating the problem 136–7
multi-disciplinary approach 2–3
problematizing approaches 56–60
range of exploitative practices 53
role of the state 54, 60, 74
socio-economic context 56
umbrella concept 1
modernity 61–2, 86
moral anxiety xxiv, 17, 24, 87, 96–7
Morales, Evo 67, 69, 70, 71, 72, 75
multi-agency collaboration 20, 177–85, 187
multi-disciplinary approach 2–3
Munck, R. 58, 61
Murchison, Julian 254
Musto, J. 153
Mutua, M. 12
Myslinska, D. 202

N

nation states 59
  methodological nationalism 19, 116–17, 135
National Human Trafficking Resource Center (NHTRC) 146
National Minimum Wage (NMW) 234
national security perspectives 150–1
National Vigilance Association (NVA) 33, 40–7
Nead, Lynda 35
negative terminology 120
Neilans, Alison 34–5, 42
neoliberal globalization 58
Nepal
  female migration 270, 271
  Gorkha earthquake (2015) 270, 280
  migration bans on domestic work 262, 276
  mobility experiences 265, 275, 276, 281
  NGOs 265, 270, 272, 276, 277, 280
  participatory action research (PAR) 23, 261–4
    action-reflection meetings 276, 278
    analysis and reflection 276–7, 281
    co-identification of pressing issues 269
    empowerment 268–9
    ethical reflections 265–7
    existing power structures 271
    methodology 267–8
    peer researchers/research companions 272–4
    placing mobility before political categories 264–5
    post-disaster 271–2
    project construction 272–4
    research findings and policy brief 278–80
    rights-based awareness-generation 275
    safe space 274
    scoping study 269–71
    steering committees 272
    training 274
Netherlands 150
NGOs 23, 152–3, 170, 181–2, 187, 263, 268
  Belize 293, 300, 302, 303, 304, 305, 306, 308, 309, 310
  Nepal 265, 270, 272, 276, 277, 280
  Palermo Protocol negotiations 291
  post-conflict societies 245
  registration requirements 302
  'volun-tourists' 310–11
Nigeria 115, 118, 119, 120, 125, 129, 130, 131, 132, 133, 137
non-state actors (NSAs) 291–2, 311
  Belize 292, 293, 297–99, 311–12
  complementary and co-produced implementation 307–9
  government-led partnerships 301–3
  non-state-led methods 305–7
  'overseer partnership' 299–300
  working outside the state 309–11
  definition 292
  historical contribution and impact 294–5
  partnerships and development in anti-trafficking 295–7
  public–private partnerships 293
Noxolo, P. 281
NSPCC Ethical Protocol 125

O

O'Connell Davidson, J. 208
OEWM 302, 310
Ongwen, Dominic 242
online footprint 156–7
Organization for Security and Co-operation in Europe (OSCE) 174
Overseas Domestic Workers (ODWs) 230, 231

P

Pain, R. 269
Palermo Protocol 8–10, 53, 82, 148, 151, 158, 174, 261, 291, 299
Panama 96
Paoli, L. 234
participatory action research (PAR) 23, 261–4
  bottom-up approach 267–8
  critiques 271
  knowledge production 268

Nepal
    action-reflection meetings 276, 278
    analysis and reflection 276–7, 281
    co-identification of pressing issues 269
    empowerment 268–9
    ethical reflections 265–7
    existing power structures 271
    peer researchers/research companions 272–4
    placing mobility before political categories 264–5
    post-disaster 271–2
    project construction 272–4
    research findings and policy brief 278–80
    rights-based awareness-generation 275
    safe space 274
    scoping study 269–71
    steering committees 272
    training 274
participatory development 309
participatory ethics 267
participatory project mapping 269–71
partnerships 293
    see also non-state actors; public–private partnerships
Patel, Priti 212
peer researchers 272–4
performance indicators 146–7, 149
personal protective equipment (PPE) 232
Peru 55, 61, 63, 94
    Chinese labourers 64
    European immigration 66
    Indigenous people 63–7
    post-independence labour: guano and rubber 63–7
    trade with Britain 63–4, 66
Phillips, N. 59
Piscitelli, A. 57
Poland 205
police investigations 20, 168–70
    complexity of human trafficking investigations 172–7
    intelligence-led strategies 176, 177, 178, 179, 182, 184, 185
    international collaboration: Joint Investigation Team (JIT) 171, 172, 183–4
    multi-agency collaboration 177–85, 187
    Operation Blue 171, 172, 183–4, 185
    Operation Green 171, 180–3, 184–5
    proactive investigation 176–7
    research methodology 170–1
        critical reflections 186
    undercover investigative strategies 171, 182
    victim engagement 175, 181–2, 185, 186
popular research 267
positionality 246–8, 257
post-conflict societies 243, 244, 255
post-trafficking 263

power relations 54, 73
    feminist methodology 244–8
    imbalances 124, 139, 154
prison industrial complex 150
private actors 59, 60
problem indicators 145–6, 149
problematizing approaches 56–60
prostitution *see* sex work
public–private partnerships 293, 294, 299

Q
qualititative data 120
quantifiable information 147–50
    see also indicator-based approaches
Quijano, Aníbal 54, 61, 63, 64, 73, 74, 83, 84, 86
Quirk, Joel 7, 57, 58

R
racial hierarchies 5
racialized discrimination 57–8, 92
    EU migrants 205, 206
racialized identities 54, 55, 61, 62, 64, 74, 84
Radford, L. 129
Ramirez, S.E. 64
rape 241
Rayment-McHugh, S. 117
recruitment advertisements 156
reflexivity 246
Reid, J.A. 157
'rescue', politics of 149, 153, 154
research xxv
    biases in participant selection 269
    feminist approaches 118, 244–8
    fieldwork *see* fieldwork
    in-depth interviews 254–6
    lack of transparency 263
    language barriers 270, 281
    methodological nationalism 19, 116–17, 135
    peer researchers 272–4
    positionality 246–8
    see also ethical research; participatory action research
research fatigue 250
resource extraction 72, 73
risk factors 56
Richardson, D. 266, 269
rights-based awareness-generation 275
risk indicators 146
risk profiling 160
Roma 120
Romania
    EU migrants in the UK 198, 204, 205, 208
    police collaboration 172, 183, 184
    rubber 65–7

S
Sakamoto, L. 57
Sansom, K. 298

'savages, victims, and saviors' (SVS) metaphor 12
Scotland 232
sensationalism xxix
sex work 31, 32, 33, 34, 82
  as gendered oppression 35, 37, 38
  Belize 305, 310
  criminalization 40, 47, 48, 153
  disproportionate focus on 150, 151
  laws regulating prostitution 35–6
  moral threat and disease 35–6
  trafficking and 87, 155
  victim-blaming 153
sexual exploitation 12, 13
  commercial sexual exploitation of children (CSEC) 146, 157–9
sexual slavery 241, 243
sexual violence *see* wartime sexual violence
Shared Learning Events (SLEs) 118–19, 120, 126, 129, 130, 131, 132, 133
Sharma, N. 75
Shih, E. 57
Siegel, D. 265
Sierra Leone 241–2
Simmons, B.A. 149
Skrivankova, K. 220
slavery
  definitions 5–8
  trans-Atlantic slave trade 58, 85
Snagge, Thomas 39
social hierarchies 84
Social Research Association 122
social norms 137–8
social stigma *see* stigma
socio-economic factors 98–9
Special Court for Sierra Leone 241
state action 291
  obligations and failures 54, 60, 74, 75
  see also non-state actors
state autonomy 59, 60
state-centred implementation 301–2
state-imposed forced labour 59
state-led regulation 301, 302–3
stereotypes 18, 153, 205, 262
  Indigenous people 83, 85, 94–6
Stewart, B. 256
stigma 120, 131–4, 137, 139, 153, 160, 174, 263, 264, 266
  re-stigmatization 250
structural issues 17–20
  causes of 'vulnerability' 137, 138, 139
subjectivity 269
Sweden 150, 203

T

tabloid press 201
taboo subjects 256
Tait, William 35
Tanzania 277

Tauri, J. 87
Taylor, Matthew 224
theoretical perspectives 15–17
Third World Approaches to International Law (TWAIL) 14
Thornton, Sara 201
torture 243, 255
Trafficking in Persons Reports (TIPRs) 17, 24
  Belize 300, 301–2, 304, 305, 311
  constructing 'Indigenous victims' of human trafficking 92, 103
  equivocality of indigeneity 92–4
  geographical clusters 99–102
  moral anxieties 96–7
  norm-setters and norm-followers 99
  reproducing stereotypes of vulnerability 94–6
  socio-economic factors 98–9
  state mechanisms 97–8
  critiques 81–3, 85, 87, 88, 102–3
  coloniality of knowledge 92–102
  epistemic violence 88–90, 91, 103
  hierarchies of victimhood 152
  imperialism 89, 90, 91, 99, 103, 149
  methodology and content analysis 90–1
  indicator-based approaches 146–7, 148, 149, 152
  methodology and data-gathering 88–90
trafficking in women
  England 31–3
  legal and social landscape of the mid-19th century 34–9
  legal framework on anti-trafficking 39–47
  women's rights activism 31, 32, 33, 34, 36–9
  feminist campaigns 295, 296
trans-Atlantic slave trade 58, 85
Transparency International 303
transparency legislation xxviii
Tummala-Narra, P. 153
Tyldum, G. 263

U

Uganda
  fieldwork 247–57
  Lord's Resistance Army (LRA) 242, 243
UK
  Brexit 21, 197, 199
    facilitating labour exploitation 199–201, 229
    see also EU migrants in the UK
  case studies 21–2
  Employment Agency Standards (EAS) Inspectorate 227
  Equality and Human Rights Commission 106
  HMRC-National Minimum Wage (NMW) Team 227
  'hostile environment' policy 138, 228–33

INDEX

Immigration Enforcement Competent Authority 213
Independent Anti-Slavery Commissioner 223
Independent Monitoring Authority (IMA) for the Citizen's Rights Agreements 211
investigation *see* police investigations
Labour Abuse Prevention Officers (LAPOs) 221, 224–6
labour market enforcement 220–2, 233–5
   Director of Labour Market Enforcement (DLME) 221, 223–4, 225, 228
   Gangmasters and Labour Abuse Authority (GLAA) 221, 224–6, 227
   'hostile environment' trumps labour security 228–33, 234
   law and policy responses 222–8
   welfare concerns 232
Labour Market Enforcement Orders (LMEOs) 221, 226–8
Labour Market Enforcement Undertakings (LMEUs) 221, 226–8
Modern Slavery Acts 5
Modern Slavery Innovation Fund (MSIF) 118
National Crime Agency 180, 183, 184
National Minimum Wage (NMW) 234
National Referral Mechanism (NRM) 118, 130, 212–13, 231
Overseas Domestic Workers (ODWs) 230, 231
police *see* police investigations
prison industrial complex 150
research ethics 122
restrictive visa regimes 230–1, 232
seasonal workers 204, 232–3
Serious Organized Crime Unit (SOCU) 170, 171
tabloid press 201
see also England
unintended harms 19
United Nations 8
   Convention against Transnational Organized Crime 151
   see also Palermo Protocol
   indicator-based approaches 147, 156
   Inter-Agency Project on Human Trafficking (UNIAP) 122
   Office on Drugs and Crime (UNODC) 146, 156, 172, 299, 305
   Sustainable Development Goals (SDGs) 4, 11, 54
   Trafficking Protocol 124, 131, 135–6, 138
UNICEF 123
Universal Declaration of Human Rights 11–12
United States
   anti-trafficking efforts in Belize 299–300, 311–12

commercial sexual exploitation and trafficking of children 146, 157–9
Human Trafficking Institute (HTI) 308
imperialism 89–90, 91, 99, 149, 150, 160, 299
Office to Monitor and Combat Trafficking 306
prison industrial complex 150
TIPRs *see* Trafficking in Persons Reports
Urry, J. 265

V

Valcarcel, Carlos 67
Valcárcel Rojas, R. 86
Venezuela 62
Ventiades, N. 68
Vertovec, S. 135, 136
victim-blaming
   children 155–9
   sex workers 153
   trans people 153
victimhood
   ideological history 268
   narratives and hierarchies 147, 152–4
victims
   control methods 173
   engagement with investigators 175, 181–2, 185, 186
   evidence-gathering 176
   identification 173
   interviewing 175–6
   problematic boundaries between 'victims' and 'non-victims' 263
   re-traumatization 254
   stigma 120, 131–4, 137, 139, 153, 160, 174, 263, 264, 266
   re-stigmatization 250
Vietnam 115, 118, 119, 120, 122, 125, 129, 130, 133, 137
visa regimes 230–1, 232
Volodko, A. 156
'volun-tourists' 310–311
vulnerability 137, 138, 139, 153
   EU migrants in the UK 207–8, 211, 213–14

W

wage theft 234
Waite, L. 207–8
Walkowitz, Judith 32
Wallace, W. 292
Walter, M. 96
war survivors 243
   see also post-conflict societies
wartime abduction 22, 249, 253, 254, 255, 256
wartime sexual violence 22, 242, 243, 245, 246
   research ethics and in-depth interviews 254–6
   taboo subjects 256
Wedgwood, Col. Josiah 46

Western hegemony 18, 149, 150, 160
  EU enlargement and 202–3
  see also coloniality; imperialism
White saviour complex 311
white slavery xxiv, xxix, 13, 32, 36, 38, 296
  Belgian scandal 34, 39, 43
  hysteria over 40
  legal framework on anti-trafficking 39–47
  racialized metaphor 32, 33, 34
Women's Library 33
women's rights 31, 32, 33, 34, 36–9
  see also trafficking in women

World Bank 147
World Health Organization (WHO) 123
world-systems analysts 60
World Wildlife Fund 294

X

xenophobia 205

Z

Zafar Ullah, A.N. 298
zero-hour contracts 233
Zimmerman, C. 117

www.ingramcontent.com/pod-product-compliance
Lightning Source LLC
Chambersburg PA
CBHW051524020426
42333CB00016B/1775